THE POLITICS OF

OLYMPUS

FORM AND MEANING IN THE

MAJOR HOMERIC HYMNS

JENNY STRAUSS CLAY

PRINCETON UNIVERSITY PRESS

PRINCETON, NEW JERSEY

Library of Congress Cataloging-in-Publication Data

Clay, Jenny Strauss.
The politics of Olympus : form and meaning in the major Homeric hymns /
Jenny Strauss Clay.
p. cm.
Bibliography: p.
Includes index.
ISBN 0-691-06775-9
1. Homeric hymns.   2. Hymns, Greek (Classical)—History and criticism.
3. Gods, Greek, in literature.   4. Politics in literature.   I. Title.
PA4023.Z5C5 1989   88-34073
883'.01'09—dc19   CIP

Publication of this book has been aided by a grant from the
Paul Mellon Fund of Princeton University Press

This book has been composed in Linotron Granjon type

Printed in the United States of America by
Princeton University Press, Princeton, New Jersey

For Andreia

ἔστι μοι κάλα πάις χρυσίοισιν ἀνθέμοισιν
ἐμφέρην ἔχοισα μόρφαν Κλέις ἀγαπάτα,
ἀντὶ τᾶς ἔγωὐδὲ Λυδίαν παῖσαν οὐδ᾽ ἐράνναν . . .

Contents

Preface

This study traces its origins to a graduate seminar on Hesiod and the Homeric Hymns in the spring of 1984 and was supported by a fellowship from the National Endowment for the Humanities as well as several summer research grants from the University of Virginia and the Earhardt Foundation.

Charles Segal and Nicholas Richardson read the manuscript with great care and thoughtfulness for Princeton University Press. I have also benefited from the suggestions and criticisms of numerous colleagues and friends who generously read all or parts of earlier drafts as the work was taking shape. I list their names here, well aware that to do so is an insufficient measure of my gratitude: D. Clay, K. Clinton, C. Dadian, W. J. Dannhauser, R. L. Hunter, H. Lloyd-Jones, P. D. Kovacs, D. Mankin, A. M. Miller, P. Sage, S. Shelmerdine, and J.-P. Vernant. Their advice immeasurably improved the results, although they cannot be blamed for the remaining shortcomings.

Thanks are also due to Megan Youngquist for the diagram at the end of chapter 4, to Gail Moore and her staff at the University of Virginia Word Processing Center for their patience in dealing with a recalcitrant manuscript, to Brian MacDonald for his editorial skill, and to David Mankin and Ward Briggs for their help in preparing the index. Finally, I owe a special debt of gratitude to Joanna Hitchcock of Princeton University Press for her tactful support and encouragement.

The text of the Homeric Hymns used throughout is the Oxford

edition of T. W. Allen. Divergences from Allen's text are signaled in the notes. Numbers in parentheses refer to the lines of the poem under discussion. For other works, book number and lines are provided as appropriate. In citing Homer, books of the *Iliad* are referred to by Roman numerals, those of the *Odyssey*, by Arabic numbers. All translations, unless otherwise indicated, are my own.

Abbreviations

AHS	T. W. Allen, W. R. Halliday, and E. E. Sikes, *The Homeric Hymns* (Oxford, 1936)
AJP	*American Journal of Philology*
ARW	*Archiv für Religionswissenschaft*
BCH	*Bulletin de Correspondence Hellénique*
BICS	*Bulletin of the Institute for Classical Studies*
CJ	*Classical Journal*
CP	*Classical Philology*
CQ	*Classical Quarterly*
CR	*Classical Review*
CW	*Classical World*
Fr.G.H.	F. Jacoby, *Die Fragmente der griechischen Historiker* (Leiden, 1923–1958)
GGR	M. P. Nilsson, *Geschichte der griechische Religion*, 2nd ed. (Munich, 1955)
GRBS	*Greek, Roman and Byzantine Studies*
HSCP	*Harvard Studies in Classical Philology*
JHS	*Journal of Hellenic Studies*
Kern	O. Kern, *Orphicorum Fragmenta* (Berlin, 1922)
LSJ	H. G. Liddel, R. Scott, and H. S. Jones, *A Greek-English Lexicon* (Oxford, 1968)

Merkelbach-West	R. Merkelbach and M. L. West, *Fragmenta Hesiodea* (Oxford, 1967)
MH	*Museum Helveticum*
Page	D. Page, *Poetae melici graeci* (Oxford, 1962)
Quandt	W. Quandt, *Orphei hymni*, 2nd ed. (Berlin, 1962)
QUCC	*Quaderni Urbinati di Cultura Classica*
RE	G. Wissowa et al., eds., *Paulys Realencyclopädie der classischen Altertumswissenchaft* (Stuttgart, 1894–)
REG	*Revue des Études Grecques*
RFIC	*Rivista di Filologia e d'Istruzione Classica*
SMSR	*Studi e Materiali di Storia delle Religione*
Snell-Maehler	B. Snell and H. Maehler, *Pindari Carmina* (Leipzig, 1975–1980)
TAPA	*Transactions and Proceedings of the American Philological Association*
West	M. L. West, *Iambi et Elegi Graeci* (Oxford, 1971–1972)
ZPE	*Zeitschrift für Papyrologie und Epigraphik*

THE POLITICS OF OLYMPUS

Introduction

No one would deny that the Western tradition is largely grounded on Greek philosophy and science. These, in turn, spring from a critical examination of Greek conceptions concerning the nature of the gods as embodied in the works of the poets—above all, Homer and Hesiod. The study of the gods in early Greek poetry is hence not merely of antiquarian or academic interest, but is justified as a necessary foundation for an understanding of the roots of Western thought. I began an investigation of the phenomenology of the Greek gods with a study of the *Odyssey*; the present examination of the Homeric Hymns constitutes a logical continuation of that earlier work.

The Homeric Hymns have generally been neglected in studies of Greek literary and intellectual history. It is, for example, striking that these poems receive short shrift in such *geistesgeschichtliche* studies as Snell's *Discovery of the Mind*, Fränkel's *Wege und Formen frühgriechischen Denkens*, and even Jaeger's *Paideia*. Moreover, in the last fifty years, only one of the major hymns has received a full-length commentary.[1] Ultimately, this neglect stems from the influence of a view that the hymns are largely derivative from the great epics and that they were in fact *prooimia*, preludes to the performance of Homer. The proem theory, first proposed in Wolf's *Prolegomena* (1795),[2] relegates the hymns to a kind of

[1] N. J. Richardson's *The Homeric Hymn to Demeter* (Oxford, 1974).

[2] See F. A. Wolf, *Prolegomena to Homer 1795*, trans. A. Grafton, G. Most, and J. Zetzel (Princeton, 1985). The proem theory remains orthodoxy. See, for example, J. M.

hors d'oeuvre of epic. Significantly, too, the language of the hymns has been labeled "sub-epic,"[3] a term that meant nothing more than post-Homeric, but the label itself suggests inferiority.

Inevitably, criticism of the hymns followed the trends of contemporary Homeric scholarship. Thus, during the nineteenth century and into the twentieth, the poems were subject to the fragmenting debates between the analysts and their opponents, the unitarians, who insisted on the integrity of these compositions. More recently, the influence of Parry's work on the Homeric epic has led to studies of formulaic diction in the hymns and attempts to ascertain whether they were composed orally.[4] Other studies, considering the hymns largely as historical documents, have focused mainly on questions of date and provenance or, in some cases, have mined the poems as source material for an understanding of Greek cult. As a result, the hymns have been stripped of their autonomy as works of literary art and significant religious thought.

However that may be, our earliest witnesses, Homer and Hesiod, both set hymn poetry on an equal footing with epic. In the first book of the *Odyssey*, Penelope remarks that the bards sing the deeds of both gods and men (1.338); in Phaeacia, Demodocus performs what may well be called our earliest example of a Homeric hymn when he recounts the "Lay of Ares and Aphrodite" (8.266–366).[5] Similarly, Hesiod defines the task of the poet as twofold:

Bremer, "Greek Hymns," in *Faith, Hope and Worship: Aspects of Religious Mentality in the Ancient World*, ed. H. S. Versnel (Leiden, 1981), p. 212; and L. Lenz, *Der homerische Aphroditehymnus* (Bonn, 1975), esp. pp. 278–86, where he gives a review of opinions. But cf. AHS, p. xciv: "it is difficult to believe that the five greater hymns can have 'preluded' a rhapsody not necessarily longer than one of them." For the ancient testimonia on the term *prooimion*, see R. Böhme, *Das Prooimion: Eine Form sakraler Dichtung der Griechen* (Bühl, 1937), pp. 11–24; also the discussion of A. Aloni, "*Prooimia, Hymnoi*, Elio Aristide e i cugini bastardi," *QUCC* n.s. 4 (1980): 23–40. I hope to discuss the proem theory and the meaning of *prooimion* in a separate paper.

[3] Cf. A. Hoekstra, *The Sub-epic Stage of the Formulaic Tradition* (Amsterdam, 1969), p. 5, who traces the term back to Allen.

[4] In addition to Hoekstra (1969), see R. Janko, *Homer, Hesiod and the Hymns* (Cambridge, 1982); and the essays collected by C. Brillante, M. Cantilena, and C. O. Pavese in *I poemi epici rapsodici non omerici e la tradizione orale* (Padua, 1981); also J. A. Notopoulos, "The Homeric Hymns as Oral Poetry: A Study of the Post-homeric Oral Tradition," *AJP* 83 (1962): 337–68. Despite its intrinsic interest, the whole question of oral versus written composition will not be considered here.

[5] U. von Wilamowitz-Moellendorff, "Hephaistos," in *Kleine Schriften* 5, pt. 2 (Berlin, 1971), pp. 10–14, believed Demodocus's song was a "Fortsetzung" of an older "Homeric Hymn to Hephaestus" (or, more likely, to Dionysus), recounting the god's binding of

But the bard,
servant of the Muses, hymns the famous deeds of men of the past
and the blessed gods who inhabit Olympus.
(Theogony 99–101)

In the *Hymn to Apollo*, the girls on Delos first hymn the divinities Apollo, Leto, and Artemis, and then sing of the men and women of old (158–61); on Olympus, the Muses themselves follow the same program: "they hymn the immortal gifts of the gods and the sufferings of men" (190–91). Here, at least, we find no evidence for subordinating hymn poetry to epic. On the basis of these passages, as well as comparative evidence, one might plausibly argue that hymn poetry is in fact prior to epic and that similarities may be due to epic adaptations of hymnic forms and motifs.[6]

Recently, the trend of neglect has begun to be reversed. Inspired in part by the growing interest in the interpretation of myth and the formal analysis of mythic narrative, a number of important studies of individual Homeric Hymns have appeared. The results of these investigations have done much to move the hymns from a marginal position into the mainstream of archaic Greek poetry. But what is still lacking is an adequate global investigation of the four major hymns as a genre.[7]

Ranging in length from 300 to 600 lines and in date from about the eighth to the sixth centuries B.C., the four long hymns contain fully developed narratives in the epic manner on mythological subjects. Each of them celebrates a divinity through a story in which the god is a protagonist. Thus, both the *Hymn to Apollo* and the *Hymn to Hermes* recount the birth of their respective deities, as does the *Hymn to Dionysus*, which stands first in the collection, but of which, unfortunately, we have only

---

Hera and his introduction into Olympus by Dionysus. Cf. R. Merkelbach, "Ein Fragment des homerischen Dionysos-Hymnus," *ZPE* 12 (1973): 212–15.

[6] As does M. Durante, *Sulla preistoria della tradizione poetica greca. Parte seconda: Risultanze della comparazione indoeuropea* (Rome, 1976), pp. 46–50 and 155–56. J. De Hoz, "Poesia oral independiente de Homero en Hesiodo y los Himnos homéricos," *Emerita* 32 (1964): 283–98, suggests that the poetry of Hesiod and the Homeric Hymns represents a tradition parallel to that of epic. W. Kullmann, *Das Wirken der Götter in der Ilias* (Berlin, 1956), pp. 10–41, argues that the Homeric epic evolved from the joining of two originally separate genres: hymn poetry and "Sage."

[7] The closest thing is probably the study of Lenz (1975). C. A. Sowa, *Traditional Themes and the Homeric Hymns* (Chicago, 1984), goes in a different direction. She analyzes plot types and typical scenes in the hymns in order to reveal their similarities to epic and folktale motifs. Useful as these comparisons may be, they ignore those elements that are specific to the hymns as a genre.

two short fragments. The abduction of Persephone is narrated in the *Hymn to Demeter*, whereas the *Hymn to Aphrodite* relates the goddess's seduction of the mortal Anchises. As the rhetorician Menander already recognized, the birth hymns merely constitute a subgroup within the class of mythological hymns.[8] Each of these poems attempts to define the essential nature and character of the god to be celebrated through a narrative sequence of his words and deeds. The peculiarity of this procedure is worth noting; one need only consider the Psalms, the shorter Homeric Hymns, or the so-called Orphic Hymns, which have little or no narrative development. Praising a divinity by no means requires telling a story about that divinity. Any interpretation of the major hymns must ultimately come to terms with the function of mythological narrative.

The first step in interpreting a poem or a group of poems is to determine, even if only provisionally, their genre.[9] There are, of course, many ways to go about defining a genre. One approach that has recently gained special currency in connection with the archaic period sets out to discover the social context or function of a given type of poetry by determining the occasion of its performance, the expectations of the audience, and the constraints on the poet. The results obtained, especially in relation to iambic and elegaic poetry, have been extremely fruitful. But, unfortunately, we now seem far less certain of the circumstances surrounding the performance of the major hymns than earlier generations of scholars.[10] For instance, it was long assumed that the *Hymn to Demeter* was performed at Eleusis in conjunction with the festival there, but recently Clinton has effectively demolished that view.[11] *Aphrodite*, on the other hand, was considered unrelated to a religious occasion, but composed to celebrate the royal house of the Aeneadae in the Troad. That

---

[8] *Menander Rhetor*, ed. D. A. Russell and N. G. Wilson (Oxford, 1981), 338.17: "I hold that all genealogies and all hymns involving genealogical elements proceed by means of mythical circumstances, whereas it is not true that all mythical hymns proceed by means of genealogies. Consequently, the class of mythical hymns will be the more generic, and that of genealogical hymns the more specific."

[9] Cf. A. Fowler, *Kinds of Literature* (Cambridge, Mass., 1982), p. 38: "when we try to decide the genre of a work, then, our aim is to discover its meaning." For the role of genre determination in interpretation, see the lucid discussion of E. D. Hirsch, *Validity in Interpretation* (New Haven, 1967), pp. 68–126.

[10] The brief discussion of T.B.L. Webster, "Homeric Hymns and Society," in *Le monde grec: Pensée littérature histoire documents: Hommages à Claire Préaux* (Brussels, 1975), pp. 86–93, remains superficial.

[11] K. Clinton, "The Author of the Homeric *Hymn to Demeter*," *Opuscula Atheniensia* 16 (1986): 43–49.

6

theory has been persuasively challenged by P. Smith.[12] In the case of the *Hymn to Apollo*, many scholars maintained that the Delian part was composed for Delos, whereas the Pythian half was performed at Delphi. The second statement can, I think, be disproved, while the first offers a possible, but by no means necessary, conclusion. If, however, we assume that *Apollo* is not two poems but one, it becomes even more questionable. *Hermes* has been linked to Athens on linguistic and other grounds, but its composition has also been localized in Boeotia and Arcadia because both are mentioned in the course of the poem. Nevertheless, no conclusive evidence links *Hermes* to a specific festival.

We must finally admit that we have very little firm knowledge about the circumstances surrounding the composition and performance of these major hymns. I would nevertheless venture to suggest that, like the account by Demodocus of Hephaestus's successful ruse against Ares and Aphrodite, they were presented at the conclusion of a feast (*dais*), or what was later called a *symposion*. Several passages in the *Hymn to Hermes*, to be discussed, corroborate this suggestion, although they may well be archaizing. They do, however, raise the possibility that hymn poetry and theogonic poetry, as well as epic, may originally have been performed at the same kind of occasion. And this really ought not to surprise us, for the metrical form and the diction of these three types of poetry is practically identical. What I am suggesting is that the hymns should not be linked to cults or specific religious festivals so much as to the ambit of *epos*.

If our attempts to discover a functional definition of the hymnic genre remain inconclusive, we might also try to define it descriptively by listing its formal components.[13] We could, for example, catalog the formal features of the major Homeric hymns, such as the opening and closing formulas, or the use of relative predication. But most of these elements can also be found in the short hymns, and the distinctive feature

[12] P. M. Smith, "Aineidai as Patrons of *Iliad XX* and the Homeric *Hymn to Aphrodite*," *HSCP* 85 (1981): 17–58 (hereafter cited as Smith [1981b]).

[13] See, for example, W. H. Race, "Aspects of Rhetoric and Form in Greek Hymns," *GRBS* 23 (1982): 5–14. For attempts to construct typologies combining both formal and thematic elements, see R. Janko, "The Structure of the Homeric Hymns: A Study in Genre," *Hermes* 109 (1981): 9–24 (hereafter cited as Janko [1981b]); W. W. Minton, "The Proem-hymn of Hesiod's Theogony," *TAPA* 101 (1970): 357–77; and P. Friedländer, "Das Proömium von Hesiods Theogonie," in *Hesiod*, ed. E. Heitsch (Darmstadt, 1966), pp. 277–94. A. M. Miller, *From Delos to Delphi: A Literary Study of the Homeric Hymn to Apollo* (Leiden, 1985), offers a detailed study of "the rhetoric of praise" in that hymn.

of the long hymn—the extended mythological narrative—is simply counted as one element among others, even though it occupies 90 percent of the poem. Or, by way of another approach, we could focus on the myth section and enumerate certain building blocks, thematic components, or recurring motifs. Lenz, for example, lists four such typical components: conflict; aetiology; epiphany; and Olympian scene.[14] Assuming that these elements are present in all four hymns, we would still have to admit that they are too vague to be of much use. Even if they were further narrowed and refined, we would be left with the question of the inner necessity of just these components and not others. We remain, so to speak, on the outside looking in.

The long hymns are basically a narrative genre, and neither a descriptive nor an analytic approach offers much help in answering some very simple questions. What kind of stories are appropriate to the hymnic genre? Will *any* story involving a god do? To this, the answer is evidently no, since, in the *Hymn to Apollo*, the poet rejects several stories concerning the god's love affairs. But then why is an erotic exploit of Aphrodite a suitable subject? What determines the choice of subject matter—its starting and end point? Do the diverse narratives contained in the long hymns have a common framework, and is that framework somehow conditioned by the generic character of the hymns?

To answer these fundamental questions, a different approach is required, one, for want of a better word, I term *contextual*. It will require a detour over some familiar territory, but one necessary to lay bare the conceptual presuppositions and generic foundations from which all four major hymns spring. Only on such a basis can the significance of their subject matter and its presentation be grasped, as well as the specific character of this genre within the context of Greek poetry.

In a famous, not to say notorious statement, Herodotus claims: "Whence each of the gods came into being, or whether they always existed, and what their forms were, the Greeks did not know until recently, only yesterday, so to speak. Hesiod and Homer ... were the ones who made a theogony for the Greeks and gave the gods their names and distinguished their honors and skills and indicated their forms" (2.53.1–2).

---

[14] Lenz (1975), pp. 9–21. Lenz makes unnecessary problems for himself by including the fifty-nine line *Hymn to Dionysus* (no. 7) among the long hymns. It contains neither aetiology nor Olympian scene. K. Keyssner, *Gottesvorstellung und Lebensauffassung im griechischen Hymnus* (Stuttgart, 1932), attempts to identify recurring motifs in all Greek hymns, both literary and cultic. His survey casts too wide a net to be of use in this study.

On the surface, this statement is patently absurd. Historians of religion assure us that the Greek gods are considerably older. Their origins are heterogeneous; some may belong to the pre-Greek Aegean substrate, whereas others are unquestionably Indo-European in origin; yet others may be imports from abroad, especially the East. Moreover, each Greek community developed its own local cults and gods in relative isolation. A divinity known under the same name may show an astounding diversity—for example, the Demeter of Eleusis and the black Demeter of Phigalia.[15] Yet around the eighth century B.C., a strong centripetal force arises, countering the centrifugal forces that splinter the individual Greek communities. It manifests itself in the emergence of the great Panhellenic shrines, like Olympia, Delphi, Delos, and Eleusis, which draw Greek speakers from every city and community. It also manifests itself in the great Panhellenic epics of Homer and Hesiod and, above all, in the creation of a Panhellenic Olympian religion.

Among modern scholars, Rohde echoes and vindicates Herodotus's words:

> No priestly teaching gave the Greeks their "theology"; at that period, popular belief, left to its own devices, must have been even more fragmented into individual conceptions according to local regions and cities than at a later date, when a few generalized Hellenic institutions offered unifying focal points. The elaboration and consequent systematization of an ordered divine community, composed of a limited number of clearly characterized gods, arranged in a permanent configuration, and assembled in one superterrestrial abode, can only be the work of the poet. If we were to trust Homer, it would seem as if the countless local cults of Greece, with their gods strictly confined to one locale, scarcely existed. Homer almost completely ignores them. His gods are Panhellenic, Olympian.[16]

More recently, Nagy (although he rejects the individual existence of Homer and Hesiod) comments on the same phenomenon: "the Olympus of Hesiodic and Homeric poetry is a panhellenic construct that elevates the gods beyond their local attributes. . . . The evolution of most major gods from most major cities into the integrated family at Olympus amounts to

---

[15] Cf. the discussion of W. Burkert, *Structure and History in Greek Mythology and Ritual* (Berkeley, 1979), pp. 125–32.

[16] E. Rohde, *Psyche*, 2nd ed. (Freiburg, 1898), pp. 38–39.

9

a synthesis that is not just artistic but political in nature, comparable with the evolution of the Panhellenic games known as the Olympics."[17]

The Olympian pantheon constitutes what Vernant calls "a system of classification, a particular way of ordering and conceptualizing the universe by distinguishing within it various types of powers and forces."[18] The formation of such a system involves the establishment of categories and hierarchies, as well as the delineation and definition of spheres of influence among the gods. In relation to each other, on a horizontal axis, each divinity has a mode and arena of action assigned to him; similarly, a hierarchical chain of being supplies a vertical axis, encompassing gods, men, and beasts.[19] In this task of systematization, the Panhellenic epic and theogonic poets, but also the poets of the hymns, played a crucial role.

A clear sign of the Panhellenic Olympian orientation of the Homeric Hymns resides in their self-conscious avoidance of local legend. For instance, at the beginning of the second half of the *Hymn to Apollo*, the poet pauses briefly to consider whether he should recount the god's erotic adventures before finally settling on his chosen subject: Apollo's founding of the Delphic oracle. The contrast here does not merely lie between the private and public exploits of the god. The amatory escapades of the Olympians are never, strictly speaking, private matters, for they produce heroes and founders of cities and cults. Yet, for the most part, these remain local concerns. The distinction between the themes rejected by the hymnist and the one he adopts resides in the difference between the local and the Panhellenic. In the *Hymn to Hermes* the newborn god steals the cattle of Apollo. The geographical setting varies in different versions of the myth, but in this hymn the cows are originally situated in Pieria near Olympus, and their destination is the vicinity of Olympia—a topography that eschews local claims but is readily intelligible to a Panhellenic audience. The fragmentary *Hymn to Dionysus* overtly rejects as lies five local claims to the birthplace of Dionysus before substituting the mythical Nysa.[20] In a far more striking manner, the two most important religious foundations described in the Homeric Hymns, that of the oracle at Delphi and that of the Mysteries of Eleusis, differ not merely in matters of detail, but massively, from the local and official

---

[17] G. Nagy, "Hesiod," in *Ancient Writers*, ed. T. J. Luce (New York, 1982), pp. 48–49.
[18] J.-P. Vernant, *Mythe et société en Grèce ancienne* (Paris, 1974), p. 106.
[19] Cf. Vernant (1974), pp. 141–76.
[20] Cf. Nagy (1982), p. 47.

legends of the founding of those shrines. In both cases, it can be shown that the deviant versions of these foundation myths contained in the hymns are motivated by their pervasive Panhellenic and Olympian orientation.

Despite their unquestionable differences in style and subject matter, the major hymns are in fact linked by a common framework or conception. Each one recounts a critical chapter in the mythological history of the Olympians. Herein lies their generic unity. Each can be said to take place in the time of origins that Eliade has called *illud tempus*.[21] Those actions and events that occurred *then* among the gods have permanent and irreversible consequences *now* and explain why the world is the way it is. The mythological framework that informs the hymns can be defined more precisely.

In Homer, we can recognize the stabilized Olympian pantheon with each god exercising his *timai* under the supreme authority of Zeus, who is both king and father of them all. Disputes and tensions arise, to be sure, especially when, in the *Iliad*, Zeus determines to carry out his promise to Thetis to honor Achilles in the face of opposition from the other divinities. But the supreme god easily deals with such challenges to his domination. We may recall that the theomachy of Book XXI is put on for his amusement.

But it was not always so. There are several allusions in the *Iliad* to earlier events in the history of the Olympians when Zeus's authority had not yet been so firmly established. Three examples will suffice. First, in Book I (396–406), Achilles suggests to Thetis that she remind Zeus what happened when Hera, Poseidon, and Athena tried to bind him: Thetis rescued Zeus by summoning up to Olympus the hundred-handed Briaraeus, "whose strength is greater than his father's." The explicit reference to the three major divinities who oppose Zeus's *boulē* is significant. In the *Iliad*, they may indeed irritate Zeus and even delay the fulfillment of his plan for a while, but they pose no genuine threat. The phrase, "whose strength is greater than his father's," hints obliquely at generational rivalries and violent successions—all of which belong to the remote past.

A second example occurs at the end of Book VIII (477–83) when Zeus orders Athena and Hera off the battlefield. In castigating his wife,

[21] See M. Eliade, *The Myth of the Eternal Return*, trans. W. R. Trask (New York, 1954); and *Myth and Reality*, trans. W. R. Trask (New York, 1963), esp. pp. 5–38.

Zeus remarks rather opaquely that he cares not a whit for her anger, even if she should go to the nethermost boundaries of the earth, where Iapetus and Cronus live in the depth of Tartarus. In his commentary, Leaf suggests two possible interpretations of Zeus's words, of which the second is to be preferred: "I should not be sorry to lose you"; and "You may try and raise a revolt in Tartarus, and I should not be afraid of your efforts."[22] The possibility of a genuine rebellion on the part of Hera in alliance with the Titans may in fact have existed some time in the past. But now Zeus's rule is unassailable.[23]

The last passage, from Book xv (187–211), alludes to events even earlier in the history of the Olympian family. When Zeus awakens from his postcoital nap, he seeks to reassert his authority over Poseidon, who has been helping the Greeks. The argument betweeen the two gods symbolizes a problematic feature of the Olympian cosmos. Zeus claims supremacy on the basis of his greater strength, age, and intelligence. But Poseidon counters by reminding his older brother of the equality of the ancient division of *timai* by lot among the three sons of Cronus. The notion of equal apportionment of *timai* stands in direct conflict with a hierarchical order under the supreme domination of Zeus. In the *Iliad*, after some initial bluster, Poseidon yields. But was it always so easy? We can readily perceive that this dual system could lead to genuine conflicts. For a true and permanent equilibrium to be achieved, the valid claims of all parties must somehow be respected and accommodated.

Homer, then, gives us only a few hints here and there of earlier, serious conflicts among the gods, but these belong to the distant past. In the world of the epic, the domination of Zeus remains unquestioned, and, despite occasional perturbations, the foundations of Olympus can no longer be shaken. The Olympian regime has achieved its final and permanent configuration.

For an outline of the prehistory of the gods, as well as human prehistory, we must turn to the Hesiodic poems. The so-called Succession Myth forms the narrative armature of the *Theogony*; similarly, the Prometheus story and its alternative, the Myth of the Ages in the *Works and Days*, serve to define and articulate the critical stages of the development

[22] W. Leaf, *The Iliad*, 2nd ed. (London, 1900–1902), p. 364.

[23] Cf. the splendid challenge Zeus pronounces before the assembled gods at the beginning of Book viii (18–27). αὖτε (26) may indicate that the cosmic tug-of-war actually took place in the past. See also *Iliad* xv.16–28; and C. H. Whitman, "Hera's Anvils," *HSCP* 74 (1970): 37–42.

of mankind in relation to the gods. These arch-myths, if I may call them that, pervade archaic Greek thought and literature, profoundly influencing the poetry of Pindar, the *Oresteia*, and the *Prometheus Bound*, to name only the most obvious examples. In turn, they form the essential background to the narratives of the major Homeric Hymns. Much that may seem elusive or obscure to the modern reader of these ancient texts was for their contemporary audience a common mythological framework embracing the divine and human past.

I cannot here give an exhaustive analysis of these myths; I can only point out some features that have a crucial bearing on the interpretation of the hymns. The stories of Uranus, Cronus, and Zeus, with their conflicts between father and son—with the strange business of impeding the birth of children and castration in the case of Uranus, the swallowing of offspring at birth on the part of Cronus, and, finally, Zeus's ingestion of Metis—all follow the same basic pattern. Equally important is the role of the female within the myth, especially that of Gaia. Gaia is the prime mover and promoter of the succession in heaven and the consistent enemy of the status quo. It is she who devises the plot whereby Cronus castrates Uranus; she, in turn, rescues the infant Zeus by a trick and assists him in deposing his father. In a last act of resistance to the victorious Olympian, she conceives Typhoeus, who "would have ruled over gods and men" (*Theogony* 837). Only after Zeus succeeds in blasting Typhoeus with his thunderbolt, does Gaia finally admit defeat and renounce her opposition by advising Zeus of the perils inherent in his marriage to Metis. To render his rule eternal, the supreme Olympian must put an end to succession by precluding the birth of a son "greater than his father." He accomplishes this by a preemptive strike, swallowing the pregnant Metis. With this act, he not only removes all future threat of a successor, but gains the permanent possession of *mētis* that renders his rule invincible.

It is, then, the female, whether as mother or wife, who relentlessly pursues change and promotes succession. In Hesiod, this pattern comes to an end with the accession of Zeus. In the major Homeric Hymns, however, as we shall see, it remains operative. Both the rebellious Hera and Demeter exploit their maternity to oppose the patriarchal order of Zeus.

If the Succession Myth provides the constitutive pattern for divine history, two myths concerning the human past play a similarly exemplary role in archaic Greek thought. The Prometheus myth, as Vernant has shown, accounts for the permanent separation of gods and men and the fundamental facts of human life as we know it: the necessity of work and the establishment of sacrifice and marriage as uniquely human institutions.[24] The *Works and Days* offers an alternative to the Prometheus myth which, though superficially quite different, follows its general contours in accounting for the present condition of mankind. The Myth of the Ages recounts the successive epochs in human history, and, like the Prometheus story, it begins from an original closeness between the gods and mankind and ends with their permanent separation and the constitution of the human condition as it is now.[25] The men of the golden race, although they resemble the gods, die out because they cannot reproduce. Zeus destroys the infantile race of silver, but the men of the Bronze Age manage to annihilate themselves. Zeus then determines to create the race of heroes, who are "better and more just" than their predecessors. These heroes, whom Hesiod calls *hēmitheoi*, are produced through the intercourse of gods and mortals. Some die in the great heroic conflicts such as the Trojan War, but they are not completely destroyed by the gods or by each other. Gradually, however, the gods withdraw from unions with mortals, and the result is the Age of Iron, our age. We are the degenerate offspring of the heroes in whose veins the divine blood has become diluted.

The two Homeric Hymns that most clearly involve human beings in their dealings with the gods, *Aphrodite* and *Demeter*, cannot be understood without reference to the fundamental conceptions underlying the Prometheus story and the Myth of the Ages, but this is equally true for the hymns in which humans appear to play only a secondary (*Apollo*) or even marginal (*Hermes*) role. The stories recounted in the hymns belong to Eliade's category of "true stories" or myths that can be differentiated from tales and fables, which "even when they have caused changes in the World . . . have not altered the human condition as such. . . . After the cosmogony and the creation of man other events occurred, and man *as he is today* is the direct result of those mythical events, *he is constituted by those events* . . . because something happened *in illo tempore*."[26]

[24] Cf. Vernant (1974), pp. 177–94; also "A la table des hommes," in *La cuisine du sacrifice en pays grec*, ed. M. Detienne and J.-P. Vernant (Paris, 1979), pp. 37–132.

[25] Cf. S. Benardete, "Hesiod's *Works and Days*: A First Reading," ΑΓΩΝ 1 (1967): 156–58; and J. Rudhardt, *Du mythe, de la religion grecque et de la compréhension d'autrui* (Geneva, 1981), pp. 245–81.

[26] Eliade (1963), p. 11.

We are now ready to define the major hymns as a genre of poetry with a specific character and function within the constellation of archaic Greek poetry. Formal elements of diction, style, and narrative technique link the hymns to *epos*, of which they form a subset. The Homeric poems show us the fully perfected and stable Olympian pantheon in its interaction with the heroes; the *Theogony* reveals the genesis of the Olympian order and ends with the triumphal accession to power of Zeus. Between theogonic poetry and epic there remains a gap, one that is filled by the Olympian narratives of the longer hymns.[27] Their appropriate motto might well be the culminating lines of the *Theogony*:

> The blessed gods ... then urged Olympian wide-seeing Zeus ... to be their king and lord of the immortals; and he divided up their *timai* well.
>
> (881–85)

The major hymns, then, serve to complete the Olympian agenda and provide the clearest account of what I would call the politics of Olympus. At the core of each lies a concern with the acquisition or redistribution of *timai* within the Olympian cosmos.[28] As critical chapters in the early history of the Olympian family, all four hymns begin from a point of crisis in the Olympian hierarchy. The birth of a new divinity (*Apollo, Hermes*) offers an ideal topic, for such an event inevitably precipitates a crisis within the existing hierarchy, which is only resolved when the new god establishes his sphere of influence and is integrated into the Olympian order. *Aphrodite* and *Demeter* pose a rather different set of problems, but each proceeds from a plan of Zeus whose eventual outcome leads to a new and permanent ordering of relations, not only among the gods but also between gods and mortals.

Each hymn describes an epoch-making moment in the mythic chronology of Olympus and, as such, inaugurates a new era in the divine and human cosmos. The state of the cosmos at the end of each of the hymns differs from that at its beginning; the intervening narrative explains the character of that change and how it came about. To apprehend the progress of the events recounted means to understand its result. The character of these narratives dictates the form that our interpretation should take. Because the narrative constitutes the vehicle of change both on Olympus

---

[27] The gap we have discerned may be analogous to the gap between the *Iliad* and the *Odyssey*, which was filled with the cyclic epics. On this question, see the Conclusion.

[28] Cf. Lenz (1975), p. 20.

and on earth, only a linear analysis of each poem can adequately describe the starting point of the mythic action, its progress, and its final goal. Therefore, despite certain drawbacks, I offer an interpretation of each of the individual hymns that begins at the beginning and proceeds through to its end and that respects the integrity and particular character of each poem.

A word, too, about my own intentions. Although the texts under investigation contain mythological narratives, I am not engaged in the study of myth per se, but in a literary study of the hymns. In a structural study of a myth in the manner of Lévi-Strauss, all variants, including parallel motifs from Greek and even other mythologies, have approximately equal standing; no one text is "privileged." In the interest of revealing an underlying structure common to them all, the precise sequence of episodes may be disregarded and certain adventitious details may be ignored.[29] But in the interpretations that follow, the text of the hymns is privileged, the exact order of events is critical, and no detail can be considered irrelevant.[30] Variant versions are, of course, of interest, but only insofar as they illuminate the text at hand. Frequently, such comparisons highlight the particular *Tendenz* of the hymnic version.

My aim throughout has been to restore the major Homeric Hymns to their rightful and central place in Greek poetic thought concerning the Olympian order and its meaning for mankind. The hymns provide a necessary complement to the Panhellenic epic and theogonic poetry of Homer and Hesiod. From these intriguing compositions, we can learn not only what the Greeks thought about their gods, but how.

[29] M. Detienne, *Dionysus mis à mort* (Paris, 1976), p. 25, offers a succinct statement of the "classic" structuralist method: "l'analyse structurale ... se donne pour tâche de déchiffrer simultanément les différentes versions d'un même mythe de manière à en reconnaître le système caché." For an exposition and critique of Lévi-Strauss's method and an attempt to overcome some of its shortcomings, see T. Turner, "Narrative Structure and Mythopoesis," *Arethusa* 10 (1977): 103–64. I am, in fact, much indebted to certain structuralist insights and attempt to combine them with a linear literary analysis.

[30] See the discussion of Vernant (1974), pp. 246–47, who clearly outlines the steps required for a full interpretation of myths embedded in highly elaborated and structured literary texts.

HYMN TO APOLLO

 The preceding chapter has offered a general framework that I believe provides a valid foundation from which to begin a consideration of the major Homeric Hymns. I do not, however, pretend that it is possible or desirable simply to impose that framework on the individual poems in a mechanical fashion. The hymns are not homogeneous compositions, and they must not be homogenized if we hope to achieve some understanding of them. While occupying their place within the ordered pantheon, the Olympian gods differ from one another in their powers and prerogatives. Moreover, each deity is distinguished by typical characteristics and a nexus of relationships to other gods as well as to mortals. Analogously, the celebration of an individual divinity—which is at the same time a definition of the god's nature—will appropriately differ both in form and in content from the praise of another god. Each hymn, then, presents a different set of problems and must be understood on its own terms. The goal of each poem is to characterize and to convey fully the essence of its chosen divinity both in speech and in action.

This study begins with the *Hymn to Apollo*, neither because of the simplicity of its structure (that prize should perhaps go to *Aphrodite*), nor because it (or parts of it) is thought to be the earliest composition in the collection. I begin with *Apollo* not on the basis of historical or stylistic criteria, but because it comes first in mythological chronology. Its temporal place within the divine history of Olympus emerges in the course of the narrative and forms an essential key to the interpretation of the poem.

In dealing with *Apollo*, it is impossible to sidestep completely the problem—which more than two centuries of scholarship have raised to the status of a Question—concerning the unity of the poem and the relation of the so-called Delian part to the Pythian. In the course of time, almost every position on this question has been occupied, with sundry modifications and permutations. It has been maintained that the Delian half is the earlier or, on the contrary, that the Pythian is; that the hymn consists in reality of two independent poems accidently joined together; or that the Pythian half was consciously composed with the Delian as its model, or vice versa. Among the analysts, there is no consensus as to where one poem ends and the second begins, or even as to how many separate pieces make up the hymn. To be sure, stout-hearted unitarians have surfaced in every generation to challenge separatist arguments. The very fact that perfectly reputable scholars have held such widely divergent views suggests that objective evidence, especially that based on ancient testimonia and diction, does not suffice to settle the case.[1] Subjective judgments of quality or taste generally convince only their propounders. At the moment, no one side can claim clear victory, and a certain fatigue has set in during the lull. Perhaps we simply no longer have the taste or energy for the old polemics. However that may be, the battle has produced a net gain; both sides have contributed acute observations that can further our understanding.

With the terrain so well strewn with the flags of philology, I see little point in planting yet another banner with a strange device. Yet an

---

[1] For a thorough and balanced account of scholarly views concerning the composition and unity of the *Hymn to Apollo* from Ruhnken (1782) to West (1975), the interested reader should consult K. Förstel, *Untersuchungen zum Homerischen Apollonhymnos* (Bochum, 1979), pp. 20–59. Förstel himself turns out to be a cautious separatist (pp. 272–84). E. Drerup, "Der homerische Apollonhymnos: Eine methodologische Studie," *Mnemosyne* 5 (1937): 81–99, also offers a summary of the earlier history of the criticism of the hymn and its relation to the Homeric question. To complete Förstel's survey, I list some studies that have appeared subsequently. Both G. S. Kirk, "Orality and Structure in the Homeric 'Hymn to Apollo,'" in *I poemi epici rapsodici non omerici e la tradizione orale*, ed. C. Brillante et al. (Padua, 1981), pp. 163–82, and Janko (1982), pp. 99–132, maintain the traditional separatist view, which assigns priority to the Delian half. Adherents to a unitarian position include M. Baltes, "Die Kataloge im homerischen Apollonhymnus," *Philologus* 125 (1982): 25–43; F. De Martino, *Omero agonista in Delo* (Brescia, 1982); W. G. Thalmann, *Conventions of Form and Thought in Early Greek Epic Poetry* (Baltimore, 1984), pp. 64–73; and Miller (1985). Finally, Sowa (1984), pp. 172–84, shows herself to be a separatist on composition while maintaining the thematic unity of the poem.

obligation persists to outline the assumptions that guide my approach. First, Apollo is a complex, even ambiguous figure, multifaceted rather than monolithic. There is every reason to expect that a poem that aims to set out a complete picture of this god will not be a simple one. Taken in isolation, neither the Delian nor the Pythian half delineates the full complexity of Apollo. It is sufficient to note that, at his birth, Apollo proclaims three areas of influence as his own: the bow, the lyre, and oracular power. Only at the end of the hymn has the god come into full possession of these three *timai*. In addition, the striking formal and thematic parallels between the first and second halves suggest a unitary conception. Finally—and to my mind the decisive consideration—certain crucial questions are raised in the first half but not satisfactorily answered until the end of the poem.[2] I conclude that, as a whole, the hymn presents a unified and comprehensible progression with a complex but nevertheless linear movement that ends when the new god has established himself and received his full definition within the Olympian order.

Prologue

Μνήσομαι οὐδὲ λάθωμαι ᾿Απόλλωνος ἑκάτοιο,
ὅν τε θεοὶ κατὰ δῶμα Διὸς τρομέουσιν ἰόντα·
καί ῥά τ᾿ ἀναΐσσουσιν ἐπὶ σχεδὸν ἐρχομένοιο
πάντες ἀφ᾿ ἑδράων, ὅτε φαίδιμα τόξα τιταίνει.

I shall remember and not forget Apollo, the far-darter,
at whose coming the gods throughout the house of Zeus tremble;
and they dart up as he comes closer—
all of them—from their seats, when he stretches his splendid bow.
(1–4)

The hymn opens with a violent and dramatic scene that vividly portrays the terrifying power of Apollo through his effect on the gods assembled on Olympus. They tremble at his approach, then leap up from their chairs, not so much from respect, but rather out of uncontrollable fear at

[2] L. Deubner, "Der homerische Apollonhymnus," *Sitzungsberichte der Preussischen Akademie der Wissenschaften, Phil.-hist. Klasse* 24 (1938): 251, emphatically poses this challenge to the unitarians: "ob es für das Verstädnis von D [the Delian half] *notwendig* ist, dass seine Motive in P [the Pythian half] wiederkehren."

the sight of the god brandishing his bow.[3] The awesome apparition of Apollo on the threshold of Olympus is, as many scholars have noted, reminiscent of the plague god of the first book of *Iliad*.[4] There his wrath has been aroused by Agamemnon's mistreatment of his priest, and his unfailing arrows rain down upon the Greeks until his anger is appeased. Here, too, his bow is poised with destructive potency; but we are told of no provocation. Why, then, is the god so violently threatening? And why are the others so frightened?

The assembly of the gods seated and feasting in the palace of Zeus has countless parallels in the epic. It evokes a picture of the stabilized (except for minor and transitory perturbations) Olympian pantheon under the supreme authority of Zeus. Yet the threatening entrance of the armed archer is unique and calls to mind ancient hostilities among the gods, the era of primeval theomachies and struggles for power, and the battles of the Giants and the Titans.[5] This hint of an earlier, more turbulent period in divine history at the very outset of the poem is by no means fortuitous but serves, as we shall see, to define its overall temporal position within the framework of Olympian history.

The ferocity inherent in these opening lines has provoked considerable critical discomfort[6] and inspired some rather lame attempts to mit-

---

[3] F. Jacoby, "Der homerische Apollonhymnos," *Sitzungsberichte der Preussischen Akademie der Wissenschaften, Phil.-hist. Klasse* 15 (1933): 727, draws a parallel between the *Hymn to Apollo*'s opening and *Iliad* 1.533–35 and xv.85–86, but the comparison is inexact. In the first case, the gods rise (ἀνέσταν) as a sign of respect when Zeus enters Olympus. In the second, the gods do indeed dart up (ἀνήϊξαν) at Hera's unexpected return, but their gesture is due to surprise and curiosity rather than fear. Cf. Förstel (1979), p. 173; and Miller (1985), p. 3.

[4] Cf. W. F. Otto, *The Homeric Gods*, trans. M. Hadas (New York, 1954), p. 75. F. Altheim, "Die Entstehungsgeschichte des homerischen Apollonhymnus," *Hermes* 59 (1924): 431, compares Apollo here to the *eidolon* of Heracles in the Nekyia, *Odyssey* 11.606–8, whereas AHS (1936), p. 200, and M. L. West, "Cynaethus' Hymn to Apollo," *CQ* 25 (1975): 163, both detect similarities to the figure of Odysseus at the beginning of Book 22 of the *Odyssey*.

[5] Förstel (1979), p. 166, comments: "Das sieht nach Himmelsturm und Götterkampf aus. Aber darum kann es sich nicht handeln. Denn die Götter sind friedlich versammelt." There is indeed a tension between the peaceful assembly on Olympus and Apollo's savage irruption. Förstel, p. 170, suggests that the motif of the god's threatening demeanor may be derived from an account of a theomachy, but its displacement in its present context "nimmt ihm die reale Kraft." "So steht das Verhalten Apollons in grotesken Widerspruch zur Situation" (p. 166). Förstel prefers a grotesque contradiction to the possibility that the reminiscence of divine hostilities here may be intentional.

[6] West (1975), p. 163, for example, calls the scene "a peculiar business," while Kirk (1981): 166–67, speaks of a "post-Homeric exaggeration," "well outside the limits of Ho-

igate them. Despite the *ipsissima verba* of the text, Baumeister insisted that the god is merely returning from the hunt and carries his bow on his shoulder.[7] Gemoll suggested that the stretching of the bow constitutes a playful gesture on Apollo's part.[8] Miller, too, believes that Apollo has only been deploying his bow against enemies outside Olympus and, I suppose, has absentmindedly forgotten to put it away before entering.[9] As Jacoby said, all such interpretations sound too "gemütlich."[10] None will do, because they render both the scene and its sequel absurd. Only by allowing the scene its full impact does its reversal in the following lines achieve its true force.

For the moment, the awesome potential for destructive violence remains unrealized. In sharp contrast to the panicked commotion of the other gods, "Leto alone remained seated by Zeus the thunderer" (5). From her place at Zeus's side, the menacing sight does not perturb her. Calmly, she disarms her son:

ἥ ῥα βιόν τ᾽ ἐχάλασσε καὶ ἐκλήϊσε φαρέτρην,
καί οἱ ἀπ᾽ ἰφθίμων ὤμων χείρεσσιν ἑλοῦσα,
τόξον ἀνεκρέμασε πρὸς κίονα πατρὸς ἑοῖο
πασσάλου ἐκ χρυσέου· τὸν δ᾽ εἰς θρόνον εἷσεν ἄγουσα.

She unstrung the bow and closed the quiver;
and, having taken it in her hands, from his strong shoulders,
she hung the bow on the column of his father's ⟨house⟩
from a golden peg; but him she led and sat on a throne.

(6–9)

---

meric *ethos*" and labels Apollo here a "figure of burlesque." Cf. G. Roux, "Sur deux passages de l'Hymne homérique à Apollon," *REG* 77 (1965): 1–2, who, with Gallic tact, describes the scene as "un burlesque très discret" characterized by "l'irrévérence légère."

[7] A. Baumeister, *Hymni homerici* (Leipzig, 1860), p. 118.

[8] A. Gemoll, *Die homerischen Hymnen* (Leipzig, 1886), p. 121: "Wir haben uns zu denken, dass Apollon mit gespanntem Bogen hereintritt und nun zum Scherz die Sehne klingen lässt." Cf. AHS (1936) on line 1: "As Apollo approaches the seated Gods he strings his bow to test it."

[9] Miller (1985), p. 15: "His bow is at the ready because he has been wielding it in the world at large and has not yet, at the moment of entering Zeus's halls, adjusted his mood and bearing to his new surroundings."

[10] Jacoby (1933), p. 727, n. 1, in response to U. von Wilamowitz-Moellendorff, *Die Ilias und Homer*, 2nd ed. (Berlin, 1920), p. 442, who claimed that Leto "lehrt den Sohn, was sich auf dem Olymp schickt." Jacoby himself, pp. 729–30, believes that the original scene was toned down by the Pythian poet in keeping with his "andersartigen Apollonbild, das den Musageten und Orakelgott an Stelle des furchtbaren Bogenschützen in den Vordergrund schob" (p. 730).

The sequence of Leto's actions is compressed but graphic.[11] The visual focus concentrates on the splendid bow, first unstrung and finally safely put away, the former object of terror now rendered innocuous. Leto's movements betray a kind of touching maternal solicitude and familiarity[12] as she brings her son to his seat, presumably next to Zeus.

τῷ δ' ἄρα νέκταρ ἔδωκε πατὴρ δέπαϊ χρυσείῳ
δεικνύμενος φίλον υἱόν, ἔπειτα δὲ δαίμονες ἄλλοι
ἔνθα καθίζουσιν· χαίρει δέ τε πότνια Λητώ,
οὕνεκα τοξοφόρον καὶ καρτερὸν υἱὸν ἔτικτεν.

To him, then, the father gave nectar in a golden cup,
welcoming his own son; then the other gods
sit down; and Leto rejoices
because she bore a bow-bearing and mighty son.

(10–13)

With the welcoming gesture of Zeus, the tension is defused and order restored to the festive scene. The joy of Leto in the mightly archer who is her son brings the action to a peaceful close, yet her maternal pride has its foundation precisely in Apollo's ability to provoke such a powerful reaction.

This remarkable little scene introduces three major figures.[13] Apollo, to be sure, dominates the stage, but Leto's calm intervention begins to dissipate the atmosphere of fear, while Zeus's gesture of acknowledgment brings the process to completion. Leto will, of course, become the central persona of the ensuing story of Apollo's birth. Zeus, however, remains peripheral as an actor in the hymn. Yet his role as master of Olympus, husband to Leto, and, above all, father of Apollo, alluded to in the three references in lines 2–8, provides the essential background of the narrative.

The hymn's short but powerful opening leaves many questions unanswered. We are given no indication of what precipitated Apollo's dramatic entrance or of the events that follow. The precise occasion remains

[11] Cf. Förstel (1979), pp. 167–70; and Deubner (1938), pp. 271–74. Miller (1985), p. 16, n. 39, correctly takes the quiver as the object of ἑλοῦα.
[12] Hesiod calls Leto "always kindly, and gentle to men and the immortal gods" (Theogony 406–7).
[13] Cf. M. Forderer, Anfang und Ende der abendländischen Lyrik: Untersuchungen zum homerischen Apollonhymnus und zu Anise Koltz (Amsterdam, 1971), pp. 63–64.

undefined. Critical opinion is fairly evenly divided as to whether the passage must be understood as Apollo's first reception into Olympus—a common hymnic motif[14]—or whether it represents a typical scene, repeated each and every time the god enters his father's halls.[15] Initially, the first interpretation may seem more attractive, for it is difficult to conceive of the gods not finally becoming blasé about Apollo's daily irruption. It follows that supporters of the second alternative are obliged to soften the impact of the scene.[16] Considerably compounding the difficulty is the odd concatenation of tenses. The gods tremble and rise from their seats in the present; Leto remains seated in the imperfect, whereas her disarming of Apollo as well as Zeus's offer of nectar are in the aorist. Yet at the end, we return to the present tense, as the gods sit down and Leto rejoices. To take the scene as a unique event in the past compels us to interpret the present-tense verbs as historical presents—which is awkward, because this usage is not attested in Greek epic poetry.[17] If, on the other hand, the action is a repeated one, then the aorists must be understood as timeless or gnomic aorists, even though the actions they depict

[14] See, for example, *Hymn to Hermes* 325ff.; *Hymn to Aphrodite* (no. 6) 14–18; *Hymn to Pan* 42–47; and *Theogony* 68–71.

[15] First time: Jacoby (1933), p. 728; F. Dornseiff, *Die archaische Mythenerzählung: Folgerungen aus dem homerischen Apollonhymnos* (Berlin, 1933), p. 10; J. Kroll, "Apollon zum Beginn des homerischen Hymnus," *Studi Italiani di Filologia Classica* 27–28 (1956): 181–84; Deubner (1938), p. 272; Forderer (1971), p. 64; A. Heubeck, "Gedanken zum homerischen Apollonhymnos," in *Festschrift K. J. Merentitis* (Athens, 1972), p. 133. Repeated or typical event: Förstel (1979), p. 166, 170; Miller (1985), p. 12; West (1975), p. 163: "It [the opening scene] is represented not just as something he [Apollo] did once but as something he does regularly; and the gods jump every time, as if they had never seen the charade before." Cf. Kirk (1981), p. 167: "If the description in the Hymn were of Apollo's *first* arrival on Olympus, then the different *ethos* and tone of the miraculous-divine-birth genre might explain things; but the tenses forbid this." Sowa (1984), p. 176, characterizes the "variety of tenses" as "timeless" "to describe a scene of the typical, conceived as taking place from time to time in the present." F. Càssola, ed., *Inni omerici* (Milan, 1975), pp. 485–86, remains undecided.

[16] Cf. nn. 8–10 above. Also Baumeister (1860), p. 119: "Assurgunt dii reverentia moti"; and C. Cessi, "L'inno omerico ad Apollo," *Atti del Reale Instituto Veneto di scienze, lettere ed arti* 87 (1928): 868: "tutti gli dei si alzano in segno di onore." Also Dornseiff (1933), p. 1: "So wird ausgemalt, dass der Gott auch bei den übrigen Göttern eine grosse Stellung hat." Cf. Deubner (1938), p. 271: "Es kann sich weder um eine ernsthafte Bedrohung der Götter handeln—denn dazu wäre nicht die leiseste Veranlassung gegeben, noch um einen Scherz—den das wäre geschmacklos. Es bleibt wohl nur eine Möglichkeit: dass der Gott sich für alle Fälle sichern will." Still too *gemütlich*, I fear.

[17] Forderer (1971), p. 167, n. 23, tries to make a case for the historical present in lines 2–4 and 12–13, but the parallels he cites are unconvincing. Förstel (1979), p. 102, correctly argues that use of the historical present nowhere occurs in the archaic epic.

do not comfortably fall into that category.[18] In any event, use of the imperfect tense presents an anomaly.[19]

Various attempts have been made to escape from this impasse, none of them very satisfactory. Wilamowitz, for example, proposed that at line 5, "the poet, who is a narrative poet by profession, converts the daily, recurring manifestation into narrative: the aorist, which one incorrectly calls gnomic, is the tense of *Sage*."[20] Similarly, according to van Groningen, the poet begins from a general description, "but the vividness of the visual representation, which characterizes his race, causes him to pass immediately into the description of a unique scene."[21] Both scholars, in different ways, imply that the poet, on account of his trade or his genes, was swept willy-nilly into narration in the past. However, they both neglect to explain his return to the present tense at the end.

[18] W. Unte, "Studien zum homerischen Apollonhymnos" (Diss., Berlin, 1968), p. 22, and Förstel (1979), pp. 102–4, consider the aorists in lines 6–10 to be "timeless" or gnomic aorists. But the study of this usage cited by Förstel, A. E. Péristérakis, "Essai sur l'aoriste intemporel en Grec" (Diss., Paris) (Athens, 1962), which claims to be exhaustive, significantly omits the opening of *Apollo*. Péristérakis clearly does not consider those aorists gnomic, nor do they fall into the categories he establishes on pp. 6–11.

[19] The imperfect μίμνε seems finally to defeat even Förstel's special pleading, as he admits the aorist ἐμεῖνε as an emendation (p. 354, n. 238.).

[20] Wilamowitz (1920), p. 442, n. 2. Cf. G. Hermann, *Homeri hymni et epigrammata* (Leipzig, 1806), on line 4: "Ita deum in actu motuque versantem intuens, incalescente animo, quod reliquum est, tamquam semel et certo quodam tempore factum ennarat." He then adds enigmatically: "Praeterita si pro praesentibus posita putantur, omnis loci venustas perit."

[21] B. A. van Groningen, *La Composition littéraire archaïque grecque* (Amsterdam, 1958), p. 305, n. 2. Cf. Unte (1968), p. 22, who believes that the poet starts from a characteristic portrait of Apollo in the present, but "falls into" the past as he describes a unique event, the first appearance of Apollo on Olympus. Later, the narrative "falls back into" the present. Compare Jacoby (1933), pp. 728–29: "Die Verse zeigen die dauernde, die charakteristische Erscheinung des furchtbaren Gottes.... Wenn ihn der Hymniker den Bogen gegen die Götter spannen lässt, so schwebt ihm doch wohl das erste Erscheinen des neuen Gottes im Olymp.... So geht der Chier vom hymnischen Präsens der vv. 1–4 ... zum Imperfecktum μίμνε für die Dauerhandlung des Sitzenbleibens und Aorist für die Einzelaktionen ... um zum Schlusse ... zu einem Präsens zurückzukehren, dass man hinter καθίζουσιν vielleicht eher als das einfache Präsens der historischen Erzählung denn als ein hymnisches auffassen wird." (Note the supposition of an inadmissible historical present at line 12.) According to Jacoby, the fluctuation between the characteristic and the unique description of the god arises from the poet's displacement of the sequence of the divinity's first entrance into Olympus from its usual place after the birth narrative. Heubeck (1972), who believes the scene describes Apollo's first entrance into Olympus, speaks of the movement of tenses from present to aorist—that is, from hymnic predication to epic narrative (p. 137, n. 10)—but he does not explain the use of the present tense at the end of the scene. In all these interpretations, the return to the present tense at the close poses a particular stumbling block.

Recently, Janko has proposed another solution. He first divides the Homeric Hymns as a whole into two categories: those with descriptive middle sections in the present tense, which he labels attributive; and those with a central mythic section narrated in the past. In the case of *Apollo* 2–13:

> The poet clumsily chose an Attributive scene incapable of narration in the present tense without absurdity. He began with present tenses in vv. 2–4, but then realized that the scene depicted could not happen once the gods were familiar with Apollo's appearance. Thus he switched to the past tenses of vv. 5–10, turning the passage into something closer to the common description of a deity's first arrival on Olympus.[22]

The resultant "débâcle" or "blunder," as Janko calls it, is then further aggravated by the return to the present tense in lines 12–13, for which he, like scholars before him, can suggest no convincing explanation. Or, rather, he offers two: "perhaps the poet is simply recalling that the scene was meant to be Attributive, and wants to make this clear before the close."[23] This suggests that our poet not only did not have the sense to cover his incompetence but positively insisted upon throwing it into relief. Alternatively, Janko proposes that the change to the present has analogies in other hymns at the end of the myth, where "a few lines are devoted to bringing it up to the present time."[24] Yet we distinctly perceive the present tenses at the beginning and end as parallel and meant to frame the scene as a whole. The gods' initial trembling and jumping up clearly correspond to their taking their seats and Leto's rejoicing.

Neither recourse to grammatical categories nor explanations based on the poet's presumed incompetence proves completely satisfactory. Apropos of a related problem, van Groningen once remarked: "in order to explain an aorist fully, one must take one's leave of the aorist, one must

[22] Janko, (1981b), p. 17; cf. Janko (1982), pp. 100–1, on the "incompetence" of the scene. The explanation of West (1975), p. 163, goes in the opposite direction from Janko's. The poet was "adapting a narrative of Apollo's first coming to Olympus.... But now he makes it into a habitual entry. Why?": Because, according to West, the Delian poet was trying to outdo the other scene on Olympus composed by the earlier Pythian poet presented in lines 184–206. For H. Herter, "L'inno a Hermes alla luce della poesia orale," in Brillante (1981), p. 186, these strange changes of tense in the passage are due to formular composition. If he were correct, one would expect to find a good number of parallels to this procedure in the Homeric epic, although Herter cites none.

[23] Janko (1981b), p. 17.

[24] Janko (1981b), p. 14.

even leave behind the realm of the verb and of language in order to enter into the soul of a people and to see how it conceives of certain aspects of reality."[25] Such advice seems well taken, for the existence of a significant number of parallels within the hymnic corpus to this apparent confusion of tenses suggests that we are not dealing merely with a superficial phenomenon.

Janko himself cites twelve other instances of anomalous past tenses within the Homeric Hymns, which he proceeds to explain away in various ways. But his observations may lead us to a deeper appreciation of what at first seems to be a grammatical oddity. In the long *Hymn to Aphrodite* 9, 10, 18, and 21 (as well as *Hymn to the Mother of the Gods* 4, *Hymn to Poseidon* 4, and *Hymn to Hestia* [no. 29] 3), "past tenses are used for the choice by or allocation to a deity of his present sphere of activity."[26] In other words, although a god received or chose a prerogative at some specific moment in the past, his influence over that sphere abides into the present. In several other cases, the customary pursuits or activities of a god are described indifferently in the past or present tense. In the *Hymn to Pan*, for instance, lines 10–11 are in the present, whereas 12–15 change into the past (cf. 29, and *Apollo* 141–42).[27] The opening of the *Hymn to Aphrodite*, a passage ignored by Janko, recounts how the goddess "aroused sweet desire in the gods and overcame the tribes of men" and beasts (2–3). The myth that follows will describe a specific instance in the past when Aphrodite made use of her particular powers, but the goddess *always* has the same effect on all creatures. For the gods, then, past and present are almost interchangeable. Each divine manifestation resembles every other. This explains the "unusual structure"[28] of the *Hymn to the Dioscuri* (no. 33), where an account of their birth leads into a description in the present tense of their power to rescue storm-bound sailors at sea. However, the divine twins' sudden saving epiphany—presumably in the

---

[25] B. A. van Groningen, "Quelques considérations sur l'aoriste gnomique," in *Studia Varia Carolo Vollgraff* (Amsterdam, 1948), p. 57. Van Groningen there coins the term "l'aoriste mythique," but perhaps "hymnic aorist" would be a more suitable label for our purposes.

[26] Janko (1981b), p. 12.

[27] In reference to the *Hymn to Pan* 10–15, Janko (1981b), p. 20, suggests that "perhaps the thought of the impending transition to Myth influenced the poet here." But in *Apollo*, no myth follows. *Pan* 29 describes the nymphs singing the birth of Pan. According to Janko, p. 19, the past tense is used "because the Nymphs cannot always be singing the same song." Why not? See below on *Theogony* 7–10.

[28] Janko (1981b), p. 20.

form of St. Elmo's fire—is narrated in the past. Each single epiphany of the Dioscuri may be a unique event, but it is simultaneously identical to all other epiphanies.

The preceding review suggests that we may be dealing with a usage peculiar to the Homeric Hymns, one not generally recognized in the grammar books. It points beyond a mere confusion of tenses to a characteristic of the gods themselves. Their actions, prerogatives, and epiphanies can be called timeless—not, however, in the sense that they are beyond or outside time, but insofar as their unique manifestations are indistinguishable from their eternal ones.

The closest analogy to the opening passage in the *Hymn to Apollo*, even including the problematic imperfect, occurs not in the Homeric Hymns but in the proem to the *Theogony*,[29] a passage that could fairly be considered the only extant *prooimion* in Greek literature. I offer a partial summary with an emphasis on the temporal alternations. Beginning from the Heliconian Muses, Hesiod describes in the present tense their haunts on Helicon and their dancing (1–4). The description of their dance on the peak of Helicon then changes to the aorist.[30] At night, shrouded in mist, they march forth in the imperfect,[31] singing of the gods all the while (5–21). At this point, Hesiod launches into an account of his meeting with the Muses and his *Dichterweihe*, a unique occasion narrated in the aorist (22–34). Breaking off abruptly, he begins again, this time in the present, describing their eternal song and its joyous effect on Olympus (35–52). Their birth, briefly narrated in the past, is followed by an account of their present abode on Olympus and their characteristic activity (53–67). However, once in the past, the Muses came to Olympus for the first time, dancing all the way and singing the song they always sing (ἄειδον), celebrating Zeus and his regime (68–76).

This outline may suffice for our purposes. Within the passage, we

---

[29] Jacoby (1933), p. 728, draws attention to the parallel but does not develop it.

[30] Jacoby (1933), p. 728, appears to connect the Muses' setting out from Helicon and the change to the aorist in lines 5–8 to their first arrival on Olympus in lines 68–74. This is incomprehensible to me. Nor can I follow Wilamowitz (1920), p. 470: "Hier ist der Übergang vom Präsens zu dem Aorist wohl nicht genau so wie im Eingang des delischen Hymnus, da die in den ersten Aoristen gegebenen Handlungen derjenigen vorausgehen, die im Präsens steht." However, on p. 469, in his paraphrase, Wilamowitz's Muses have been dancing on Olympus, whereas Hesiod's are on Helicon (*Theogony* 7).

[31] M. L. West in his commentary on the *Theogony* (Oxford, 1966), p. 155, calls both the aorists and the imperfect "timeless," but admits that "this use of the imperfect [in line 10] in a typifying sense does not seem to be recognized by the standard grammars" (p. 156).

discover a variety of descriptions, ranging chronologically from the remote past (the birth of the Muses and their introduction to Olympus), the nearer past of their encounter with Hesiod, and their present and eternal activity. Moreover, their presence embraces two locations: both Helicon and Olympus. Logic may dictate that the Muses cannot be at two places at once, but there is no question that the Olympian and Heliconian Muses are identical. It is, after all, the Olympian Muses who address Hesiod (25), although they meet him on Helicon. Whether on Helicon or on Olympus, or anywhere else, the Muses exercise the same characteristic activity. Hence, past and present become in a sense indistinguishable. The problematic past tenses in lines 7–10 refer *both* to their ever-repeated activity *and* to the unique occasion of their meeting with Hesiod. Their essential nature, embodied in their dance and song, remains always the same, from the moment of their birth through all time to come. Janko claims that the past tenses are necessary because the Muses "cannot always be singing this particular song."[32] But this is exactly what they do—although sometimes they sing it backward and sometimes forward, which explains why Hesiod so firmly insists on their beginning from the beginning for *his* theogony (114–15). For the gods themselves, however, it is a matter of indifference whether the Muses sing their history from its end or from the beginning.

The preceding rather technical analysis has not been undertaken to try the reader's patience, but rather to expose an essential feature of mythic narrative and mythic time, of events that occur *in illo tempore*. The apparent confusion of tenses in descriptions of the gods constitutes no mere aberration, but points rather to a fundamental aspect of their nature. The time of the gods differs from ours.[33] This is clear from the paradox that the gods, although they are born and thus have come into being, henceforth exist forever: αἰὲν ἐόντες. Mortals, on the other hand, are universally liable to change, development, growth, decline, and, ultimately, death. At the mercy of countless accidents, our individual acts are hemmed in by circumstances and, rarely, if ever, do they have the occasion to become, in Pindar's words, who we are. For the gods, however, each and every act, every epiphany and intervention, forms a full expression of the divine being. Hence, an event in the past—say, the birth of a god, his first reception on Olympus, or his first epiphany among

[32] Janko (1981b), p. 20.
[33] Cf. P. Vidal-Naquet, "Temps des dieux et temps des hommes," in *Le Chasseur noir: Formes de pensée et formes de société dans le monde grec* (Paris, 1981), pp. 69–94.

men—is not to be distinguished from his characteristic repeated actions. Each conveys the god's essential nature in all its fullness.

In defiance of our mortal temporal categories, but in complete harmony with those of the divine, the opening scene of the *Hymn to Apollo* portrays *both* the first epiphany of the new god on the threshold of Olympus *and* his eternally repeated entrance into his father's house. In this unique but recurring sequence, the god manifests himself fully, as he did the first time, and as he will forever. The progress from terror to delight constitutes the eternal response to the manifestation of Apollo's divinity. Initial fear yielding to subsequent joy accompanies his manifestations throughout the hymn and forms the identifying feature of the god.[34] Even though the main narrative takes up elsewhere, the first scene, far from being unmotivated,[35] must be understood as a programmatic presentation of the characteristic and paradigmatic response to the divinity the hymn sets out to celebrate.

In the first of the many surprising transitions the poet evidently delights in, he turns to address Leto directly.[36] The joy of Leto (χαίρει), which brought the first scene to an end, is taken up in the poet's apostrophe (χαῖρε μάκαιρ᾽ ὦ Λητοῖ). The verbal link reinforces the substantive one—Leto as the mother of "splendid children." But the technique goes beyond a mere association of ideas or chain of thoughts that may be likened to beads on a string. There the first motif introduces a second, which, in turn, has connections to a third; but the third need have no direct relation to the first.[37] Our poet, on the other hand, seems to have a

---

[34] Sowa (1984), p. 324, cites words signifying "joy" and "rejoicing" as key terms in the hymn. She does not, however, list words for "fear" or "trembling," which are equally prevalent and are the preliminary to rejoicing. For the "joy" motif, see also Forderer (1971), pp. 149–50.

[35] Cf. H. Fränkel, *Dichtung und Philosophie des frühen Griechentums*, 2nd ed. (Munich, 1962), p. 288, n. 7, who calls the opening "eine unmotivierte Szene. . . . Warum Apollon so im Olymp auftreten soll, wird nicht angedeutet." Cf. Lenz (1975), p. 75, who believes that the two Olympian scenes in the hymn "jeweils am Anfang der Gedichte, haben keinen Motivzusammenhang mit der anschliessende erzählten heiligen Geschichte." Miller (1985), p. 28, claims that the initial scene is "self-contained and makes no advance toward the poet's narrative goal."

[36] See Förstel (1979), pp. 114–15, for a summary of older, usually analytic, views on these lines. Cf. Càssola (1975), pp. 486–87. Förstel, pp. 116–18, attributes Leto's prominence in the hymn to her prominence in Delian cult, whereas van Groningen (1958), p. 306, imagines the rhapsode saluting a statue of Leto near the place of his recital. This seems unnecessary. Cf. Miller (1985), pp. 16–17, for a defense of the passage on rhetorical grounds.

[37] Cf. van Groningen (1958), pp. 29–50, on the "chain" style in archaic literature; and

clear sense of his direction and ultimate goal.[38] Thus Leto's role in the Olympian assembly and her pride in her son lead to her address as mother of the "splendid children," Apollo and Artemis. This notice, in turn, expands into a description of their respective birthplaces (16–18). The poet's range of vision continues to expand in the following lines in which he will describe the universality of Apollo's power. Then, his focus will again narrow, as the whole movement culminates in the fully developed narrative of Leto's giving birth to Apollo (30–139). The appropriate metaphor for this complex procedure might not be the stringing of beads, but rather a sophisticated musical modulation from one key to another. In composing his work, the hymn-poet similarly exploits certain recurrent themes, complexes of ideas, and progressions.[39]

Although my main interest in studying the *Hymn to Apollo* and the other hymns focuses on their narrative content, it is nonetheless essential to deal with some of the stylistic peculiarities of *Apollo*. The poet's unusual transitions constitute one such characteristic, but equally striking is his use of apostrophe. In the epic, the interposition of the poet into his narrative through direct address is extremely rare except in the invocation. However, what Norden labeled the "Du-" and "Er-Stil" is abundantly attested throughout Greek hymnodic composition.[40] But the direct address of a divinity is severely limited in the major Homeric Hymns.[41] Moreover, the frequent oscillation between these two modes in the first half of *Apollo*, though common enough in later literary hymns, is unparalleled in the longer Homeric Hymns. No one, it appears, has seriously inquired why the poet of the hymn should alternate between them. Variety in and of itself affords an insufficient explanation. We can, in any case, perceive the effect: the poet insists on his immediate involvement with his subject matter and repeatedly draws attention to his presence, a presence culminating in the self-description of lines 172–76. Once again,

---

the discussions of H. Fränkel, *Wege and Formen frühgriechischen Denkens* (Munich, 1960), pp. 40–82; W. J. Verdenius, "L'Association des idées comme principe de composition dans Homère, Hésiode, Théognis," *REG* 73 (1960): 345–61; and Thalmann (1984), pp. 4–6.

[38] Cf. Förstel (1979), p. 119: "Kein Zweifel, dem Dichter schwebte schon in dieser Partie die Geburt Apollons vor Augen."

[39] Cf. van Groningen (1958), pp. 94–97, for what he calls "le réseau entrelacé"; also Thalmann (1984), pp. 22–24, on "spiral structure."

[40] E. Norden, *Agnostos Theos* (Berlin, 1923), esp. pp. 157–58.

[41] In the long hymns, apostrophe usually occurs only in the final salutation to the deity. The fragmentary *Hymn to Dionysus* offers what may be a significant exception (see below) insofar as the seven opening lines contain a direct address to the god.

the proem to the *Theogony* offers the nearest analogy. Yet perhaps more can be said. Norden suggested that the "Du-Stil" might have originated in the dithyramb, a hymn dedicated to Dionysus.[42] However, direct address may be equally native to the genre of composition dedicated to the god Apollo, which the Greeks called the paean.[43] It is well known that the paean was characterized by a recurrent refrain invoking the god directly. In addition, the resemblance between certain stylistic features of the hymn and lyric poetry has frequently been noted:

> The bold jumps in thought, the harsh transitions, the constantly changing themes, the short, even obscure, allusions, the frequent change between apostrophe and narrative, between direct and indirect address, the numerous repetitions that sound like refrains . . . all this and other features as well find their only true analogy in Lyric, not in the Epos of the Greeks.[44]

The *Hymn to Apollo* itself alludes to several lyric forms: not only the paean itself (517–19), but also to the choral and mimetic song of the Delian maidens (156–64) and the complicated singing and dancing that goes on in Olympus (188–203). To be sure, the poet of the hymn shows himself fully capable of composing in the epic narrative manner when he so desires. Would it be too far-fetched to suggest that he consciously modifies his essentially epic hexameter style to the manner of composition traditionally associated with the divinity he celebrates? In any event, the hymn attests not only to the poet's virtuosity, but also to the sophistication of his audience, who may be presumed to appreciate his artfulness.

I return to the immediate context that gave rise to these reflections. There is one place in the Homeric Hymns where apostrophe is canonical: at the end. In fact, χαῖρε sounds for all the world like a closing formula; we now expect the poem to come to an end. But two considerations immediately undermine our expectation: the apparent close goes on rather

---

[42] Norden (1923), p. 160.

[43] For the paean, see A. Fairbanks, *A Study of the Greek Paean* (Cornell Studies in Classical Philogy 12) (1900); and A. von Blumenthal, "Paian," *RE* 18, pt. 2 (1942): 2345–62.

[44] A. Ludwich, *Homerischer Hymnenbau* (Leipzig, 1908), p. 162. (The ellipsis omits an unfortunate statement about the hymn's strophic structure.) On pp. 165–67, Ludwich discusses the possible relation between the hymn and the style of the paean. For the lyric style of *Apollo*, see also Gemoll (1886), p. 111; and Drerup (1937), pp. 131, 133. Dornseiff (1933), pp. 3–4, notes the frequency of the priamel in the hymn, a device he finds characteristic of the lyric but not found elsewhere in rhapsodic poetry.

longer than usual; and it is addressed to the *wrong* divinity—that is, to Leto rather than to Apollo, the subject of the poem.[45] χαῖρε, of course, can mean both "farewell" and "rejoice," and the poet teases us with its ambiguity. We first interpret it in the former sense, but as the passage progresses, we realize that it does not signal the end of the composition and reinterpret it as a greeting to Leto.[46] The apparent closing formula becomes a bridge to further development. This peculiar procedure bears emphasizing, because the poet will exploit the same device on a larger scale toward the end of the Delian section (166ff.). There, he bids an apparent goodby to the Delian maidens—again, not to the god of the hymn—only to continue his composition in an unexpected direction.

At line 19, the poet again breaks off abruptly, this time to apostrophize *Apollo*:

Πῶς τάρ σ᾽ ὑμνήσω πάντως εὔυμνον ἐόντα;
πάντῃ γάρ τοι, Φοῖβε, νομὸς βεβλήαται ᾠδῆς,
ἠμὲν ἀν᾽ ἤπειρον πορτιτρόφον ἠδ᾽ ἀνὰ νήσους.

How shall I hymn you, you who are everywhere well hymned?
For in all directions, Phoebus, the range of song has been set down
    for you,
both on the calf-nurturing mainland and throughout the islands.

(19–21)

Some have found this transition from Leto to Apollo impossibly harsh. But Apollo has never completely receded from view in the intervening lines, and he remains the center of the composition. After all, Leto hardly exists independent of her children.[47] Confronted with the choice of subject matter appropriate to the celebration of his god, the poet first pauses as if overwhelmed with the vast possibilities open to him. The metaphorical "range of song" introduces a list of geographical features, all of which are pleasing to Apollo (22–24). Since a god favors a place because he is honored there, the catalog attests to the universality of Apollo's worship. At the same time, it hints that the narrative the poet will finally choose for his theme will focus on one of the places where Apollo commands

[45] Cf. E. Bethe, "Der homerische Apollonhymnos und das Prooimion," *Berichte der Sächsischen Akademie der Wissenschaften, Leipzig. Phil.-hist. Klasse* 83, no. 2 (1931): 14; and West (1975), p. 163, speaks of the poet's making "farewell noises here," but also notes that "if it were really the end of a hymn, he would not have added" lines 16–18.

[46] Cf. Unte (1968), p. 24.

[47] This is certainly true of her cult on the Greek mainland and islands. Cf. F. Wehrli, "Leto," *RE* Suppl. 5 (1931): 555–65.

special veneration—perhaps a myth describing the foundation of one of Apollo's many cult places.[48] But which one, since the material for celebration abounds everywhere? The poet now makes an altogether reasonable choice. With the wealth of possible locations, why not begin with the first? That can only mean the birthplace of the god. The previous references to Leto render the final choice inevitable.

ἢ ὥς σε πρῶτον Λητὼ τέκε χάρμα βροτοῖσι,
κλινθεῖσα πρὸς Κύνθου ὄρος κραναῇ ἐνὶ νήσῳ
Δήλῳ ἐν ἀμφιρύτῃ· ἑκάτερθε δὲ κῦμα κελαινὸν
ἐξίει χέρσον δὲ λιγυπνοίοις ἀνέμοισιν·
ἔνθεν ἀπορνύμενος πᾶσι θνητοῖσιν ἀνάσσεις.

or how Leto first bore you, a joy to mortals,
leaning against Mount Cynthus on the rocky isle,
on sea-girt Delos? And on both sides the dark wave
poured forth[49] unto the land, with the winds blowing shrilly;
arising from there, you rule over all mortals.

(25–29)

Delos, Leto, the story of Apollo's birth, and his progress from the inhospitable island to universal rule—these are to be the poet's theme.

The Birth of Apollo

The lengthy geographical catalog that begins from Crete and describes a great arc around the Aegean offers another instance of the peculiar gliding transitions favored by the poet. At first, the sonorous toponyms seem to continue and exemplify the motif of the universality of Apollo's power and honor. Only fifteen lines later do we discover them to be a list of places visited by the pregnant Leto as she searched in vain for a place to give birth to the new god. The double linking of the catalog both to what precedes and to what follows serves to blur the division between prologue and narrative.[50] The numerous disagreements among

[48] Cf. Jacoby (1933), p. 703: "an jeden der Kultorte knüpft sich eine Geschichte, von jedem kann man singen." Cf. Miller (1985), p. 22.

[49] I accept the emendation ἐξίει for the ἐξῄει of the manuscripts proposed by M. Cantilena, "Due versi dell' inno omerico ad Apollon," in *Perennitas: Studi in honore di Angelo Brelich* (Rome, 1980), pp. 109–13.

[50] The pause postulated by Förstel (1979), p. 112, and Baltes (1982), p. 26, would ruin the effect. For the deliberate syntactical ambiguity, see E. Kalinka's review of Bethe (1931), *Philologische Wochenschrift* 52 (1932): 390; Forderer (1971), pp. 70–72; and Miller

scholars who attempt to outline the hymn demonstrate that the poet frequently disguises his transitions.

τόσσον ἔπ᾽ ὠδίνουσα ῾Εκηβόλον ἵκετο Λητώ,
εἴ τίς οἱ γαιέων υἱεῖ θέλοι οἰκία θέσθαι.
αἱ δὲ μάλ᾽ ἐτρόμεον καὶ ἐδείδισαν, οὐδέ τις ἔτλη
Φοῖβον δέξασθαι καὶ πιοτέρη περ ἐοῦσα
πρίν γ᾽ ὅτε δή ῥ᾽ ἐπὶ Δήλου ἐβήσετο πότνια Λητώ.

over such an expanse did Leto in labor with the Archer wander
    and entreat
whether any land would be willing to establish a home for her son.
But they trembled greatly and were afraid, nor did any land dare
to receive Phoebus, even one that was very rich,
until, indeed, the lady Leto set foot on Delos.

(45–49)

Due to an unspecified fear, every land rejects Leto's supplication. For the moment, the cause of the universal dread remains unexplained. Although the prosperous lands, which might offer a suitable site for the birth of a new divinity, refuse the goddess in her distress, she will finally convince impoverished Delos to welcome her son. In the full epic style, the poet now narrates the charming exchange between Leto and the island, which leads to the hammering out of an agreement acceptable to both parties. Addressing Delos in a tone alternately wheedling and threatening, the goddess begins: "if you should be willing to be the seat of my son," but then she switches to the minatory future, warning the island that no one else will pay her any attention or entreat her[51] if she passes up this opportunity:

(1985), pp. 31–33. If all the sites named can be considered cult places of Apollo (cf. AHS [1936], p. 205, and Forderer, p. 70), then the ambiguity is hightened into an ironical contrast, as Forderer, p. 71, emphasizes: "Die Orte, die zunächst als Herrschaftsbereich Apollons erschienen waren und die es tatsächlich auch sind—sie haben ihm erst einmal sämtlich versagt." Cf. Miller, p. 33: "The catalogue of *inclusions* adumbrating Apollo's present magnificence becomes retrospectively a catalogue of *exclusions* that defines the sorely straitened circumstances of his first appearance in the world." H. Koller "Πόλις Μερόπων ᾽Ανθρώπων," *Glotta* 46 (1968): 22, claims that the catalog in lines 30–44 is a preexisting traditional piece of poetry that the poet used for Leto's wanderings.

[51] Forderer (1971), p. 174, n. 44, defends the manuscript reading λίσσει; cf. Förstel (1979), p. 427, n. 489. AHS (1936) print λήσει; Baumeister (1860), Gemoll (1886), J. Humbert, *Homerè: Hymnes* (Paris, 1936), and Càssola (1975) all print τίσει.

οὐδ' εὔβων σέ γ' ἔσεσθαι ὀΐομαι οὔτ' εὔμηλον,
οὐδὲ τρύγην οἴσεις, οὔτ' ἄρ φυτὰ μυρία φύσεις.

nor, in fact, do I think you will be good for cattle or sheep,
nor will you produce grain nor indeed bring forth abundant crops.

(54–55)

If, on the other hand, Delos should agree to establish a temple of Apollo, then Leto foretells the island's future prosperity: all men will bring offerings, and the savor from sacrifices will rise ceaselessly, while her inhabitants will flourish with wealth imported from abroad, "since you have no richness in your soil" (56–60). Noticeably, Leto does not ask for pity or kindness—perhaps she had tried that tack unsuccessfully in more prosperous climes—nor does she refer to her delicate condition. Instead, she bases her entire argument on Delos's poverty and immediate self-interest.

At first, Delos receives Leto's proposal with pleasure (χαῖρε), for the island is well aware of her poor reputation among men; in this way, "I might become honored round about" (61–65). Something, however, holds her back from accepting and makes her waver:

ἀλλὰ τόδε τρομέω Λητοῖ ἔπος, οὐδέ σε κεύσω·
λίην γάρ τινά φασιν ἀτάσθαλον Ἀπόλλωνα
ἔσσεσθαι, μέγα δὲ πρυτανευσέμεν ἀθανάτοισι
καὶ θνητοῖσι βροτοῖσιν ἐπὶ ζείδωρον ἄρουραν.

But the following story causes me to tremble, Leto, nor shall I hide
    it from you;
for they say that Apollo will be excessively overbearing
and greatly lord it over the immortals
and mortal men on the barley-giving earth.

(66–69)

The reason for the universal fear that gripped all lands and caused them to reject Leto's entreaties is now made explicit. A rumor, whose source remains obscure, has it that her son will be brutally violent and tyrannical.

Critics have vainly tried to tone down the shocking implications of the text by suggesting that these lines merely form a somewhat hyperbolic expression for Apollo's great power. For example, Kirk finds the use of ἀτάσθαλος "extravagant, or insensitive" although "the theme of Apollo's

35

majesty . . . is here introduced quite plausibly."[52] Forderer, on the other hand, detects lighthearted humor in Delos's grotesquely exaggerated characterization of Apollo's might.[53] Förstel and Miller offer more sophisticated explanations, but both fail to persuade. The former claims that the rumor about the god describes his nature but contains no specific threat that motivates the rejection of the lands. The lands, however, compare themselves with the announced terrible greatness of the god and sense their absolute inferiority to him. This sense, in turn, gives rise to their fear. The main point for Förstel remains the presentation of Apollo's surpassing greatness.[54] Miller's interpretation (to the extent I can follow it) involves the disparity between Apollo's greatness and his humble need for a place to be born or, as Miller calls it, his "humiliating dependency": "The poet contrives to suggest that Apollo might conceivably have felt the discrepancy between his fully realized divinity and the zero-point of his emergence into being as an intolerable affront to his dignity and so have been prompted to wreak his resentment on the surroundings in which he first found himself."[55] None of this fancy footwork can sidestep the transparent sense of the text, which dwells not on Apollo's grandeur, but on his savagely lawless and overbearing nature.

It is a shocking paradox to hear ἀτάσθαλος applied to Apollo. No single English term can convey the full range of this Greek word. "Overbearing," "violent," "reckless," or "lawless" offer only partial translations for this highly charged term. In Homer, it is frequently linked with a form of *hybris*.[56] Although in the epic, Apollo may on occasion display

---

[52] Kirk (1981), p. 170. Wilamowitz (1920), p. 442, paraphrases λίην ἀτάσθαλος as "der gewaltige und gewalttätige Gott." Cf. Dornseiff (1933), p. 5: "der zu erwartende Letosohn stehe im Ruf, recht ungebärdig zu werden."

[53] Forderer (1971), p. 74: "Das Furchtbare ist freilich gemildert durch den Humor, mit dem alles gezeichnet ist. . . . Apollons Gewalt aber bespricht sie [Delos] mit grotesker Wendung . . . und die drohende Gefahr malt sie vollends in grotesken Farben."

[54] Förstel (1979), p. 183: "Es ist eine Aussage über das *Wesen* des Gottes, enthält also keine bestimmte Bedrohung, die automatisch die ablehnende Haltung der Länder hervorrufen müsste. Die Länder vergleichen sich mit der angekündigten furchtbaren Grösse des Gottes und fühlen sich ihr nicht gewachsen. Erst aus diesem Gefühl der vollkommenen Unterlegenheit heraus fühlen sie sich bedroht, resultiert ihre Furcht." Ibid., p. 184: "Vor allem tritt aber die alles Irdische übersteigende Grösse Apollons anschaulich hervor."

[55] Miller (1985), p. 41.

[56] See, for example, *Iliad* XIII.633–34; *Odyssey* 16.86; 24.282 and 352. For its startling application to Apollo, see Kroll (1956), p. 185: "Apollon ἀτάσθαλος? Der Gott von grosser Erhabenheit und Würde, der in der Religion der archaischen Zeit die Strömung des Legalismus und Ritualismus trägt, kann das nicht sein." Also Miller (1985), p. 39: "it

an uncanny or distant side, yet for the most part he is precisely the god who maintains order. Thus, it is he who intervenes to check the hybristic onslaughts of Diomedes and Patroclus;[57] and in the theomachy Zeus stages for his own entertainment, Apollo refuses to join in the frivolous fighting.[58] The un-Homeric character of the ἀτάσθαλος god delineated here does, however, resemble the violent archer introduced at the beginning of the hymn.[59] The divinity who there caused the gods to leap from their seats in terror is the same one whose birth inspires fear throughout the earth. Both images of Apollo have been thought so completely alien to the spirit of Greek religion that some scholars have posited an Oriental source.[60] But there is no need to look so far afield: these verses, correctly understood, fit squarely into the Greek tradition—not, however of epic, but of theogonic poetry.

Delos, as well as the rest of the world, is terror stricken that Apollo "will greatly lord it over" not only mankind, but even the gods. Occurring here for the first time in Greek, πρυτανεύω carries a suggestion of despotic rule.[61] Yet Zeus and Zeus alone rules over gods and men.[62] The

---

remains remarkable to find so negative a term used in connection (however indirect) with a god who as promulgator of the maxims Γνῶθι σεαυτόν and Μηδὲν ἄγαν was to archaic Greek belief the arch-enemy of *hubris* in human beings." Förstel (1979), p. 416, n. 459, makes a lame attempt to render the term "wertneutral" "und nur ein ausserordentliches Mass von Stärke, Macht usw. ausdrücken." He can, of course, find no parallel for such a neutral sense.

[57] *Iliad* v.438–44; xvi.705–11.

[58] *Iliad* xxi.461–67.

[59] Cf. Baumeister (1860), p. 132; Gemoll (1886), p. 133; Wilamowitz (1920), p. 442; Altheim (1924), p. 431; Unte (1968), p. 31; Forderer (1971), p. 76; Càssola (1975), p. 492; and Förstel (1979), p. 170. Although all these critics note a connection between the Apollo of the proem and the Apollo of the rumor, none makes a serious attempt to understand their connection, as if noting the parallel were in itself sufficient.

[60] See Kroll (1956), pp. 184–91; and F. Guida, "Apollo arciere nell' inno omerico ad Apollo Delio," *Studi Omerici ed Esiodei* (Rome) 1 (1972): 7–25.

[61] The root *prytan*-, like that of *tyrannis*, is presumably of Anatolian origin. In *Iliad* v.678, Prytanis is the name of a Lydian warrior. Cf. J. Liderski, "Etruskische Etymologien: zilaθ und purθ," *Glotta* 40 (1962): 157–59; A. Heubeck, *Praegraeca* (Erlangen, 1961), pp. 67–68; and M. Hammarström, "Griechisch-etruskische Wortgleichungen," *Glotta* 11 (1921): 214–15. In the *Prometheus Bound* 169, Zeus is called μακάρων πρύτανις. Cf. Pindar, *Pythian* 6.24: κεραυνῶν τε πρύτανιν; and Euripides, *Trojan Women* 1288: Κρόνιε, πρύτανι Φρύγιε.

[62] Cf. *Iliad* xii.242: (Zeus) ὃς πᾶσι θνητοῖσι καὶ ἀθανάτοισιν ἀνάσσει. Cf. Kroll (1956), p. 190: "Macht über Götter und Menschen kommt nur dem Zeus zu, dem πατὴρ ἀνδρῶν τε θεῶν τε. Von keinem anderen Gotte lässt sich sagen, dass er μέγα πρυτανεύει ἀθανάτοισι." Cf. Förstel (1979), pp. 171–72. "Diese Darstellung des Gottes ist einmalig." Förstel goes on to note that in hymns "wird oft die Universalität der Macht

nations dread nothing less than that the newborn Apollo will depose the Olympians and succeed to the kingship in heaven. Furthermore, they fear that his reign, unlike the regime of Zeus, will be both violent and lawless. The full significance of the poem's first scene now emerges. The awesome god who interrupts the peaceful banquet of the Olympians and strikes terror in the hearts of the divine assembly appears as the potential violator of the Olympian order and usurper of Zeus's dominion. Only Zeus's welcoming gesture of acknowledgment restores tranquillity. It indicates unmistakably that his son, far from being an enemy to be feared, is a friend and ally of the established order. On earth, that same new god is rumored to be none other than a brutal successor to Zeus.

These lines have critical consequences for the interpretation of the hymn as a whole. First, the poem situates itself firmly within the theogonic tradition or, more precisely, within the framework of the Succession Myth in which each generation of the gods is overthrown by a new god or gods. Furthermore, we can now place the hymn in its proper temporal setting within the history of the Olympians. For the possibility of an enemy and successor to Zeus implies that the Olympian regime is only recently established and not yet fully stabilized into its final configuration. Zeus's reign is still in its childhood, and genuine disturbances and challenges to his authority remain conceivable.

On the basis of the generalized rumor going around (τῷ), Delos explains her immediate fears for her own well-being. As soon as he sees the light of day, the new god, brutal and ἀτάσθαλος as he is foretold to be, may despise the craggy island; in an act of hybristic violence, he may kick it into the sea (70–73). While the god goes off elsewhere to establish his cult, she will become a mere deserted reef, habitable only by seals and octopodes (74–78). Acutely aware of her present poverty and unattractiveness, Delos is afraid that, if she accepts Leto's offer, she will be worse off than before.

For all her apparent helplessness and simplicity, Delos displays a certain cleverness in exacting an oath from Leto; the goddess should swear that Apollo "will first build his most beautiful temple there to be an oracle of men, but then [build temples]⁶³ among all men, for he will

---

eines Gottes, ihre Erstreckung auf Götter und Menschen betont; allerdings ist dabei stets . . . an *die spezielle Tätigkeit des Gottes* gedacht, während die Hymnos die Überlegenheit Apollons als *allgemeinen Machtvorrang* darstellt" (italics mine).

[63] Delos speaks elliptically here, but there is no need to assume with Hermann (1806), AHS (1936), and Càssola (1975) a lacuna. Cf. Baumeister (1860) and Gemoll (1886).

be famous."[64] Delos modestly sets her sights not on exclusivity, but on priority. Acceding to this request, Leto swears by "the greatest and most dreadful oath of the gods" (85–86). Swearing by the water of the Styx has many parallels, but the oath here is not treated in the usual epic manner.[65] Not bereft of cunning herself, Leto modifies the phrasing of the proposed oath, promising the island both more and less than she requested.

ἦ μὴν Φοίβου τῆδε θυώδης ἔσσεται αἰεὶ
βωμὸς καὶ τέμενος, τίσει δέ σέ γ᾽ ἔξοχα πάντων.

Truly, here the fragrant altar of Phoebus will be forever
and his sanctuary, and he will honor you exceedingly, above all
  others.
    (87–88)

The goddess promises Delos not merely Apollo's first temple, but one that will abide forever, and have supreme honor among his cult places. She silently rejects Delos's bold request for an oracular shrine.[66] Yet its mention here foreshadows its foundation in the second part of the hymn.[67]

  The bargain has been sealed, and Delos "rejoiced greatly at the birth of the lord archer" (90). The unquestionable humor in this little exchange arises for the most part ἐκ προσώπων, from the characterization: the hard-headed bargaining of the goddess and the talking island, Leto's bald in-

---

  [64] πολυώνυμος, literally, "of many names," hence, "famous." Here the word presumably refers to the many cult names Apollo will acquire. Dornseiff (1933), p. 14, found this line to offer evidence for the unity of the hymn by pointing to the fact that Apollo acquires the titles "Telphousios," "Delphinios," and "Pythios" in the course of the second half of the poem. See also his "Nochmals der homerische Apollonhymnos: Eine Gegenkritik," *Greifswalder Beiträge zur Literatur- und Stilforschung* 8 (1935): 12.
  [65] The formula in line 89 occurs six times in Homer (*Iliad* xiv.280; *Odyssey* 2.378, 10.346, 12.304, 15.438, 18.59), but in none of these instances is it preceded by a rephrasing of the previously dictated oath.
  [66] There is evidence for an oracle at Delos, but it is Hellenistic, and there is no reason to assume its great antiquity, let alone its priority over Delphi. Cf. AHS (1936), pp. 212–13. Bethe (1931), pp. 19–20, and S. Eitrem, "Varia, 87: Ad Homericum hymnum in Apollinem," *Symbolae Osloenses* 18 (1938): 130, doubt the existence of a Delian oracle in the archaic period. Wilamowitz (1920), p. 446, n. 2, and Jacoby (1933), p. 717, n. 3, both believe in it. The important thing, however, is that Leto does *not* promise Delos an oracle. Cf. Heubeck (1972), p. 146; and Ch. Floratos, "Ὁ ὁμηρικὸς ὕμνος εἰς Ἀπόλλονα," Ἀθηνά 56 (1952): 295–96.
  [67] Cf. Gemoll (1886), p. 134; Ludwich (1908), p. 183; Forderer (1971), p. 75; and Heubeck (1972), p. 136, n. 8—obviously, all unitarians.

dictment of Delos's poverty, the island's sense of her own humility and her timorous worries about her future, and, finally, the touch of earthy cunning exhibited by both parties.[68] Yet a deeper irony is at work here. Both Leto's wanderings and Delos's fears arise from a rumor that is manifestly untrue.[69] The poet's audience knew this, as do we. For in announcing his subject matter, the poet does indeed proclaim Apollo's universal rule over *mankind*, πᾶσι θνητοῖσιν ἀνάσσεις (29), but the new god will prove to be not a terror but a joy to men: χάρμα βροτοῖσι (25). The dreadful rumor that accompanied Apollo's birth has no solid foundation; we remain puzzled as to its source.

With the expression of Delos's joy, the typical progress from fear to rejoicing, which is the very hallmark of Apollo and which characterized his epiphany in the proem, seems to be accomplished. For Leto, however, a new impediment suddenly appears. For nine days, the goddess was wracked by labor pangs with no hope of relief.[70] To our surprise, we learn that she was not alone in her travail:

θεαὶ δ᾽ ἔσαν ἔνδοθι πᾶσαι
ὅσσαι ἄρισται ἔσαν, Διώνη τε ʽΡείη τε
ἰχναίη τε Θέμις καὶ ἀγάστονος ᾽Αμφιτρίτη,
ἄλλαι τ᾽ ἀθάναται, νόσφιν λευκωλένου ῞Ηρης·
ἧστο γὰρ ἐν μεγάροισι Διὸς νεφεληγερέταο.

The goddesses all were within,
all those who were the best, Dione and Rheia,
tracking (?)[71] Themis and loud-sighing Amphitrite,
and the other goddesses, apart from white-armed Hera;
for she sat in the halls of cloud-gathering Zeus.

(92–96)

The presence of a whole host of goddesses to keep Leto company has not been anticipated, and the phrasing betrays a certain awkwardness.[72] The

---

[68] For the humor in the exchange, see Forderer (1971), p. 74, and the discussion of Miller (1985), pp. 34–45.

[69] Miller (1985), p. 42, refers to "the contrafactuality of his ἀτασθαλία."

[70] Cf. Gemoll (1886), p. 135.

[71] On this obscure epithet of Themis, see Forderer (1971), p. 176, n. 48.

[72] The ἔνδοθι of the manuscripts was emended to ἐνθάδε by Hermann (1806). Kirk (1981), p. 171, expresses surprise at the omission of "Athena, Aphrodite, and even Artemis with her special associations with birth." The goddesses named in the hymn, of course, all belong to the previous generation of divinities. J. Schröder, *Ilias und Apollonhymnos*

poet has abandoned the pathetic possibilities inherent in the picture of Leto's giving birth in solitude on a rocky island. He has a purpose: the attendance of the immortals at the birth suggests that Leto is not as god-forsaken as first appeared. Of the named goddesses, Themis, who will also nurse the newborn god, is the most important. Her name means law, order, and propriety. The *Theogony* calls her the second wife of Zeus, and her children are the Horai, Eunomia, Dike, and Eirene (*Theogony* 901–02). Traditionally, she has close ties to Zeus as his most trusted advisor;[73] on one occasion, she is said to have warned both Zeus and Poseidon of the dangerous consequences of a marriage to Thetis.[74] Finally, Themis has a special connection to Delphi and its oracle.[75] Her active presence at Apollo's birth lends a divine sanction to the whole proceeding.

Hera, however, remains "apart." Here, as in the *Hymn to Demeter*, νόσφιν reflects a division in heaven, a state of conflict among the gods.[76] While all the other goddesses have left Olympus for Delos, Hera, well aware of what is going on below, stays aloof.[77] Only Eileithyia, the birth goddess, knew nothing:

ἧστο γὰρ ἄκρῳ Ὀλύμπῳ ὑπὸ χρυσέοισι νέφεσσιν
Ἥρης φραδμοσύνης λευκωλένου, ἥ μιν ἔρυκε
ζηλοσύνῃ ὅ τ᾽ ἄρ᾽ υἱὸν ἀμύμονά τε κρατερόν τε
Λητὼ τέξεσθαι καλλιπλόκαμος τότ᾽ ἔμελλεν.

For she sat on the peak of Olympus under golden clouds,
through the plans of white-armed Hera, who held her back

(Meisenheim, 1975), pp. 13–14, believes the list of goddesses in the hymn derives from *Theogony* 11–21.

[73] Wilamowitz (1920), p. 449, calls her "die Vertreterin der ewigen Weltordnung, mit der Zeus sich zu beraten pflegt." As such, she is the appropriate figure to be Apollo's nurse. Cf. R. Hirzel, *Themis, Dike und Verwandtes* (Leipzig, 1907), pp. 2–7.

[74] Cf. Pindar, *Isthmian* 8.26a–37.

[75] At line 394, Apollo's oracles are called θέμιστες. Cf. lines 253 and 293. Cf. Hirzel (1907), pp. 20–21. According to one tradition, Apollo took over the Delphic oracle from Themis. Cf. for example, Aeschylus, *Eumenides* 2–19. For Themis and Delphi, see Hirzel (1907), pp. 7–9.

[76] See, below, chapter 4, esp. n. 68.

[77] Most editors (Baumeister, Gemoll, Humbert, and Càssola—an exception is AHS) find lines 96 and 98 redundant and eject 96. Cf. the discussion of Förstel (1979), pp. 120–23. Forderer (1971), pp. 79–80, defends the text. The poet is at pains to emphasize the irony in the fact that only the envious Hera and her unwitting accomplice remain on Olympus.

out of jealousy, because lovely haired Leto was then about
to give birth to a son, mighty and without blemish.

(98–101)

Hera's envy and her jealous scheming keep Eileithyia in ignorance. Yet
the situation admits of an easy resolution. The goddesses dispatch Iris—
elsewhere, Zeus's own messenger—to fetch the birth goddess and, with
womanly wiles, to offer her a gold necklace as a bribe, all without attract-
ing Hera's attention (102–14). The mission is quickly accomplished;[78] and
as soon as Eileithyia sets foot on Delos, Leto at long last gives birth (115–
19):

ἐκ δ' ἔθορε πρὸ φόως δέ, θεαὶ δ' ὀλόλυξαν ἅπασαι.

and out he lept into the light, and all the goddesses let out a cry of
jubilation.

(119)

In the *Hymn to Apollo*, then, the impediments to the god's birth are
twofold: the jealousy of Hera and the fear of the lands. Hera's persecu-
tion of Zeus's *amours* constitutes a common mythological motif in, for
example, the story of Io or Semele. In the *Iliad*, Hera delays the birth of
Heracles and thereby dooms him to his multiple trials (*Iliad* xix.96–133).
In other versions of Apollo's birth, and doubtless traditionally, Leto's
wanderings and sufferings are caused by Hera's jealousy alone.[79] The
summary fashion in which the poet alludes to this motif and his cursory
handling of its resolution suggests that it was well known to his audience.[80] To the traditional motivation for Leto's troubles, our poet has
added a second impediment, and he spends more than twice as many
lines to unfold it. To most critics, the two seem independent of each
other, a kind of gratuitous doubling of motifs. The divine hostility of
Hera to the new god[81] runs parallel to the terrestrial fear. Both, presum-

[78] Cf. Miller (1985), p. 46, who speaks of "the baldness and the business-like haste of
the narrative style."

[79] Compare Callimachus's *Hymn to Delos*; Apollodorus 1.4.1; and Ovid, *Metamorphoses* 6.332–36.

[80] Cf. Förstel (1979), pp. 185–86. West (1975): 169–70, seems to stand alone in considering the motif of Hera's jealousy secondary.

[81] Förstel (1979), p. 187, calls Hera's opposition "eine olympische Familienintrige,"
which tends to trivialize it.

ably, do no more than amplify the greatness of Apollo.[82] But we have already seen that the fear of the nations, which may be our poet's innovation, introduces a whole new cosmic and theogonic dimension into the hymn. Perhaps our question should rather be why the hymn-poet retains the theme of Hera's enmity at all.

Long awaited with both fear and hostility, the birth of Apollo releases a flood of joy. Apparently sharing in this joyous rapture, the poet addresses the god directly (120) and describes how the attendant goddesses washed and swaddled the newborn with golden bands. As a god, Apollo receives no mother's milk, but Themis offers[83] him nectar and ambrosia. Then Leto rejoices "because she bore a mighty and a bow-bearing son" (126). Her joy at his birth is identical to her maternal joy in the prologue (cf. 12–13); every epiphany, even the first, elicits the same reaction.

While the gods have parents and must be born, unlike mortals they quickly mature and reach their prime; then they remain "unaging and immortal for all time."[84] So, as soon as he has swallowed the immortal food, Apollo bursts the golden bands that restrain him (127–29). No longer an infant but the full-grown divinity he will henceforth always be, Apollo speaks:

εἴη μοι κίθαρίς τε φίλη καὶ καμπύλα τόξα,
χρήσω δ᾽ ἀνθρώποισι Διὸς νημερτέα βουλήν.

Let the lyre be mine and the bent bow,
and I shall prophesy the unfailing will of Zeus to men.

(131–32)

In his very first words, the new god lays claim to his triple *timai*: music, archery, and prophecy.[85] The first scene of the hymn introduced the awesome archer; we have every reason to suppose that it will also display

---

[82] Cf. Forderer (1971), p. 86: "Beides, die Furcht der Länder und die Eifersucht der Hera, weist auf Apollons Grösse." See also Förstel (1979), p. 185; and Miller (1985), p. 46.

[83] For the sacral connotations of ἐπήρξατο (125), see Gemoll (1886), pp. 138–39.

[84] Cf. J. S. Clay, "Immortal and Ageless Forever," *CJ* 77 (1981–1982): 112–17.

[85] Verses 131–32 have been recognized to be Apollo's "Lebensprogram," which is completed in the second half of the hymn. Cf. Bethe (1931), pp. 8–9; Jacoby (1933), p. 720, n. 1; Dornseiff (1933), p. 10, and (1935), p. 12; Unte (1968), pp. 38–39; Forderer (1971), p. 88: "Das sind seine künftigen Werke, sein geistiger Machtbereich, sein Wesen." See also Heubeck (1972), p. 146; and Miller (1985), p. 54.

Apollo practicing his other prerogatives. The assumption of prophetic power clearly forms the climax of the series,[86] and the phrasing of Apollo's declaration demands special attention. The god does not simply say that he will predict the future or that he will offer various kinds of advice on the basis of his superhuman knowledge of events. Rather, he claims that he will convey to mankind "the unfailing will of Zeus." This pronouncement has important consequences for both gods and men. In his first declaration, the mighty god, feared as a potential enemy or usurper of the existing order, allies himself unambiguously with his father and the Olympian regime whose spokesmen he will be. Furthermore, as the mouthpiece of Zeus, Apollo will be a mediator between his father and mankind. It is reasonable to assume that the power Apollo here adopts as his own constitutes a cosmic innovation. It follows that prior to Apollo—and prior to the founding of his oracle—no means of communicating the will of the gods to mankind existed. Mortals lived in a state of ignorance concerning the divine will. The hymn has already supplied a signal example of the prevailing human ignorance: the universal misapprehension concerning the new god at the time of his birth. Henceforth, however, the oracular powers of Apollo will alleviate such ignorance. As we shall see, the hymnist's insistence on the innovative character of Delphi diverges significantly from alternative traditions of the founding of Apollo's oracular shrine.

Having claimed the *timai* that will be his, the god, now fully grown and with the flowing locks (ἀκερσεκόμης) that characterize him, strides from the earth. With the response typical of the epiphany of a god, all the goddesses are amazed (θάμβεον) at the sight. Yet what happens to Delos now is far from typical:

χρυσῷ δ' ἄρα Δῆλος ἅπασα
ἤνθησ' ὡς ὅτε τε ῥίον οὔρεος ἄνθεσιν ὕλης,
βεβρίθει δέ θ' ὁρῶσα Διὸς Λητοῦς τε γενέθλην,
γηθοσύνῃ ὅτι μιν θεὸς εἵλετο οἰκία θέσθαι
νήσων ἠπείρου τε, φίλησε δὲ κηρόθι μᾶλλον.

Behold, with gold all of Delos
flowered, like a mountaintop with the flowers of the forest,

[86] Cf. J. T. Kakrides, "Zum homerischen Apollonhymnos," *Philologus* 92 (1937): 108; and Miller (1985), p. 54.

[with gold] she had grown heavy as she beheld the offspring of
Zeus and Leto
in her pleasure that the god chose her to establish his dwelling
above the islands and the mainland, and she loved him in her
heart all the more.

(135, 139, 136–38)

The miraculous gilding of Delos serves as a radiant expression of her joy
in Apollo.[87] At the same time, it fulfills the promise of Leto and foreshadows the future wealth of the island. Lines 136–38 are generally assumed to be variants of 139. Editors usually adopt one set or the other,
even though they are not strictly doublets.[88] I accept the text but print
136–38 after 139.[89] This reading restores the proper sequence and brings
out the agricultural metaphor, as well as providing a climax to the passage. Delos first blooms with gold and then grows heavy with it. Gold,
to be sure, is a mark of divinity and, like the gods, imperishable. But the
verbs ἤνθησ᾽ and βεβρίθει are both drawn from the context of vegetation.[90] To flower with gold and to grow heavy, not with fruits or with
crops, but with gold, vividly presents the paradoxical nature of Delos's
future riches.[91] As Leto promised, they will derive not from the island's

[87] Cf. Förstel (1979), p. 192, who points out that this presents the third and climactic
expression of Delos's joy. Cf. lines 61 and 90. See also Forderer (1971), p. 92. But we must
recall her initial fear and trembling in lines 66 and 70 to comprehend the complete and
characteristic sequence that progresses from terror to joy.

[88] Lines 136–38 are found in the margins of several manuscripts. Hence, Baumeister
(1860), pp. 139–40; Jacoby (1933), pp. 710–11; AHS (1936), p. 222; Deubner (1938), pp.
261–62; van Groningen (1958), p. 321, n. 3; and Förstel (1979), p. 125, consider 139 original
and 136–38 a variant. Wilamowitz (1920), pp. 449–50; Bethe (1931), p. 21; M. H. Van der
Valk, "A Few Observations on the Homeric *Hymn to Apollo*," *L'Antiquité Classique* 46
(1977): 449–50; and Kirk (1981), p. 172, defend the opposite view, and Càssola omits line
139 from his text. Unte (1968), pp. 40–41, defends the order 136–39, whereas Forderer
(1971), pp. 89–93, reads 135, 139, 137, 138, and believes that 136 may be the poet's own
variant. Gemoll (1886), p. 141, inserts 136–38 after 139 as I do, but he reads βεβρίθη and
repunctuates the lines, drawing the word into the simile: ἤνθησ᾽, ὡς ὅτε τε ῥίον οὔρεος
ἄνθεσιν ὕλης / βεβρίθη.

[89] A. Kirchhoff, "Beiträge zur Geschichte der griechischen Rhapsodik II: Der Festhymnos auf den Delischen Apollon," *Sitzungsberichte der Preussischen Akademie, Berlin*
(1893): 910, prints βέβριθεν followed by a comma. My reading restores Delos as the
subject of βεβρίθει and emends καθορῶσα to δέ θ᾽ ὁρῶσα.

[90] For βρίθω in conjunction with vegetation, see *Iliad* VIII.307, XVIII.561; *Odyssey*
15.334, 19.112; *Hymn to Demeter* 473, *Hymn to Earth the Mother of All* 9; Hesiod, *Works
and Days* 466, and the *Shield of Heracles* 290, 295, 300.

[91] Cf. G. Dumézil, *Apollon sonore et autres essais* (Paris, 1982), pp. 27–33.

natural resources, but be imported from abroad by the throngs of Apollo's worshipers. Delos's wealth will ultimately have an "unnatural" but divine source in the island's relation to the god.

Lines 140–214

The birth narrative has now come to an end. The entire section that follows (140–214) may be considered a highly elaborate transition to the second, longer, mythological narrative concerning the founding of the Delphic oracle.[92] Bringing the first half to a close and preparing the way for the second, the transitional material points both forward and backward; the devices of verbal repetition and thematic correspondences bind together what might otherwise seem a sprawling composition.

Two extended set pieces arrest the somewhat restless movement of the passage and form its double foci. Both celebrate the first of the *timai* claimed by the newborn god. Apollo, the god of music, dominates both the festival held in his honor at his birthplace and the divine gathering on Olympus. The two tableaux mirror each other; the terrestrial poet on Delos corresponds to the divine poet on Olympus. Thus, the poet of the hymn, in praising himself and his art, resumes his praise of Apollo.

First continuing his celebration of Apollo and Delos, the poet skillfully modulates from the god's birth in the mythical past to the present. The geographical priamel (141–46) begins from Delos in the past ("Sometimes, you came to rocky Cynthus") and proceeds to move farther afield ("Sometimes you wandered among islands and men"). The list of geographical features that are dear to the god forges a link to the present and the climax of the series:

ἀλλὰ σὺ Δήλῳ Φοῖβε μάλιστ᾽ ἐπιτέρπεαι ἦτορ.

But you in Delos, Phoebus, most take pleasure in your heart.

(146)

Beginning and ending his priamel with Delos, the poet also manages to reecho the theme of Apollo's universality, which now frames the entire Delos episode (144–45; cf. 22–23). The god's special affection for Delos alludes to the circumstances of his birth and, abiding into the present, leads to the description of the great festival held there quadrennially in

[92] For an analysis of the organization of this section, see Miller (1985), pp. 56–70.

Apollo's honor. The Ionians gather on Delos "mindful of you" and take their pleasure in "boxing, dancing, and singing" (149–50). It is the last item that will occupy the poet's attention in the sequel;[93] and we may even surmise that the Delian *panegyris* has been introduced to prepare for the following discussion of ἀοιδή. But in its immediate context, the festive gathering of the Greeks fulfills Leto's ancient promise to Delos of unending wealth from abroad. The selfsame nations who trembled at the news of the impending birth of the god now joyfully gather to celebrate him. Their fear has been transmuted into the pleasure (τέρπουσιν [150]) of the participants in the contests and the pleasure (τέρψαιτο δὲ θυμόν [153]) of the observer. Such is the splendor of the scene that:

φαίη κ' ἀθανάτους καὶ ἀγήρως ἔμμεναι αἰεὶ
ὅς τότ' ἐπαντιάσει' ὅτ' Ἰάονες ἀθρόοι εἶεν·
πάντων γάρ κεν ἴδοιτο χάριν, τέρψαιτο δὲ θυμὸν
ἄνδρας τ' εἰσορόων καλλιζώνους τε γυναῖκας
νῆάς τ' ὠκείας ἠδ' αὐτῶν κτήματα πολλά.

He would declare that they were immortal and ageless forever
whoever would encounter the Ionians when they are gathered
    together;
for he would see the grace of all and take pleasure in his heart,
gazing at the men and the lovely girdled women,
and their swift ships and their many possessions.

(151–55)

The festive occasion lends a divine radiance and an aura of transcendence that makes the mortal participants momentarily resemble the gods.[94]

It has been widely assumed that the *Hymn to Apollo*, or at least the Delian section, was specifically composed for the Delian festival.[95] Accordingly, the wandering bard, participating in the Ionian *panegyris* at-

[93] Cf. Forderer (1971), p. 105: "Der Nachdruck liegt auf dem letzten Glied, dem Gesang, der auch als einziges noch weiter ausgeführt wird." For the poet's preference for tricola with climactic emphasis on the last item, see Kakrides (1937), pp. 107–8.

[94] The thought is Pindaric. Cf. Miller (1985), p. 58, n. 143. For the correspondence between the Delian gathering and the opening assembly on Olympus, see J. D. Niles, "On the Design of the Hymn to Delian Apollo," *CJ* 75 (1979): 37–39.

[95] The hymn itself provides the source of this tradition, which goes back to antiquity and is preserved in the *Contest of Homer and Hesiod* 315 (in T. W. Allen, ed., *Homeri Opera* [Oxford 1912], 5: 237) and Hesiod, fr. 357 (Merkelbach-West). Cf. the discussion of Förstel (1979), pp. 71–84.

tempted to win the goodwill of his audience by celebrating them in his poem and predicted his own victory in the rhapsodic contest (173). Such an interpretation may be plausible, but it is unnecessary. The description of the celebration of Apollo on Delos arises quite naturally from the context. Moreover, it draws together into a vivid tableau certain motifs used in the hymn thus far and introduces new ones that will dominate the second half. The description itself remains quite general and refers to a repeated event rather than to a specific occasion. Its inclusion in the hymn can be sufficiently justified on poetic grounds.[96] In addition, as we shall see, the poetic performance singled out as characteristic of the Delian festival is emphatically *not* rhapsodic.[97] But, in any case, the assumption of a Delian locale for the hymn's original performance does not entail the conclusion that the subsequent story of the founding of the oracle of Delphi could not form part of the original composition. We should not foist off a nineteenth-century parochialism on the Greeks.[98] The major Homeric Hymns are all consciously Panhellenic in their orientation. In fact, along with the great sanctuaries and the Homeric epics, these poems constitute precious documents of the movement that decisively molded Greece in the archaic period. It is scholars who insist on trying to tie these compositions to specific locations and occasions: *Aphrodite* to the Troad, *Demeter* to Eleusis, and *Hermes*—unsuccessfully—to various places.[99] In their eyes, Apollo, a Panhellenic god if ever there was one, can only be

[96] Cf. Miller (1985), p. 59, n. 145: "Only if one has on *a priori* grounds restricted the poet's announced subject-matter to Apollo's *birth* rather than (in Heubeck's words) 'den Gott selbst in seinem überzeitlichen Wirken' does it become necessary to invoke hypothetical 'circumstances of performance' in order to account for the passage."

[97] Thucydides 3.104.3–5, often cited as evidence for the separate existence of a Delian hymn, explicitly mentions only the choral competitions on Delos on the testimony of the hymn. It does *not* suggest that the hymn itself was performed as part of a rhapsodic competition held there.

[98] Cf. Dornseiff (1935), p. 13: "Gegen die Einheit liegt jene naive Gepflogenheit vor, als Verfasserort den Ort anzunehmen, der in einem Gedicht vorkommt oder gar eine Rolle spielt. Das ist im Anfang Delos. Also muss das Andere, worin Delphi vorkommt, in Delphi entstanden sein und natürlich auch von einem andern Dichter stammen." Van Groningen (1958), p. 312, offers a striking example of what he calls "chauvinisme" by inventing a version of the hymn for presentation at Miletus.

[99] For *Aphrodite*, see Smith (1981b), who rightly rejects the view of the hymn's composition for patrons in the Troad. For the *Hymn to Demeter* as an Eleusinian composition intended for one of the Eleusinian festivals, see Richardson (1974), p. 12. For attempts to localize the *Hymn to Hermes*, see Herter (1981), pp. 198–201. Jacoby (1933), p. 695, calls the poet of the Delian hymn "ein panhellenischer Dichter."

Delian *or* Pythian. On the other hand, the poets—and the composer of
the *Hymn to Apollo* above all—go to considerable pains to universalize
the divinities they celebrate. His aim, to depict the totality of Apollo,
embraces both Delos and Delphi.

The vivid description of the festival on Delos is capped by "a great
marvel whose fame will never perish" (156). The twenty-two lines (157–
78) that immediately follow doubtless make up the most controversial
section of the hymn. Discussion has been focused on whether the poem
was originally intended to end here[100] and on speculation concerning "the
blind man of Chios," as the poet calls himself.[101] I have already expressed
my conviction concerning the unity of the hymn as we have it and have
little to add to the controversy about the poet's identity. I would instead
like to turn to an issue at least as intriguing as the traditional ones, but
which has not received sufficient attention: the poetics implied by the
passage, both in general terms and in specific reference to the hymn.

The Delian Maidens, we are told, begin by hymning the gods,
Apollo and, in second place, Leto and Artemis; then they sing of the
"men and women of old" (158–61). The order of their song—first gods,
then men—appears to be canonical and is common to both epic/rhap-
sodic and choral poetry. The poet calls the girls "maiden servants of the
Far-Darter." Were it not for the inclusion of the adjective "Delian" we
would take the expression as a reference to the Muses—and rightly so,
since the later description of the Muses on Olympus corresponds to that
of the singers of Delos. The girls' terrestrial song reflects the divine music
on Olympus. Although there is no explicit mention of their dancing, the
performance of the Maidens is clearly choral, and it is in some sense mimetic. Its effect lies in its ability to "enchant the races of men" (161):

---

[100] For a review of opinion, see Förstel (1979), pp. 20–53.
[101] Antiquity believed the blind man of Chios to be Homer. Drerup (1937), pp. 121–
22, revives this possibility. On the basis of the scholium to Pindar, *Nemean* 2.2, the *Hymn
to Apollo* has been ascribed to Cynaethus, who is taken to be either a Homerid of the
eighth century (AHS [1936], pp. 183–86) or a late sixth-century forger (West [1975], pp.
165–68). Dornseiff (1933), pp. 36–43, had a rather bizarre theory that Cynaethus's ascrip-
tion of the poem to Homer was not a forgery, but a joke. For a discussion of the Pindar
scholium, see Förstel (1979), pp. 92–101. See also the theories of H. T. Wade-Gery, "Kynaithos," in *Greek Poetry and Life: Essays Presented to Gilbert Murray on His Seventieth
Birthday* (Oxford, 1936), pp. 56–78; R. Dyer, "The Blind Bard of Chios (*Hymn Hom. Ap.*
171–76)," *CP* 70 (1975): 119–21; and W. Burkert, "Kynaithos, Polycrates, and the Homeric Hymn to Apollo," in *Arktouros: Hellenic Studies Presented to Bernard M. W. Knox*
(Berlin, 1979), pp. 53–62.

πάντων δ' ἀνθρώπων φωνὰς καὶ βαμβαλιαστὺν
μιμεῖσθ' ἴσασιν· φαίη δέ κεν αὐτὸς ἕκαστος
φθέγγεσθ'· οὕτω σφιν καλὴ συνάρηρεν ἀοιδή.

The voices of all men and their chatter[102]
they know how to imitate; and each man would declare that he
   himself
was speaking; thus is their lovely song fitted together.

(162–64)

Here, then, the doctrine of *mimesis* finds, if not its first expression, then surely its earliest explicit statement.[103] The girls' perfect representation of the voices of all men renders art and reality indistinguishable. Finally, the beauty of their song derives from the way all its parts—content, form, presentation—are "fitted together" into a harmonious whole.

In what appears to signal the end of the hymn, the poet asks Apollo along with Artemis to "be gracious" (165). A conventional closing sequence follows, including a salutation (χαίρετε), a request, and, finally, the poet's promise to continue his praise.[104] Here, as at line 14, but on a larger scale, the poet manipulates hymnic conventions to create a false close, which turns out to be a transition. For the salutation is addressed not to Apollo but to the singing girls of Delos, as is the request that follows: "remember me even hereafter" (166–67). In this context,

[102] βαμβαλιαστύν is to be preferred to the variant κρεμβαλιαστύν. Cf. Wilamowitz (1920), p. 450, n. 4. Wilamowitz, pp. 450–52, thinks the "babble" of the Delian Maidens refers to incomprehensible words adopted from foreign, probably Anatolian, cult songs, but preserved on account of their sacredness. Bethe (1931), p. 39, rightly rejects Wilamowitz's "glossolalia." Forderer (1971), p. 180, n. 66, thinks the term refers not to the song but the rhythm of the dance. Yet lines 163–64 say nothing of the girls' dancing. On the mimicry of the Delian Maidens, Forderer, p. 100, cites *Odyssey* 4.279, where Helen is said to imitate the voices—and presumably, the speech habits—of the wives of the Greeks in the wooden horse. The girls are surely singing in Greek, but their imitative powers may embrace the various local dialect peculiarities. We should not forget that the rhapsodic *Kunstsprache* contains a good number of dialectal isoglosses. It, like the festival described in the poem, is a Panhellenic institution.

[103] Cf. Dornseiff (1933), p. 8: "Es ist die früheste Stelle für den in der antiken Ästhetik so wichtigen Mimesisbegriff." Cf. Forderer (1971), p. 101; also the discussion of A.L.T. Bergren, "Sacred Apostrophe: Re-Presentation and Imitation in the Homeric Hymns," *Arethusa* 15 (1982): esp. 92–94.

[104] Cf. A. M. Miller, "The 'Address to the Delian Maidens' in the *Homeric Hymn to Apollo*: Epilogue or Transition?" *TAPA* 109 (1979): 176–81, whom I follow closely on the rhetorical configuration of this pasage. See also Altheim (1924), p. 437; and De Martino (1982), pp. 63–75, who likens the whole passage to the comic parabasis.

μνήσασθ᾽, can only mean "include me in your song."¹⁰⁵ In instructing the girls how they are to accomplish his request, the poet assumes the role of a *chorodidaskalos*, composing a short responsive dialogue for his chorus.¹⁰⁶ He tells them what to say whenever a stranger of broad experience should come and ask them,

ὦ κοῦραι, τίς δ᾽ ὔμμιν ἀνὴρ ἥδιστος ἀοιδῶν
ἐνθάδε πωλεῖται, καὶ τέῳ τέρπεσθε μάλιστα;

"O maidens, who in your opinion is the sweetest singer
who frequents this place, and in whom do you take the greatest
pleasure?"
(169–70)

In answer to the two-line question, the girls are to give a corresponding reply:

ὑμεῖς δ᾽ εὖ μάλα πᾶσαι ὑποκρίνασθε ἀφ᾽ ἡμέων
τυφλὸς ἀνήρ, οἰκεῖ δὲ Χίῳ ἔνι παιπαλοέσσῃ,
τοῦ πᾶσαι μετόπισθεν ἀριστεύουσιν ἀοιδαί.

All of you answer well from us:¹⁰⁷
"A blind man who lives on rugged Chios,
all of whose songs hereafter are always the best."
(171–73)

¹⁰⁵ Cf. line 1 (μνήσομαι οὐδὲ λάθωμαι) and line 160, concerning the song of the Delian Maidens: μνησάμεναι ἀνδρῶν τε παλαιῶν ἠδὲ γυναικῶν. See the discussion of J.-P. Vernant, "Aspects mythique de la mémoire et du temps" in *Mythe et pensée chez les Grecs* (Paris, 1965), 1: 80–107; and W. S. Moran, "Μιμνήσκομαι and 'Remembering' Epic Stories in Homer and the Hymns," *QUCC* 20 (1975): 195–211. Also De Martino (1982), pp. 66–71.

¹⁰⁶ Cf. Förstel (1979), p. 404, n. 415: "die Anrede des Dichters an die delischen Chormädchen und die vorhergehende Lob ihres Gesanges erinnern an die Art, wie Alkman in seinen Gedichten seine Choreutinnen sprechen lässt und zu ihnen spricht." Cf. the remarks of Bethe (1931), pp. 39–40: "Ich komme immer wieder auf den Schluss, dieser Blinde von Chios hat den delischen Mädchen selber das Lied gemacht und mit ihnen gesungen wie Alkman. . . . Dieser Vermutung steht allein das ungerechtfertige Vorurteil entgegen, der Rhapsode der homerische Aoide sei vom Chormeister zu trennen." Bethe, as well as Dornseiff (1933), pp. 44–45, draw parallels to Demodocus's singing of the "Lay of Ares and Aphrodite" among the dancing Phaeacians (*Odyssey* 8.256–367). The whole notion of the separation of choral and rhapsodic genres in the archaic period should be reassessed in the light of this passage.

¹⁰⁷ Forderer (1971), p. 104 and n. 69, interprets ἀφ᾽ ἡμέων as "from us" rather than "about us." In other words, the answer the girls are to deliver is a message from the poet. For the hiatus, see Forderer, p. 173, n. 38. ὑποκρίνασθαι might also be possible.

The poet's boast that all of his songs are the best would appear to include not only the hymn but also the mimetic choral song of the Delian Maidens themselves. In other words, embracing both the lyric and rhapsodic modes, the poet proclaims his universal mastery of all music.[108] Indeed, he has just given a playful display of his comprehensive mastery of the art by imitating a choral performance within the framework of his hexameter hymn.[109]

From their fixed point on Delos, the girls will announce the poet's excellence by singing the song he composed for them to the visiting strangers who frequent the island. The poet, for his part, will disseminate their fame throughout the world, as he passes through "the well-inhabited cities of men" (174–75). Whereas the girls' medium will be choral lyric, his will inevitably be solo—presumably, rhapsodic—song. Surely the song to which he refers and the one that contains the *kleos* he promises to convey to the ends of the earth (cf. 156) can be none other than the hymn itself[110]—a portable version of the composition performed on Delos. We may conclude that the *Hymn to Apollo*, far from being tailored for performance on Delos, is composed for presentation to the Greek world at large. Like his patron god, the itinerant poet and his hymn begin from Delos and, through his worldwide journeyings, win universal recognition (cf. line 29: ἔνθεν ἀπορνύμενος πᾶσι θνητοῖσιν ἀνάσσεις). The hymn, which celebrates a universal, Panhellenic Apollo, likewise declares itself to be Panhellenic.

An unparalleled degree of self-consciousness on the part of the poet concerning himself and his art marks the preceding passage. There is nothing like it within the hymnic corpus, although the so-called Hymn

---

[108] Cf. Forderer (1971), p. 109: "damit beansprucht der Dichter, der ja gewissermassen ein Abbild Apollons ist, mit spielerischem Humor, auf seine Weise teilzunehmen an der Allkraft des Gottes."

[109] Cf. Dornseiff (1933), p. 16: "wir sehen hier eine *Verchorung* der epischen Rhapsodenkunst." Also H. Koller, "Das kitharodische Prooimion," *Philologus* 100 (1956): 166: "im delischen Hymnus handelt es sich um eine Umsetzung von Chorlyrik in epische Sprache."

[110] ἡμεῖς δ' ὑμέτερον κλέος οἴσομεν ὅσσον ἐπ' αἶαν (174) is surely an example of the so-called encomiastic future so frequently found in Pindar. Cf. E. Bundy, *Studia Pindarica I: The Eleventh Olympian Ode* (Berkeley, 1962), p. 21: "The laudator's use of the future indicative in the first person . . . is, in fact, a conventional element of the encomiastic style. It never points beyond the ode itself." S. Fogelmark, *Studies in Pindar with Particular Reference to Paean VI and Nemean VII* (Lund, 1972), pp. 93–94, cites several examples of such conventional futures from the opening formulas of the Homeric Hymns (*Apollo* 1, *Aphrodite* [no. 6] 2, *Dionysus* [no. 7] 2, *Aphrodite* [no. 10] 1, *Heracles* 1, *The Son of Cronus* 1, and *Earth the Mother of All* 1), but he neglects to mention our passage.

to the Muses that forms the proem to the *Theogony* offers equally self-conscious, albeit different, reflections about the nature and function of poetry and the poet. The similarity is not accidental;[111] both Hesiod and the hymn-poet celebrate their patron deities and the source of their art:

ἐκ γὰρ τοι Μουσέων καὶ ἑκηβόλου Ἀπόλλωνος
ἄνδρες ἀοιδοὶ ἔασιν ἐπὶ χθόνα καὶ κιθαρισταί.

For from the Muses and far-casting Apollo
men are singers on earth and lyre players.
(*Theogony* 94–95 = *Hymn to the Muses and Apollo* 2–3)

In both cases, the relationship between the singer and the object of his song is peculiarly intimate. In praising Apollo, the hymn-poet is naturally led to reflect on his own art; such reflections cannot be construed as digressions from the task of praise, but instead constitute one of its essential components. Finally, as the mortal representative of the divine Olympian singer, the poet can proclaim his own excellence and fame and simultaneously enhance the greatness of his patron god. Far from abandoning his subject in the interest of peripheral personal or occasional considerations,[112] the poet here expounds his understanding of the significance of Apolline music for mankind.

Now reassuring his audience that he will not leave off hymning his god,[113] the poet returns with the apostrophe, ὦ ἄνα, to the direct representation of Apollo. A brief transitional passage, involving a geographic priamel that mentions Delos for the last time and Pytho for the first,[114]

[111] Both Bethe (1931), p. 36, and Jacoby (1933), p. 700, note the similarity between the hymn's *sphragis* and the proem to the *Theogony*. Jacoby goes so far as to postulate Hesiod's influence on the hymn-poet. For the correspondences between Hesiod and the Muses of Helicon and the hymn-poet and the Deliades, see Nagy (1982), pp. 55–56.

[112] Unte (1968), p. 57, calls the entire description of the Delian festival "ein Exkurs," while Forderer (1971), p. 110, labels it a "fast privaten Abschweifung," and Baltes (1982), p. 29, n. 19, speaks of a "privaten Vorstellung und Bitte" after which the poet returns "zu seiner eigentlichen Aufgabe zurück." But cf. Miller (1985), pp. 64–65.

[113] Cf. Miller (1979), pp. 178–79, for the meaning of οὐ λήξω. Koller (1956), p. 198, speaks of the "gewollt spielerischer Zweideutigkeit." Cf. Heubeck (1972), p. 140, for the poet's playing with hymnic conventions. For the transitional character of lines 177–78, see Dornseiff (1933), p. 9, and (1935), p. 11; Jacoby (1933), p. 719, n. 3; Floratos (1952), p. 301; Unte (1968), pp. 47–49; Forderer (1971), pp. 110–11; and Heubeck (1972), pp. 138–40.

[114] Unte (1968), p. 50, and Forderer (1971), p. 111, see the list of geographical names in lines 179–81 as a complement to the other geographical catalogs in the hymn. Less convincingly, Forderer (1971), p. 114, and Baltes (1982), pp. 28–30, argue that the passage must be understood as a resumption of Apollo's wanderings from line 146.

prepares for the poem's second scene on Olympus. Somewhat abruptly, we discover "the splendid son of Leto" making his way to rocky Pytho while playing the lyre. Thence,"quick as thought," he proceeds to Olympus:

εἶσι Διὸς πρὸς δῶμα θεῶν μεθ᾽ ὁμήγυριν ἄλλων·
αὐτίκα δ᾽ ἀθανάτοισι μέλει κίθαρις καὶ ἀοιδή.

and he comes to the house of Zeus among the gathering of the
    other gods;
and straightway lyre and song are the immortals' concern.

(187–88)

The scene of musical festivity on Olympus forms the counterpart to the poem's opening (2–13), which depicted a very different reaction to Apollo's arrival in the halls of Zeus. There, his entrance provoked panic and commotion among the peacefully assembled gods; here, it produces harmonious song and dance, serene play and pleasure.

The activity inspired by Apollo on Olympus constitutes the most perfect musical performance, of which all earthly performances are only imperfect representations. Its complex form is characterized by a clear articulation of parts, harmoniously fitted together. The Muses sing responsively (ἀμειβόμεναι ὀπὶ καλῇ [189]); meanwhile, the Graces and the Horai as well as other female divinities who embody grace, beauty, and pleasure—Harmony, Hebe, and Aphrodite—dance in a circle. Among them, Artemis, Apollo's sister, stands out for her size and beauty. Inside the ring, Ares and Hermes, youthful models of male beauty, "play."[115] Finally, in their midst, "high-stepping" Apollo plays the lyre; a divine radiance surrounds his person, and his feet and clothing sparkle (189–203). Song, dance, and the accompaniment of the lyre form clearly articulated but perfectly joined components of this divine concert.

The division of roles among the Olympian participants sheds light on several peculiarities in the earlier scene of musical activity on Delos. Like their divine counterparts, the Muses, the Delian Maidens were said to sing, but nothing was said of their dancing.[116] So too, the "blind man

---

[115] For Ares' and Hermes' play as some kind of acrobatic display, compare *Odyssey* 4.15–19 and *Iliad* xviii.604–6. Cf. the discussion of Forderer (1971), pp. 206–13.

[116] The separation of singing and dancing in the hymn is all the more striking because the Muses traditionally do both. Consider, above all, Hesiod's Muses. Dornseiff (1933), p. 8, notes that the dance of the Deliades, while not mentioned, "muss aber wohl ange-

of Chios," while instructing his chorus, does not appear to join in their song.

Like his divine model, Apollo *Musagetes*, the poet depicts himself directing and accompanying the song of *his* earthly muses. These formal correspondences convey the paradigmatic character of the Olympian performance. Like the girls on Delos, the Muses sing of gods and men. Yet, inevitably, the song of the Muses embodies an Olympian perspective.

> ... ὑμνεῦσίν ῥα θεῶν δῶρ᾽ ἄμβροτα ἠδ᾽ ἀνθρώπων
> προφύλαχθε, δέδεχθε δὲ φῦλ᾽ ἀνθρώπων
> ζώουσ᾽ ἀφραδέες καὶ ἀμήχανοι, οὐδὲ δύνανται
> εὑρέμεναι θανάτοιό τ᾽ ἄκος καὶ γήραος ἄλκαρ.

> ... they hymn the deathless gifts of the immortals and men's
> sufferings, as many as they have at the hands of the immortal
>   gods;
> they live ignorant and without resources, nor are they able
> to find a remedy for death or a defense against old age.

$$(190–93)$$

The gods' celebration of their own "deathless gifts" is enhanced or at least remains incomplete without a reminder of the afflictions of mankind.[117] The gulf between gods and mortals, which seemed momentarily bridged or abolished amid the splendor of the Delian festival (cf. 151–52), reappears on Olympus; the apparent exemption from old age and death was only an illusion. Mortality abides as the condition of human life. But human folly and helplessness will be somewhat alleviated by the estab-

---

nommen werden" and suggests (p. 15) that, because the poet was blind, he was unable to observe their dancing! While recognizing the correspondence between the Delian and Olympian festivities and using it as an argument for the unity of the hymn, Kakrides (1937), pp. 104–5, insists that the Delian Maidens dance and that the dancers on Olympus take part in the singing. Koller (1956), pp. 160–61, is also inaccurate on this point. Förstel (1979), p. 227, is more precise: "nur von ihnen [the Muses] wird gesagt, dass sie singen; am Reigentanz dagegen scheinen sie nicht teilzunehmen." For the correspondences between the poet and Apollo and the Delian Maidens and the Muses, see Forderer (1971), pp. 129–30; and Nagy (1982), pp. 55–56.

[117] Cf. J. Griffin, *Homer on Life and Death* (Oxford, 1980), pp. 189–92. For the Olympian view of mankind as a corrective to the beautiful illusion of the Delian festival, see Kakrides (1937), p. 105, and Heubeck (1972), pp. 143–44. Charles Segal has suggested to me that ἄκος in line 193 may allude to Apollo's link with medicine and healing.

lishment of Apollo's oracle, which will convey "the unerring will of Zeus" to mankind.[118]

Our passage concludes with the joy of Leto and Zeus as they observe their "dear son playing among the immortals" (204–6). In the hymn's opening scene, Apollo's parents were the only ones exempt from the general terror that engulfed the gods. But here, their pleasure and pride in their son forms part of the universal joy of Olympus under the benign influence of Apollo's music. The two epiphanies of the god on Olympus, then, reproduce on a grand scale the characteristic progress from fear to joy that the manifestation of Apollo inspires.

Apollo's Search for His Oracular Shrine

With both bow and lyre sufficiently celebrated as dual aspects of the god, a resting point of sorts has been reached.[119] A new beginning is required to introduce the last of Apollo's *timai*. The fresh start is signaled by the same question that preceded the birth narrative:

πῶς τ' ἄρ σ' ὑμνήσω πάντως εὔυμνον ἐόντα;

How shall I hymn you, you who are everywhere well hymned?

(207 = 19)

Once again, the abundant possibilities seem to bewilder the poet. In the earlier passage the "range of song" led naturally to a list of places pleasing to Apollo until finally an appropriate topic was chosen: the story of the god's birth on Delos. Here, the poet adopts a different strategy. First, he suggests a general theme, the erotic exploits of Apollo among mortals (208) and then offers a catalog of specific examples, filled with obscure names and allusions to what appear to be local variants of better-known myths (209–13).[120] But the second topic proposed and the one finally adopted seems to have no connection with the god's *amours*:

[118] Cf. Förstel (1979), p. 233: "Eben diese so umfassend zu verstehende menschliche Blindheit und Hilflosigkeit ist Grund und Voraussetzung für die Orakeltätigkeit des Apollon in Pytho."

[119] For a new beginning at line 207, see Forderer (1971), p. 154. Drerup (1937), pp. 123–24, sets the beginning of the Pythian poem at line 206.

[120] For the difficulties, see AHS (1936), pp. 230–32; and Càssola (1975), pp. 499–501. Cf. L. Bodson, "Hymne homérique à Apollon, 209–213: Un 'locus desperatus'?" *L'Antiquité Classique* 40 (1971): 12–20, who believes the passage alludes to local Peloponnesian

ἢ ὡς τὸ πρῶτον χρηστήριον ἀνθρώποισι
ζητεύων κατὰ γαῖαν ἔβης ἑκατηβόλ᾿ Ἄπολλον;

Or shall I sing how first seeking an oracle for men
on earth you came, far-darting Apollo?

(214–15)

According to Miller, the contrast between the final choice—the founding of the Delphic oracle—and the erotic subjects rejected lies in the difference between public and private πράξεις.[121] Yet the amatory escapades of the gods are not strictly speaking private—at least not the way those of mortals might be. As the *Odyssey* has it, the courtships and loves of the Olympians are never unproductive.[122] In fact, heroes and founders of cults and cities arise from such encounters, but generally they remain tied to the specific communities and locales where they are worshiped. The real distinction between the themes rejected by the hymn-poet and the one he takes up is not between the public and the private spheres, but between the local and the Panhellenic.

The chosen topic, Apollo's search for a site for his oracle, begins with a catalog of places the god visits in the course of his quest.[123] The list both parallels and contrasts with the enumeration of stations in Leto's search for Apollo's birthplace. While Leto's journey took her along the coastal and island locales that skirt the Aegean, her son proceeds through the interior of the Greek mainland as he makes his progress from Olympus to Pytho. A third geographic catalog (409–39) will round the Peloponnese. Together, they will cover the whole of Greece. The hymn, then, gives concrete expression to its claim of Apollo's universality; no part of the Greek world remains untouched by the god.[124] There are also significant differences in the techniques of the two catalogs. The first offers a

---

traditions. Dornseiff (1933), p. 11, calls the allusions in these lines "ehoienmässig angedeuteten Geschichten."

[121] Miller (1985), p. 71. Forderer (1971), p. 159, notes that the rejected themes deal with "bestimmte ausgezeichnete Menschen der Vorzeit," while the oracle founding deals with mankind in general.

[122] *Odyssey* 11.249–50: οὐκ ἀποφώλιοι εὐναὶ ἀθανάτων.

[123] Cf. Baltes (1982), pp. 31–34. Apollo's journey from Olympus to Pytho is anything but direct, but we must remember that the god remains as yet unaware of the goal of his quest. For the problems surrounding Apollo's route, see Baltes, p. 32, n. 37, and the map in D. Kolk, *Der pythische Apollonhymnus als aitiologische Dichtung* (Meisenheim, 1963), p. 15. Altheim (1924), pp. 443–45, assumes the conflation of two versions.

[124] Cf. Baltes (1982), p. 42.

static enumeration of the places traversed by the pregnant Leto, as the goddess was passively buffeted from place to place, rejected by all, until she finally persuaded Delos. Here, however, the catalog is full of movement as it traces the majestic progress of the god. Moreover, Apollo takes active charge of his quest, inspecting and choosing a site that will suit him. On one occasion, he too will meet with rejection, but his reaction will be far from passive.[125]

The god's quest begins from Olympus and proceeds in a generally southern, then southeasterly direction, traversing Euboea. As he comes to the Lelantine plain, we are told that "it did not please him" (220).[126] In fact, none of the places appeals to Apollo until he reaches the spring of Telphousa:

βῆς δ᾽ ἐπὶ Τελφούσης· τόθι τοι ἅδε χῶρος ἀπήμων
τεύξασθαι νηόν τε καὶ ἄλσεα δενδρήεντα.

Then you came to Telphousa; there the untroubled place pleased
you
to build a temple and a wooded grove.

(244–45)

Along the way, two sites, implicitly rejected by the god, receive extended descriptions. Apollo first passes the future site of "holy Thebes," which was not yet inhabited and did not contain "paths or roads" but was choked with virgin forest (225–28). Traditionally, Thebes was considered one of the oldest cities in Greece, founded, according to legend, by Cadmus on orders from the Delphic oracle.[127] The apparent digression on Thebes thus has a twofold function: it coordinates the divine narrative of the founding of Delphi with human history. The events recounted in the hymn take place in the remote past, not only early in the reign of Zeus, but also long ago in the earliest phases of human history.[128] The allusion to Thebes also points forward to one of the most important functions of

[125] Cf. Baltes (1982), p. 32, n. 36.
[126] On the reasons for Apollo's rejection, see Jacoby (1933), pp. 739–40; and Miller (1985), pp. 73–75 and n. 187. Cf. Eitrem (1938), p. 128: "Apollo in insula parva saxosaque natus neque campos (cf. Lelantium campum, v. 220) neque agros fertiles omnino deligere videtur, scopulis autem montibusque delectatur (v. 145 etc.)."
[127] Cf. F. Vian, *Les origines de Thèbes* (Paris, 1963), esp. pp. 76–87.
[128] Cf. Förstel (1979), p. 243, and p. 464, n. 645, who notes that the poet not only wants to indicate the great antiquity of the oracle, but also "dass mit der Frühzeit der Orakelgründung auch ein qualitativ anderer Zustand auf der Erde angedeutet wird."

the Delphic oracle: its political role in the establishment of cities and the colonization of the Greek world in the archaic period.[129] The description of Poseidon's grove at Onchestus and the strange rite practiced there (230–38) has often been dismissed as an excursus motivated merely by the poet's antiquarian interest.[130] But it too sheds light on Apollo's ultimate choice for the site of his shrine. First, Onchestus is already sacred to another divinity; Delphi, a godforsaken spot, will belong to Apollo alone. Second, Poseidon's grove with its riderless horses and chariots careening through the woods hardly offers the "untroubled spot" for which Apollo searches. Finally, if, as has been suggested, the mysterious ritual at Onchestus constitutes a primitive form of divination,[131] then the violent and costly means employed there for discovering the divine will offer a striking contrast to the oracular practices to be established at Delphi.

Apollo arrests his search at the spring of Telphousa, the "untroubled place" that he favors. The god's address to the spring parallels Leto's supplication of Delos, but his tone is lordly and imperious rather than entreating; he makes no attempt to strike a bargain with the nymph:

Τελφοῦσ᾽ ἐνθάδε δὴ φρονέω περικαλλέα νηὸν
ἀνθρώπων τεῦξαι χρηστήριον, οἵ τέ μοι αἰεὶ
ἐνθάδ᾽ ἀγινήσουσι τεληέσσας ἑκατόμβας,
ἠμὲν ὅσοι Πελοπόννησον πίειραν ἔχουσιν
ἠδ᾽ ὅσοι Εὐρώπην τε καὶ ἀμφιρύτους κάτα νήσους,
χρησόμενοι· τοῖσιν δέ τ᾽ ἐγὼ νημερτέα βουλὴν
πᾶσι θεμιστεύοιμι χρέων ἐνὶ πίονι νηῷ.

Telphousa, here then I think to build my splendid temple
as an oracle for men, who will always to me
bring hither perfect hecatombs,
both those who inhabit the rich Peloponnesus
and those who live in Europe and throughout the sea-girt islands,

[129] Cf. H. W. Parke and D.E.W. Wormell, *The Delphic Oracle* (Oxford, 1956), 1: 49–81.

[130] So, for example, West (1975), p. 161: "When he gets to Onchestus, the poet cannot refrain from describing a curious ceremony to be seen there, although it has nothing to do with Apollo."

[131] For a thorough discussion of interpretations of the ritual at Onchestus, see A. Schachter, "*Homeric Hymn to Apollo*, lines 231–238 (The Onchestus Episode): Another Interpretation," *BICS* 23 (1976): 102–13. However, Schachter does not believe that the rite involved either divination or propitiation of the god.

as they come to consult the oracle; to them I myself will lay down
the unerring will, prophesying to them all in my rich temple.

(247–53)

Without waiting for a response, Apollo immediately begins to lay out the
huge foundations. Observing all this, Telphousa becomes "angered in her
heart." But cloaking her anger in apparent goodwill, she advises Apollo
that, despite its appearance, the site is in fact not suitable for his purpose.
Far from being a trouble-free spot (cf. χῶρος ἀπήμων [244]), the place is
always troubled (πημανέει, [262]) by the din from the horses and mules
who come to drink at the springs. The noise from the traffic will disturb
the god and distract his worshipers. With a flattering acknowledgment
of Apollo's superiority, Telphousa suggests that the god locate his shrine
"in Crisa" "under the fold of Parnassus" where neither chariots nor
horses will bother him:

ἀλλά τοι ὡς προσάγοιεν Ἰηπαιήονι δῶρα
ἀνθρώπων κλυτὰ φῦλα, σὺ δὲ φρένας ἀμφιγεγηθὼς
δέξαι' ἱερὰ καλὰ περικτιόνων ἀνθρώπων.

But to you, all the same, Iepaean, they will bring gifts,
the famous tribes of men, and warmed in your heart, you
will receive fine sacrifices from the men who live round about.

(272–74)

Telphousa's motives are by no means benevolent. As the poet tells us, she
wants to have all the glory on earth for herself, and leave none for Apollo
(275–76). Nevertheless, something in her argument persuades the god; he
too desires a place free from the distractions of an established watering
place.[132] As it turns out, the spot he finally elects for his sanctuary has no
natural attractions, but will derive all its fame and splendor from the god
himself.

Proceeding to the site of Delphi, Apollo passes the "city of the Phlegyans, hybristic men who have no respect for Zeus" (278–79). According
to legend, the same Phlegyans later attacked Delphi and were defeated
by the god. For the moment, Apollo has no time for these outlaws and
enemies of Zeus, as he quickly hurries toward his goal:

[132] Cf. Förstel (1979), pp. 245–46; and Miller (1985), pp. 71–72.

ἔνθεν καρπαλίμως προσέβης πρὸς δειράδα θύων,
ἵκεο δ᾽ ἐς Κρίσην ὑπὸ Παρνησὸν νιφόεντα
κνημὸν πρὸς ζέφυρον τετραμμένον, αὐτὰρ ὕπερθεν
πέτρη ἐπικρέμαται, κοίλη δ᾽ ὑποδέδρομε βῆσσα
τρηχεῖ᾽.

Thence swiftly you went toward the ridge, panting,
and you came to Crisa under snowy Parnassus,
its shoulder turned westward, but from above
a rock hangs over, and hollow is the glen that runs under it
and harsh.

(281–85)

The harsh and forbidding spot appeals to the god. He determines
to build his "lovely temple" here. The hymn emphasizes the desolate and
uninviting character of the site. Why it should have such appeal to Apollo
remains as yet unclear.

In other accounts of the establishment of Apollo's oracle at Delphi,
the god is said to take over—either by force or by peaceful means—a
preexisting oracular shrine of Gaia or Themis.[133] This tradition has apparently been confirmed by the archaeological evidence, but, more important, it forms the canonical version incorporated into official Delphic
lore.[134] The *Hymn to Apollo*, on the contrary, insists on Apollo's innovation: no oracle or settlement preceded the god's installation at Delphi; the
place did not even have a name and has no prehistory. Förstel acknowledges that the version of the founding told in the hymn constitutes a
radical "Sagenkorrektur,"[135] but he does not appreciate the full implica-

[133] The main literary sources are Aeschylus, *Eumenides* 1–20; Euripides, *Iphigenia in
Tauris* 1234–83; and the *Paean* of Aristonous (*Collectanea Alexandrina*, ed. J. U. Powell
[Oxford 1925], pp. 162–64). Cf. Förstel (1979), pp. 212–17; O. Panagl, "Stationen hellenischer Religiosität am Beispiel des delphischen Sukzessionsmythos," *Kairos* 11 (1969):
161–71; and J. Defradas, *Les Thèmes de la propagande delphique* (Paris, 1954), pp. 86–95.

[134] Best represented in Aristonous's *Paean*. Cf. Panagl (1969), pp. 168–69, and Förstel
(1979), p. 216. C. Sourvinou-Inwood, "Myth as History: The Previous Owners of the
Delphic Oracle," in *Interpretations of Greek Mythology*, ed. J. Bremmer (London, 1987),
pp. 215–41, strenuously rejects the historicity of the Previous Owners myth. Her argument does not necessarily undercut mine. For there is no way of telling whether the
Previous Owners myth is earlier or later than the foundation story recounted in the hymn.

[135] Förstel (1979), p. 235; cf. Defradas (1954), p. 86, who admits that our later testimonia may contain older traditions, which the hymn "aurait volontairement laissés dans
l'ombre."

tions of this drastic departure from what was, after all, the tradition officially sanctioned at Delphi. Panagl admits that "the cause of this fundamental alteration in the actual significance of the Delphic myth presumably lies in the particular character of the old hymns themselves."[136] Noting that the Homeric Hymns contain many new foundations and inventions on the part of the gods, Panagl goes on to suggest that the takeover of an existing oracle would be deemed unworthy of so great a divinity as Apollo. But no one else in the Greek world or, least of all, at Delphi thought the tale of Apollo's conquest beneath the dignity of the god.

The poet's departure from orthodox Delphic tradition has a deeper cause. It is the necessary consequence of his definition of Apollo's oracular *timē* and of the overall Olympian framework of the hymn. To put it simply, as his prerogative, Apollo chooses to become the prophet of Zeus.[137] Obviously, that choice can only be made after Zeus's establishment on Olympus. Thus, the radical revision of accepted Delphic dogma betrays the profoundly Olympian orientation of the hymn. The founding of the oracle becomes a unique event with the unique purpose enunciated by Apollo at the moment of his birth: to convey the unerring will of Zeus to mankind (cf. 132). By ignoring Delphic tradition and denying any continuity or connection between Apollo's establishment and a prior prophetic seat on the same spot, the hymn proclaims Apollo's oracle to be a uniquely Olympian institution and an essential component of the Olympian dispensation.

Repeating once more his proclaimed intent (287–93 = 247–53), Apollo again sets about laying the great foundation for his sanctuary. Almost miraculously, the splendid temple is constructed before our eyes.[138] Upon the divine foundation, the legendary builders, Trophonius and Agamedes, "dear to the gods," set the great stone walls, "to be a subject of song forever." And straightway, the "numberless tribes of men" settle the area around the great temple, which before Apollo's com-

[136] Panagl (1969), p. 164.

[137] Panagl (1969), p. 167, is incorrect in asserting that Aeschylus was the first to make Apollo a "Zeusprophet." It is, however, true that in the prologue to the *Eumenides*, Apollo is both the peaceful successor to the old oracular gods *and* the recipient of Zeus's unique prophetic gift.

[138] Jacoby (1933), p. 740, correctly claims that the building of Apollo's temple is not the climax or center of the Pythian poem, but he is wrong to say that "dieser Hymnus hat keinen Höhepunkt, weder künstlerisch noch sachlich." Apollo's proclamation of the first oracle to mankind forms the altogether appropriate climax of the poem.

ing had been uninhabited and uninhabitable (294–99).[139] The proleptic description of Apollo's temple reflects the great hierarchy embracing gods, heroes, and men that informs Greek thought.[140] It also sets Apollo's sanctuary at Delphi apart from other temples and shrines. Here, the god himself lays out the foundation, whereas usually a divinity simply orders a temple to be built in his honor.[141] Apollo's active participation at Delphi will not cease with the construction of his temple. For when men come to consult the oracle, the god himself will respond. In conveying the will of his father, Apollo creates a new bond between gods and mortals and a new mode of communication. The temple at Delphi thus inaugurates a new era in the history of the relations between gods and men.

Pytho and Typho

ἀγχοῦ δὲ κρήνη καλλίρροος ἔνθα δράκαιναν
κτεῖνεν ἄναξ Διὸς υἱὸς ἀπὸ κρατεροῖο βιοῖο.

Nearby was a fair-flowing stream where
the lord son of Zeus killed a dragoness with his mighty bow.

(300–1)

Far from being a place free of trouble, the site commended by Telphousa turns out to be occupied by a savage serpent who destroys both men and flocks, "since she was a blood-reeking bane" (ἐπεὶ πέλε πῆμα δαφοινόν [304]). Apollo's combat with the dragon forms a canonical component of the Delphic tradition. Yet in other versions, the huge serpent is the guardian of the primeval oracle of Earth or Themis; the defeat of the monster signifies the takeover of the ancient shrine by the new god. However, as we have seen, the hymn-poet insists that Apollo's oracle is a new foundation. The hymn also departs from the usual tradition by

[139] I follow A. von Blumenthal, "Der Apollontempel des Trophonios und Agamedes in Delphi," *Philologus* 83 (1927–1928): 220–24, in transposing lines 228 and 229. Förstel (1979), pp. 252–57, sees in the references to Trophonius and Agamedes as well as "the numberless tribes of men" "einem eklatanten sagenchronologischen Widerspruch" and a "kühne Verachtung der Logik," because both heroes belong to a later generation, and no men yet inhabit the site of Delphi. There is no reason to assume that the dragon allows the temple to be built in peace before she seizes Apollo's attention. Surely, lines 295–99 must simply be understood proleptically. Jacoby (1933), p. 741, assumes the lines are an interpolation.

[140] Cf. Eitrem (1938), p. 129; and Förstel (1979), p. 252.

[141] Cf., for example, *Hymn to Demeter* 270–74.

making the dragon female.[142] This change is clearly motivated in the sequel: the Delphic serpent turns out to be the foster mother of an even greater monster, Typho. But, perhaps most striking, the hymn drastically curtails the description of the actual combat, which, on the evidence of artistic representations, must have been a very popular set piece, and formed the narrative core of the Delphic *nomos*.[143] The hymn, however, goes off in an unexpected direction. We learn that the she-dragon, herself a πῆμα, once received from Hera and nursed "the terrible and dreadful Typho, a bane (πῆμα) to the gods.[144] An elaborate digression of fifty lines enlarges on the origins of Typho.

Almost all commentators have condemned the passage (305–55) out of hand as an intrusion into the text;[145] the ranks of its defenders are thin and generally feeble. Some concede its irrelevance to the hymn and retreat to the weak outpost of "association of ideas." Thus the unitarian Dornseiff considered the episode a caricature of the manner in which mythological digressions are inserted in lyric poetry—"dragged in by the hairs, but then remaining strangely pointless."[146] According to van Groningen, "the fortuitous association of ideas causes the insertion of an inorganic element." One might well ask why? Because "on adore les récits."[147]

Those who maintain that the account of Typho serves to character-

[142] Cf. J. Fontenrose, *Python: A Study of Delphic Myth and Its Origins* (Berkeley, 1959), p. 14, n. 4, and p. 21, where Fontenrose outlines five major versions of the myth of Apollo and the dragon. Only in the *Hymn to Apollo* is the serpent female, but some later accounts seem to be influenced by the hymn's version.

[143] For the *nomos pythikos*, see the discussion in Kolk (1963), pp. 41–47. Jacoby (1933), p. 743, explains the omission of the combat with the dragon as due to the poet's desire not to compete with similar descriptions. For the compression, see also Förstel (1979), p. 249.

[144] See n. 166, below. For the mythological parallels between Pytho and Typho, see Fontenrose (1959), pp. 77–93. Their familial association appears unique to the *Hymn to Apollo*.

[145] For example, Hermann (1806), pp. xxx–xxxvii; Baumeister (1860), p. 117; Gemoll (1886), p. 165; Bethe (1931), p. 12; U. von Wilamowitz-Moellendorff, *Pindaros* (Berlin, 1922), p. 75, n. 3; Jacoby (1933), pp. 743–45 ("das Stück ... ist ohne jede Verbindung mit der Apollongeschichte"); Drerup (1937), p. 126, who believes the Typho story may be part of the "pythischen Kultlegende"—for which there is not a shred of evidence; O. Regenbogen, "Gedanken zum homerischen Apollon-Hymnus," *Eranos* 5 (1956): 52–53; Càssola (1975), p. 505; and Kirk (1981), p. 176.

[146] Dornseiff (1933), p. 17.

[147] Van Groningen (1958), pp. 317–18. Cf. AHS (1936), p. 189, n. 1, and p. 244; and Humbert (1936), p. 92, n. 1, for equally halfhearted defenses of the passage. Janko (1982), pp. 116–19, finds the episode uncommonly "clumsy" but "not incomprehensible" and detects no "literary nor linguistic grounds for supposing that it is an interpolation by a different poet."

ize obliquely the Delphic dragon and to enhance Apollo's heroic accomplishment offer a stronger line of argument.[148] While true as far as it goes, this defense does not quite justify the extraordinary length of the digression or its indirection. Its shortcoming lies in its limited focus, a kind of philological tunnel vision, which looks only at the immediate context rather than to wider implications. While continuing to emphasize the close link uniting Pytho and Typho, the recent studies of Förstel and Miller reveal an awareness of the relevance of the Typho passage to the hymn as a whole, although neither pursues the question sufficiently. Förstel, for example, alludes to the theogonic and theological significance of the lines and points to the contrast between the divisive state of affairs here and the harmony that reigns on Olympus in lines 182–206. He further notes that the Typho story reveals a "time of crisis in the establishment of the Olympian family,"[149] but he does not elaborate. Miller recognizes that the Hera of the Typho episode resembles the jealous goddess who persecuted Leto;[150] in addition, "the poet contrives to have his audience discern a relation of analogy between Apollo and Zeus as enemies of disorder."[151]

The preceding remarks point the way to a more comprehensive interpretation of the Typho passage. Far from being either a pointless digression or one of limited relevance, it illuminates crucial aspects of the hymn by setting the story of Apollo's birth and his founding of the oracle, as well as his role among the Olympians and his meaning for mankind, into their proper framework. The poem's central concern, the emergence of Apollo, receives its full definition through the portrayal of what may be called his opposite number.[152] The legitimate and mighty son who furthers his father's Olympian agenda stands in powerful contrast to the unnatural offspring, would-be usurper, and destroyer of the Olympian order.

At this point, it may be useful to review briefly the account of Typho

---

[148] Ludwich (1908), p. 190: "Dieser unheimliche Pflegesohn dient dazu, die Drachin selber zu charakterisiren." Cf. Unte (1968), pp. 80 and 104; and Floratos (1952), pp. 305–7.

[149] Förstel (1979), pp. 262–63.

[150] Miller (1985), p. 87. Cf. Unte (1968), p. 80: "Hera ist natürlicherweise die Gegenspielerin Apollons, dessen Geburt sie schon Hindernisse in den Weg legte."

[151] Miller (1985), p. 88. Cf. Thalmann (1984), p. 72; and Unte (1968), p. 80: "Zeus und Apollon stehen hier zusammen gegen Hera und ihre Ungeheuer Typhon und Drakaina."

[152] Drerup (1937), p. 126, suggests that the Typho story "vielleicht auch eine bewusste Parallele zur Geburt Apollons aus der Leto enthält." Forderer (1971), p. 196, considers "die Geburt des Typhaon als dämonisches Gegenbild zur Geburt Apollons."

and its sequel in the *Theogony*. I believe, as does Miller,[153] that the poet of the *Hymn to Apollo* was well acquainted with the Hesiodic version or, at least, with the traditions on which the *Theogony* is based. As will become clear, the hymn-poet seems to have known others as well. At any rate, a comparison with the account in the *Theogony* throws light on the version recounted in the hymn. It contains many similar components; however, they are recounted in a different configuration and sequence, which drastically modifies their meaning. The hymn, moreover, alludes to several motifs drawn from other points in the Hesiodic Succession Myth. This telescoping, as Miller calls it,[154] of diverse elements into a unified whole lends a peculiar density and concentration to the narrative told in the hymn. It is as if the poet had attempted to roll all succession stories into a single paradigmatic account.

In Hesiod, Typhoeus presents the last violent threat from without to the establishment of the Olympian order. After the Titans have been defeated and thrust into the nether world, Gaia conceives the monstrous Typhoeus, her last child, by Tartarus. His parentage suffices to reveal his significance: this hundred-headed monster with blazing eyes and bizarrely bestial voices represents the final opposition on the part of the primordial gods to Zeus's regime:

καί κεν ὅ γε θνητοῖσι καὶ ἀθανάτοισιν ἄναξεν,
εἰ μὴ ἄρ' ὀξὺ νόησε πατὴρ ἀνδρῶν τε θεῶν τε.

And in truth he would have been lord over mortals and
    immortals,
if the father of gods and men had not taken sharp notice.

(*Theogony* 837–38)

The swift reaction of Zeus prevents the monster from becoming ruler of the universe in his stead and blocks forever the recrudescence of the primeval forces of disorder. After Typhoeus's fiery defeat at the hands of Zeus's thunderbolt, Zeus is immediately elected to the supreme kingship in heaven, and he distributes the various *timai* among the other gods. Henceforward, no further challenge to his domination can arise outside the Olympian order. Nevertheless, an internal danger remains: Zeus's

---

[153] Miller (1985), p. 85. Cf. Janko (1982), p. 119: "we conjecture *P Ap.* is consciously altering his [Hesiod's] version."
[154] Miller (1985), p. 85.

marriage to Metis ("Contrivance").[155] She is destined to bring forth first a daughter "equal to her father in strength and counsel" (896), and then a son who is to be "king of gods and men" and possess a violent and overbearing nature (897–98). By swallowing Metis when she is on the point of giving birth to Athena, Zeus prevents the birth of a successor and at the same time, by incorporating Metis, ensures the permanence of his rule. Hesiod now recounts in order the further marriages of Zeus and their respective offspring; his second wife is Themis, who is followed by Eurynome, Demeter, and Mnemosyne; Leto comes fifth, and "last he made Hera his flourishing wife" (921).[156] At this point, Zeus, who, it seems, has been incubating her all along, gives birth to Athena from his head. In rage at her husband, Hera, in turn, produces the master crafts-man Hephaestus parthenogenically.

In adapting and modifying many of these Hesiodic motifs, the *Hymn to Apollo* produces a very different account of the early history of the Olympians. Most striking, according to the hymn, not the primordial Earth but Hera herself conceives the terrible Typho.[157] We are accus-tomed to a jealous, spiteful Hera who resents her husband's countless affairs and persecutes his bastard children. Often enough in the *Iliad*, the bickering of the Olympian couple offers a moment's relief from the in-cessant slaughter on the battlefield. Yet even there, Hera's savage hatred of the Trojans hints at a darker side. Behind the comic, largely impotent figure of the epic stands an older, more powerful one, the true heiress of her grandmother Gaia, who was once kingmaker among the gods. Hera's claim to the queenship of heaven does not depend on Zeus; her lineage is as august as his. Yet the permanence of Zeus's reign requires

---

[155] For the meaning of *mētis*, see M. Detienne and J.-P. Vernant, *Les Ruses de l'intelli-gence: La Mètis des Grecs* (Paris, 1974), esp. pp. 9–10.

[156] In the *Theogony* the birth of Apollo and Artemis appears to precede Zeus's mar-riage to Hera; Hesiod thus precludes the jealousy motif as we have it in the *Hymn to Apollo*.

[157] Stesichorus evidently recounted a similar version (fr. 62, Page). A scholium to *Iliad* II.783 tells a curious variant, which perhaps was intended to harmonize both accounts of Typho's birth from Earth (as in Hesiod) and from Hera. Earth, distressed at the defeat of the Giants, denounced Zeus to Hera. Hera, in turn, told Cronus, who gave her two eggs smeared with his own semen and instructed her to bury them in the earth. Because Hera was angry at Zeus, she carried out these orders. From these eggs Typho was born, but then Hera told everything to Zeus who promptly blasted the monster with a thun-derbolt. The T Scholium to *Iliad* XIV.296 reports a tradition that Hera gave birth to an-other enemy of Zeus, Prometheus, whom she conceived by the Giant, Eurymedon. See now the discussion of W. Pötscher, *Hera: Eine Strukturanalyse im Vergleich mit Athena* (Darmstadt, 1987), pp. 95–103.

an end to succession and entails the establishment of a patriarchal order and the consequent subordination of the female. Under the Olympian dispensation, Hera may continue to try to sabotage Zeus's plans, but her opposition remains ultimately ineffectual. The most telling indication of her demotion resides in the inferiority of her offspring, especially her sons: Hephaestus, the cripple, and Ares, most hateful of the Olympians to Zeus (cf. *Iliad* v.890). Yet at the dawn of the Olympian regime, during the epoch of the *Hymn to Apollo*, Hera, not yet domesticated, offers the ultimate challenge to Zeus's new order by attempting to reproduce the ancient cycle of succession.[158]

The threat to Zeus's rule arises not from the old gods as in the *Theogony*, but from within the Olympian family itself, in fact, at its very center. Enraged at Zeus after the birth of Athena, Hera makes a solemn proclamation before the assembled gods and denounces her husband. By bringing forth Athena "apart from me," Zeus has taken the first step in dishonoring her, even though she is his lawful wife (312–13). Hera complains that she has been stripped of her *timē* and her legitimate wifely prerogative to bear children to her husband. Because he was the first to dishonor her, she is justified in taking revenge. The same argument is used by Hesiod's Gaia under similar circumstances. When Uranus prevented Gaia's children from emerging from her womb, she justifies her plot against her consort: "he was the first to devise unseemly deeds" (*Theogony* 166). Hera continues her indictment: as if adding insult to injury, Zeus's daughter, Athena, "stands out among the blessed immortals" (315), while Hera's own son, Hephaestus, is a weakling with twisted feet. In Hesiod, the parthenogenic birth of Hephaestus is Hera's response to Zeus's outrage, but in the *Hymn to Apollo*, his birth clearly precedes that of Athena.[159] The disparity between the two gods—Zeus's splendid daughter and her own crippled son—serves to fuel Hera's rage; and the latter's existence is a continual reminder of her own inferiority. Once in disgust, Hera hurled him into the sea, but Thetis and her Nereids rescued him—a rescue Hera bitterly regrets:

ὡς ὄφελ᾽ ἄλλο θεοῖσι χαρίσσασθαι μακάρεσσι.

Would that she [Thetis] had done some other favor to the gods!

(321)

---

[158] Cf. C. Ramnoux, *Mythologie ou la famille Olympienne* (Paris, 1959), pp. 49–52.

[159] Cf. Miller (1985), p. 85, n. 221. The hymn-poet follows the Homeric (cf. *Iliad* xiv.338 and *Odyssey* 8.312) version of Hephaestus's lineage. Note καὶ νῦν in the *Hymn to Apollo* 314; the immediate context of Hera's rage is the recent birth of Athena.

Homer mentions the tale of Thetis's rescue of Hephaestus in the *Iliad*,[160] but its prominence here in the *Hymn to Apollo* may allude to another story as well in which Thetis is a doublet of the Hesiodic Metis. Zeus had intended to marry her but learned that she was destined to bear a son greater than his father; thereupon, she was married off to the mortal Peleus.[161] If Hera has this story in mind, her otherwise lame reference to "some other favor" assumes a threatening dimension.[162] Rather than saving the wretched Hephaestus, Thetis ought to have brought forth the son who would have toppled Zeus. As it is, Hera will attempt to accomplish what Thetis failed to do.

At any rate, Hera now turns to vent her boundless rage against Zeus directly:

σχέτλιε ποικιλομῆτα τί νῦν μητίσεαι ἄλλο;
πῶς ἔτλης οἶος τεκέεν γλαυκώπιδ᾽ Ἀθήνην;
οὐκ ἂν ἐγὼ τεκόμην; καὶ σὴ κεκλημένη ἔμπης
ἦν ἄρ᾽ ἐν ἀθανάτοισιν οἳ οὐρανὸν εὐρὺν ἔχουσι.

Wretch, of varied contrivances, what other thing do you now
    contrive?
How could you dare to bring forth gray-eyed Athena alone?
Couldn't I have borne her? And, even so, she would have been
    called
yours[163] among the immortals who inhabit the broad heaven.

(322–25)

It is crucial to follow carefully the progress of Hera's indictment of Zeus. What begins as an offense to her wifely honor becomes a challenge to the patriarchal principles of Olympus. Even if Hera had participated in the birth of Athena, Zeus would nevertheless receive the credit for so splendid an offspring, although the disgrace for an imperfect child falls upon

---

[160] *Iliad* XVIII.395–405.

[161] Cf. Pindar, *Isthmian* 8.27–37; and J. S. Clay, *The Wrath of Athena* (Princeton, 1983), p. 176, n. 78. For Thetis's double role as the ultimate threat to Olympus and its protector, see L. Slatkin, "The Wrath of Thetis," *TAPA* 116 (1986): 1–24.

[162] Consider also the erotic overtones of χαρίζομαι, and the remarks of Plutarch, *Amatorius* 751d: χάρις γὰρ ἡ τοῦ θήλεος ὕπειξις τῷ ἄρρενι κέκληται πρὸς τῶν παλαιῶν. Cf. J. Latacz, *Zum Wortfeld "Freude" in der Sprache Homers* (Heidelberg, 1966), pp. 107–16.

[163] I adopt the reading ἦν ἄρ᾽ as opposed to ἦα ῥ᾽ accepted by most editors. Cf. Càssola (1975), p. 506, who defends the absence of a modal particle. Förstel (1979), p. 288, also prefers this reading.

Hera. What Hera ultimately disputes—and what motivates her subsequent actions—is the subordination of the female to the male, of wife to husband. From this perspective, the portrayal of Leto in the two earlier Olympian scenes gains in significance. In the first, she displays maternal pride in her mighty son; in the second, she shares her husband's pleasure as both parents observe Apollo leading the concert of the gods. Leto thus exemplifies the conduct appropriate to the consort of Zeus, conduct characterized by quiet concord rather than rivalry and opposition. Once kindled, Hera's indignation goes beyond its immediate cause to a cosmic questioning of the natural hierarchy between the sexes and within the family. The violent, disorderly offspring she defiantly produces on her own will unambiguously demonstrate the validity of that hierarchy, a hierarchy that extends also to the proper relation between father and son, for which Apollo forms the model.

If Zeus dared to bring forth Athena without her, Hera will avenge herself by another contrivance: on her own, without sexual intercourse, she will produce a son who, like Athena, will "stand out among the immortal gods" (327). The repeated occurrence of words connected with *mētis* in these lines—μητίσεαι in line 322, μητίσομ' in line 325a, τεχνήσομαι in line 326 (cf. Διὸς . . . μητιόεντος in line 344)—inevitably recalls the story of Metis, Athena's would-be mother. By swallowing her and thus permanently incorporating Contrivance, Zeus became μητίετα Ζεύς, "Zeus who possesses Metis," and forever invincible. In the *Hymn to Apollo*, Hera proposes to counter Zeus's contrivance with one of her own, but μητίετα Ζεύς can neither be overcome by force nor outwitted by guile. As Hesiod puts it, "there is no way to escape the mind of Zeus or to surpass it" (*Theogony* 613). Hera's plan is ultimately doomed to failure.

Hera now cuts herself off not only from the bed of Zeus, but also from the gods—or at least the Olympians.[164] Yet she cannot bring her plan to fruition without help. Beating the ground in a gesture of cursing,[165] she invokes Earth and Sky and the "Titans who live under the earth around great Tartarus" and prays that they grant her a son:

[164] Ludwich (1908), p. 192, suggested οὐδέ for οὖσα at line 330. At first glance, this emendation seems attractive, but I prefer to leave the text unchanged. Hera's last words to Zeus contain a riddling challenge; while she will leave Olympus, she will nevertheless consort with gods, but these will not be Olympian divinities.

[165] Cf. *Iliad* ix.568–69 and, perhaps, *Odyssey* 11.423.

νόσφι Διός, μηδέν τι βίην ἐπιδευέα κείνου·
ἀλλ’ ὅ γε φέρτερος ἔστω ὅσον Κρόνου εὐρύοπα Ζεύς.

apart from Zeus, one who is in no wise inferior in force to him;
but let him be stronger—as much as wide-seeing Zeus is stronger
than Cronus.

(338–39)

As her rage assumes cosmic proportions, Hera allies herself with the primordial chthonic powers who have only recently been defeated by Zeus.
When the earth moves in answer to Hera's prayer, the full enormity of
Hera's enterprise becomes manifest: she intends to produce a son might-
ier than Zeus, one strong enough to depose him—just as Zeus once over-
threw his father Cronus. The goddess envisions nothing short of the destruction of the Olympian order.

Retiring to her temples, Hera "takes pleasure in her sacrifices" (347–
48). It appears that she too has her devotees among mortals. Could her
worshipers resemble the overbearing Phlegyans who "pay no heed to
Zeus" (cf. 278–79)? In any case, the division in heaven may well have its
counterpart on earth. In due season, the monstrous offspring is born:

ἡ δ’ ἔτεκ’ οὔτε θεοῖς ἐναλίγκιον οὔτε βροτοῖσι
δεινόν τ’ ἀργαλέον τε Τυφάονα πῆμα θεοῖσιν.

And she brought forth one that resembled neither gods nor men,[166]
Typhaon, terrible and dreadful, a bane to the gods.[167]

(351–52)

In the sequel, the hymn-poet seems to adapt a motif from the *Theogony*.
He has already drawn an explicit parallel between Cronus–Zeus and
Zeus–Typho. Now, just as Zeus's mother Rheia entrusted her newborn
son to Gaia to nurse and to hide him from his father Cronus, so Hera
entrusts her offspring to the dragoness at Delphi, "an evil to an evil"
(354).[168]

[166] Cf. the description of Echidna in *Theogony* 295–96. She is said (304–15) to produce
various monstrous offspring from her union with Typho.
[167] Ludwich (1908), pp. 190–91, suggested that the reading of M at line 352, πῆμα
θεοῖσιν, was changed to πῆμα βροτοῖσιν by homeoteleuton. He further recommended
that πῆμα βροτοῖσιν be restored at line 306 and that ἥ be read for ὅς at line 355 on the
grounds that Typho is a bane to the gods while the serpent constitutes a bane to men. In
slaying the latter, Apollo becomes a savior of mankind.
[168] With equal appropriateness, Themis is Apollo's nurse in the hymn.

71

At this point, the return to the main narrative commences. Foster mother and child lead similar careers of destruction: she works many evils among mankind,[169] bringing death to all who approach her, until, that is, the mighty arrow of Apollo puts an end to her murderous activity. Apollo's defeat of the serpent will be commemorated eternally at Delphi. From it will derive a cult title of the god, and the place, heretofore nameless, will take its name from the rotting of the monstrous corpse:

τὴν δ' αὐτοῦ κατέπυσ' ἱερὸν μένος Ἡελίοιο·
ἐξ οὗ νῦν Πυθὼ κικλήσκεται, οἱ δὲ ἄνακτα
Πύθειον καλέουσιν ἐπώνυμον οὕνεκα κεῖθι
αὐτοῦ πῦσε πέλωρ μένος ὀξέος Ἡελίοιο.

The holy force of the Sun putrified her on the spot;
whence now it is called Pytho, and they call the lord
Pythian as a byname because here
the force of sharp Helios putrified the monster.

(371–74)

The chthonic creature of darkness rots when exposed to the light of the sun. Yet Apollo's boast over the dying dragon makes it clear that Typhaon and other monsters still inhabit the world. His destruction by the thunderbolt of Zeus remains undescribed in the poem not only because it would detract from Apollo's accomplishment,[170] but also because the threat he poses still abides.[171] The violent overthrow of the Olympian order remains a possibility.

With the monster dead, Apollo recognizes the extent of Telphousa's malicious deception. Enraged, he rushes back to the stream. In sending Apollo off to the serpent's lair, Telphousa was motivated by the desire to be the only one to have *kleos* at the spring and to exclude Apollo (275–76). Now, Apollo responds in word and deed. First, he declares that he too will have *kleos* there and not she alone (381); then, he appropriately punishes the spring by pushing rocks into the streams that are the source of her pride and glory. The god's treatment of Telphousa reminds one of Delos's earlier fears for her own safety. The island was terribly frightened that the new god would scorn her on account of her poverty and contemptuously push her into the sea (70–73). The parallel between Tel-

---

[169] Cf. above, n. 166.
[170] Cf. Miller (1985), pp. 87–88.
[171] Cf. Förstel (1979), p. 263.

72

phousa and Delos illustrates the character of Apollo. Whereas Delos joyfully receives the god and is amply rewarded, Telphousa's mean-spirited rejection meets with ignominy and punishment. If in slaying the dragon Apollo becomes "Pythian," so in punishing the spring he becomes "Telphousian" (385–87). The god uses his great power not for random violence, but employs it purposefully to punish pride and wickedness.

It has long been recognized that the entire sequence that begins with Apollo's first meeting with Telphousa and ends with her punishment is constructed according to the principle of ring composition.[172] The two encounters with Telphousa frame the account of the Delphic serpent, which, in turn, encloses the story of Typho. Miller has likened the disposition of narrative material here to the famous digression on Odysseus's scar in the nineteenth book of the *Odyssey*.[173] The comparison is apt because, here as there, the core element—in the one case, Odysseus's naming, in the other, the Typho episode—radiates significance out to the concentric framing components. As Thalmann has said of a different passage employing the same technique: "by the end of the passage, when the same ideas are recapitulated, they are understood more fully, in all their implications, because the development in the middle part has shed new light upon them."[174] Just as the dragon's nature is illuminated by her association with Typho, so the meaning of Telphousa's actions only becomes fully manifest from the perspective of the Typho episode.[175] By sending Apollo to his presumed destruction, she too reveals herself to be on the side of the enemies of Olympus.[176]

Yet the ramifications of the Typho story fan out far beyond its immediate context. The tale of his birth reveals deep divisions on Olympus. As Hera's alliance with them shows, the old chthonic powers, although defeated, remain potent. Typho himself has not yet been annihilated, and the danger of a violent overthrow of the regime of Zeus continues. Uni-

[172] Cf. Unte (1968), p. 83; Thalmann (1984), pp. 70–71; and Miller (1985), p. 94.
[173] Cf. Miller (1985), pp. 82–83. For Odysseus's scar, see Clay (1983), pp. 56–59.
[174] Thalmann (1984), p. 16, apropos of *Apollo* 14–29.
[175] Without the Typho story, they remain merely puzzling. Cf. Jacoby (1933), p. 740: "Wir haben entschieden das Gefühl, dass hinter dem Rencontre mit der Quelle . . . irgend etwas steckt, was über den Märchentypus des bösen Rates hinausgeht, wissen nur nicht was." Like most scholars, Jacoby considers the Typho story an interpolation.
[176] Baltes (1982), p. 43, aptly calls Telphousa "eine Komplizin der Hera." According to a tradition preserved in the Scholia to Sophocles' *Antigone* 126, Telphousa or Tilphossa was the mother of the Theban dragon slain by Cadmus. This would make the nymph a counterpart of both Hera and the Delphic serpent. For Telphousa's chthonic associations, see Vian (1963), pp. 107–8; and Fontenrose (1959), pp. 366–74.

versal instability, disharmony, and fear still prevail. It is in this atmo-sphere of crisis that Apollo has come into the world. His entrance into Olympus in the hymn's opening scene resembled nothing so much as the violent irruption of the usurping son destined to depose his father. That threat proved illusory as Apollo, disarmed and welcomed, took his place at his father's side. The apprehension that filled the earth at the time of Apollo's birth was the fear of a violent and lawless successor to Zeus. The source of the malicious rumor turns out to be none other than Leto's persecutor, Hera, no mere jealous wife, but the mother of Typho and an avowed enemy of Zeus's cosmos. However, with his very first words, the newborn Apollo declares his allegiance to his father: his lyre will bring harmony to Olympus; his bow, far from challenging his father's domin-ion, will defend it and destroy its enemies;[177] and his oracle will com-municate his father's will to mankind. The hymn thus sets Apollo in the broadest possible context and defines his role as a critical component in the constitution and preservation of the Olympian order.

The Acquisition of the Cretan Priesthood

Even though his temple is built, Pytho slain, and Telphousa pun-ished, Apollo's task is not yet completed. In order to function, his sanc-tuary requires a priesthood to look after the temple, disseminate the god's decrees, and receive his worshipers.

καὶ τότε δὴ κατὰ θυμὸν ἐφράζετο Φοῖβος Ἀπόλλων
οὕς τινας ἀνθρώπους ὀργιόνας εἰσαγάγοιτο
οἳ θεραπεύσονται Πυθοῖ ἔνι πετρηέσσῃ.

And then Phoebus Apollo considered in his heart
what men he might bring in to be his ministers,
who would be his servants in rocky Pytho.

(388–90)

The final section of the hymn focuses on the establishment of Apollo's priesthood in Delphi and culminates in the pronouncement of the first oracle. At the same time, it enlarges on a motif that has been peripheral to the main action of the poem thus far. Up to now, the hymn

---

[177] Cf. Miller (1985), p. 121; and Unte (1968), p. 81.

has embraced Olympus and even the nether world, the divine and the bestial, as well as the whole earth. Thus, all nations trembled at the god's birth, and all men are subject to him (cf. 29). The Delian festival portrayed mortals momentarily exalted in the splendor of their celebration of the god. It culminated in the praise of the Delian Maidens, the servants of Apollo and counterparts of the Muses, and of the poet himself, the earthly representative of the god. On Olympus, the Muses revealed a less sanguine view of the limitations of mortals. Yet the relationship between Apollo and mankind has not yet been explored fully, even though it constitutes the basis of his third *timē*. For Apollo's oracular function resides precisely in disseminating the divine will to mankind and thus alleviating the human ignorance and misery of which the Muses sang. The last section of the hymn, then, records the ironic contrast between human ignorance and helplessness in the time before Delphi and the divine knowledge of Apollo. The gulf between the two will to some extent be mitigated by the god's oracular decrees. As men receive access to the gods' intentions, they become capable of moral choice, which their previous ignorance had precluded. The *Hymn to Apollo* thus points forward to a new era not only in the history of Olympus, but also for mankind.

Here we should pause for a moment to point out a striking omission that has elicited surprisingly little notice from commentators: the absence within the hymn of any reference to the Pythia, Apollo's prophetess at Delphi. Humbert and Càssola, who date this part of the hymn to the beginning and end of the sixth century respectively, simply ignore the problem, while Allen, Halliday, and Sikes set the poem's silence concerning Pythia on a par with its omission of other accoutrements of the cult— for example, the chasm, the holy tripod, the *omphalos*—and attribute it to "the epic manner" and the early date of the hymn (late eighth century).[178] Yet the Pythia's absence cannot be regarded in quite the same light: in the historical period at least, she, not the Delphic priests, was the mouthpiece of the god. The function of the priesthood was to interpret her responses and transmit them to the oracle's consultants. The hymn, however, gives the clear impression that the Cretan ministers themselves constitute the spokesmen of the god:

[178] AHS (1936), pp. 185 and 192. Cf. C. A. Lobeck, *Aglaophamus* (Königsberg, 1829), 1: 264–65; and Rohde (1898), 2: 57, n. 4. The hymn's silence concerning Apollo's role in healing and purification, while also striking, falls into a different category, since the god himself does not claim these *timai* within the confines of the poem.

Κρῆτες ἀπὸ Κνωσοῦ Μινωΐου, οἵ ῥά τ᾽ ἄνακτι
ἱερά τε ῥέζουσι καὶ ἀγγέλλουσι θέμιστας
Φοίβου Ἀπόλλωνος χρυσαόρου, ὅττι κεν εἴπῃ
χρείων ἐκ δάφνης γυάλων ὕπο Παρνησοῖο.

... the Cretans from Minos's Cnossos, who to the lord
perform sacrifices and announce the decrees
of Phoebus Apollo of the golden sword, whatever he may say
as he prophesies from the laurel under the hollows of Parnassus.

(393–96)

The hymn's silence concerning the Pythia can be explained in one
of two ways: she did not exist at the time of the poem's composition and
was not considered part of the original organization of the oracle; or the
prophetess did exist and was known to the poet but was consciously sup-
pressed and omitted from his account. The main arguments for the first
interpretation can be reviewed here briefly. If it is correct, it is of interest
for the earliest period of Delphi and the history of Greek religion, but
has little bearing on the interpretation of the hymn. For if there was no
Pythia, her omission from the poem is not significant but completely natural.

Some scholars have suggested that the Pythia must be considered a
later addition to Delphic cult, and they point to traces of primitive oracular practices that do not appear to involve the Pythia. It is perhaps significant that Homer does not mention her, although Theognis, dated by
West to the seventh century, does.[179] Her absence has been taken as evidence of the high antiquity of the hymn.[180] According to one view, the
original oracle consisted of a tree cult, like that of Dodona, but the prophetic tree was Apollo's sacred laurel; his priests interpreted its rus-
tling.[181] To be sure, the laurel was important at Delphi. According to one
legend, the first temple was built of laurel wood; the Pythia was said to
shake a branch of the tree while delivering her responses and even to

[179] Theognis 807 (West) calls her the ἱέρεια.
[180] Cf. J. Fontenrose, *The Delphic Oracle* (Berkeley, 1978), p. 215: "Since the Hymn
does not mention the Pythia, it may reflect an early period when male prophets received
Apollo's inspiration."
[181] Cf. H. Pomtow, "Delphoi," *RE* 4, pt. 2 (1901): 2527. Cf. Parke and Wormell (1956),
1: 9. AHS (1936), p. 254, express doubts, as does P. Amandry, *La Mantique Apollinienne
à Delphes: Essai sur le fonctionnement de l'Oracle* (Paris, 1950), p. 131.

chew its leaves in preparation; and laurel fueled Apollo's sacred hearth.[182]
Yet the evidence for a primitive tree cult at Delphi remains meager; the
ἐκ δάφνης of line 396 offers too slender a reed on which to hang this
theory. One form of prophecy that is attested during the historical period
involved the drawing of lots by the Pythia. It is assumed by some that
cleromancy may have been practiced at Delphi by the priests before the
installation of the prophetess, although the hymn offers no evidence for
or against this hypothesis.[183] Finally, Rohde suggested that the mantic
frenzy of the Pythia was inspired by the ecstatic practices of Dionysiac
worship that penetrated Apolline cult at a fairly late date.[184] Since then,
the evidence of the Pylos tablets has cast serious doubts on the view of
Dionysus as a relative newcomer and foreign import into the Greek pantheon.[185] Thus, the arguments for the late arrival of the Pythia at Delphi
are inconclusive at best. Admittedly, our evidence for the earliest phases
of the cult are extremely scanty. Yet it remains striking that no legends
detailing the arrival of the Pythia subsequent to Apollo's establishment
at Delphi or traditions concerning the reorganization of the oracle that
her installation would have entailed have come down to us.

The alternative explanation of the Pythia's absence from the hymn,

[182] For the use of the laurel at Delphi, see Fontenrose (1978), pp. 224–25; Parke and
Wormell (1956), 1: 26; and Amandry (1950), pp. 126–34.

[183] For a lot oracle at Delphi, see Lobeck (1829), 2: 814–16; Rohde (1898), 2: 57; Parke
and Wormell (1956), 1: 9, 18–19; Nilsson, *GGR* (1955), 1: 167: "In Delphi war das Los-
orakel die älteste Orakelform." Cf. pp. 170–71; and Amandry (1950), pp. 25–36. Both
K. Latte, "Orakel," *RE* 18, pt. 1 (1939): 831–32, and Fontenrose (1978), pp. 220–23, reject
this view. In Euripides' version of the early history of the shrine (*Iphigeneia in Taurus*
1259–83), Earth is said to establish a dream oracle in order to avenge herself on Apollo
who had removed her daughter Themis and taken over the oracle. Zeus, however, sup-
pressed Earth's nocturnal oracle. Rohde (1898), 2: 58, accepts the existence of incubation
rituals at Delphi, but Amandry (1950), pp. 37–40, expresses doubts. Finally, Forderer
(1971), pp. 170–71, n. 28, suggests that fire prophecy may be the original form of prophecy
implied in the hymn.

[184] Rohde (1898), 2: 56–61. For a more cautious formulation of possible Dionysiac influence, see Parke and Wormell (1956), 2: 12–13. Compare L. R. Farnell, *The Cults of the
Greek States* (Oxford, 1907), 4: 192. K. Latte, "The Coming of the Pythia," *Harvard Theological Review* 33 (1940): 9–18, rejects Rohde's thesis of the Dionysiac origins of *Inspira-
tionsmantik* and insists that the Pythia's arrival at Delphi coincides with that of Apollo.
Both, he claims, are Anatolian in origin; her mantic powers derive from the Oriental
notion of her being the concubine of the god. There is no evidence for such a conception
of the Pythia. Amandry (1950), pp. 41–56, and Fontenrose (1978), pp. 204–12, reject the
idea of any kind of prophetic frenzy on the part of the Pythia.

[185] See, for example, W. Burkert, *Griechische Religion der archaischen und klassischen
Epoche* (Stuttgart, 1977), pp. 252–53.

then, merits consideration. It should be noted that the later the presumed date of the poem's composition, the more glaring the omission becomes. The supposition that the poet consciously omitted all mention of the Pythia in his account of the founding of the Delphic oracle fits in with other tendencies of the composition. We have already noted that the hymn suppresses the tradition of an older cult or oracle of Gaia/Themis at the site of Delphi. The Pythia, as some scholars plausibly argue, was originally a priestess of Gaia.[186] Her chthonic origins appear to be borne out by her traditional associations with clefts, caverns, underground chambers, and vapors.[187] These stubbornly persist despite their lack of apparent connection with Apollo.[188] Whatever the truth of the matter, the hymn-poet may well have perceived the Pythia as a holdover from the ancient rituals of the Earth goddess. The conscious omission of Gaia in the hymn would then seem to entail the suppression of her priestess as well.

Thus, it appears all traces of pre-Olympian chthonic and female associations are purged from Delphi in the interest of the Olympian and male. The opposition between Olympian and chthonic and male and female similarly informs the hostility of Telphousa and the dragoness to Apollo, as well as the story of Hera and Typho in which the rebellious female allies herself with the pre-Olympian chthonic powers to produce the enemy of the Olympian order. The champion of that order, Apollo, confines his oracular power to announcing the will of his *father*. In the

[186] Cf. Parke and Wormell (1956), 1: 10–11; and Farnell (1907), 4: 192.

[187] Excavations under the floor of Apollo's temple at Delphi have conclusively disproved the existence of any subterranean *adyton* or cave at the site. Nevertheless, traditions linking the Pythia to underground chasms and chthonic exhalations are remarkably consistent. A. P. Oppé, "The Chasm at Delphi," *JHS* 24 (1904): 214–40, considers them to be later rationalizing explanations for the Pythia's mantic ecstasy; but he admits that they were based on old Delphic legends of the cult of the earth goddess (p. 237). Cf. Fontenrose (1978), pp. 197–203. Parke and Wormell (1956), 1: 11, note that "the persistence of the tradition that the Pythia sat above a cleft or entered a cavern points to some similar ritual, which as we may suppose was originally employed by a priestess of Ge at Delphi in the second millennium B.C." Cf. also pp. 19–24. A most impressive chasm does, of course, exist at Delphi a short distance from Apollo's *temenos*: the Castalia gorge. Remains of a prehistoric cult of a female divinity were discovered below Castalia in the area of the later temple of Athena Pronaia. It is an easy hypothesis to assume that when the priestess of Ge was transformed into Apollo's prophetess, she retained some of her chthonic associations. Cf. G. Roux, *Delphes: Son oracle et ses dieux* (Paris, 1976), pp. 28–29.

[188] Cf. Farnell (1907), 4: 193: "What strikes us as most alien to Apollo in the Delphic ritual is the idea that the source of the inspiration is in the subterranean world." Farnell also speaks of "chthonian divination" "inherited by the Pythian Apollo from the older system."

hymn, Apollo's foundation constitutes a purely Olympian innovation that owes nothing to pre-Olympian antecedents. His priesthood consists exclusively of males who come from abroad and have no previous connection with Delphi; that is, they are decidedly not autochthonous.[189] The god's choice of ministers thus stands in complete accord with the hymn's fundamental orientation.

As Apollo ponders his need for ministers, he notices a ship on the open sea, full of Cretans from Cnossos who are destined "to carry out his sacrifices and announce his decrees" (394). The wide gaze of the god, which evidently can take in the Cretan sea from the Greek mainland, stands in marked contrast to the mortals who are incapabable of comprehending even what is immediately before their eyes. The Cretans are engaged in a decidedly commonplace activity: sailing to Pylos for private gain and commerce rather than the public weal. Nothing is said of their peculiar suitability to the god's service. They excel neither in piety or wisdom, and they are not even assigned individual names. Apollo's choice seems to be completely random. Far from being heroic founders of a new cult, the Cretans turn out to be anonymous, unheroic representatives of mankind in general.[190] Just as Delos and Delphi are singled out by the god despite their unpromising appearance, and both sites are to derive their splendor and wealth not from any natural advantages but solely from the god, so too Apollo chooses as his ministers unremarkable men, whose position, honor, and livelihood will depend on the god alone.

The unheroic character of the Cretan sailors offers a perfect model of the human ignorance and helplessness described by the Muses. Their conduct, both during the journey and upon their arrival at Delphi, reveals a complete lack of awareness of their singular destiny and an inability to rise above the petty concerns of human life. From the divine perspective, their all-too-human shortcomings appear comic or, occasionally, pathetic, but clearly untragic. The lack of a tragic dimension accompanies the absence of the heroic. The blindness of the Cretans is a source of amusement; as men worse than us, they are, as Aristotle would have it, fit subjects for comedy. The humor of the episode arises from our sense

---

[189] For alternate traditions of the autochthony of the Delphic priesthood, see Förstel (1979), p. 222, and my discussion below.

[190] Cf. Förstel (1979), p. 268. Förstel, pp. 221–22, points out that other versions have the Cretans setting out to found a city; they are rescued by Apollo from a storm at sea and finally become his priests. Such accounts present the Cretans in a more heroic light. For the Cretans' "deracination," see also Miller (1985), p. 97.

of superiority to the ignorant Cretans. *We* recognize the god and understand his intentions. Our ability to laugh at the Cretans reveals how far we have come as a result of Apollo's innovation. Because of Apollo, the decrees of the gods are no longer completely hidden from us. In a sense, then, the Cretan sailors represent the helpless state of mortals before Apollo inaugurated his oracle.

Be that as it may, Apollo, now in the likeness of a dolphin, leaps into or alongside the Cretan's boat—"a great and terrible monster" (401) whose presence might well be taken as a poor omen for the success of their journey.

τῶν δ' ὅς τις κατὰ θυμὸν ἐπιφράσσαιτο νέεσθαι
πάντοσ' ἀνασσείασκε, τίνασσε δὲ νήϊα δοῦρα.

But whoever of them would think in his heart of turning back,[191]
[the beast] would shake him in all directions and shake the ship's
planks.
(402–3)

Quite naturally, the sailors think of returning home, but they are fated never to resume their former lives. Their first (mental) resistance to the god's design calls forth a violent reaction on the part of the huge fish on board, who seems to have an uncanny ability to read their minds. Reduced to a fearful silence, they sit too paralyzed to haul in their sails; a brisk south wind keeps them to their original course. After rounding Malea, the Cretans attempt to put in at Taenarum to see whether the "great marvel" would stay on the ship or jump back into the sea. The alternatives point to a test of sorts: if the dolphin returns to his natural habitat, then he is presumably a real dolphin; if he does not, then he must surely be something other than what he appears. However, the experi-

---

[191] The manuscripts offer νοῆσαι, which is unintelligible to me, although Kirk (1981), p. 177, says it "must be intended to mean 'decided to take some notice (and therefore some action).'" Cf. AHS (1936), p. 255, who render: "whoever thought to observe"; similarly, Humbert (1936), p. 95. Càssola (1975), p. 509, adopts, unconvincingly, βοῆσαι, which he interprets in the sense of "give orders." But neither νοῆσαι nor βοῆσαι jibe with κατὰ θυμόν, which suggests a pondering or consideration of an appropriate course of action. νέεσθαι in the sense of "return home" appears to suit the immediate situation of the Cretans; they cannot as yet be very far from Crete. Furthermore, their loss of a homecoming plays an important thematic role in the sequel. νέεσθαι is usually found at line end in Homer. For the meaning "return home," see *Odyssey* 2.238, 3.60, and 24.460. For parallels to the *Hymn to Apollo* passage, see esp. *Odyssey* 4.260 (κραδίη τέτραπτο νέεσθαι) and *Odyssey* 1.205 (φράσσεται ὥς κε νέηται).

ment is never carried out, for, despite their efforts, "the ship does not obey the rudder" (418),

πνοιῇ δὲ ἄναξ ἑκάεργος Ἀπόλλων
ῥηϊδίως ἴθυν᾿.

but with his breath, the far-working lord Apollo kept it straight on course with ease.

(420–21)

With the god now in complete control of the ship, the journey continues. Pylos, which had been the sailors' original goal is left behind (424),[192] and they quickly round the whole Peloponnese.

The final geographic catalog in the hymn (421–29) both complements and contrasts with the two earlier ones.[193] In the first, Leto searched for a place that would accept her; in the second, Apollo sought a place acceptable to *him*. The present journey is different: the goal is predetermined by the god. But the Cretans are not searching at all; they have no notion where they are going, or why. From afar, the Ionian islands and "the steep mountain of Ithaca appeared to them from under the clouds" (428). Förstel calls the line "an exceptionally fine example of 'literary' reminiscence,"[194] but he offers no explanation of its meaning, although it is no isolated phenomenon. Numerous echoes of the epic and the *Odyssey* in particular occur throughout the last 150 lines of the hymn. They point to conscious imitation and allusion rather than to formulaic coincidence.[195] The explicit mention of Ithaca as well as the other allusions are intended to evoke by way of poignant contrast another journey: no Odyssean homeward voyage or return is vouchsafed the Cretans. Swept away by a demonic force they do not comprehend, they pursue a destiny as yet hidden from them.

The ship passes the Peloponnese, "exalting in the fair wind from

---

[192] Line 398 = 424. Cf. Unte (1968), p. 87.

[193] For the geographical problems in this third catalog, see Baltes (1982), p. 39. He assumes (pp. 37–38) that Telemachus's journey in *Odyssey* 15.292–300 is the model for the hymn. Cf. Wilamowitz, (1922), p. 75, n. 3; and Altheim (1924), pp. 445–47. Both believe the journey in the hymn is derived from Homer.

[194] Förstel (1979), p. 266.

[195] Cf. Janko (1982), pp. 129–32, who argues that the echoes of the *Odyssey* throughout this section of the poem cannot be ascribed to a shared tradition or a traditional use of epic formulas, but indicate that the poet knew the *Odyssey*. Kirk (1981), pp. 177–80, speaks of a *literary* imitation of the *Odyssey*.

Zeus" (427) and approaches the gulf of Corinth. There, a great westerly wind "from the destiny of Zeus" (433) rapidly drives it toward its goal, "and the lord, son of Zeus, Apollo guided them" (437). Zeus's active complicity receives due emphasis; his son carries out and completes his father's design.[196] Upon arrival, the god, assuming the likeness of a meteor "at midday," leaps from the ship, "and many sparks flew from him, and the glow came unto heaven" (441–42). Entering the *adyton* of his temple, Apollo, "showing forth his bolts," himself lights his sacred flame. This miraculous epiphany again underlines Apollo's intimate involvement with his Delphic shrine. Not only does he lay its foundations, his own brightness ignites his sacred hearth. As the divine glow engulfs all of Crisa, the women cry out, "for great was the fear he inspired in each" (447). Repeating the characteristic progress that accompanies Apollo's manifestations, the frightening aspect of the god will, in due course, yield to joy.[197]

Returning to the ship "quick as thought," Apollo puts aside his wondrous disguises and appears anthropomorphically as a *kouros* with his characteristic flowing locks. For the first time, the god speaks to human beings as he addresses his future priests. The ensuing exchange between god and mortal is marked by the ironic disparity between human ignorance and divine providence. Apollo asks who they are and whence they come. Are they engaged in commerce, or are they pirates? While the lines are formulaic, their irony is not, for the god, who has brought them, knows all the answers. Then, with a hint of mockery, he inquires why they are behaving so strangely; why don't they disembark and beach their ship, "as is the way of men who eat bread" (458) after a long voyage, "and straightway, desire for sweet food seizes their hearts" (460–61). Strangers in a strange land, unwitting and unwilling hostages of an unknown god, the Cretans remain prey to the fear and paralysis that suspends ordinary human activity. Yet encouraged by the god's words, their leader finally responds. Noting that the youth before him resembles the immortals, he immediately undercuts his correct intuition by praying that "the gods grant you prosperity" (466).[198] Again, formulaic phrases

---

[196] Cf. Miller (1985), p. 93.

[197] Unte (1968), p. 96, compares the fright of the Crisaeans to the similar reaction of the divine assembly in the opening scene and comments: "es ist der Wesenszug des Gottes." The light-epiphany at Crisa also parallels the joyful gilding of Delos on the occasion of Apollo's birth.

[198] Consider the similar irony in the *Hymn to Demeter* and the *Hymn to Aphrodite*, where mortals are incapable of recognizing the god before them.

are used with ironic point. Answering Apollo's questions, the captain asks their own whereabouts and explains that they are Cretans who were heading for Pylos. They have come

νόστου ἱέμενοι ἄλλην ὁδὸν ἄλλα κέλευθα·
ἀλλά τις ἀθανάτων δεῦρ᾽ ἤγαγεν οὐκ ἐθέλοντας.

seeking a different route and different paths of return;
but someone of the gods brought us here against our will.

(472–73)

Of course, the unknown god stands before them, unrecognized.

In his reply, Apollo reveals both his own identity and the Cretans' destiny. They are not fated to return again to their "lovely city, fine houses, and their own wives" (477–78). Stripped of family, home, and city, the Cretan sailors are to be cut off from all normal human attachments, but, by way of compensation, they will have the god's rich temple in their charge. Now declaring himself to be "the son of Zeus, Apollo" (480), the god reveals that he himself brought them over the sea "with no evil intent":

βουλάς τ᾽ ἀθανάτων εἰδήσετε, τῶν ἰότητι
αἰεὶ τιμήσεσθε διαμπερὲς ἤματα πάντα.

you will learn the plans of the immortals, by whose will
you will always be honored continually for all time.

(484–85)

In exchange for their loss of natural human associations, the priests are to have access to the divine will and receive eternal honor. After describing the Cretan's future privileges and functions, Apollo turns his attention to their immediate situation. They are to beach their ship and build an altar to him as *Delphinius*, commemorating his first appearance to them as a dolphin; then, with due prayer and sacrifice, they are to eat before accompanying him to his rich temple. Again, the diction here is dense with epic formulas and contains, as Miller has noted,[199] a touch of pathos. This is, after all, the last time that the strangers from Crete carry out these commonplace activities before they begin their new existence as servants of the god.

[199] Miller (1985), pp. 98–99.

83

The Cretans dutifully carry out Apollo's orders. Their earlier resistance to the god has been replaced by obedience to his commands. Thereafter, they proceed toward Pytho. Apollo leads the way, playing the lyre and striding high. They follow, dancing and intoning the *iepaian*,

οἷοί τε Κρητῶν παιήονες οἷσί τε Μοῦσα
ἐν στήθεσσιν ἔθηκε θεὰ μελίγηρυν ἀοιδήν.

like the paeans of the Cretans,[200] in whose breast the goddess Muse
has placed the sweet-sounding song.

(518–19)

The joyful musical procession of the god and his priests constitutes the final example of the characteristic and universal response to Apollo's manifestations. As on Olympus and on Delos, so also at Delphi, initial dread gives way to harmonious concord and pleasure. Under the god's tutelage, the Cretans arrive quickly and without fatigue at Parnassus and the "lovely place, where the god intended to abide, honored by many men" (521–22). However, when Apollo shows them his holy *adyton* and rich temple, their hearts are troubled. Although the Cretans have up to now obeyed the god and willy-nilly accepted his call, they remain, as before, ordinary men, concerned more about their immediate material needs than his great promises of divine knowledge and eternal honor. Finally, their captain speaks up again: How are they to live far from their friends and native land in this place to which the god has seen fit to bring them?

οὔτε τρυγηφόρος ἥδε γ᾽ ἐπήρατος οὔτ᾽ εὐλείμων,
ὥς τ᾽ ἀπό τ᾽ εὖ ζώειν καὶ ἅμ᾽ ἀνθρώποισιν ὀπηδεῖν.

For all its loveliness, it is neither crop bearing, nor does it contain
     good meadows
that one could live on comfortably and, at the same time, serve
     men.[201]

(529–30)

[200] The paean and paeonic meter was thought to originate from Crete. For the connection of the metrical paean to the so-called Cretic, see von Blumenthal (1942), cols. 2361–62. For mythological and historical relations between Crete and Delphi, see Förstel (1979), pp. 220–22.

[201] ὀπηδεῖν usually means "follow," "accompany," or "attend." The necessary sense here, "look after," is unparalleled, and ὀπάζειν and even ἀθανάτοισιν ὀπηδεῖν have been suggested. See Baumeister (1860), p. 179. But the general meaning is clear: How can

Delphi, like Delos, possesses few natural resources, yet the presence of Apollo's "lovely temple" there has already transformed the harsh and unpromising site into a "lovely place" (ἐπήρατος, [529]; cf. χῶρον ἐπήρατον in line 521).²⁰² It will soon become a place of wealth and abundance as well.²⁰³

By way of a response, Apollo smiles a smile of amused condescension, which attests to his divine superiority. Then he scolds:

νήπιοι ἄνθρωποι δυστλήμονες οἳ μελεδῶνας
βούλεσθ᾽ ἀργαλέους τε πόνους καὶ στείνεα θυμῷ. . .

Foolish men and impatient, who choose in your heart
worries and painful toils and cares. . .

(532–33)

But an "easy word" from the god suffices to relieve their unnecessary anxieties. Their right hands will be constantly engaged in sacrificing the flocks that worshipers will bring in abundance. The presence of the god assures his ministers' livelihood.

In his last words, Apollo gives his final exhortation and pronounces a solemn warning to his priestly servants:

νηὸν δὲ προφύλαχθε, δέδεχθε δέ φῦλ᾽ ἀνθρώπων
ἐνθάδ᾽ ἀγειρομένων, κατ᾽ ἐμὴν ἰθύν γε μάλιστα.
εἰ δέ τι τηὖσιον ἔπος ἔσσεται ἠέ τι ἔργον,
ὕβρις θ᾽, ἢ θέμις ἐστὶ καταθνητῶν ἀνθρώπων,
ἄλλοι ἔπειθ᾽ ὑμῖν σημάντορες ἄνδρες ἔσονται,
τῶν ὑπ᾽ ἀναγκαίῃ δεδμήσεσθ᾽ ἤματα πάντα.
εἴρηταί τοι πάντα, σὺ δὲ φρεσὶ σῇσι φύλαξαι.

Look after my temple and receive the tribes of men,
who gather here, in accordance, above all, with my direction.
But if any rash word or deed shall occur,

---

they live off this poor land and at the same time carry out the god's orders? Cf. Miller (1985), p. 100.

²⁰² For the misinterpretation of ἐπήρατος, see Càssola (1975), p. 515; and Förstel (1979), p. 473, n. 690. However, the site is not just naturally lovely, but becomes so through the presence of Apollo's "lovely temple." Cf. νηόν . . . ἐπήρατον in line 286. Similarly, Delos is proleptically called a "well-built island" (102), which she will become through the presence of Apollo's sanctuary there.

²⁰³ For the parallel Delos–Delphi, see Unte (1968), pp. 96–97. The wealth of both sites is not natural but imported by the god's worshipers.

that is, hybris, which is customary for mortal men,
others then will be your leaders, men from whom you take orders,
to whom you will be subject perforce for all time.
All has been spoken to you; but you guard it in your hearts.

(538–44)

Taken together, these verses constitute the first oracle and thus form an appropriate climax to the entire hymn. The passage itself poses many problems, some due to textual corruptions and others due to the opacity of the god's words. The latter need not surprise us, given the notorious obscurity of Delphic pronouncements. But the main impediment to an understanding of these lines derives from the refusal of commentators to grasp the unity of the passage. Although a single line may have dropped out of the text after line 539,[204] its overall coherence remains undisturbed. However, in separating Apollo's exhortation from his prophetic warning, critics ignore their interconnection and misconstrue both.

A few minor textual emendations and judicious punctuation render the verses intelligible.[205] Apollo first instructs his ministers to attend to his temple and to receive his followers under the god's direction and authority. The word ἰθύς, which means "straight course," is fully appropriate in Apollo's mouth. Earlier, he had literally directed (ἴθυνε [421]) the ship of the Cretans on a straight course, just as he is later said to guide them (ἡγεμόνευε [437]). A warning concerning the future follows immediately and logically upon this positive exhortation. Any deviation from the straight course dictated by the god, any unconsidered word or deed on the part of his priests, any act that constitutes *hybris*, will meet with punishment. Yet the capacity, one might even say, inclination, to commit *hybris* is part of man's nature (541). The Cretans whom Apollo has chosen as his ministers are, we remember, in no wise exceptional men of exceptional endowments but, on the contrary, fully representative of

---

[204] Cf. AHS (1936), p. 266.

[205] I read κατ' ἐμὴν ἰθύν γε μάλιστα followed by a period, and εἰ δέ τι at line 540. There is no need to postulate a lacuna, but if one retains the manuscripts' τε μάλιστα, one could supply something like: "and above all, perform my sacrifices and announce my decrees" (cf. 394). A common critical error arises from myopically limiting κατ' ἐμὴν ἰθύν to the preceding word, ("men gathered here according to my direction"). Cf. AHS (1936), p. 266; Humbert (1936), pp. 100–1; and Càssola (1975), pp. 515–16. The last two join 540–41 to the preceding sentence so that the lines continue to refer to the "tribes of men." This is completely unintelligible to me. Moreover, it makes Apollo's prophetic warning in 542–43 a totally unmotivated and disconnected bolt from the blue. Cf. Förstel (1979), p. 441, n. 538.

human limitations and frailties.[206] Moreover, the wealth, honor, and exalted status the god's election has bestowed upon them render them prime candidates for transgressing the proper bounds of human conduct, which the Greeks called *hybris*. *Koros* (satiety), as the Greeks also knew, is the breeding ground of *hybris*. The talismans against it are the two maxims inscribed on Apollo's temple: γνῶθι σεαυτόν and μηδὲν ἄγαν, "know thyself" and "nothing in excess." Apollo's message to his priests is also a message to mankind.[207]

Divorced from its context, Apollo's oracular warning (540–43) has become mired in historical speculation concerning the date of the hymn or, rather, the Pythian half. Assuming that the god's pronouncement must be taken as a *vaticinium ex eventu*, scholars generally have detected a reference to the so-called First Sacred War, dated around 590 B.C.[208] At that time, we are told, the people of Crisa, who had previously controlled the sanctuary of Delphi, had misbehaved in some way; the combined forces of the Amphictyonic League defeated the Crisaeans, razed their city, and took over the administration of the shrine. According to this view, the "other leaders" in line 542 refer to the new Amphictyonic administrators of the site. A few scholars, however, maintain that Apollo's words indicate the period just before the war when the Crisaeans were threatening to take over the sanctuary. The so-called oracle, then, in reality constitutes "a warning in time of imminent danger."[209]

To review the evidence for the First Sacred War would lead too far afield. It suffices to mention a few immediate objections. First, in the hymn, Crisa is referred to as still standing.[210] Second, there is no clear evidence that Crisa ever controlled Delphi[211] (if the Crisaeans did at some point pose a threat to the sanctuary, the danger must have passed quickly with Crisa's defeat). Third, if, as the historical testimonia imply, the Am-

---

[206] Cf. Förstel (1979), pp. 267–71.

[207] For the universality of Apollo's message, see Förstel (1979), p. 271; and Miller (1985), p. 110.

[208] According to Gemoll (1886), p. 180, Ilgen (1796) was the first to propose this interpretation, which has become the *communis opinio*. Cf., among others, Wilamowitz (1920), p. 441; (1922), p. 74; Altheim (1924), p. 449; Dornseiff (1933), pp. 14–15; Humbert (1936), p. 77; Eitrem (1938), pp. 133–34; Parke and Wormell (1956), 1: 108; and Càssola (1975), p. 101. G. Forrest, "The First Sacred War," *BCH* 80 (1956): 34–44, goes so far as to identify the ἔπος, ἔργον, and ὕβρις that brought about the war.

[209] West (1975), p. 165, n. 2; cf. Förstel (1979), p. 202. Jacoby (1933), p. 731, remains uncertain whether the poem was composed before or after the First Sacred War.

[210] Cf. Förstel (1979), pp. 200–2.

[211] Cf. N. Robertson, "The Myth of the First Sacred War," *CQ* 72 (1978): 49.

phictyonic campaign against Crisa was intended to protect and liberate Delphi from its Crisaean oppressors, why should the hymn refer to the supposed liberators as masters who subjugate the Delphians "by compulsion"?[212] Finally, Apollo's prophetic warning is not addressed to Crisa but to his Delphic priesthood. It is their potential crimes that are threatened with punishment; Crisa has nothing to do with the case. Recently, Robertson has put forth arguments that suggest that the First Sacred War never took place, but was a fourth-century invention to justify Philip of Macedon's interference in Delphian affairs.[213] But even if we assume it did, the traditions surrounding it will not square with our text. As far as the hymn is concerned, the First Sacred War has always been a red herring.

I digress for a moment. To understand why this interpretation arose in the first place means to confront an impulse fundamental to the modern study of ancient texts. Classical philology has always regarded itself primarily as a historical discipline. The question a classicist initially asks of a text is not what does it mean, but when was it composed and by whom. In dealing with anonymous texts of unknown date, these questions become the focus of inquiry. Clues are sought everywhere, and lack of evidence becomes a goad to ingenuity. Any passage that can be construed to contain a contemporary allusion or to betray the author's circumstances or prejudices is wrenched from its context. Interpretation of the *Hymn to Apollo* offers several examples of this distorting procedure. For instance, when Apollo passes through the future site of Thebes, and the place is described as still uninhabited, the poet is claimed to reveal an anti-Theban bias.[214] Similarly, Telphousa's remark that the noise from

[212] Cf. Förstel (1979), pp. 201–2: "Die starke Betonung des Zwanges und der Unterwerfung in v. 543 . . . passt überhaupt nicht zu der Rolle, die . . . die Amphiktyonen zur Zeit des Heiligen Krieges gespielt haben." See also Humbert (1936), p. 101, n. 1: "la sujétion du sacerdoce au Conseil [the Amphictyonic League] est exprimée avec une brutalité un peu suspecte." Forrest (1956), p. 45, does some fancy footwork here. He assumes that the hymn's brutal description of the Amphictyonic League derives from the defeated Crisaeans. Cf. Eitrem (1938), p. 134, who explains the menacing tone as a warning to the priesthood, who had sided with the Crisaeans. Robertson (1978), p. 49, assumes the "other leaders" must be the Amphictyonians who "administered Delphi from at least the Late Archaic period onward," but he does not explain why they are described in such unflattering terms.

[213] Robertson (1978), pp. 38–73. Cf. Parke and Wormell (1956), 1: 103 and 99. Robertson's thesis has been challenged by G. A. Lehmann, "Der 'Erste Heilige Krieg'—Eine Fiktion?" *Historia* 29 (1980): 242–46. See also M. Sordi, "La prima guerra sacra," *RFIC* n.s. 31 (1953): 320–46.

[214] Cf. Eitrem (1938), pp. 128–29; and Defradas (1954), pp. 59–62.

traffic around her spring would distract Apollo's worshipers has been used—ludicrously—to date the poem. For, it is argued, the nymph could not make such a statement if the poem was composed after the establishment of chariot races at Delphi (ca. 586 B.C.)—as though the god's aversion to noise was such that games instituted in his honor would disturb him.[215] Critics who reject this view and the date it imposes on the poem point out, with a straight face, that the chariot contests were held in the plain below the sanctuary and thus would not trouble the god in his temple.[216] Be that as it may, the First Sacred War never had any bearing on the interpretation of the hymn; the earliest history of Delphi remains cloaked in obscurity.[217] Nevertheless, most commentators still cling to some sort of political interpretation of Apollo's words involving a change from one form of administration to another. The god's pronouncement does indeed warn of a change, but it is of a different kind.

Like so many oracles, this first one has a conditional form; if the condition is met, the consequences are inescapable. Apollo, however, does not predict the future; he merely conveys the will of Zeus and his decrees to mankind. If the priests veer from the straight path of the god, retribution will inevitably follow. While presently they are subject to the god alone and answerable only to him, they will, if they err, be brought under the authority of *men*. In other words, Apollo presages his ministers' loss of autonomy. Not from Apollo, but from these other σημάντορες—literally, "those who give the signals"—will the priests take their orders and to them will they be beholden. The true counterpart to these "others," whoever they may be, is the god himself. The oracle, then, appears to announce a change in the status of Apollo's Cretan priesthood, a change from autonomy to subservience. Moreover, that change will be eternal (ἤματα πάντα) and, presumably, irreversible. The priests, for

---

[215] Cf. Gemoll (1886), p. 119; Humbert (1936), pp. 76–77.

[216] Cf. Càssola (1975), p. 102. West (1975), p. 165, n. 2, points out the absurdity of this line of argument. A similarly frivolous attempt to date the poem is based on line 299 where Apollo's first temple is called ἀοίδιμον ἔμμεναι αἰεί. Because the archaic temple was burned in 548 B.C., the poem must have been composed prior to that date. Cf. Wilamowitz (1922), p. 74, n. 3; Gemoll (1886), p. 164; Dornseiff (1933), p. 14. Of course, the poet says nothing about whether the temple was standing in his time, only that it will always be the subject of song. Drerup (1938), pp. 108–9, and Càssola (1975), p. 102, to their credit, express doubts. Cf. West (1975), p. 165, n. 2.

[217] Cf. the cautionary remarks of Unte (1968), p. 98, n. 3: "Mit einer historischen Deutung ... muss man sehr vorsichtig sein. Aus dem Text lässt sich nur herauslesen, wenn man die Voraussage ex eventu interpretiert, dass die delphischen Priester zur Zeit des Dichters nicht selbstständig, sondern abhängig waren."

their part, have a choice: either to follow the god, ἕπου θεῷ,[218] or to become subject to men.

If this interpretation of the general thrust of Apollo's prophecy is correct, the question remains as to whether it was fulfilled. The parallel warning at the end of the *Hymn to Aphrodite*, though not an oracle, suggests that it was.[219] If, as critics insist, we do in fact have before us an oracle *post eventum*, that event cannot be dated. As we have seen, Apollo's words seem inappropriate to describe the role of Crisa or the Amphictyonic League in the affairs of Delphi either before or after the Sacred War.[220] In any case, the god would be ill-advised to refer to a passing political crisis in this manner, nor is there any reason to suppose that an oracle of such limited validity would be piously preserved. The forging of oracles was, after all, a common practice in antiquity. It is far more likely that Apollo refers to the internal religious organization of his shrine than to any external political event. Because the oracle was consulted more often on religious matters than on political or private affairs,[221] it would be altogether appropriate if the first oracle pronounced at Delphi dealt with a religious issue.

On the basis of the foregoing remarks, I should like to revive an old suggestion of K. O. Müller that the "other leaders" to whom the Cretans will be subject are the *Hosioi*.[222] Our evidence concerning these "Pure Ones" is, to be sure, late and sparse, but it is suggestive.[223] They were five

---

[218] U. von Wilamowitz-Moellendorff, *Der Glaube der Hellenen* (Darmstadt, 1959), 2: 41, calls ἕπου θεῷ the complement to the Apolline "know thyself."

[219] For the end of the *Hymn to Aphrodite*, see my discussion in chapter 3. For the parallel between the warning there and here, see Unte (1968), p. 97. Miller (1985), pp. 109–10, believes that Apollo's words only constitute a warning rather than a prophecy.

[220] Cf. Robertson (1978), p. 49: "Is it conceivable that a passage so topical and partisan could survive both the period of transmission after the Sacred War and the final redaction by Cynaethus or another? δεδμήσεσθ' ἤματα πάντα says the Hymn." Robertson is here rejecting the possibility that the oracle refers to Crisa, but his statement is equally true in reference to the Amphictyony.

[221] Cf. Fontenrose (1978), pp. 26–27, who calculates that three-fourths of all historical oracles (as opposed to legendary ones) concerned religious matters.

[222] K. O. Müller, *Geschichten hellenischer Stämme und Städte II: Die Dorier* (Breslau, 1824), 1: 211–12.

[223] The main testimonia are from Plutarch *Quaestiones graecae* 9 (292d); *De Iside et Osiride* 35 (395a); *De defectu oraculorum* 49 (437a) and 51 (438b); and Euripides, *Ion* 413–16. H. W. Parke, "A Note on the Delphic Priesthood," *CQ* 34 (1940): 86–87, doubts whether the Ion passage refers to the *Hosioi*. But the very fact that Ion uses the plural, "those within," suggests that he means the *Hosioi* because there were only two *prophets* (and he seems to be one), whereas there were five *Hosioi*. Cf. A. S. Owen, *Euripides Ion* (Oxford, 1939), p. 101. For the inscriptional evidence, see *BCH* 20 (1896): 716, line 9; *BCH*

in number and drawn by lot from the noblest families in Delphi who claimed descent from Deucalion and hence would be considered autochthonous. Their duties at the sanctuary appear to have consisted in overseeing the activities of the "prophets" and priests. Thus, while the priests performed the sacrifices preliminary to consultation, the *Hosioi* would determine whether the victim's behavior permitted the consultation to proceed, or even when the oracle could be consulted. In view of their role, the rather unusual term used by Apollo, σημάντορες, "those who give the signal," becomes significant.[224] For the duties of the *Hosioi* seem to involve giving the signals, either positive or negative, as to whether a sacrifice was acceptable or consultation of the oracle permissible. The priests and "prophets" would be subject to their decisions "perforce." Nothing could be done without their consent.

The preceding interpretation reveals an attempt on the part of the hymn-poet to harmonize his version of the Cretan origins of Apollo's ministers with the Delphic claims of an autochthonous priesthood. And as we have seen, the poet's insistence on the importation of a foreign priesthood from abroad depends on his determination to present the site of Delphi as deserted prior to the founding of the oracle by Apollo. The Delphian claim to autochthony had to be ignored in the narrative but is finally accommodated in the oracle that warns the Cretans of their future subservience.

The interpretation set forth here jibes, I believe, better with both the spirit and the letter of the text than the traditional views. But one should also recognize that this oracle transcends an immediate occasion or circumstance to become a paradigm for all Apolline prophecies. By exhorting not only his ministers, but all of mankind, to heed the gods' decrees, and warning of punishment for misconduct, Apollo for the first time introduces men to their place within the divine scheme.

With the pronouncement of the first oracle, the *Hymn to Apollo* comes to an end. The god's last words suggest completion and impose the task of both keeping and understanding his message—"everything

---

49 (1925): 83–87; and *Fouilles de Delphes* 3, pt. 2: 118, line 5; pt. 3: 300 and 302. Roux (1976), pp. 59–63, has the best discussion of the role of the *Hosioi* at Delphi. See also Fontenrose (1978), p. 219; and Amandry (1950), pp. 123–25, who gives the main testimonia in his appendix.

[224] It is intriguing to note that the activity of the oracle is designated by the verb σημαίνω "to signal," "indicate," by both Theognis 808 (West) and Heraclitus, fr. 93 (H. Diels and W. Kranz, *Die Fragmente der Vorsokratiker*, 5th ed. [Berlin, 1934]).

has been spoken to you; but you guard it in your hearts" (544). Apollo has accomplished the *Lebensprogram* he articulated at the moment of his birth, while the hymn-poet has, at the same time, completed his agenda of praise. Apollo has acceded to his *timai* and taken his place among the Olympians; and, through his role as mediator of the divine decrees to mankind, he has inaugurated a new epoch in the relations between gods and mortals. The birth of any new divinity inevitably and irreversibly alters the status quo both on Olympus and on earth—but perhaps none more than the birth of Apollo. For in his case, the circumstances surrounding his birth as well as his choice of *timai* define his cosmic significance as the defender par excellence of Zeus and the Olympian order.

The theogonic character of the hymn is further determined by the Succession Myth, which casts a threatening shadow over the emergence of Apollo. The terrifying apparition of the god in the hymn's opening alludes to the possibility of the overthrow of the Olympian pantheon. At the time of his birth, the entire world is gripped by fear that the child Leto carries will be a despotic and violent ruler over men and gods. The ominous and oblique allusions to a divine usurper do more than merely emphasize Apollo's greatness; they provide the essential background for an understanding of the god. These puzzling hints move into the foreground in the story of Typho, where the dark outlines of the Succession Myth finally stand fully illuminated. The monstrous son of Hera proves to be the real enemy of Olympus, whereas his equally powerful counterpart, the mighty son of Zeus, takes his place, so to speak, at the right hand of his father. Moreover, Apollo chooses as his prerogatives the bow, which annihilates his father's enemies like Pytho, the doublet of Typho and his mother Hera, and the lyre, which ensures Olympian harmony. Finally, far from posing a challenge to his father's authority, Apollo proposes to propagate it among mankind by transmitting his father's ordinances. From a terrestrial perspective, the whole earth first feared Apollo's brutal violence. Yet the new divinity puts his triple *timai* at mankind's service by liberating it from monstrous and destructive creatures like Pytho and by sharing with it the pleasures of music, which free men—if only momentarily—from their human cares. In addition, Apollo's oracle raises mortals up from their helpless ignorance and, by making them aware of the consequences of their actions, renders them capable of moral choice.

The presentation of Apollo in the hymn is thoroughly Olympian in its perspective. The poem's Olympianism goes hand in hand with its Panhellenic orientation. In fact, these tendencies can be considered two facets of the same phenomenon; together, they illuminate almost every aspect of the poem and account for many of its peculiarities. Throughout, the hymn conveys Apollo's universality by means of the geographic catalogs that cumulatively cover the whole Greek world. The poet himself promises to carry his composition—his praise of Apollo—to the ends of the earth. Thus, both the poem and the god it celebrates are explicitly Panhellenic.

The hymn's Panhellenism is most clearly manifested in the topics the poet chooses to treat and those he rejects. Although he repeatedly emphasizes the vast, almost overwhelming, choice of material suitable to Apollo's praise, the poet excludes local myths involving the god as well as cult centers of only local importance. Of relevance here is Jacoby's comment:

> For every hymn-poet, when he composes primarily for a particular local cult or a local cult festival, there exists a tension between the demands of the local cult and the Panhellenic celebration of the god. For every hymn-poet, but perhaps most of all for the poet of Apollo; for Apollo is, in contradistinction to Zeus, for example, or Hera or Athena, nowhere in a precise sense a local divinity, but ... universal.[225]

In the *Hymn to Apollo*, the tension between the local and universal manifestations of Apollo is resolved on the side of Panhellenism not only through the avoidance of local traditions and cults. The poet adopts a peculiar strategy that precludes *all* local exclusivity, by singling out not one, but two cult places: Delos *and* Delphi. Moreover, both sites are emphatically characterized as having *no* local traditions at all but being purely Apolline and Panhellenic. Thus, on account of her poverty, Delos can support only a minimal indigenous population; the island acknowledges her poor reputation among men. Her negotiations with Leto reveal that up to now no divinities have dignified the island with their presence. This suggests that Delos, prior to Apollo, possessed no local religious traditions whatsoever. The godforsaken site acquires all of its future wealth and splendor from the sole presence of Apollo. Thus the hymn presents the Delian *panēgyris* as a Panhellenic affair rather than a local festival. The Ionians and their wives gather there to celebrate Apollo; the

---

[225] Jacoby (1933), p. 713.

only local inhabitants mentioned are the Delian Maidens, servants of the god.

The case of Delphi is even clearer; when Apollo arrives there, the place has neither inhabitants nor a name. Not only is it rocky and infertile, but a murderous dragon occupies the site. After disposing of the beast, Apollo must import a foreign priesthood from Crete, since Pytho remains uninhabited. The hymn ignores the Delphians' claim to autochthony, just as it insists on the absence of any previous cult on the site, despite the fact that such a cult was recognized by official Delphic tradition. Here, the poet's Panhellenic orientation impels him to contradict canonical Delphic lore; the hymn reinterprets the founding of Apollo's oracle as an Olympian innovation.

The fame and divinely ordained splendor of both Delos and Delphi derive from their character as Panhellenic shrines, where men and women gather from throughout the inhabited world to celebrate and consult Apollo. The god universally honored at both locales is the Olympian son of Zeus whose birth aroused universal consternation on heaven and earth. The mighty offspring of Zeus, whose power is such that it poses a potential threat to the Olympian regime, proves to be a formidable guarantor of his father's order. By the end of the hymn, the cosmos has been transformed: Apollo's presence at his father's side neutralizes all future challenges to Olympus and thus renders it stable and eternal. In addition, the god of bow and lyre, who produces both fear and joy, has through his oracle extended his father's dominion to include mankind within the cosmic hierarchy.

CHAPTER 2

HYMN TO HERMES

ὡς ἀγαθόν ἐστ' ἐπωνυμίας πολλὰς ἔχειν·
οὗτος γὰρ ἐξηύρηκεν αὐτῷ βιότιον.

How good it is to have many names;
for he has got himself a fine little living.

— Aristophanes, *Ploutos* 1164–65

 Generally assumed to be substantially later than the other major Homeric Hymns, the *Hymn to Hermes* displays numerous peculiarities of diction as well as an apparently erratic narrative progress. Recalcitrant textual problems considerably compound the difficulties of interpretation. Although the poem's playful, occasionally even broad, humor has charmed readers, many critics have denied the hymn a serious intent.[1] The looseness of the narrative line and its many inconsistencies are thus excused by the comic character of the composition.[2] Its unity has repeatedly been called into question, and earlier scholars constructed elaborate theories to account for the poem's present disarray.[3] Even uni-

---

[1] For example, W. Schmid and O. Stählin, *Geschichte der griechischen Literatur* (Munich, 1929), I, pt. 1: 236, claim that "von religiösem oder sittlichem Ernst fehlt jede Spur." H. van Herwerden, "Forma antiquissima hymni homerici in Mercurium," *Mnemosyne* 35 (1907): 181, calls the hymn a "priscae impietatis documentum."

[2] Cf. Baumeister (1860), p. 185: "hic [in the hymn] autem, ut in comoedia, laxioribus vinculis res contineri, aliquoties consulto expectationem falli, non raro diversa et contraria inter se componi, denique iocum serio misceri."

[3] For a review of earlier analystic scholarship, see Baumeister (1860), pp. 182–84; Ludwich (1908), pp. 27–30; and Humbert (1936), p. 105. The analysis of C. Robert ("Zum homerischen Hermeshymnos," *Hermes* 41 [1906]: 389–425) reduced the "original" hymn to less than half its length. See Herwerden (1907), pp. 181–91, for the resulting truncated text. Ludwich (1908) and J. Kuiper, "De discrepantiis hymni homerici in Mercurium," *Mnemosyne* 38 (1910): 1–50, attempted to refute Robert's arguments, but Ludwich's drastic transposition theory convinced no one. Among the unitarians should be listed: Baumeister (1860); Gemoll (1886); L. Radermacher, *Der homerische Hermeshymnus*, Sitzungs-

CHAPTER 2

tarians were at a loss.⁴ Thus, Allen, Halliday, and Sikes conclude "that the search for a single theme giving unity to the hymn is a mistake" and end up labeling the poem's subject "a day in the life of Hermes."⁵ Yet Gemoll was surely closer to the truth when he called the "real subject" of the hymn "how the newborn Hermes won recognition as a powerful god on Olympus."⁶

However much *Hermes* may differ from the other long hymns in tone, style, and structure, nevertheless, on the whole the poem conforms to the main generic features of the extended Homeric Hymn. First, it sets out to convey the essential nature of the chosen divinity through a narrative of his words and deeds. Furthermore, it manifests the hymns' characteristic concern with the acquisition and (re)distribution of *timai* among the Olympians that leads to a permanent and irreversible reorganization of the divine cosmos. Finally, like the *Hymn to Apollo*, *Hermes* recounts the birth of a new god who at first appears to threaten the stability of the established pantheon but who ultimately accedes to his prerogatives and takes his destined place within the divine order. Yet the differences between these two birth hymns are equally striking and important. As we have noted, Apollo is born at an early stage of Zeus's regime, before the supreme god has completely consolidated his power; Hermes, on the other hand, within the context of his hymn, is the last-born of the Olympians.⁷ The *timai* of the others have all been divided and distributed. Nothing remains for Hermes, who is thus obliged to acquire his honors by theft or exchange. *Apollo* and *Hermes*, then, are set at opposite poles of the mythological history of the Olympian family.

---

berichte (Akademie der Wissenschaften in Wien 213, no. 1) (1931); Humbert (1936); AHS (1936); and Càssola (1975), although some doubt the authenticity of the last seventy lines. Janko (1982), p. 133, characterizes the present situation as follows: "despite various attempts to dissect it in the past, the integrity of the Hymn to Hermes is not nowadays seriously disputed."

⁴ Cf. Radermacher (1931), p. 234: "der Dichter selbst ist ausgesprochener Impressionist; er sieht nur das Nahe, und das Augenblickliche gilt ihm so viel, dass er, dies ausmalend, den Zusammenhang im grossen vergisst; so kommt es zu Widersprüchen in seiner Schilderung der Dinge." With a nod to Lévy-Brühl, Humbert (1936), p. 107, dubs the hymnist "un demi-primitif."

⁵ AHS (1936), p. 268.

⁶ Gemoll (1886), p. 184. Ludwich (1908), p. 27, approvingly cites Ilgen's (1796) judgment on the hymn's unity: "finis totius actionis hic est, ut honorem consequatur, eo quo alii dii conspicui sunt, non inferiorem." "Ohne Zweifel," adds Ludwich, "ist dies das Grundthema."

⁷ Cf. S. C. Shelmerdine, "Hermes and the Tortoise: A Prelude to Cult," *GRBS* 25 (1984): 205, n. 22.

96

One may indeed wonder why Hermes should be the last-born member of the pantheon. Historically, his presence on Greek soil seems very old; he cannot be considered a recent arrival or import from abroad.[8] Indeed, there has been considerable speculation concerning Hermes' primary or original function. He has been identified as the god of herdsmen, a fertility god with chthonic associations, a fire god, a wind god, the divine trickster, and the god of the stone heap or marker.[9] Attempts to derive Hermes' multiple manifestations from a single origin have not met with success. There is not even a consensus as to whether Hermes should be considered a pre-Greek or Indo-European divinity.[10] Hermes' primitive nature remains obscure, but we can be fairly confident that it was transformed or modified when the god became incorporated into the Olympian family.

To be sure, members of that "family" also have diverse origins and multiple local manifestations. Only when they become organized into the Panhellenic pantheon do they acquire their final aspects and configurations. Vernant has noted aptly:

Every study that sets out to define the Greek gods independently of one another as separate and isolated figures runs the risk of missing

[8] Cf. Nilsson, *GGR* (1955), 1: 501.

[9] For a survey of scholarship concerning Hermes' "original" function, see H. Herter, "Hermes," *Rheinisches Museum* 119 (1976): 193–204. As Herter remarks: "er [Hermes] hat die religionswissenschaftlichen Moden der vorigen Jahrhunderts treulich mitgemacht" (p. 194). A useful catalog of the god's prerogatives comes from an inscription on a bust of Hermes from the Villa Albani: Interpres divom, caeli terraeque meator / sermonem docui mortales atque palaestram ... sermonis dator atque somniorum / Iovis nuntius et precum minister (*Inscriptiones Graecae* 14.978). Horace, *Odes* 1.10, demonstrates a genuine understanding of the meaning of Hermes. Burkert's ([1977], p. 246) concise definition is also helpful: "so ist denn Hermes, als Gott des Grenzbereichs und des tabubrechenden Übergangs, Patron der Hirten, der Diebe, der Gräber und der Herolde."

[10] For example, É. Benveniste, "Le sens du mot ΚΟΛΟΣΣΟΣ," *Revue de Philologie* 6 (1932): 129–30; J. Orgogozo, "L'Hermès des Achéens," *Revue de l'historie des religions* 136 (1949): 170–76; and C. Ruijgh, "Sur le nom de Poséidon et les noms en -ᾱ-ϝον-, -ᾱ-ϝον-," *REG* 80 (1967): 12, all argue that Hermes cannot be Indo-European. On the other hand, A. Kuhn, *Die Herabkunft des Feuers und des Göttertranks*, 2nd ed. (Gütersloh, 1886); A. Hocart, *Kings and Councillors* (Cairo, 1936), pp. 18–23; and R. Mondi, "The Function and Social Position of the Kêrux in Early Greece" (Ph.D. diss., Harvard, 1978), pp. 109–46, all equate Hermes with the Indic fire god Agni. But C. Watkins, "Studies in Indo-European Legal Language, Institutions, and Mythology," in *Indo-European and Indo-Europeans*, ed. G. Cardona and H. Hoenigswald (Philadelphia, 1970), pp. 345–50, detects a parallel between Hermes and the Vedic Pusan. Wilamowitz (1959), 1: 156, calls Hermes "ein urhellenischer und ein rein hellenischer Gott." Cf. A. Van Windekens, "Sur le nom de la divinité grecque Hermès," *Beiträge zur Namenforschung* 13 (1962): 290–92.

the essential. . . . As with a linguistic system, one cannot understand a religious system except by studying the place of the gods in relation to each other. One must replace a simple catalog of divinities with an analysis of the structures of the pantheon, elucidating the manner in which the different divine powers are grouped, associated, opposed, and distinguished. Only in this way can the relevant features for each god or group of gods appear—that is to say, those that are significant from the perspective of religious thought.[11]

Vernant emphasizes the necessity of such an approach, especially when examining a figure as complex as Hermes.

We may now return to our initial question: Why, from the perspective of the *Hymn to Hermes*, is Hermes presented as the last-born of the gods? The assignment of *timai* among the gods is accomplished, and the organization of the Olympian cosmos more or less complete. Yet something essential to its functioning is still lacking. The nature of the missing element emerges as soon as we observe that the fully articulated Olympian system of divisions and boundaries remains static and lifeless unless it acquires the possibility of movement between its spheres and limits. Introduced only after the hierarchical configuration of the cosmos has been achieved and its boundaries defined, Hermes embodies that principle of motion.[12] Hermes thus allows the cosmos to retain its ordered structure while simultaneously instituting movement between its articulated components. It is along these lines that Vernant tried to define the god's fundamental characteristics in terms of his opposition to Hestia, goddess of the hearth:

> In view of the profusion of his epithets and variety of attributes, the figure of Hermes appears unusually complex. Scholars have found him so bewildering that they have supposed that there were originally several different Hermeses who subsequently became fused. However, the diverse characteristics that make up the physiognomy of the god become clearer if we consider him in relation to Hestia. . . . To Hestia belongs whatever is interior, closed and fixed, the turning in on itself of the human community; to Hermes, whatever

[11] Vernant (1974), pp. 110–11.
[12] Interestingly enough, on the basis of a probably incorrect etymology (deriving Hermes from ὁρμᾶν), F. G. Welcker, *Griechische Götterlehre* (Göttingen, 1857), 1: 342, called Hermes the god of "die lebendige Bewegung." Càssola (1975), p. 154, comments that "un aspetto tipico di Ermes è la mobilità."

is outside, openness, mobility, the contact with something other than oneself. One can say that the pair Hermes–Hestia expresses through its polarity the tension that characterizes the archaic representation of space; space requires a center, a privileged fixed point, from which one can orient and define directions, which all differ qualitatively. But space also represents itself as the locus of movement, which in turn implies the possibility of transition and passage from any one point to another.[13]

Significantly, tradition assigns to Hestia the role of the firstborn of the Olympians;[14] Hermes, her counterpart and opposite number, becomes the last.

Vernant has not dealt directly with the *Hymn to Hermes*; but by elaborating his insights in light of the hymn, Kahn has established a framework for a reconsideration of this most enigmatic of the Olympians.[15] According to Kahn, the nature of the movement that constitutes Hermes' typical mode of action is characterized by penetration and passage between boundaries and limits and hence also by mediation between a host of oppositions: among them, inner/outer, gods/men, life/death, and male/female. Yet although Hermes crosses or penetrates boundaries, he does not destroy them or even call them into question. His characteristic activity is passing and piercing. The limits, once traversed, remain intact.

If the movement across boundaries defines Hermes' domain, his characteristic means of effecting such a passage is *mētis*.[16] The intimate connection between penetration and *mētis* can be illustrated by the familiar tradition of the conquest of Troy. A dispute arose among the besieging Greeks: Should the city's defenses be breached by force (*biē*) or by guile and trickery (*mētis*)? The strategem of the wooden horse prevails. All unsuspecting, the Trojans open the gates to haul in the "hollow ambush," as the *Odyssey* calls it, which quickly disgorges its murderous crew. Even while its walls remain intact, the city, which could not be taken by frontal assault, is penetrated by the enemy. *Mētis* triumphs over *biē*, and

---

[13] J.-P. Vernant, "Hestia–Hermès: Sur l'expression religieuse de l'espace et du mouvement chez les Grecs," in *Mythe et pensée chez les Grecs* (Paris, 1965), 1: 128.

[14] Cf. Hesiod, *Theogony* 454, and the *Hymn to Aphrodite* 22–23. See the discussion of *Aphrodite* 22–23 below.

[15] L. Kahn, *Hermès passe ou les ambiguïtés de la communication* (Paris, 1978).

[16] For *mētis* in general, see Detienne and Vernant (1974); in relation to Hermes, see Kahn (1978).

the mastermind of the victory is Odysseus, the hero closest to Hermes, and who shares with the god his epithet πολύτροπος.[17]

As youngest of the Olympians, Hermes comes into being only after the general distribution of *timai*. The new god must thus acquire his own by theft or bargaining with the other gods. It would seem natural for the originally disenfranchised Hermes to extort a variety of prerogatives from a host of different divinities. Yet the hymn presents Hermes only in his dealings with Apollo. Why should Apollo be Hermes' sole antagonist? To be sure, the hymn does not neglect to exploit the many comic possibilities inherent in the confrontation of the clever babe and his wealthy, established, older brother.[18] But beyond that, many critics have sought to detect an underlying cultic rivalry between the two gods. Eitrem, for example, attempts to explain almost every feature of the *Hymn to Hermes* in this manner.[19] For Brown, on the other hand, the conflict between the two divinities reflects the political ferment in late sixth-century Athens and the displacement of the old aristocracy by the merchant class who viewed Hermes as their special patron.[20] Along similar lines, Herter, who however localizes the composition of the hymn at Delphi, discovers a tension between the aristocratic priests and worshipers of Apollo and the more plebeian devotees of Hermes[21]—for which there is no evidence at Delphi or elsewhere. Granted that Hermes acquires the clearly subordinate prophetic shrine of the Bee Maidens on Parnassus, he nowhere poses a real threat to the prestige of the Delphic oracle. Nor is

[17] Consider also the Cyclops's cave, which is easy to enter, but hard to escape from without *mētis*. Cf. Clay (1983), pp. 29–34. For the connection between *polytropos* Hermes and Odysseus, see Thalmann (1984), pp. 173–74; and P. Pucci, *Odysseus Polutropos* (Ithaca, 1987), pp. 23–26.

[18] Cf. K. Bielohlawek, "Komische Motive in der homerischen Gestaltung des griechischen Göttermythus," *ARW* 28 (1930): 203–9.

[19] S. Eitrem, "Der homerische Hymnus an Hermes," *Philologus* 65 (1906): 248, claims that the poet depicts "die Concurrenz zweier Göttergestalten und zweier Kulte," which renders the hymn an important "Dokument der griechischen Religionsgeschichte." Cf. Radermacher (1931), p. 217: "Religionsgeschichtlich verstanden, bedeutet dieser erste und grösste Teil der Dichtung den Einbruch der Hermesreligion in eine Sphäre, die bis dahin Apollo allein gehörte."

[20] N. O. Brown, *Hermes the Thief* (Madison, Wis., 1947). Cf. G. Graefe, "Der homerische Hymnus auf Hermes," *Gymnasium* 70 (1973): 515–26, who takes the rivalry and final reconciliation of the two Olympians to represent the political relations between the democratic Themistocles and the aristocratic party of Cimon around 475 B.C. Readers will note that I have taken no position on the supposed date of the *Hymn to Hermes*. I simply do not know.

[21] Herter (1981), pp. 198–99.

it persuasive to claim, as Càssola and others have, a genuine rivalry between two originally pastoral divinities.[22] Apollo's involvement with
herdsmen and his role as protector of flocks remain secondary and derivative.[23] Similarly, despite his invention of the lyre, Hermes is never identified with the art of music in any intimate manner. Thus the opposition
between the two gods cannot be reduced to a simple overlap in their
religious functions or spheres. Finally, we must note that the hymn's
overall movement proceeds from antagonism to reconciliation; it ends
with the repeated assertion of the brothers' *philia* and intimacy. In cult,
they share one of the six altars to the twelve gods in Olympia, an arrangement suggesting not rivalry but harmonious unity.[24] Although the evidence is scant, the Homeric epic also points to their peaceful association.
In the theomachy, Hermes laughs off a confrontation with Apollo's
mother, Leto (*Iliad* xxi.497–501), while the close relationship of the two
brothers is implied by their playful banter at *Odyssey* 8.334–42.

The preceding observations suggest that the reasons underlying the
conflict between Hermes and Apollo in the *Hymn to Hermes* must be
sought elsewhere. In this context, it may be useful to compare what seems
to be a genuine religious tension localized at Delphi—that between
Apollo and Dionysus. To explore fully the complex interrelationships
between these two figures would lead too far afield. I mention only the
well-known fact that Dionysus is said to reign at Delphi during the winter months when Apollo is absent. This alternation suggests that these
two gods coalesce uneasily. Although a mutual accommodation is finally
achieved, a certain tension abides that cannot readily be resolved. In
Apollo, the Greeks recognized the god who maintains order and observes
hierarchies and distinctions, especially those separating gods and mortals.
The presence of Dionysus blurs and dissolves such boundaries and brings
in its wake ecstatic liberation but also chaos.[25] The case of Hermes and
Dionysus differs fundamentally. Whereas Dionysus tends to threaten the
system from without, Hermes extends its flexibility *within* the established
order, which he has the ability to traverse. Hermes' movements of pas-

[22] Càssola (1975), p. 153; cf. J. Duchemin, *La Houlette et la lyre* (Paris, 1960).
[23] Cf. Nilsson, *GGR* (1955), 1: 536.
[24] Cf. the Scholium to Pindar, *Olympian* 5.10a, who cites the grammarian Herodorus
(*Fr.G.H.* 34a) for the arrangement of the double altars at Olympia. Cf. Pausanias 5.14.8.
[25] See, for example, C. Segal, *Dionysiac Poetics and Euripides' Bacchae* (Princeton,
1982), p. 12: "as Apollo imposes limits and reinforces boundaries, Dionysus, his opposite
and complement, dissolves them. From the *Iliad* on, Apollo embodies the distance between god and man. Dionysus closes that distance."

sage and penetration neither negate the Olympian hierarchy nor abrogate Apollo's insistence on orderly limits and bounds. While permitting mediation and movement between boundaries, Hermes' passage leaves them in place unchallenged and, in fact, reaffirms their presence. As transgressor of limits, Hermes simultaneously becomes their guardian and as such finally becomes Apollo's helpmate. The reconciliation of Apollo and Hermes ultimately represents their necessary complementarities and interdependence.

To find his place on Olympus, Hermes must discover his particular sphere of activity—the traversing of boundaries—and, appropriately, he must wrest his privileges from the god whose business it is to ensure those boundaries. Hermes, then, introduces dynamic movement and vitality into what might otherwise be a beautifully ordered but static cosmos.

By their character, Hermes' *timai* differ from those of the other gods; they involve not so much a particular sphere or even several spheres of influence as a mode of activity that cuts across and moves between individual domains. As Welcker recognized long ago, "Hermes is the only one of the great gods who possesses no visible substratum, whose mythological nature is not based on the material."[26] The abstract character of Hermes' *timai* poses peculiar problems for the hymn-poet who works in what is essentially a narrative medium. He cannot be satisfied simply to label such an abstract conception, although early on he does enumerate and circumscribe some of its particular manifestations through a long string of epithets (13–15) unique to the narrative Homeric Hymns.[27] Instead, he manifests and incorporates it into the dramatic movement of the narrative, in which Hermes *becomes* his function by enacting it. The erratic progress of the poet's account with its abrupt leaps and discontinuities may be only partially due to textual lacunae, for it appears to offer a perfect vehicle for conveying the restless movement of the god and his shifting thoughts and motivations. It is through these that Hermes discovers and acquires his role and *timai*. Unlike Apollo who can lay claim to his prerogatives moments after his birth, Hermes must invent them and, even before that, he must discover his proper place. For it is by no means immediately clear whether he belongs with the gods or among men.

[26] Welcker (1857), 1: 343.

[27] Some of the so-called Orphic Hymns are little more than a string of epithets. The *Hymn to Ares* in our collection is assumed to be Hellenistic and opens with a list of seventeen epithets.

Although a good number of details may admittedly remain obscure and some vexing problems unresolved, nevertheless I believe the preceding observations offer an adequate starting point for a general consideration of the *Hymn to Hermes*.

Famous Deeds

The poem begins with an invocation to the Muse to sing of Hermes and then names the god's parentage and two of his cult places, Cyllene and Arcadia, as well as one of his functions—"swift messenger of the gods." After this brief identification of its subject, the hymn modulates into narrative through the characteristic relative construction: "whom Maia bore ... mingling in love with Zeus." The names of Hermes' parents occur twice in the first four lines. By the fifth, it becomes apparent that we are dealing with a birth story.[28]

As in the case of Apollo, the circumstances surrounding the god's conception and birth go a long way in explaining his nature and the course of the subsequent narrative. Maia herself lives in a shadowy cave,[29] a natural enough habitat for a nymph; but she also actively avoids the "converse of the blessed gods." Whether she is one of them remains unclear. However that may be, her union with Zeus takes place in secret, far from Olympus, in the dead of night. Both time and place conspire to keep the *amour* hidden not only from the presumably jealous Hera, but from other gods and mortals as well. But as the nymph is dignified with

[28] There are alternate traditions localizing Hermes' birth in Tanagra. See L. Preller and C. Robert, *Griechische Mythologie*, 4th ed. (Berlin, 1887), 1, pt. 1: 397, for the testimonia. Philostratus, *Imagines* 26, on the other hand, sets Hermes' birth below Olympus. Neither of these versions would be appropriate to our hymn. In the first case, the god, called *Promachos* in Tanagra, is much too closely linked to local cults and foundation traditions. If, on the other hand, Hermes were born on or near Olympus, he would have no difficulty asserting his Olympian status. The hymn, however, insists on the remoteness of the god's birthplace.

[29] Consider, for example, Calypso (*Odyssey*. 5.57–74), who also dwells in a cave, and Thoosa, the mother of Polyphemus, who "mingled with Poseidon in hollow caves" (*Odyssey* 1.71–73). For parallels between Maia's cave and that of Calypso, see S. C. Shelmerdine, "The 'Homeric Hymn to Hermes': A Commentary (1–114) with Introduction" (Ph.D. diss., University of Michigan, 1981), p. 15; and S. C. Shelmerdine, "Odyssean Allusions in the Fourth Homeric Hymn," *TAPA* 116 (1986): 55–57. Note also that Maia, like Calypso, is a daughter of Atlas (cf. *Hymn to Hermes* (no. 18) 4, and *Odyssey* 1.52). Although our *Hymn to Hermes* does not mention this fact, one may surmise that Hermes' Titanic lineage on his mother's side may exert some influence on the infant god's character.

the epithet "revered" (5),[30] so the affair is distinguished from Zeus's many dalliances by its duration.[31] This is no one-night fling.

The first nine lines of the hymn are recorded with some minor variants as number 18 of the Homeric Hymns. As is generally recognized, the latter is an abbreviation of the longer version.[32] The studied emphasis on the secrecy accompanying Hermes' conception is inconsequential in the shorter composition but is crucial to the development of the fuller account. The supreme god's clandestine union with the lowly nymph and his nocturnal deception of his legitimate consort will ultimately find its reflection in the character of his offspring[33]—a trickster who operates at night and is illegitimate to boot, neither fully Olympian nor simply terrestrial, a perfect go-between. And all this, the poet assures us, is in accord with the intention of great Zeus (10), which is on the way to being accomplished[34] with Hermes' birth, but will not be complete until the end of the hymn.

καὶ τότ᾽ ἐγείνατο παῖδα πολύτροπον, αἱμυλομήτην,
ληϊστῆρ᾽, ἐλατῆρα βοῶν, ἡγήτορ᾽ ὀνείρων,
νυκτὸς ὀπωπητῆρα, πυληδόκον, ὃς τάχ᾽ ἔμελλεν
ἀμφανέειν κλυτὰ ἔργα μετ᾽ ἀθανάτοισι θεοῖσιν.

[30] The enjambed position of αἰδοίη draws attention to the fact; it is by no means a common epithet of νύμφη. In Homer and Hesiod, the feminine adjective is most commonly applied to wives as well as goddesses, housekeepers and maidens. For the close connection between αἰδοῖος and φίλος, see É. Benveniste, Le Vocabulaire des institutions indo-européennes (Paris, 1969), 1: 340–41. I wonder whether the unusual ἔσω in line 6 is not meant to emphasize that not only does Maia inhabit her cave, but she remains inside it.

[31] As is brought out by the iterative μισγέσκετο (7) and the optative ἔχοι (8). On the force of the latter, see Gemoll (1886), p. 195; and Càssola (1975), p. 517. Shelmerdine (1981), pp. 50–51, notes only two Homeric parallels: Iliad IX.450, where the duration of his father's affair causes Phoenix's mother to beg her son to lie with Amyntor's concubine; and Odyssey 18.325, where Melantho's ongoing affair with Eurymachus attests to her ingratitude and disrespect toward Penelope.

[32] Cf. Baumeister (1860), pp. 187–88; Gemoll (1886), p. 331; Ludwich (1908), p. 76; AHS (1936), p. 401; and Shelmerdine (1981), p. 47.

[33] Cf. Eitrem (1906), p. 249: "übrigens ist die Geburt des Hermes prototypisch für das ganze spätere Auftreten des Kleinen: er ist Frucht gestohlener Liebe, im Dunkel der Nacht empfangen." See also Lenz (1975), p. 73; "die ... Zeugungsgeschichte ... ist bedeutungsvoll für das Handeln des Kleinen, weil in ihr seine Physis festgelegt wird: bei diesen Eltern und unter solchen Umständen geht in Hermes' Wesen das Nächtlich-Betrügerische ein." The emphasis on the secrecy of Hermes' birth seems to be unique to the hymn.

[34] The full force of the imperfect ἐξετελεῖτο should be retained. Cf. A. Pagliero, "Il proemio dell' Iliade," in Nuovo saggi di critica semantica, 2nd. ed. (Florence, 1971), p. 19, for its force in the proem to the Iliad.

And then she bore a child of many turns, of wheedling wiles,
a robber, a cattle rustler, a leader of dreams,
one who keeps watch for night and lurks at gates, who would soon
show forth famous deeds among the immortal gods.

(13–16)

From the darkness of the shadowy cave, Hermes emerges into the light.
In a sense, the entire hymn constitutes the revelation of the new god. The
prologue now comes to a close with a short overview of the "famous
deeds" accomplished on the god's first day:

ἠῷος γεγονὼς μέσῳ ἤματι ἐγκιθάριζεν,
ἑσπέριος βοῦς κλέψεν ἑκηβόλου Ἀπόλλωνος,
τετράδι τῇ προτέρῃ τῇ μιν τέκε πότνια Μαῖα.

Born at dawn, he played the lyre at midday;
in the evening he stole the cattle of far-shooting Apollo,
on the fourth day of the month on which lady Maia bore him.

(17–19)

This summary of Hermes' *kluta erga* is striking for two reasons. First, in
the other versions that contain both motifs, the theft of the cattle precedes
the invention of the lyre. In fact, the slaughtered cows are used in the
manufacture of the instrument.[35] In the *Hymn to Hermes*, however, the
order is reversed with the result that the lyre is given special prominence.[36] Once manufactured, the lyre will remain hidden, a secret
weapon that will later become the means for resolving the confrontation
between Hermes and Apollo. The instrument of reconciliation is, then,
prior to the conflict of the two brothers and guarantees its ultimate resolution.

There is an additional peculiarity in the summary account of
Hermes' activities during his first day on earth. Extending from lines 20
to 153, the narrative of those events includes not only the lyre and the
cattle theft, but also the bizarre "sacrifice" Hermes performs by the Alpheus, yet the preview makes no allusion to the latter event. Its exclusion

[35] Cf. Sophocles, *Ichneutae* 376–77 (E. V. Maltese, *Sofocle Ichneutae* [Florence, 1982]),
and Apollodorus 3.10.2. According to some commentators (e.g. Robert [1906], p. 400, and
Radermacher [1931], p. 184), Apollodorus's version "corrects" the *Hymn to Hermes* and
puts the story into "eine verständigere Ordnung." On the other hand, Ludwich (1908), p.
4, maintains that the hymn cannot be Apollodorus's source; and Burkert (1984), p. 835,
suggests that Apollodorus may actually transmit a version older than the hymn.

[36] Cf. Shelmerdine (1984), p. 202.

from the enumeration of the god's actions raises the suspicion that the butchering of the cows does not rank among Hermes' *kluta erga*. We shall have to keep that possibility in mind when we examine that enigmatic episode.

Hermes displays his characteristic restlessness from the moment he emerges from his mother's womb. Rejecting the comfort of his cradle, he darts up, crossing the threshold of the cave to go after the cattle of Apollo. His motive remains undefined. In any case, the search is abruptly interrupted by a chance encounter with a tortoise grazing at the cave's entrance. With childish glee, Hermes welcomes the chance find—what the Greeks called a *hermaion*—as a source of great future profit to himself. As the infant god is easily distracted from his original purpose, so the narrative is momentarily diverted. Its zigzag course mirrors the movements of the god as he sets about acquiring his *timai* through indirection. The apparent detour will nevertheless lead to his final goal.

Now for the first time, Hermes begins to speak. Speech, insofar as it involves communication or mediation between individuals, belongs to Hermes' domain. But the rhetoric of Hermes is of a peculiar sort; persuasive, seductive, and deceptive, it is characteristically ambiguous and riddling, concealing as much as revealing, and abounding in double and ulterior meanings. Addressing the tortoise as one who "beats out the rhythm of the dance" and "companion of the feast," Hermes already envisions the use to which he will put the "lovely toy." Turning the creature into a lyre demands multiple transformations. First, it must be brought within from outdoors, exchanging its previous mountain habitat for a domestic existence; but contrary to the proverb with which Hermes entices the creature indoors, safety does not reside within.[37] Second, the mute, living beast must surrender its life to become a singer in death.[38] If in life the tortoise constitutes a charm against evil spells, once transformed into the lyre she will herself cast enchantment over her auditors. Full of flattery and riddling paradox, Hermes' seductive rhetoric masks the violence of these metamorphoses.

The god quickly dispatches the tortoise in a mode peculiarly his

[37] The phrase, doubtless proverbial, occurs in Hesiod's *Works and Days* 365. For the erotic overtones of Hermes' address to the tortoise, see W. Hübner, "Hermes als musischer Gott," *Philologus* 130 (1986): 161. The tortoise's seductive powers will emerge later.

[38] Cf. Sophocles, *Ichneutae* (Maltese), who plays on this conceit: θανὼν γὰρ ἔσχε φωνήν, ζῶν δ᾽ ἄναυδος ἦν ὁ θήρ (300); οὕτως ὁ παῖς θανόντι θηρὶ φθέγμ᾽ ἐμηχανήσατο (328).

own by "piercing out its life."[39] Penetrating the slender boundary between life and death, Hermes manages to leave the tortoise's shell intact
so that it can become the sounding board for the lyre. A simile conveys
the speed of the god's actions:

ὡς δ᾽ ὁπότ᾽ ὠκὺ νόημα διὰ στέρνοιο περήσῃ
ἀνέρος ὅν τε θαμιναὶ ἐπιστρωφῶσι μέριμναι,
καὶ τότε δινηθῶσιν ἀπ᾽ ὀφθαλμῶν ἀμαρυγαί,
ὡς ἅμ᾽ ἔπος τε καὶ ἔργον ἐμήδετο κύδιμος Ἑρμῆς.

As when a swift thought pierces through the breast
of a man whom dense cares whirl about,
and then beams whirl from his eyes:
so did glorious Hermes devise both word and deed.

(43–46)

The point of comparison is the swiftness with which Hermes executes
his intentions.[40] The saving thought penetrates the breast of a man beset
by anxieties and straightway resolves them; almost simultaneously, his
eyes light up, sparkling with triumphant intelligence. But the whole image also characterizes Hermes' mental alertness, his restless powers of
observation, a glance that swiftly lights on all relevant details and misses
nothing of importance,[41] and a lightning-swift intelligence that cuts
through all obstacles and impediments to reach its goal.

[39] For the association of τορέω with Hermes, see lines 119 and 283 of the hymn; also
Iliad x.267, where it is applied to Hermes' favorite, Autolycus (cf. Odyssey 19.395–98);
Aristophanes Peace 381; and Aratus Phaenomena 268–69. αἰών in lines 42 and 119 should
be understood generally as "life force" or "seat of life" rather than "spinal marrow." Cf.
Gemoll (1886), p. 200; Ludwich (1908), p. 96, n. 1; and Càssola (1975), p. 519. For the
sense, compare Iliad xix.27. Shelmerdine (1984) interprets the killing of the tortoise as a
kind of sacrifice and the preceding address to the tortoise as a kind of hymn, both paralleled in the later cattle sacrifice. The two actions do indeed resemble one another, but I
consider neither one a sacrifice, as will be discussed later in this chapter.

[40] I follow Ludwich's ([1908]), p. 85) interpretation of the simile and read καὶ τότε at
line 45. Most editors (Radermacher, AHS, Càssola, and Shelmerdine) read ἦ ὅτε and take
the passage as a double simile, the first referring to the speed of thought, the second to
the speed of the glance. M. Treu, Von Homer zur Lyrik (Zetemata 12), 2nd ed. (Munich,
1968), p. 252, accepts the usual text but coordinates the two images, citing Schmid (1929),
1: 237, n. 1: "das Aufblitzen des Auges bei einem guten, hilfreichen Einfall."

[41] Baumeister (1860), p. 192, offers αἱ δέ τε and remarks that "the poet has a special
fondness for describing the movement of eyes as indications of a quick intelligence" ("vi-
brationes autem oculorum, mobilis ingenii indices, in deliciis habet hic poeta"). Compare
lines 278–79 describing Hermes' glance.

Upon the thought follows the deed, as the infant god sets about transforming the dead animal into a singing lyre through his *technē*. Assembling a collection of diverse objects—not only the tortoiseshell, but reeds, an oxhide, and sheep guts as well—Hermes pierces, cuts, fits, stretches, and joins them, piecing together a novel invention. Hermes' *bricolage* resides in his ability to exploit whatever happens to be at hand and to devise from chance finds an instrument of salvation. The hallmark of *mētis* is precisely such a device, a *mēchanē* or *poros*, that can resolve a situation of helplessness and resourcelessness, *amēchania* or *aporia*. It may, furthermore, have to be held in reserve, patiently hidden, until the right moment, *kairos*, for its most effective use, so as to disarm and catch off guard even the strongest adversary.[42] Such, then, is the use to which Hermes, master of devices and wiles, will put his wonderful invention.

As soon as the "lovely toy" is completed, Hermes tries it out, singing to its accompaniment and performing a kind of "hymn to Hermes." The god's impromptu performance is likened to the improvisations of young men at feasts who "provoke each other with side meanings" (παραι-βόλα).[43] While improvisation forms the immediate *tertium comparationis*, the simile extends beyond it to draw a comparison between two different genres of music, on the level of form or performance and on the level of content. At first glance, the parallel seems unsuitable on both counts. Yet later on, when he first hears the lyre, Apollo similarly likens Hermes' playing to the "skillful deeds of young men at feasts" (454).[44] Evidently, the closest available analogy to Hermes' new mode of making music is improvisational verse accompanying symposiastic occasions. Such poetry, however, was usually accompanied by the flute, as is also implied by Apollo's explicit mention of the "lovely moan of flutes" (452). In likening Hermes' performance to the activity of a plurality of participants (κοῦροι, νέοι), the poet indicates the infant god's decisive inno-

[42] One again thinks of Odysseus in the Cyclops's cave, where he must wait patiently, even while his companions are eaten, to use the olive-wood stake.

[43] Radermacher (1931) and AHS (1936) interpret παραιβόλα as "impudent." Cf. J. Hooker, "A Residual Problem in *Iliad* 24," *CQ* n.s. 36 (1986): 34: "like impudent retorts uttered by young men at festivals." But the parallel from *Iliad* iv.6 suggests a different sense. There, Zeus tries to provoke Hera κερτομίοις ἐπέεσσι, παραβλήδην ἀγορεύων by suggesting that the gods initiate peace between Greeks and Trojans. His aim, of course, is just the opposite.

[44] Possibly to be connected with a feast of Hermes celebrated on the fourth of the month. Cf. Aristophanes, *Ploutos* 1126, and Hesychius, *s.v.* τετραδισταί· σύνοδος νέων συνήθων κατὰ τετράδα γινομένῳ. C. Diano, "La poetica dei Faeci," in *Saggezza e poetiche degli antichi* (Vicenza, 1968), p. 210, speaks of Hermes' first song as a "canto giambico."

vation. Prior to the invention of the lyre, song and accompaniment were necessarily distributed among two or more performers, a singer and a musician. Hermes' unique discovery entails not only a new way of producing music, but a completely different *kind* of music that, with the ingenuity characteristic of its inventor, involves the union of two hitherto distinct activities. Henceforth, one and the same person can exercise complete control over both words and music.

In addition to comparing two modes of poetic performance, the simile draws attention to the unique character of this particular song composed by Hermes. The god sings the beginning of a hymn to Hermes, one much like the composition of the professional bard before us. But although superficially resembling such a typical performance, Hermes' "hymn" diverges in crucial respects. Normally, of course, the mortal hymn-poet praises and celebrates a god, but here we have a god—whose precise status is still ambiguous—praising himself. On Olympus, it is the function of the Muses to sing the *dora ambrota*[45] of the gods, and the terrestrial poet invokes the Muse for assistance at the beginning of his composition. Hermes, to be sure, has no need to do so. Finally, no audience attends the precocious god's performance. The anomalousness of Hermes' song reflects his anomalous position: not a mortal, but not yet fully a god.

If we compare Hermes' hymn to himself to that of the Muse-inspired bard, it becomes apparent that the god goes well beyond the hymnist in glorifying the circumstances of Hermes' birth and legitimizing it. Singing of his parentage, Hermes emphasizes not only the duration of their union, but the equality of the partners. Downplaying the purely sexual component of their relationship, Hermes describes how Zeus and Maia were "wont to converse ἑταιρείῃ φιλότητι" (58). The phrase implies the mutual and reciprocal obligations between equals.[46] Represented as a lasting union between equal partners rather than as a fleeting sexual escapade, the relationship of Hermes' parents and his own begetting are thus legitimized, and his own lineage exalted (γενεὴν ὀνομακλυτόν, [59]).[47] The god continues his self-glorification in the description of his

---

[45] Cf. *Hymn to Apollo* 190. In the *Hymn to Pan* 27–47, the nymphs sing of the god's birth, while in the *Hymn to Artemis* (no. 27) 18–20, the Muses and Graces hymn Leto and her children. See also *Theogony* 43–49.

[46] For the implications of ἑταιρία, see H. Jeanmaire, *Couroi et courètes* (Lille, 1939), pp. 97–111.

[47] Cf. Radermacher (1931), p. 76, who speaks of the "Unverschämtheit" of Hermes: "denn vorläufig ist er noch νόθος; in einem σκότιον λέχος erzeugt, muss er sich die Anerknnnung des Vaters verdienen. Wer keinen Vater hat, hat auch keine γενεή."

birthplace. In Hermes' account, the shadowy cave becomes a splendid place, furnished with maidservants and other accoutrements. Scholars have long noted that Hermes' description of Maia's grotto appears to contradict the earlier one and, indeed, that both are at odds with subsequent references. These contradictions have, in turn, been cited as evidence for multiple authorship.[48] But here surely Hermes' idealization of his birthplace is of a piece with the god's self-aggrandizement. He does not simply celebrate himself, but γέραιρε (60), which means to offer a *geras* or a tangible gift symbolizing honor or esteem.[49] The song itself constitutes the gift.

Like the sideways meanings of the young men in the simile, Hermes' "hymn" constitutes an act of oblique provocation that simultaneously hides and reveals a purpose beyond the literal meaning of his words. A perversion of the usual function of a hymn, the god's composition contains an ulterior purpose and proclaims a hidden agenda, laying claim to a divine status he has yet to acquire. Even as he plays, Hermes "intends other things" (62). Despite his invention of the lyre, Hermes cannot become the patron of poetry. Although aware of music's potential for charming others, the god himself is impervious to its charm, because for him, poetry—and all language—constitutes primarily a means to an end. Hermes' lyre playing resembles the storytelling of his human counterpart, Odysseus. Both possess the power to enchant their listeners, like the genuine bard, with whom Odysseus is explicitly compared.[50] But both figures also mask an oblique purpose in their songs, and this purpose shapes the contents of their recital, whether it be, as in the case of the hero, to obtain a homeward journey, or a cloak, or to test his auditors, or with Hermes, to obtain his *timai* among the Olympians. Hermes' domain, then, is not the sphere of language that lays claim to truth,[51] but

---

[48] See especially Robert (1906), pp. 389–90, for whom these contradictions form the basis of his analysis of the hymn. Ludwich (1908), pp. 7–8; Kuiper (1910), pp. 7–9; and Humbert (1936), pp. 106–8, attempt to answer Robert's objections, but their defense of the text is unsatisfactory. Yet an adequate solution is not hard to come by; depending on the circumstances, Hermes may glorify the cave, as here, or denigrate it, as he does later.

[49] Cf. Benveniste (1969), 2: 43–49.

[50] Cf. *Odyssey* 11.367–69.

[51] Cf. M. Detienne, *Les Maîtres de vérité dans la Grèce archaïque*, 2nd ed. (Paris, 1973), pp. 61–80. For the similar distinction between poetry intended to charm its audience and that which contains an ulterior motive, see G. B. Walsh, *The Varieties of Enchantment: Early Greek Views of the Nature and Function of Poetry* (Chapel Hill, N.C., 1984), pp. 18–21. What Walsh, p. 22, calls Odysseus—"an unbeguiled audience and a deceptive story-

rather that use of language whose goal extends outside itself and which is a means to an end: persuasion, seductive rhetoric, lies, oaths, perjuries, and even magical incantations.

καὶ τὰ μὲν οὖν ἤειδε, τὰ δὲ φρεσὶν ἄλλα μενοίνα.
καὶ τὴν μὲν κατέθηκε φέρων ἱερῷ ἐνὶ λίκνῳ
φόρμιγγα γλαφυρήν· ὁ δ᾽ ἄρα κρειῶν ἐρατίζων ...

These, then, were the things he sang, but in his heart he was intent
on others.
And then he carried and set the hollow phorminx
into his holy cradle; but he, desirous of meat ...

(62–64)

It is completely obscure what connection there might be between Hermes' lyre playing and his hunger, but it is worth at least considering the possibility that his musical performance reminds the god of food.[52] At any rate, his appetite for meat now causes him to break off his song.

The mention of the cradle frames and encloses the invention of the lyre.[53] Returning to his point of departure, the god once more sallies forth. Earlier, we were told that he "sought the cattle of Apollo" (22), although no explanation was given as to why Hermes has a particular interest in Apollo's herds. Here we learn that the infant god is hungry or, rather, ravenous, because the expression "desirous of meat" is elsewhere used of lions.[54] Hermes' human—or animal—craving could presumably be satisfied by any meat,[55] but his interest in Apollo's cattle arises from a different motive: a desire for divine timai. The dual motives for the cattle theft—one human, one divine—are in a sense at cross-purposes, but they point to Hermes' liminal position between god and man. Hermes straddles the boundary between human and divine until he fi-

---

teller"—could be applied equally well to Hermes. Cf. Diano (1968), pp. 208–12, who compares Hermes' poetics of *mētis* and *apatē* to those of Odysseus.

[52] Note the balanced pairs of μέν ... δέ ... μέν ... δέ in these lines. The intimate connection between lyre and *dais* will emerge subsequently.

[53] Cf. Shelmerdine (1981), p. 95.

[54] Cf. *Iliad* XI.551 and XVII.660. Gods, of course, can be said to desire meat only insofar as they enjoy the *knisē* from sacrifice. For Hermes' anomalous devotion to his *gastēr* (which again connects him to Odysseus), see also lines 130–32 and 296, where he emits a "message from his *gastēr*." The *gastēr* motif, especially in relation to Odysseus, is discussed by Pucci (1987), pp. 157–87.

[55] As we later learn, there are in fact sheep grazing on Cyllene (232).

nally resolves the problem of his identity. At first, both the obscure circumstances of his birth and his role as mediator render uncertain
whether Hermes belongs among the gods. Only after he has unambiguously ascertained his divinity can he single-mindedly pursue his divine
prerogatives.

"Pondering a steep ruse in his heart" like a thief in the night,
Hermes springs into action (65–67). The nocturnal theft of Apollo's cattle
divides into three phases, each marked by an indication of time.[56] At
dusk, Hermes sets off for Pieria; after midnight, he arrives at the Alpheus; and at dawn, he returns to the cave on Cyllene. The geography of
the theft reveals the Olympian *tendenz* of the hymn. The site of the cattle's pasturage varies in different versions,[57] but here the god steals the
cows from Pieria, "the shadowy mountain of the gods," below Olympus.
In the *Hymn to Apollo*, Pieria is where Apollo first touches down as he
makes his way from Olympus. (216). Similarly, the Muses, born in Pieria
at the foothills of Olympus, ascend from their birthplace to their Olympian homes (*Theogony* 53–62). Constituting a common hymnic motif, the
introduction of a new god into Olympus signifies his induction into the
Olympian order.[58] For now, Hermes approaches, but does not yet enter,
Olympus; his reception there is postponed. Accounts likewise vary as to
where he finally conceals the stolen herds.[59] In the *Hymn to Hermes*, the
god hides the cows in a cave along the Alpheus, a site closely associated
with the Panhellenic shrine of Zeus at Olympia. Thus, both the starting
point and goal of Hermes' nocturnal journey reinforce the Olympian orientation of the hymn.[60]

[56] For supposed contradictions in the temporal indications, see Robert (1906), pp. 390–
91. Ludwich (1908), pp. 9–13; Kuiper (1910), pp. 9–16; and Humbert (1936), pp. 108–9;
all offer adequate defenses of the text as it stands.

[57] Apollodorus 3.10.2 follows the *Hymn to Hermes* in giving the locus of the theft as
Pieria. Cf. Philostatus, *Imagines* 26 (ἐν τῷ τοῦ Ὀλύμπου πρόποδι). But in Antoninus
Liberalis 23, Apollo is grazing his cattle in Pereia in Magnesia, along with those of Admetus. Ovid, *Metamorphoses* 2.679–85, has Apollo herding in Messenia and Elis, but the
theft takes place "Pylios . . . in agros." For the geography of the various versions, see AHS
(1936), pp. 272–73.

[58] Cf., for example, the *Hymn to Aphrodite* (no. 6), the *Hymn to Pan*, presumably also
the fragmentary *Hymn to Dionysus* 1, and *Theogony* 68–71.

[59] In the *Ichneutae*, the cattle are hidden in a cave on Cyllene. Antoninus Liberalis 23
and Ovid, *Metamorphoses* 2.684, both locate their hiding place in Messenian Pylos. Eitrem
(1906), p. 264, believes that in the original myth Hermes concealed the cows in the underworld and that Pylos refers to the entrance to the lower world. Cf. R. Holland, "Battos," *Rheinisches Museum* 75 (1926): 165–66.

[60] W. Burkert "Sacrificio-sacrilegio: Il 'trickster' fondatore," *Studi Storici* 4 (1984):
842, succinctly describes the movement of the cattle as "dall' Olimpo verso Olimpia."

Like the herds of Helios in the *Odyssey* who are exempt from the natural cycle of birth and death, Apollo's cattle are immortal and feed on inviolate meadows.[61] Elsewhere, they are called *admētēs*; presumably, they do not reproduce. Of the fifty cows Hermes will drive from Pieria, Hermes will slaughter only two. The remainder will be transformed into domestic animals who graze on ordinary grasses and who increase and multiply. Removing them from the divine sphere, their domestication will simultaneously introduce them into the realm of men and mortality.[62] The vehicle of this metamorphosis is Hermes who mediates between the mortal and divine and who makes possible movement between those spheres.

Despite some textual obscurities, it is clear that Hermes adopts three different devices to conceal the direction of his theft. First, he drives the cattle on a zigzag path, avoiding the normal roads (πλανοδίας δ' ἤλαυνε [75]; ὁδοιπορίην ἀλεείνων [85]); then, he turns them around, so that their tracks are reversed (ἀντία ποιήσας ὁπλάς [77]); and finally, he disguises his own tracks by tying branches to his feet (ὑπὸ ποσσὶν ἐδήσατο σάνδαλα [83]). Hermes' sandals, the θαυματὰ ἔργα, resemble the god's other inventions in that disparate things, in this case tamarisks and myrtles, are joined together (διέπλεκε, συμμίσγων, συνδήσας) to produce something new and unheard of (ἄφραστ᾽ ἠδ᾽ ἀνόητα). The *technē* of Hermes remains the same, but unlike the lyre and the later fire drill, these sandals constitute an ad hoc invention, a μηχανή, which is discarded as soon as its usefulness is exhausted, whereas both the lyre and the fire drill are cultural innovations that will permanently enhance the character of human life. These two aspects of Hermes' inventiveness can again be illustrated by a parallel from the *Odyssey*. In the Cyclops's cave, Odysseus transforms the branch of olive wood into a weapon to blind Polyphemus. The techniques employed are likened to the arts of shipbuilding and ironworking, both of which define the human condition.[63] Hermes' inventions thus attest to two aspects of his ingenuity and *mētis*,

---

[61] Most commentators do not allow ἄμβροτοι (71) its full force. The cattle are not merely possessions of the gods but are themselves immortal. For their resemblance to the cattle of the Sun in *Odyssey* 12, see J.-P. Vernant, "Manger aux pays du Soleil," in *La Cuisine du sacrifice en pays grec*, ed. M. Detienne and J.-P. Vernant (Paris, 1979), p. 241 (hereafter cited as Vernant [1979b]). Cf. Kahn (1978), pp. 48–50. Note that in those versions where Apollo herds the cattle of Admetus, they are not immortal. Cf. Brown (1947), p. 140.

[62] See especially Kahn (1978), p. 50; also Burkert (1984), p. 842.

[63] Cf. Clay (1983), pp. 118–19.

the one linked to the enduring discoveries of the culture hero, the other, to the quick-witted exploitation of the needs of the moment.

That Hermes functions not only as a trickster but also as a culture hero may shed some light on the puzzling Onchestus episode that follows.[64] While driving Apollo's cattle, Hermes encounters an old man on the plain of Onchestus (87–88). In pursuit of his cows, Apollo will later stop to question the same individual. The two encounters thus frame the strange proceedings by the Alpheus. Moreover, the episode is unique to the *Hymn to Hermes*. In other versions, Hermes meets a certain Battos in Arcadia whom he bribes to remain silent about what he had witnessed.[65] When Hermes returns to test him, Battos betrays the god and is punished by being turned into stone. The point of the story seems to lie in Battos's punishment for informing on the god, and it contains a local Arcadian version of how a rock formation came to be known as "Battos's Watch."

Some scholars have assumed that the account given in the hymn is a truncated version of the Battos story, which is at least as old as the Hesiodic *Catalog of Women*.[66] Although the old man has no name in the hymn, Apollo may allude to it when he calls him *batodrope*, but the localization of the incident at Onchestus remains mysterious.[67] More significant, not only is the old man never punished for his betrayal, but he simply disappears from the narrative. The omission of Hermes' revenge completely alters the meaning of the incident.[68] Its function within the hymn must thus be sought elsewhere.

To begin from that most obvious point: the anonymous old man of Onchestus is the only human being to play a role of any importance in the hymn. For the most part, the hymn-poet concerns himself with the revelation of Hermes' *kluta erga* among the gods (cf. 16); mankind is only

[64] Cf. Eitrem (1906), p. 256: "die Episode hat, wie wir sie hier lesen, keine grosse Bedeutung für die Composition des Ganzes." According to Radermacher (1931), p. 214, the incident is merely meant to amuse and entertain: "auf die Entwicklung der Dinge übt sie keinerlei Einfluss." Cf. Shelmerdine (1981), p. 119.

[65] The story is preserved in Antoninus Liberalis 23 and Ovid, *Metamorphoses* 2.687–707, but the Scholiast to Antoninus informs us that the tales goes back to Hesiod. Cf. Holland (1926), pp. 156–62. In Apollodorus 3.10, 2, Apollo seeks information from the inhabitants of Pylos.

[66] Cf. Brown (1947), p. 137; but Holland (1926), pp. 173–75, believes the *Hymn to Hermes* is older than the Hesiodic version.

[67] Holland (1926), p. 167, halfheartedly suggests that Hermes may have had special cultic associations with the region around Onchestus. Cf. Càssola (1975), p. 523.

[68] Radermacher (1931), pp. 193–96, believes that the incident in the hymn is drawn from the tradition of the disguised or unrecognized god and is completely distinct from the Battos story.

of marginal interest. As the sole mortal in the poem, the old man takes on a representative role, and a peculiar one at that. His significance has been misinterpreted in part because the text describing his activities is not only corrupt, but has been further altered and misconstrued by scholars.[69] As Hermes passes, the old man is "building a flowering orchard" and evidently terracing it with curved logs. Later, when Apollo accosts him, he is similarly engaged, enclosing or fencing the orchard and picking berries. The activities of the solitary "old brute," as he is called, resemble those of Laertes in the last book of the *Odyssey* (24.226–31).[70] In his despair over his absent son, Laertes has retired from the city, living in rustic degradation and devoting all his energies to tending his orchards. Old Laertes' pitiful existence, born of his grief, constitutes a rejection of civil society and political life. There is, however, no reason to suppose that the old man of the *Hymn to Hermes* has likewise turned his back on a more civilized life. Rather, he seems to represent a primitive phase of human existence, preagricultural, prepastoral, and prepolitical.[71] In fact, the Odyssean Cyclopes offer the closest parallel to the hymn's monstrous old man. They too are characterized by their solitariness, their lack of technology and political institutions, as well as a certain bluntness of intellect and a total absence of curiosity. The old man does not recognize the infant god, and he reveals himself too slow-witted to comprehend Hermes' riddling warning.[72]

καί τε ἰδὼν μὴ ἰδὼν εἶναι καὶ κωφὸς ἀκούσας,
καὶ σιγᾶν, ὅτε μή τι καταβλάπτῃ τὸ σὸν αὐτοῦ.

[69] At line 90, I read: ὦ γέρον, ὥστε φυτὰ σκάπτεις ἐπικαμπύλα κᾶλα (cf. Radermacher [1931], p. 85, but κᾶλα means logs or stumps and cannot refer to vines); and translate: "Old man, you dig curved logs as if they were plants; you'll have lots of wine when all these bear" (i.e., never). At line 188, I read δέμοντα for AHS's νέμοντα. δέμων at line 87 as well as 188 does not mean arranging or extending, but building. Finally, I understand βατοδρόπε at line 190 to mean "berry picker" rather than "bramble picker" or "weeder," as generally assumed.

[70] Cf. Shelmerdine (1981), pp. 17, 119, 123–24; now also Shelmerdine (1986), pp. 59–60.

[71] The old man evidently lives on fruits from his orchard and wild berries. I was long troubled by the presence of vineyards and grapes in this otherwise primitive diet, although the Homeric Cyclopes also possess wine (cf. *Odyssey* 9.357–58). But the description in Pausanias 7.42.5–12 of a preagricultural sacrifice confirms that the fruit of the vine (ἀμπέλου καρπόν) belongs to a preagricultural environment. For a discussion of the Pausanias passage and its implications, see L. Bruit, "Pausanias à Phigalie," *Mètis* 1 (1986): 71–96.

[72] See above, n. 69. Hermes' riddling speech to the old man is paralleled by his earlier enigmatic words to the tortoise.

Seeing, be unseeing and deaf, having heard,
and keep silent, when no harm is done to your interest.

(92–93)

Perhaps one can see here an allusion to the petrification of Battos found
in other versions or, more generally, to the stone piles or herms found
along Greek roads. But these verses also bear a striking resemblance to
Prometheus's description of mankind's primeval state: "At first, seeing,
they saw in vain, and, hearing, they heard not" (*Prometheus Bound* 447–
48).

I believe we can now see why the whole incident should be set in
Onchestus. In the *Hymn to Apollo*, the site is one of primeval antiquity,
even antedating the ancient foundation of Thebes.[73] The old man of Onchestus thus embodies the primitive condition of mankind antedating the
introduction of the arts and ingenuity of Hermes.[74] The hymn-poet, then,
transforms a local tale of limited interest into a dramatic account of the
brutish status of human life prior to the advent of Hermes.

After midnight, Hermes and the cows reach the ford of the Alpheus. The cattle are fed and watered and driven into a lofty cave. The
god then gathers wood and devises a fire drill made of laurel and pomegranate wood.[75] Hermes is expressly credited with being the first to discover this technique of making fire (πυρὸς τέχνη); he does not, however, in any sense invent fire. To be sure, a certain parallelism exists
between Hermes and Prometheus. Both figures share the traits of the
wily trickster and culture hero, but it is their differences that are illumi-
nating. Prometheus attempts to use his craft and guile to deceive Zeus
and ultimately to undermine the Olympian order; Hermes, on the other
hand, succeeds in using his trickery and cunning to establish his place
within that order. In the first case, mankind ends up being the loser; but
Hermes' success entails, as we shall see, an improvement in the human
condition.

Many commentators view the following episode, in which Hermes
first slaughters and butchers two of the cows, then divides the meat into

[73] *Apollo* 225–30. See the previous discussion of this passage.

[74] Compare the catalog of Prometheus's arts in *Prometheus Bound* 454–506. The *tech-
nai* of Hermes likewise include the domestication of herds, but exclude agriculture.

[75] I adopt the text of Càssola (1975) and Radermacher (1931) who, following the suggestions of Ludwich (1908), read δάφνης ἀγλαὸν ὄζον ἑλὼν ἐν δ᾽ ἴλλε σιδείῳ (109).
Once again, Hermes' characteristic *technē* resides in his ability to combine disparate
things—here, two different types of wood with opposing qualities.

twelve portions but fails to eat any of it, and finally tries to efface all traces of his activity, as a self-contained incident with little bearing on the progress of the poem. According to Brown, "the episode contributes nothing to the development of the plot."[76] Radermacher considers both the theft and slaughter of the cattle as a local *aition* explaining the peculiar rock formation of an unidentified cave near the Alpheus.[77] Generally, it is thought that the hymn here depicts Hermes exercising his functions as herald-butcher and founding a sacrificial ritual in honor of the twelve gods either at Olympia or elsewhere. But in any case, the god's activity is considered incidental or parenthetical to the narrative. It is one of the great merits of Kahn's analysis to have recognized the critical importance of the proceedings for the hymn's presentation of Hermes as the god of passage and mediation, although she pays less attention to its significance in the dynamic of the narrative movement. Nevertheless, her overall conclusion regarding the scene is completely persuasive: "Hermes is able to affirm not only the divinity of the Twelve Gods, but also his own. But, defined by his own history, he will become a god 'friendly to man.' "[78]

I do not pretend to be able to solve all the textual and interpretive difficulties in this passage and indeed wonder whether some questions can be answered with certainty without new evidence. But before becoming entangled in problems of detail, I think it well to state what I consider to be the general import of this episode within the total economy of the hymn. Up to now, Hermes' precise status has remained in doubt: Is he a god or a mortal? While laying claim to divinity in his improvised hymn to himself, Hermes is simultaneously beset with an all-too-human hunger, which, however, he insists on appeasing with none other than the immortal cattle of Apollo. Moreover, the one mortal he has encountered has failed to recognize the new god. Hermes' "identity crisis" is only resolved when he finds himself unable to swallow the meat he had prepared for himself. With this unmistakable evidence of his divinity, Hermes returns to Maia's cave, which now is called a "rich temple" (πίονα νηόν [148]), because it has proved to be the habitation of a god.

It remains to attempt to interpret the details of Hermes' treatment

[76] Brown (1947), p. 102.
[77] Radermacher (1931), pp. 190–91. K. O. Müller, "Die Hermes-Grotte bei Pylos," in *Hyperboreisch-römische Studien für Archäologie*, ed. E. Gerhard (Berlin, 1833), pp. 310–16, believed he had discovered the cave described in the hymn in the vicinity of Pylos. For persuasive arguments against this identification, see Ludwich (1908), pp. 100–1; and Radermacher, p. 190.
[78] Kahn (1978), p. 66.

of the cows he slaughters by the banks of the Alpheus. In two recent studies, Kahn and Burkert have examined the scene with great thoroughness but have arrived at rather different conclusions.[79] In Kahn's subtle but sometimes confused analysis, Hermes' actions represent a pseudo- or antisacrifice in which the rules governing Olympian sacrifice, established to define the distinctions between gods and mortals, are perverted. The conscious inversion of ritual norms, expressed through the systematic confusion of sacrificial vocabulary, permits Hermes to create a breach in the boundaries separating mortals from the gods and thus to effect a passage between them. In so doing, Hermes enacts his essential function as a liminal and mediating divinity.

Disputing Kahn's interpretation of the scene as a pseudosacrifice, Burkert returns to the more conventional view that the episode offers an account of the origins of a local ritual in honor of Hermes and the twelve gods celebrated in the vicinity of Olympia.[80] After noting that our knowledge of Greek sacrifice is extremely fragmentary and that many local practices diverge from those described in Homer and Hesiod, Burkert adduces parallels to those elements in the hymn that Kahn has labeled uncanonical deviations from Olympian sacrificial practice. He concludes that there is no reason to suppose that Hermes' activity by the Alpheus does not represent an actual ritual. In the absence of corroborating evidence, Burkert's contentions can be neither proved nor disproved, yet certain doubts arise on the basis of the very parallels he cites. For example, although the use of the pit hearth can be paralleled in hero cult, Hermes clearly intends an offering to the twelve Olympians. It is not each element, but the *conjunction* of elements that appears contradictory. Moreover, I would contend that, even if the actions performed by Hermes provide an etiology for a specific ritual (and certain elements can indeed be linked to cult practices associated with Hermes), nevertheless the description of those acts must manifest some kind of coherence on the narrative level. A mythological hymn does not resemble the text of a sacred law. Thus, even if we knew that the activity described in the poem was exactly reenacted in cult, we would not be excused from interpreting that activity in the context of the mythological narrative.

Finally, a more general consideration: I have argued that, as a genre,

[79] Kahn (1978), pp. 41–73; Burkert (1984), pp. 835–45.

[80] Cf. Eitrem (1906), p. 257. Brown (1947), pp. 102–22, insists that the hymn depicts the cult of the Twelve Gods as practiced in Athens in the third quarter of the sixth century B.C.

the major Homeric Hymns display a marked Panhellenic/Olympian tendency. Despite its many eccentricities, the *Hymn to Hermes* does not constitute an exception to this rule. It is perhaps clearest in the role the poem assigns to Zeus,[81] but it is equally evident in its geographical orientation, which situates Apollo's cattle originally near Olympus and makes their destination the vicinity of Olympia—a topography readily intelligible to a Panhellenic audience. Burkert, on the other hand, posits a local Arcadian cult that has left no traces. It is, I submit, inherently improbable that a Panhellenic document like the *Hymn to Hermes*, which self-consciously avoids or transforms local legend, would incorporate a description of an obscure ritual, comprehensible only to a limited local audience.

The interpretations of Burkert and Kahn, as well as those of other scholars, share a common assumption that what transpires by the Alpheus must be understood as a sacrifice of one kind or another.[82] I suggest, however, that the operative model is a different institution, one, to be sure, closely associated with sacrifice, but nevertheless sufficiently distinct to have its own set of rules and norms: the *dais* or feast.

The conventions governing the *dais* have been clearly spelled out by Saïd.[83] As she points out, the name itself refers not to the consumption of food but derives from the act of division or apportionment; hence the fomulaic expression, δαὶς ἐΐση, referring to a fair or equable distribution. As a social institution, the *dais* affirms the communal bonds and mutual obligations of those admitted to participate in it.

> Commensality is, in effect, a sign of belonging to a common community. A proof of this is that the gods do not take part in the banquets of men except in a mediated and distant way. "They take their share of the hecatombs" (*Il.* ix.535) through their altar, which

---

[81] Cf. Lenz (1975), pp. 69–75, and my discussion of the end of the hymn later in this chapter.

[82] AHS (1936), p. 269, speak of Hermes' "institution of burnt sacrifice." Humbert (1936), p. 111, refers to "l'invention du feu et le sacrifice." Cf. Càssola (1975), p. 525. T. Van Nortwick, "The Homeric *Hymn to Hermes*" (Ph.D. diss., Stanford University, 1975), pp. 108–10, compares the diction of the episode to the traditional sacrifice sequence in Homer and notes that "not only does the poet neglect to include even one line from the Homeric feast/sacrifice scenes, he even seems at times willfully to avoid using an obvious Homeric phrase." This "perverse attitude," as Van Nortwick calls it, may be due to the fact that Hermes is not performing a sacrifice at all.

[83] S. Saïd, "Les Crimes des prétendants, la maison d'Ulysse et les festins de l'Odyssée," in *Études de littérature ancienne* (Paris, 1979), pp. 13–22. Cf. G. Berthiaume, *Les Rôles du mágeiros* (Leiden, 1982), pp. 50–51, and the comments in the preface (p. xvi) by M. Detienne.

receives the offerings of wine and fat that are burned, but they are no longer truly the guests of men as they were before the intervention of Prometheus.[84]

According to Saïd, the fair or equable *dais* involves two distinct kinds of apportionment. The first is the division into strictly equal parts (*moirai*), which affirms the parity of all the members of the banquet. The second constitutes the portion of honor, the *geras*, assigned in recognition of individual worth or esteem. Thus the *dais eisē* declares, on the one hand, the equality of the participants as members of a social group and, on the other, the pervasive presence of a social hierarchy based on *timē*. It is in light of the conventions of the *dais* that much of Hermes' activity becomes intelligible.

With his newly manufactured fire sticks, Hermes first ignites the dry wood he has piled into a pit hearth. Such a *bothros* is used for sacrifices to the dead and in hero cult and thus may be contrasted with the raised altar of Olympian sacrifice, but it also resembles the simple domestic hearth, the *eschara*.[85] It suggests that Hermes may not be engaged in performing either an Olympian or chthonic sacrifice, but may simply be cooking dinner. Then, in an act demanding considerable force, the god drags[86] two of the cows near the fire and hurls them on their backs. With their bellowing and panting, the victims appear to protest the violence of their treatment. Kahn is surely correct to contrast this procedure to the usual preliminaries of sacrifice in which everything is done to make it appear that the victim consents to his own immolation.[87] Rolling the beasts over, Hermes now pierces their spines. His method of dispatching the cattle closely parallels his procedure with the tortoise whereby he transformed the living, silent, wild creature into a dead, domestic, instrument of song, the δαιτὸς ἑταίρη (31). But in the case of the cows, the transition is not merely from life to death: the immortal cows become mortal; they are transferred from the possession of the gods to the domain of men. In sacrificial ritual, the victim is removed from the mortal

---

[84] Saïd (1979), pp. 17–18.

[85] Cf. Kahn (1978), p. 53. For the ancient testimonia, see J. Rudhardt, *Notions fondamentales de la pensée religieuse et actes constitutifs du culte dans la Grèce classique* (Geneva, 1958), p. 250.

[86] I do not understand why Burkert (1984), p. 837, detects here an allusion to the practice of "sullevare i buoi." The text speaks only of dragging (ἕλκε in line 116).

[87] Cf. Kahn (1978), p. 58; Burkert (1984), p. 837, n. 15, cites *Iliad* xx.404 as a parallel.

sphere and submits to becoming the possession of the gods; here, by contrast, a desacralization of the previously sacred cows occurs.

The god proceeds to butcher and cook the desacralized meat. Then stretching the hides on a boulder, where "even now" they remain visible, Hermes divides the cooked meat into twelve portions. This division stands in sharp contrast to the division of sacrifice, where different parts receive different treatment depending on the recipient, with the gods assigned their share before the mortal celebrants. We could say that Hermes simply omits the sacrifice, that is, the offering to the gods, except that the meat has already been desacralized; no part of it could properly be offered to the gods.[88] As at a *dais*, all the edible meat is divided into equal portions. Hermes aims not at establishing a vertical hierarchy based on distinctions of rank and status, but a horizontal distribution affirming equality. Acting not as a priest or sacrificer, but as a host who gives a feast among *philoi* deemed to be equals, by his hospitality Hermes creates a bond of *philotēs*.[89] An unusual epithet, χαρμόφρων, "with joyous spirit" or "cheerful" (127), describes the god as he prepares the food. It points to his dual role as both steward and host of the feast and finds a parallel in the Homeric formula describing the housekeeper who serves her guests, χαριζομένη παρεόντων. The *dais* itself is the very locus of *charis*.[90] Having gone to great pains to divide each of the twelve portions equably, Hermes now adds a "perfect portion of honor," τέλεον γέρας, to each, refusing thereby to make any distinctions among the intended recipients.[91] In addition, to ensure absolute equality, he has assigned the portions by lot. The casting of lots presupposes a community of equals and ignores the existence of hierarchical differences among its members.[92]

[88] Cf. M. Mauss, "Les fonctions sociales du sacré," in *Oeuvres* 1, ed. V. Karady (Paris, 1968), pp. 193–307, who defines sacrifice as both a consecration followed by a deconsecration. Hermes' actions involve only the latter. The cows are originally *hiera*, that is, they belong to the gods; their slaughter and butchery constitutes an act of desacralization.

[89] Cf. Benveniste (1969), 1: 341–44.

[90] Cf. Saïd (1979), p. 23. See also *Odyssey* 15.319–24 where the disguised Odysseus advertises to the suitors his stewardly skills, which he owes to the "will of Hermes, who grants *charis* and *kudos* to the works of all men."

[91] Incorrectly identifying the *geras* with the portion reserved for the gods, Kahn (1978), p. 63, argues that Hermes here promiscuously confuses the portions destined for men and gods, which ought to be kept separate. But as the text makes clear, the *geras* is equivalent to the νῶτα γεράσμια (122), the portion destined for the guest of honor. Hermes' procedure follows the conventions of the *dais*, but not the sacrifice. Kahn, p. 65, is correct when she notes that "en tirant au sort leurs parts, Hermès traite donc le groupe divin comme une communauté humaine."

[92] Eitrem (1906), p. 258, misunderstands Hermes' recourse to lots: "um so komischer

Thus in the *Iliad*, when Zeus seeks to impose his supremacy over Poseidon on the basis of his greater age and intelligence, Poseidon tries to establish his equality with his brother by reminding Zeus of the ancient division by lot of the cosmos among the three sons of Cronus.[93] Significantly, the appeal to lots is most effective in the mouth of an underdog.

Hermes, then, does not perform a sacrifice, but hosts a *dais* for the Olympians as *par inter pares*. His division of the portions reflects his claim to equality within the community and denies any valid distinction in *geras*, and hence in *timē*, among his guests. The god's actions express a kind of wishful thinking. In rejecting the notion of a stratified pantheon, Hermes implies that *all* the Olympians are equally deserving of *timē*—a claim fully intelligible on the part of the youngest and least honored among them. It expresses a desire to enter the company of the gods on an equal footing.

The banquet is ready, but the guests do not arrive. For all his elaborate preparations, Hermes has ignored a fact of fundamental importance: the gods do not eat meat. In fact, as Hermes soon discovers, the inability to consume meat is a hallmark of divinity:

ἔνθ᾽ ὁσίης κρεάων ἠράσσατο κύδιμος Ἑρμῆς·
ὀδμὴ γάρ μιν ἔτειρε καὶ ἀθάνατόν περ ἐόντα
ἡδεῖ᾽· ἀλλ᾽ οὐδ᾽ ὥς οἱ ἐπείθετο θυμὸς ἀγήνωρ
καί τε μάλ᾽ ἱμείροντι περῆν᾽ ἱερῆς κατὰ δειρῆς.

Then glorious Hermes desired the desacralized portion of meat;
for the sweet smell weakened him, even though he was immortal;
but not even so could his valiant heart persuade him,
despite his great desire, to allow it to pass down his holy throat.

(130–33)

It is not, as Hermes intended, the communal consumption of the *dais* that establishes Hermes' membership in the company of the Olympians, but, on the contrary, his *inability* to partake of it that confirms his divinity.[94] In recognition of Hermes' newly established status, the poet now calls

---

wird die Wirkung sein, wenn man den Hermes eben durch diese Entscheidung des Looses sich selbst die beste und erste Portion zuteilen lässt." But Burkert (1984), p. 839, rightly emphasizes that the use of lots presupposes the equality of the participants.

[93] *Iliad* xv.187–95.

[94] Cf. Vernant (1979b), p. 242: "Hermès se garde de manger les viandes qu'il a préparées. S'il y goûtait, il deviendrait un homme."

him a *daimōn* (138). Whereas the immortal cattle have crossed from the divine to mortal realm, Hermes has passed into the domain of the gods, thus enacting his essential function as traverser of boundaries.

The remnants of the failed *dais* attest to Hermes' egregious error concerning the nature of his own divinity. The god therefore quickly moves to conceal the evidence of his embarrassing mistake.[95] The meats are placed high inside the cave, suspended appropriately "in midair," between heaven and earth, gods and men, as a "sign of his recent theft." Hermes then burns the head and feet of the cattle, throws his wonderful sandals into the Alpheus, and tries to efface all traces of the fire. In the sequel, it will turn out that his efforts are only partially successful. Although the banquet beside the Alpheus constitutes an essential preliminary to the god's acquisition of *timai*, it also remains an enduring source of embarrassment, attesting to a lasting ambiguity in Hermes' divine status. We can now understand why the poet omitted mention of the nocturnal events by the banks of the Alpheus in his catalog of the god's *kluta erga* (16).

The young Olympian's inventions, the fire sticks and the *dais*, in a sense parallel those of Prometheus—but in reverse order. In the Hesiodic account, Prometheus likewise divides a great ox (μέγαν βοῦν ... δασσάμενος [*Theogony.* 536–37]) at the time when gods and mortals still feasted together (cf. *Catalog of Women*, fr. 1 Merkelbach-West). The wily Titan attempted to trick Zeus by offering the gods the bones hidden in shining fat, but giving men the edible parts. The Promethean *dais* institutes the permanent separation of gods and men, symbolized in the sacrifice.[96] Hermes' *dais*, on the other hand, presupposes that separation and inaugurates a purely human institution, the apportionment of edible meats at a human banquet, the *dais eisē*. Similarly, the fire produced by Hermes differs from the Promethean fire that was stolen from the gods after Zeus had "hidden" it from men (*Theogony.* 563–67; *Works and Days* 50). Whereas the fire stolen by the Titan is the product of *hybris* and attests to the impossibility of successfully deceiving the *mētis* of Zeus, Hermes' fire, the product of *mētis* and *technē*, has a human and civilizing

[95] Radermacher (1931), p. 100, says, not quite accurately, that Hermes attempts "die Spuren des Diebstahls zu vernichten." Not the theft of the cattle, but their butchering, is concealed.

[96] Rudhardt (1981), pp. 216–17, insists, I think rightly, that Prometheus does not invent Olympian sacrifice but, rather, that his actions entail a series of consequences that lead to its foundation. Ultimately, Prometheus's acts of separation lead to a new form of communication between gods and men.

function.[97] To be sure, Hermes' new method of producing fire presupposes Prometheus's theft, just as the young Olympian's *dais* presupposes the ancient Promethean division. The action of the *Hymn to Hermes* takes place in a decidedly post-Promethean era; the precise moment in which the narrative is set can be further pinpointed and specified. The old man of Onchestus offers an emblem of post-Promethean man, separated from the gods and reduced to a level of solitary brutishness.[98] According to the hymn, it is not Prometheus, but Hermes whose *technē* and *mētis* will alleviate that state. Hermes' new πυϱὸς τέχνη allows mankind to manufacture and control fire at will. Moreover, far from being an instrument of separation, the new *dais* becomes a means of uniting men into social communities through the fundamental human institution of commensality.

The *Hymn to Hermes* thus suggests that the Titan Prometheus brought mankind down to a brutish state, but the Olympian Hermes, a true friend to man, enabled him to ascend to the level of civilization. By crediting Hermes with mankind's technological advances, the hymn-poet dissolves the disturbing ambiguities inherent in the traditional Prometheus figure, who is both an enemy of Zeus and a friend to man. While mankind's loss of intimacy with the gods arises from Prometheus's hybristic challenge to Olympus, Hermes' beneficent actions are in complete harmony with the mind of Zeus (cf. 10). Olympus is blameless.

I have argued that the scene by the Alpheus represents neither a sacrifice in the usual sense nor a pseudo-sacrifice, but a *dais*, a primarily human institution. Yet Hermes' actions also impinge upon the relations between gods and mortals and therefore possess a religious dimension. Whereas at the *dais* at Mecone, commemorated in Olympian sacrifice, Prometheus precipitated the alienation of the gods from mankind, through his *dais* by the Alpheus Hermes draws them closer together. As divine mediator and friend to man, the new god's conciliatory action also finds an appropriate commemoration within the context of the *dais*.

The main literary testimony comes from Book 14 of the *Odyssey*,

[97] Cf. Kahn (1978), p. 52: "ainsi le feu d'Hermès est bien un feu technique: fabriqué par *technē* et produit par *mētis*, il s'oppose au feu volé par Prométhée."

[98] Burkert (1984), p. 842, acknowledges the similarity between Prometheus and Hermes: "il *trickster* che constituisce la *condicio humana* in opposizione agli dei." But he does not recognize the exemplary function of the old man of Onchestus when he adds: "certo il nostro testo non fa alcuna esplicita menzione degli uomini." Horace, who understood much about Hermes, would have recognized in the old man the "feros cultus hominum recentum" (*Odes* 1.10.2).

where the pious Eumaeus slaughters a pig in honor of his new guest, the disguised Odysseus (14.418–56).[99] The swineherd's sacrifice begins with a prayer "to all the gods" followed by a modest version of the usual Olympian sacrifice of meat wrapped in fat and burned on the hearth (*eschara*). The remaining meat is then roasted. Eumaeus, whose expertise in such matters is emphasized,[100] proceeds to distribute the cooked meat into seven portions, setting one aside for Hermes and the Nymphs, before serving the other guests. For Odysseus he reserves the portion of honor: νώτοισιν δ᾽ Ὀδυσῆα διηνεκέεσσι γέραιρεν (437).

The portion assigned to Hermes is exactly equivalent to that of the other participants. Whereas the other gods receive their canonical offering of burnt meat as a preliminary to the feast, Hermes is simply counted as one of the guests invited to take part in the *dais eïsē*—and not even as the guest of honor. In his analysis of the passage, Kadletz connects the offering to Hermes with the common practice of leaving bits of food for travelers at the stone markers or herms along country roads.[101] The hungry traveler who came upon these tidbits would consider them a lucky find, a *hermaion*, a gift from Hermes, the protector of voyagers. However that may be, offerings of cooked food stand midway between Olympian sacrifice and chthonic holocausts and imply an intimacy between the giver and the intended recipient.[102] Not surprisingly, these so-called *tra-*

---

[99] I follow the analysis of E. Kadletz, "The Sacrifice of Eumaios the Pig Herder," *GRBS* 25 (1984): 99–105. Orgogozo (1949): 157, perceptively remarks: "pour avancer dans la connaissance du dieu [Hermès], les quelques vers sur le sacrifice d'Eumée ont plus de signification que la grande scène chez Calypso." But she goes on to characterize Hermes as the god of Dumézil's third function, the protector of those who labor.

[100] *Odyssey* 14.432–34: "the swineherd stood up to distribute the feast. For he excelled in the knowledge of appropriate shares. And apportioning them, he divided them all into seven parts." αἴσιμα here has its root meaning of "appropriate shares or portions."

[101] Kadletz (1984), pp. 103–5.

[102] K. Meuli, "Griechische Opferbräuche," in *Phyllobolia für Peter von der Mühll* (Basel, 1946), p. 196, believes that all such food offerings originated in the cult of the dead or heroes and only were transferred to the gods when the Olympians became more human and more intimate with their worshipers. On Eumaeus's meal for Hermes and the Nymphs, he comments: "ihm sind diese dunklen, oft unheimlichen Mächte . . . nah und vertraut wie die Heroen des Landes" (p. 214). Nilsson, *GGR* (1955), 1: 145, n. 2, denies that *Speiseopfer* must be connected with chthonic or hero cult. D. Gill, "*Trapezomata*: A Neglected Aspect of Greek Sacrifice," *Harvard Theological Review* 67 (1974): 135–36, also expresses doubts and suggests that such meals may have had their origins in popular religion or house cults. Cf. Kadletz (1984), p. 105, who characterizes Eumaeus's offering as "rustic." Burkert (1977), p. 176, similarly suggests that these "Göttermahle" belong "mehr um Familienbrauch als um Polis-Religion." Gill, p. 137, further notes that "the earlier evidence . . . seems to indicate that the god was thought of as himself being present

pezomata are widely attested for certain other mediating figures such as Hecate and the Dioscuroi as well as Hermes.[103] While Hermes ultimately becomes a full member of the Olympian community, nevertheless, as "companion of the feast," δαιτὸς ἑταῖρος (436), he continues to participate in the human *dais* he has founded. That institution, as we have seen, constitutes the basis for all human associations. In this context, we should recall the proverbial wisdom mentioned by Plutarch: "whenever a sudden silence falls during a meeting or an assembly, people say that Hermes has come in."[104] Hermes' sudden, uncanny, one might almost say, demonic, presence attests not only to his patronage of social institutions,[105] but also to his power to mediate between the Olympians and mankind.

The new Olympian, then, invents neither fire nor the sacrifice. Rather, he reinstitutes the *dais* that Prometheus had perverted, but with an important modification: gods and mortals will never again feast together as they did at Mecone. However, a new link between them has been forged through the action of the divinity who "keeps company with all mortals and immortals" (576).

Thus far, I have considered the consequences of Hermes' *dais* for human society and for the relations between gods and mortals. But the proceedings by the Alpheus also have an unquestionable significance for the gods themselves. Although Hermes in no sense founds the cult of the twelve Gods,[106] through his actions he establishes the community of the

---

at the meal in some way." The common denominator in all such offerings may, in fact, be intimacy.

[103] For the Dioscouroi as "Hausgötter," see Nilsson, *GGR* (1955), 1: 409–10. For Hecate as a mediator, see J. S. Clay, "The Hecate of the Theogony," *GRBS* 25 (1984): 24–38. The *deipna* of Hecate, deposited at crossroads, resemble those left at the herms. See T. Kraus, *Hekate* (Heidelberg, 1960), pp. 71, 85, 101, 151, for the relation between Hecate and Hermes: "mit Hermes hat Hekate viel gemein" (p. 71). For the *deipna* of Hecate, see Kraus, pp. 88 and 91; and Meuli (1946), p. 200. Consider also the discussion of Burkert (1977), pp. 175–76, who draws attention to the meal offerings to Zeus *Philios*: "dieser Zeus, mit dem man so vertraut verkehrt, ist offenbar nicht ohne weiteres identisch mit dem blitzeschleudernden Himmelsgott." For a Roman parallel, see G. Dumézil, *Archaic Roman Religion*, trans. P. Krapp (Chicago, 1970), 1: 182–83. Cf. also the discussion of *daps* by É. Benveniste in *Problèmes de linguistique générale* (Paris, 1966), 1: 323–25.

[104] *De garrulitate* 502: ὅταν ἐν συλλόγῳ τινί σιωπὴ γένηται τὸν Ἑρμῆν ἐπεισεληλυθέναι λέγουσι. On Kahn's ([1978], p. 184) misinterpretation of this proverb, see Hübner (1986), p. 157.

[105] Cf. J. Toutain, "Hermès, dieu social chez les Grecs," *Revue d'Histoire et de Philosophie Religieuses* 12 (1932): 297–98; and Watkins (1970), p. 345, who calls Hermes "the patron god of the fundamental anthropological and sociological principle of *reciprocity*."

[106] Pindar ascribes the foundation of the cult in Olympia to Heracles (*Olympian* 10.49); Hellanicus (*Fr.G.H.* 4, fr. 6) names Deucalion as its founder.

twelve Olympians as a complete and permanent society. Henceforth, there will always be twelve Olympians, no more and no less.[107] With Hermes' birth and acceptance into that society, the divine cosmos, hitherto incomplete and lacking, arrives at its final form and *telos*. With its threefold impact on both the divine and human community, as well as their interrelationships, Hermes' nocturnal *dais* thus introduces a *novus ordo rerum*.

Confrontations

Just at dawn, Hermes returns to the cave on Cyllene, now called a rich temple (148), slipping through the keyhole without a sound.[108] Quickly settling back into his cradle and wrapping himself in his swaddling clothes, the god plays the babe-in-arms, clutching his "lovely tortoise" all the while. The return to cave and cradle signals the end of the god's *kluta erga*. After deeds will come words. Three confrontations, first with his mother, then with Apollo, and finally with Zeus—clearly an ascending sequence—will occupy the center of the poem. With the sure knowledge of his divinity, Hermes' status has changed. But it remains anomalous: he is indeed a god, but one without *timai*. The rest of the hymn will depict his acquisition of *timai*.

Hermes' consciousness of his new status informs his conversation with Maia.[109] For the first time, he clearly states his intention of acquiring the privileges that by rights accompany it. The poet underlines the changed situation by introducing Maia's speech as an exchange between gods, θεὰν θεός (154). No doubts remain concerning Hermes' divinity

[107] The number twelve remains canonical despite the varying personnel. See O. Weinreich, "Zwölfgötter," in *Ausführliches Lexikon der griechischen und römischen Mythologie* 6, ed. W. H. Roscher, esp. cols. 838–41. Cf. Wilamowitz (1959), 1, 323, n. 3, who, oddly enough, believes that the hymn-poet does not count Hermes among the twelve; so also Radermacher (1931), p. 99. Welcker (1857), 2: 164–65, suggests that the cult of the twelve Gods may have been founded by Solon.

[108] Cf. Càssola (1975), pp. 160 and 527, who notes the similarity between Hermes' movements and the dream in *Odyssey* 4.802 and 836, and Hermes' relation to dreams (cf. *Hermes* 14).

[109] Robert (1906), p. 406, claimed the passage was an interpolation; Radermacher (1931), p. 214, finds the conversation between Maia and Hermes to have no bearing on the narrative. But Kuiper (1910), p. 45, recognizes its importance, calling lines 166–75 the *summa carminis*. F. Dornseiff, "Zum homerischen Hermeshymnos," *Rheinisches Museum* 87 (1938): 83, regards the verses as Hermes' "Lebensprogramm" and compares them with lines 131–32 of the *Hymn to Apollo*.

127

or Maia's. Scolding her infant son, Maia, who is well aware of what he
has been up to, predicts either that Apollo will take him away in
ἀμήχανα δεσμά, or that Hermes will become a thief in the glens. Binding in chains, of course, constitutes the traditional punishment for insubordinate gods, and Apollo will, in fact, try to tie up the new god, but
without success. Maia's second prediction will in a way be fulfilled. The
liminal god always remains a bit of an outlaw, inhabiting the marginal
spaces between city and wilds. Maia concludes:

μεγάλην σε πατὴρ ἐφύτευσε μέριμναν
θνητοῖς ἀνθρώποισι καὶ ἀθανάτοισι θεοῖσι.

Your father begot you to be a great trouble
to mortal men and to the immortal gods.

(160–61)

Her words remind us that Hermes' birth is in accordance with Zeus's
intentions (cf. 10).[110] Despite the trouble he causes, the thievish god is a
necessary component of the divine plan.

Although Hermes has played the helpless child before and soon will
again in his confrontation with Apollo, here he brushes off his mother's
rebuke by telling her not to treat him like a baby. In his reply, he unveils
his intention to get the *timai* appropriate to his newly ascertained divinity.
He will use whatever means (τέχνης ... ἤ τις ἀρίστη) are necessary
to attend to their best interests. Hermes proposes to exchange their habitation, from what he disparagingly calls a "moldly cave" (172), for Olympus; their present isolation, for full participation in the company of the
gods; and, finally, their status as gods who receive neither prayers nor
gifts from men, for the wealth and prosperity due divinity. He sums up
his intentions:

ἀμφὶ δὲ τιμῆς
κἀγὼ τῆς ὁσίης ἐπιβήσομαι ἧς περ Ἀπόλλων.

As for *timē*,
I too will enter in on the same *hosiē* as Apollo possesses.

(172–73)

The word *hosiē* has caused considerable perplexity here. Most commentators translate it simply as "cult," although the context suggests

[110] See S. C. Shelmerdine's forthcoming commentary.

128

something more precise. Hermes just complained that he gets neither nor gifts nor prayers from men (168). Here, he stakes a claim to *hosiē*—that is, precisely those offerings due the gods, equivalent to those of Apollo. This interpretation of *hosiē*, however, seems to contradict its usage in an earlier passage where the ὁσίη κρεάων, the "desacralized portion of meat,"[111] would not go down the god's "holy throat" (130). This passage as well as numerous others in which *ta hosia* are juxtaposed to *ta hiera* led Jeanmaire and Benveniste to define *hosiē* as "that which the divine law concedes to men"—that is, that which is profane, as opposed to *hiera*, that which belongs to the gods or is sacred.[112] When we apply this sense of *hosiē* to the present passage, a problem arises. Both Benveniste and Kahn believe that Hermes here *misuses* the term by speaking as a mortal rather than as a god. The *hosiē* Hermes covets are the profane goods that belong properly to men. Accordingly, the god's malapropism attests to his ambiguous status and his continued uncertainty as to whether he rightly belongs to the human or the divine realm.[113] But if our interpretation of the preceding scene is correct, Hermes returned from the Alpheus without the slightest remaining doubt concerning his divinity, firmly determined to acquire the prerogatives due his position—including *hosiē*.

If *hosiē* refers only to the profane goods the gods concede to mortals, our passage makes no sense. If, however, we adopt Benveniste's broader definition, "that which the divine law prescribes for men,"[114] we can elicit not only a satisfactory meaning from Hermes' pronouncement, but also one that illuminates the new god's dilemma. For what the divine law prescribes for men is first and foremost worship of the gods in the form of sacrifice and prayer; only secondarily does it concede profane goods to

[111] Cf. Burkert (1984), pp. 837–38, who translates *hosiē kreaon* as *daps profanata*: "si tratta della disponibilità della carne per la consumazione normale dopo il compimento dei riti sacri (*hiera*)." Of course, in the butchering of Apollo's cattle, no *hiera* had been performed; the immortal cows had been rendered intrinsically profane by their removal from the divine sphere. They could only be made *hiera* (i.e., resacralized) if they were ritually slaughtered and sacrificed. But this, as we have seen, Hermes fails to do. Kahn (1978), pp. 61–66, insists that in line 130 "l'usage du terme *hosios* est déplacé" and involves a "jeu de mots efficace" (p. 66). But I think her interpretation, for all its subtlety, is misconceived. *hosiē kreaon* has the expected meaning of "desacralized portion of meat" and coincides with its meaning in other passages where *ta hosia* are contrasted to *ta hiera*.

[112] Cf. Benveniste (1969), 2: 198–202; and H. Jeanmaire, "Le Substantif *hosia*," *REG* 58 (1945): 66–89. See also M. H. Van der Valk, "Zum Worte "ΟΣΙΟΣ,' " *Mnemosyne* 10 (1942): 113–40; Rudhardt (1958), pp. 30–38; and A. Pagliaro, "'Ιερός in Omero e la nozione di 'sacro' in Grecia," in *Saggi di critica semantica* (Messina, 1953), pp. 92–96.

[113] Benveniste (1969), 2: 201; and Kahn (1978), pp. 68–71.

[114] Benveniste (1969), 2: 198.

men for their own use. The specific context determines the precise meaning in each instance. *Only in a linguistically marked context* where *hosia* are explicitly or implicitly contrasted with *hiera* does *hosiē* mean *profanus*. Thus, the term *hosiē* encompasses *both* offerings to the gods *and* those things for the exclusive enjoyment of mortals.

Hermes' words do indeed betray a kind of confusion, not, however, in respect to his divine status, but rather in reference to the distinction between *hosiē* and *timē*.[115] Having amply affirmed his divinity, Hermes now desires to obtain the privileges and honors, that is, the *timai*, that go with it. These include membership in the company of the gods on Olympus and offerings from men (*hosiē*). Now, in the vocabulary of Olympus, *timē* denotes a god's sphere of influence. For example, archery constitutes one of Apollo's *timai*. Consequently, human success in archery depends on Apollo's goodwill, which can be ensured by appropriate offerings and prayers (*hosiē*). Their omission, on the other hand, may lead to failure.[116] Hermes' predicament arises from the anomalousness of his situation; he is unquestionably a god, but one as yet without recognized *timai*. When he lays claim to *hosiē* equivalent to Apollo's, Hermes, to be sure, betrays a kind of crude materialism, but, more important, he reveals his ignorance of the Olympian system: *hosiē* depends on *timai*. What Hermes ought to say is: "I want *timai* (e.g., prophecy or cow-herding) equal to

---

[115] The relation between *hosiē* and *timē* is also brought out in lines 469–72, a passage for which neither Jeanmaire nor Benveniste can offer a convincing explanation. Hermes is there describing, somewhat enviously, Zeus's special relationship to Apollo (I print the Greek text as I think it should be punctuated and propose γέ for δέ, the manuscript reading at line 470):

> ... φιλεῖ δέ σε μητίετα Ζεύς·
> ἐκ πάσης ὁσίης ἔπορεν γέ τοι ἀγλαὰ δῶρα
> καὶ τιμάς· σὲ δέ φασι δαήμεναι ἐκ Διὸς ὀμφῆς
> μαντείας.

> ... and Zeus who has *mētis* loves you;
> from every *hosiē* he [Zeus] has granted you splendid gifts
> and *timai*; they say you have learned from the voice of Zeus
> prophecies.
> (469–72)

Prophecy goes closely with *timai*, while *hosiē* produces splendid gifts, i.e., from men. Zeus, then, not only grants Apollo his *timai*, but also enjoins upon men the obligation to make offerings to his favorite son.

[116] Cf., for example, *Iliad* xxiii.862–83, where Teucer fails to promise offerings to Apollo and loses the archery contest, while Meriones remembers and wins.

those Apollo possesses, and then I will be as rich in *hosiē* as he." By demanding *hosiē* rather than *timai*, Hermes makes manifest his anomalous position vis-à-vis the established gods who already possess their clearly defined domains. As yet, Hermes possesses no *timai* and remains ignorant of what *timai* will be his. He does, however, know how he intends to go about acquiring them: through his wits, *technē* and *mētis*. Ironically, the young god is unaware that every action he has performed since the moment of his birth, from the making of the lyre to the butchering of the cattle, will ultimately become a component of his *timai*. Thus, Hermes is already well on his way to becoming the god of skillful invention, of trickery and theft, of piercing and penetrating, and of transitions and mediations.

In pronouncing the threat that follows (174–81), Hermes reveals a new awareness of the governance of Olympus. It is Zeus's place to assign and guarantee *timai*, and Hermes must ultimately receive them from him. If Zeus should refuse, then Hermes intends to become the "leader of thieves" by penetrating (ἀντιτορήσων, [178])[117] Delphi itself and stealing Apollo's countless treasures. Here again we find the confusion between *timai* and the gifts due the gods from men. To achieve full divine status and thus to get *timai*, Hermes must somehow insinuate himself into Olympus; failing that, he intends at least to acquire the *hosiē*, that is, the material offerings due the gods, by plundering Apollo's shrine. To be sure, the threat is never realized, for in the sequel Hermes will manage to finagle his way into Olympus, characteristically, by a devious and indirect route.

At dawn, when Hermes has retired to his cradle, Apollo sallies forth in search of his cattle and comes to Onchestus. One cardinal fact stands out: despite the information given by the old man (who has suddenly become garrulous, for Hermes' passage seems to have endowed him with speech), despite the god's divinatory powers, and despite his discovery of the tracks, Apollo remains unable to discover the whereabouts of the contraband cows. For all intents and purposes, they have vanished into thin air;[118] Hermes alone can lead his brother to their hiding place.

In hot pursuit, Apollo is repeatedly obliged to marvel at Hermes' exploit, first, because only the bull and dogs were left behind. (Presumably, the bull would normally have followed the cows, while the dogs

[117] Cf. above, n. 39.
[118] Note that Autolycus, Hermes' favorite and, in some traditions, his son, has the same power. Cf. Hesiod, fr. 66–67 (Merkelbach-West).

would have pursued the thief.) Wonder, of course, is the typical reaction to an act of *mētis*.[119] When Apollo asks what *man* may have passed by with the cattle, the old man of Onchestus seems at first to sidestep the god's question, perhaps remembering Hermes' injunction, but then he reveals that he "thought he noticed" a *child* walking in a peculiar zigzag fashion and driving the cattle backward. As Apollo wordlessly continues on his way, an omen appears to him, indicating the thief to be a son of Zeus.[120] Apollo then rushes off in the direction of Pylos until he encounters the marvelous tracks (μέγα θαῦμα, [219]), first of the cattle, and then of Hermes, which do not resemble those of human beings or of wild animals, or even those of the half-human, half-bestial centaurs. If the tracks take after neither man nor beast, the perpetrator must indeed be divine, or at least semidivine. Now Apollo abruptly changes his course, in effect abandoning the pursuit of the tracks, and darts off to Cyllene. Of course, the tracks cannot lead him there, and we must assume that, just as Apollo learned through divination that the thief was Zeus's son, so he also knew that his home was in the Arcadian cave. Apollo's inability to discover his cattle renders his confrontation with Hermes inevitable.

The account of his search that Apollo later gives to Zeus (334–61) displays far greater coherence than the one contained in the narrative. Its order is clear and logical.[121] There, Apollo claims that he followed the tracks until he lost sight of them on the hard ground, then learned from the old man that Hermes was headed toward Pylos where (and here the god's account becomes vague) he hid the cattle and returned to Cyllene. Before Zeus, then, Apollo covers his own tracks and disguises his *aporia* and his inability to find his cows. In fact, Hermes has led Apollo on a wild goose chase, one that ends exactly as Hermes had desired—with his entrance into Olympus.

The confrontation between Apollo and Hermes (233–318) centers

[119] Cf. θαῦμα in lines 196 and 219. On the connection between *thauma* and *mētis*, see Kahn (1978), p. 75; and Clay (1983), p. 179.

[120] Cf. Shelmerdine's forthcoming commentary on lines 213–14, who notes that the formula Διὸς παῖδα Κρονίωνος "is new" and "could apply to any of Zeus' sons." Van Nortwick (1975), p. 36, notes that the poet could have used the metrically equivalent Διὸς καὶ Μαιάδος υἱόν here, but he misses the point of the poet's choice. What Apollo discovers through divination is the paternity of the cattle thief and hence his fraternal relationship to himself (cf. Διὸς υἱὸς ᾿Απόλλων in the next line).

[121] According to Robert (1906), p. 407, the contradictions between the narrative of Apollo's search (186–227) and his account to Zeus are due to textual transposition. In the inconsistencies, Radermacher (1931), pp. 138 and 211, detects traces of an earlier version that has not been fully integrated into the hymn.

on the contrast between the bullying, self-confident, older brother and the supposedly innocent, helpless, babe. For all its broad humor, the episode nevertheless offers a paradigm of the opposition of *biē* and *mētis*. *Mētis*, to be sure, loves to hide itself, pursuing its goals while dissembling as weakness and childlike innocence. As Apollo enters the cave, Hermes rolls himself up in his swaddling clothes, making himself appear even smaller and playing the sleepy newborn, "but, in truth, he was wide awake, clutching the tortoise under his arm" (242). Another of the hymn's extraordinary similes likens the infant god to the burning embers hidden under a pile of ashes.[122] The glowing spark of the god's ever-watchful *mētis* lies concealed under his infantile bearing:

παῖδ᾽ ὀλίγον δολίης εἰλυμένον ἐντροπίῃσι.

a tiny child, wrapped in guileful twistings.[123]

(245)

In violation of all human and divine etiquette, Apollo brusquely proceeds to rifle through the nooks and crannies of the cave, evidently still hoping to find his stolen cows, but discovering only the usual paraphernalia and treasures "such as the holy houses of the blessed gods contain" (251).[124] When his search proves unsuccessful, Apollo rudely and imperiously demands his cattle and immediately adds a brutal threat to hurl Hermes into the depths of Tartarus from which there can be no escape. Hermes answers Apollo's threat of force with "crafty words" (260). Boldly denying any knowledge of the cattle, he points out that he is an unlikely suspect.[125] In fact, he cares only for sleep and milk and other things appropriate to an infant. In any case, Apollo's accusation lacks credibility: no one would believe that a newborn could pass through

[122] Cf. *Odyssey* 5.488–91, where the exhausted Odysseus, hidden in a bed of leaves, is likened to a glowing ember. See Shelmerdine (1986), p. 58.

[123] Hermes is, of course, literally wrapped in swaddling clothes. Cf. line 151. The playful inversion of abstract and concrete is characteristic of the hymnist's style.

[124] There is no contradiction between the personal wealth of Maia, appropriate to a goddess, and the "loot" Hermes desires in lines 171–81. The latter comes from men and is a token of their honor and esteem for the god.

[125] H. Görgemanns, "Rhetorik und Poetik im homerischen Hermeshymnus," in *Studien zum antiken Epos*, ed. H. Görgemanns and E. A. Schmidt (Meisenheim, 1976), pp. 113–19, tries to develop a criterion for dating the hymn on the basis of Hermes' rhetoric and, especially, the argument from probability. But even if the early sophistic rhetoricians were the first to categorize this kind of argumentation, its basis—the distinction between appearance and reality—goes back to Homer.

a door with a herd of cattle; he is far too weak and tender to undertake such an exploit. Finally, Hermes offers to swear "on the head of his father" that he has neither committed the deed nor been a witness to it. In fact, he does not even know what cattle are; he has only heard rumors. The wily god has chosen his words carefully; neither here nor later, in the presence of Zeus, does he actually perjure himself; he never drove the cows through the door.[126]

Hermes' pose of wounded innocence, coupled with the brazen disclaimers, which, in turn, are belied by his restless and sparkling glance of intelligence (278–79), provokes Apollo to laughter. As Maia did before him, Apollo prophesies a career as cattle rustler and thief, "often penetrating (ἀντιτοροῦντα) at night well-inhabited houses" (283–84), for the wily-minded deceiver.

> τοῦτο γὰρ οὖν καὶ ἔπειτα μετ' ἀθανάτοις γέρας ἕξεις·
> ἀρχὸς φηλητέων κεκλήσεαι ἤματα πάντα.

> Such, then, even hereafter will be your privilege among the
>   immortals:
> to be called the prince of thieves for all time.
>
> (291–92)

The only prerogative Apollo is presently willing to concede to his little brother is the one the god has already claimed as his own. Then, reasserting his physical superiority, Apollo picks up the child, presumably with the intention of forcing him to reveal the hidden cows. But, this time, Hermes counters not with words, but with a Rabelaisian expression of gastric distress that compels the finicky Apollo to drop the infant—as Hermes had intended. For while Apollo is concerned only with the recovery of his cattle, Hermes has all along had another agenda: to exploit the issue of the theft to gain access to Olympus, as was already hinted at in his offer to swear on the head of Zeus. Repeating his brazen denials, Hermes demands that the case be brought before Zeus.

Although Apollo's accusation is just and Hermes wants nothing more than "to deceive with crafty and wheedling words" (317–18), the confrontation has ended in a standoff. *Polymētis* Hermes has encountered

---

[126] Cf. Baumeister (1860) and Gemoll (1886) on line 379. On "sophistische Eide," see R. Hirzel, *Der Eid: Ein Beitrag zu seiner Geschichte* (Leipzig, 1902), pp. 41–52, and esp. p. 43, for his definition of "die Kunst des Schwörens": "jene feinen Netze, die kunstvoll aus Worten geworben werden und in denen sich Thoren und Arglose fangen."

an opponent who is himself *polymēchanos* (319). Hermes briskly leads the way to what has been his goal all along, but now, for the first time, the erstwhile opponents are joined in the expression, "lovely children of Zeus" (Διὸς περικαλλέα τέκνα, [323]), foreshadowing their ultimate reconciliation.

On Olympus the company of the gods is gathered together in good fellowship.[127] It is, of course, this community that Hermes seeks to penetrate, smuggling himself in, so to speak, through the unorthodox means of a trial.

κεῖθι γὰρ ἀμφοτέροισι δίκης κατέκειτο τάλαντα.

There for both the scales of justice were established.

(324)

By bringing the case before Zeus, Hermes affirms his standing in the court of Olympus. At the same time, the scene replaces and parodies the standard hymnic motif describing the first entrance of a new divinity into Olympus.[128]

Low comedy is by no means absent from Olympus as Zeus opens the proceedings by jocularly inquiring where Apollo got "this substantial booty, a young child who resembles a herald in appearance" (330–31). Surely, a weighty matter has come before the divine assembly. Retorting that he is not the only greedy one, Apollo lays out his charges against the "piercing plunderer" and recounts his pursuit of the thief in a fashion that, as we have seen, masks his *aporia*. When Apollo has completed his presentation of the indictment, Hermes rises in his own defense. His speech constitutes a little masterpiece of equivocation. Opening with assurances of his truthfulness, he first avoids a direct refutaton of the allegations by countercharging Apollo with improper procedure—he brought no witnesses—and threats of violence against one far weaker than himself. Then Hermes again exploits the argument from probability: a mere infant would be unlikely to have the strength sufficient to rustle cattle. As before, the god's rebuttal is carefully worded: he did not, in fact, drive the cattle home, nor did he cross the threshold. Once again,

---

[127] This I take to be the meaning of the hapax εὐμιλίη (325) and the sense required by the passage, despite the metrical anomaly. The company of the gods is precisely what Hermes had desired (ἤματα πάντα μετ᾽ ἀθανάτοις δαρίζειν [170]) and what he finally achieves (πᾶσι δ᾽ ὅ γε θνητοῖσι καὶ ἀθανάτοισιν ὁμιλεῖ [576]).

[128] See above, n. 58.

while boldly proclaiming his innocence, Hermes skillfully avoids perjuring himself with an equivocal oath "by the foregates of the immortals" (384).[129] Finally, emphasizing his present helplessness, he closes with an appeal: someday, he hopes to be able to pay Apollo back, but, in the meantime, Zeus should protect the younger.

On hearing the expert denials of his naughty son, Zeus bursts into laughter (389–90) and renders his verdict: without further tricks, Hermes must lead the way and reveal the whereabouts of the cows. Legally, then, they remain the property of Apollo. If Hermes has further designs upon them, he must resort to other means to acquire them. To be sure, Hermes quickly accedes to Zeus's judgment. After all, he had never expected to refute Apollo's charges but, instead, had manipulated the situation to gain access to Olympus and thereby to win official recognition of his divine status and the paternity of Zeus.[130]

Deeds of Exchange

The last section of the poem (397–580) presents the final reconciliation of the two brothers. With Zeus's blessings, his two "lovely children" race off to the ford of the Alpheus. But, here again, the narrative takes a totally unexpected turn. Its interpretation remains obscure unless we keep in mind the events that transpired there on the previous night. As Hermes drives the cattle from their hiding place, Apollo suddenly notices the hides of the two slaughtered cows, which had been left lying outside of the cave. How on earth, marvels Apollo, could a mere infant muster

---

[129] Compare Hera's equivocal oath in *Iliad* xv.36–44 and Zeus's amused response. Here, Hermes' oath by the gates of Olympus seems especially appropriate for the young god who is seeking to penetrate them. For the parallels between the speeches to Apollo (261–77) and to Zeus (368–86), see Hübner (1986), pp. 169–71.

[130] Radermacher (1931), p. 200, recognizes that the scene on Olympus has a double function and presents not only the quarrel between the two brothers, but also "die Anerkennung des heimlich Geborenen, des σκότιος Hermes als eines grossen Gottes." The Olympian family resembles *mutatis mutandis* the Greek family, where the father retains the sole right to acknowledge his children as his own, to legitimize them, and to admit them into the family. Cf. J. Rudhardt, "La Reconnaissance de la paternité dans la société athénienne," *Museum Helveticum* 19 (1962): 51: "un enfant grec, en effet, n'appartient pas à la famille de son père, il n'est pas reconnu, du simple fait de sa naissance dans la maison familiale.... Il doit lui donner un nom et accomplir pour lui plusieurs rites qui ont pour effet de l'introduire dans la communauté familiale, de le faire connaître aux différents circles de ses proches et enregistrer parmi eux."

the requisite force to "cut the throats"[131] of the cattle. If he is so strong now, he may well grow even stronger in the future. Apollo's discovery entails a sudden shift in the relations between the two gods. Hitherto, he had taken for granted, and Hermes had insisted upon, the disparity in their physical strength. However, the evidence of the cowhides suggests that Hermes is a greater threat than previously assumed. Consequently, Apollo now tries to do what Maia had earlier predicted: to bind Hermes in mighty bonds. At this point, Hermes manages to divert the withies; first, they take root in the ground, and then they wind around the herd of cattle, immobilizing them "by the plans of thievish-minded Hermes" (413).[132] With his binding magic, Hermes demonstrates a power that transcends the simply physical and which, once again, arouses Apollo's wonder.

Apollo's marveling has not yet come to an end, for suddenly the plot takes another unforeseen twist. Out of the corner of his eye, Hermes has caught sight of the fire, apparently still glowing from the *dais* of the previous night.[133] In order to hide the remnants of the fire from Apollo, Hermes diverts the god's attention by producing his ultimate weapon: the lyre, which all along he has kept hidden on his person under his swaddling clothes.[134] We may well wonder why Hermes goes to such lengths to distract Apollo from the sight of the fire. If the evidence of the cowhides attested to Hermes' hitherto unsuspected strength, then the traces of the fire point to an event whose revelation would prove an acute embarrassment to the young god, for they attest to Hermes' earlier uncertainty concerning his divinity. In the meantime, Hermes has been accepted into Olympus, and now he wants only to acquire those *timai* that

---

[131] δειροτομῆσαι (405) makes clear that Apollo assumes that his younger brother had ritually slaughtered the cattle.

[132] Kuiper (1910), p. 43, compares the withies here to the vines and ivy in the *Hymn to Dionysus* (no. 7) 39–42. On binding and its relations to *mētis*, see Kahn (1978), pp. 81–117. For its connection with magic, see Brown (1947), pp. 12–13.

[133] At line 415, the manuscripts read πῦρ ἀμαρύσσων, which is retained by Radermacher (1931), AHS (1936), and Humbert (1936). Baumeister (1860) and Gemoll (1886) adopt the emendation, πύκν' ἀμαρύσσων, but all assume a reference to Hermes' sparkling or fiery glance and postulate a lacuna containing the object that Hermes was trying to hide: the lyre (Gemoll, Radermacher, Humbert), or the portions of meat (AHS). However, both Ludwich (1908) and Càssola (1975) were on the right track in reading πῦρ ἀμαρύσσον, but they continue to interpret the phrase in reference to the glance that the god is trying to conceal. Hesiod, *Theogony* 827, describing the fire flashing from the eyes of the monster Typhoeus, does not constitute a parallel. For Hermes' eyes may twinkle or flash, but they do not literally produce fire.

[134] Cf. Gemoll (1886), p. 186.

are the necessary appurtenances of a full-fledged member of the divine community. All signs of his earlier ignorance of his status, his cooking and attempting to consume the meat of the slaughtered cows, must at all costs be concealed from Apollo.

At this critical moment, Hermes unveils the lyre. The appearance of the instrument, long held in readiness, precipitates a sudden and unforeseen reversal in the situation, which is the characteristic mark of a successful ruse of *mētis*. The one who seemed the weaker and in imminent jeopardy unexpectedly manages to disarm and triumph over his opponent who is caught off balance and rendered without resources. Previously amazed by Hermes' ruses of *technē* and rhetoric, Apollo *polymēchanos* now falls victim to the ruse of desire.[135] The enchantment of Hermes' music binds Apollo more tightly than any chains. Its spell ensnares not just the body, but entrances the spirit with desire. Both the sound of the lyre and Hermes' singing are described as "lovable" (ἐρατόν [423]; ἐρατή [426]). Seduced by the new combination of words and music, Apollo surrenders to irresistible *eros* (434).

Whereas earlier Hermes improvised a hymn to himself, for Apollo he performs a theogony. Why should the god choose this particular song at this particular moment? The verb describing Hermes' activity, κραίνων (427), implies more than merely "to celebrate" or "sing"; it literally means "to bring to accomplishment with words," "to fulfill."[136] In a sense, Hermes' song has the power to bring order to the world. Beginning from primordial beginnings (ὡς τὰ πρῶτα γένοντο [428]) and proceeding in order of seniority (κατὰ πρέσβιν, [431]), it awards due honor to the gods (ἐγέραιρε [432; cf. 429]), and describes the whole, πάντ' ἐνέπων (433). Hermes' theme is nothing less than the ordered cosmos and the pantheon, in which each god possesses his own share or *moira*. Organized as it is on the principle of seniority, the song must end with the culminating event of theogony: Hermes' own birth and his accession to his own destined *moira* within the pantheon. The song itself is the vehicle of its own ends, for it will bring about the exchange that will form the basis for Hermes' *timai*.

Hermes appears to violate his own organizing principle by giving pride of place to Mnemosyne:

Μνημοσύνην μὲν πρῶτα θεῶν ἐγέραιρεν ἀοιδῇ
μητέρα Μουσάων, ἣ γὰρ λάχε Μαιάδος υἱόν.

[135] Cf. Kahn (1978), pp. 127–53.
[136] Cf. Benveniste (1969), 2: 35–42.

Mnemosyne he honored first of the gods in song,
the mother of the Muses, for she received as her lot the son of
Maia.

(429–30)

To be sure, the god's procedure is reminiscent of the practice of invocation, which normally introduces song. But the statement that Mnemosyne
"received Hermes as her lot" seems oddly contorted.[137] What it suggests
is that the god's new technique of making music renders possible the
kind of song over which Mnemosyne presides—namely, the song that
the Greeks called *epos*, hexameter verse, which embraces not only epic
but theogonic and hymnic poetry as well. Or perhaps we should say,
hymn poetry in particular. For the hymnist's characteristic vocation is to
"remember and not forget" the divinity he celebrates; and after complet-
ing his praises, he carefully reassures the deity that he will "remember"
him on another occasion. The birth of *epos*, then, is coeval with Hermes'
theogony. But as we have seen, this particular song could not be sung
until the theogonic process had come to completion. Song, to be sure,
does not create the cosmos, but it reveals and celebrates its order and
perfection, thereby "bringing to completion the immortal gods and the
dark earth" (427).[138] Hermes is the first to be able to sing a theogony,
because only with his birth is the configuration of the divine cosmos complete. As hymn poetry is coterminous with, and a continuation of, theo-

[137] I cannot understand Thalmann's ([1984], p. 154) statement that "in the extrava-
gance of Hermes' claim to be Maia's [*sic*, read Mnemosyne] allotted portion, the whole
concept of inspiration becomes a subject of sport." On a papyrus in the British Museum
(Pap. Gr. 46, 415–16) = K. Preisendanz and A. Henrichs, eds., *Papyri graecae magicae*,
2nd ed. [Stuttgart, 1973] 1: 194), Hermes is called a son of Mnēmē.

[138] A similar conceit underlies *Theogony* 68–74, where the Muses come to Olympus
after their birth and sing of Zeus's kingship after his defeat of Cronus and how Zeus εὖ
δὲ ἕκαστα / ἀθανάτοις διέταξε νόμους καὶ ἐπέφραδε τιμάς. Cf. Wilamowitz (1920),
p. 468. See also the testimony of Aristides 2.420 (= Pindar, fr. *31 [Snell-Maehler]):
"Pindar . . . says that at Zeus's wedding, when Zeus asked the gods if they lacked anything, they asked him to make some gods for himself, who would adorn all those great
works and his whole arrangement with words and music." This testimony is usually
associated with Pindar's first *Hymn to Zeus* (cf. Snell-Maehler and A. Turyn, *Pindari
Carmina* [Cracow, 1948]) and probably alludes to the birth of the Muses or, perhaps,
Apollo (cf. Wilamowitz [1920], p. 468, n. 2). But in any case, it suggests that the ordering
of the cosmos is not complete until it is celebrated in song. On Pindar's first *Hymn to
Zeus*, see B. Snell, "Pindar's Hymnos auf Zeus," in *Die Entdeckung des Geistes*, 4th ed.
(Göttingen, 1975), pp. 82–94. What Snell says of Pindar is equally valid for our hymnist:
"was Dichtung für die Welt bedeutet, konnte Pindar nicht eindrucksvoller sagen: am
Tag, da sich die Welt vollendet, stellt er fest: alle Schönheit ist unvollkommen, wenn
niemand da ist, sie zu preisen" (p. 87).

gonic poetry, Hermes' performance inevitably ends with a hymn to Hermes. We can now recognize that the god's earlier song, when he had not yet securely established his divinity or gained access to Olympus, was premature. His present song reveals that the divine hierarchy is henceforth complete.

Soon the lyre will pass from Hermes to Apollo, but Hermes will keep the epithet, "companion of the feast" (436). Just as he remains master of the craft that produced the lyre, so too Hermes retains possession of the seductive and enchanting art that forms an essential component of song. If his inventiveness and *technē* link him with Hephaestus and Athena, his spellbinding powers of persuasion, charm, and seduction join him to the realms of Aphrodite and Apollo, *eros* and music. *Mētis*, in fact, embraces them all.[139] Hermes unites their disparate domains in his own person, while retaining his distinctive mediating capacity to move between them.

Wonderstruck and racked with desire to possess Hermes' enchanting instrument, Apollo immediately declares his willingness to strike a bargain and to resolve their differences peacefully: the lyre is well worth the price of fifty cows. In rapid succession, Apollo questions his younger brother concerning the nature of "these wondrous works" (440). Were they his from birth, or did he receive them from a god or man who taught him "divine song" (442)? Of course, the answer to both questions is no: Hermes' *mētis* created both lyre and song; both involved joining together previously separate elements into a "wondrous new voice" (443). In fact, Apollo answers his own questions when he inquires what *technē* and expertise[140] could produce this song, which arouses such irresistible passions.[141] Its effects parallel those of love: happiness, desire, and sweet sleep. As companion of the Muses and patron of music, Apollo is, of course, no novice to such arts, but no performance has ever stirred him so deeply.

After this outburst of enthusiasm, Apollo begins to collect himself and subtly reasserts his superiority over Hermes who, while very clever, is still young and should listen to the counsel of his elders. Apollo can use

[139] For the *mētis* of Aphrodite, see chapter 3.

[140] τρίβος in line 448 is equivalent to τριβή, "study," "practice," and does not mean "path" as LSJ. would have it. Cf. M. Kaimio, "Music in the Homeric Hymn to Hermes," *Arctos* 8 (1974): 36.

[141] I am convinced by Càssola's (1975) argument, p. 537, that μοῦσα ἀμηχανέων μελεδώνων cannot mean a "song that soothes irresistible cares." After all, Hermes' performance has just *aroused* "irresistible *eros*" in Apollo (434).

his influence on Olympus to give *kleos* to both Hermes and his mother, and he further offers to make Hermes famous and prosperous among the gods[142] and to give him splendid gifts without deception.

To Apollo's vague promises, Hermes responds with "crafty words" (463). A deal is about to be made, a mutually agreed-upon exchange, but, despite their courteous words, both partners drive a hard bargain. In flattering tones, Hermes declares himself willing to introduce his older brother to his new art immediately. After all, Apollo has the ability to master any art he may wish. Even Hermes has heard of his brother's exalted status among the immortals. Zeus himself has conceded to him splendid gifts from men,[143] as well as *timai*. Among Apollo's prerogatives, Hermes singles out prophecy:

σὲ δέ φασι δαήμεναι ἐκ Διὸς ὀμφῆς
μαντείας θ᾽ Ἑκάεργε· Διὸς πάρα θέσφατα πάντα.

And they say that you have learned from the mouth of Zeus prophecies, Far-Darter; all oracles are from Zeus.

(471–72)

In passing, the wily Hermes hints broadly at the nature of the gift he would like to receive from Apollo. But because Apollo presently desires to learn to play the lyre, Hermes will hand it over; however, Apollo, in turn, should grant his younger brother *kudos*.

Kahn has noticed the anomalousness of Hermes' request.[144] After all, *kudos* is what gods grant to mortals. By adopting the term, Hermes places himself in the position of Apollo's inferior, but in addressing his older brother as *philos*, he slyly implies his equality. In fact, Hermes is responding to Apollo's earlier offer of *kleos*, a term that likewise belongs to the human sphere and hence constitutes a subtle putdown; but at the same time he rejects Apollo's insinuation of his inferior status. A little game is being played here; Hermes wants neither *kleos* or *kudos* nor even the fine gifts Apollo offers. He is after bigger fish for which the exchange of lyre and cattle forms only a preliminary step: the *timai* that must ultimately be guaranteed by Zeus (cf. 470–71 and 516).

Henceforth, Apollo will bring the "gentle-voiced companion" into

---

[142] The corrupt ἡγεμονεύσω in line 461 may have arisen by homeoteleuton from ἦ μὲν ἐγώ σε in the previous verse. Hence most of the proposed emendations must be rejected.

[143] For the punctuation and meaning of the text here, see above, n. 115.

[144] Cf. Kahn (1978), pp. 159–64.

the "flourishing feast and lovely dance and into the splendid revel" (480–81).[145] From the outset, Hermes' invention has been destined to become the "companion of the feast" (31) and has been closely associated with it throughout the hymn (cf. 56 and 454). The lyre is thus intimately linked to the other institution founded by Hermes and becomes an inseparable component of its harmonious functioning. As Odysseus says to the Phaeacians:

> I proclaim there is no more pleasing goal
> than when festive good fellowship (εὐφροσύνη) possesses the
>   whole
> people; and feasting throughout the house, they listen to the singer,
> sitting in order; and nearby are tables full of
> bread and meats, and drawing wine from the mixing bowl,
> the steward brings it and pours it into the cups.
>
> (*Odyssey* 9.5–10)

Banquet and lyre combine to create the sense of benevolent good fellowship, εὐφροσύνη (cf. 449 and 482).[146] Although the lyre will soon pass into the hands of Apollo, the discovery of the gentle force that joins mortals and even gods[147] together in the spirit of *philotēs* belongs to Hermes,

[145] On the basis of his analysis of the figure of the *kēryx* in Indo-European society, Mondi (1978), p. 135, puts forward the intriguing suggestion that "Hermes and Apollo represent two types of song, ritual and secular. The passing of the lyre from Hermes to Apollo reflects not only the transference of the patronage of song from one god to the other, but the historical development of secular, i.e. epic, song out of ritual hymn." I can find no concrete evidence for such a transfer in the *Hymn to Hermes*, and we may note that in the *Hymn to Apollo*, the god accompanies the Muses' song, which embraces both gods and men (189–93). I would rather argue that *Hermes* presents the integrity of *epos*, which includes theogonic, hymnic, and epic poetry, within the context of the *dais*.

[146] See Saïd (1979), p. 22, for the association of the *dais* and *euphrosynē*. Cf. *Iliad* xv.99 and *Odyssey* 2.311.

[147] For the intimate connection between the lyre and the feast, see, for example, *Odyssey* 8.99: "the lyre ... which is the consort of the flourishing feast" (φόρμιγγός θ᾽, ἣ δαιτὶ συνήορός ἐστι θαλείη); *Odyssey* 17.270–71: "the lyre, which the gods made the companion of the feast" (φόρμιγξ ... ἣν ἄρα δαιτὶ θεοὶ ποίησαν ἑταίρην). Cf. *Theogony* 917: the Muses ... who take pleasure in festivities and the enjoyment of song" (Μοῦσαι ... τῇσιν ἅδον θαλίαι καὶ τέρψις ἀοιδῆς). On Olympus, the gods seem to be engaged in continual feasting. On occasion, in the *Iliad*, a god complains that their pleasure in the *dais* will be jeopardized by their quarrels over mortals (1.575–79; xv.95–99). In the *Theogony*, exclusion from the assembly and *dais* of the gods is the punishment for a god who has perjured himself (802). Hübner (1986), p. 161, n. 32, suggests that δαιτὸς ἑταῖρος (*Hermes* 436) may originally have been a ritual epithet of Hermes.

the god not only of boundaries and separations, but also of alliances and unions.

Hermes now proceeds to instruct his older brother in the art of the lyre.[148] Patience, skill, and gentleness are required to elicit from the instrument "all kinds of varied things, pleasing to the mind" (484), but to ignorant and violent treatment, she will respond raucously. Throughout his music lesson, Hermes emphasizes the reciprocal and harmonious interaction of musician and lyre: the two engage in a kind of dialogue, the lyre player questioning and inquiring, the instrument, responding and giving instruction.[149] Revealing himself again in his role of civilizer and mediator, Hermes demonstrates the communicability of his *technē*. His arts do not remain his exclusive preserve, but can be freely transmitted to those eager to learn.

In exchange for the lyre, Hermes receives the cattle, which, henceforth domesticated, will reproduce under his tutelage. Removed from the divine sphere, they will multiply in the world of mortals. To the accompaniment of Apollo's lyre playing, Zeus's lovely children return to Olympus, and their father rejoices in their newly established but eternal friendship, whose emblem is the lyre, itself a veritable instrument of harmony.

Three signs remain of the young god's activity on the first day of his life: the lyre is taken to Olympus as a token of reconciliation (509); the hides of the slaughtered cattle remain eternally on earth (124–26); and the meats stay hidden within the cave, suspended between heaven and earth (136), offering a silent, invisible testimony to the new divinity's mysterious mediating powers.

The quarrel between the two divinities, precipitated by Hermes' theft, has apparently been resolved to everyone's satisfaction. Since Groddeck (1786), a good number of scholars have believed that the *Hymn to Hermes* originally ended here and that the present closing section (512–80) was added at a later date by a devotee of Apollo, anxious to redress the balance between the two Olympian brothers in favor of the great god

---

[148] Thalmann (1984), p. 155, sees the exchange of cattle for lyre as a kind of *Dichterweihe* and invokes the traditional story of Archilochus's encounter with the old women who take his cow and leave him with the lyre. But it should be noted that the events in the hymn offer a playful *inversion* of this traditional motif of poetic initiation. In handing over the lyre to Apollo, Hermes abandons poetry in order to become a herdsman—just the opposite of Hesiod and Archilochus.

[149] For lyre playing as a dialogue, see Kaimio (1974), p. 39. On Hermes' musical instruction of Apollo, see Görgemanns (1976), pp. 123–27.

of Delphi.[150] Several inconcinnities and awkwardnesses, it is argued, reveal the hand of the latecomer, who tried unsuccessfully to attach his tendentious endpiece to the existing composition. The haphazard stitching is particularly visible at line 533 where Apollo apparently refers to a request on the part of Hermes for a share of his oracular art, although no such request has been made. We will return to this problem shortly, but we must openly confess that the close of the poem is fraught with daunting textual and interpretive problems. It is these, I suspect, that have attracted critics to the view that the entire ending constitutes a later interpolation.

Let us quietly admit that no passage in this most difficult of the hymns offers so many perplexities. Ludwich, who believed in the unity of the poem, resorted to wholesale transpositions to bring coherence to the text.[151] However, his procedure rests on an optimistic but unwarranted assumption: that all the pieces of the puzzle, while scrambled, remain intact. Moreover, his method is vitiated by his refusal to give any account of how and why a given error in the sequence of verses occurred. Be that as it may, I feel convinced that the text contains at least one major gap at line 568 and a tranposition of six lines (507–12) that belong at the end of the poem between lines 575 and 576.[152] But we must also acknowledge that the hymn cannot simply come to a close with the exchange of cattle and lyre. That episode constitutes a preliminary—albeit an important one—to the goal of the poem and its divinity: Hermes' full accession to his *timai*. Moreover, the text itself makes this clear. After Apollo has declared his willingness to trade cows for lyre, Hermes answers him with μύθοισιν . . . κερδαλέοισιν (463), words both crafty and aiming at further profit.[153] In fact, he hints openly at his object by emphasizing

[150] For a summary of earlier views on the end of the hymn, see Gemoll (1886), pp. 187–88. He, Baumeister (1860), and AHS (1936) are basically unitarians; Radermacher (1931), Humbert (1936), and Càssola (1975) all argue against the authenticity of the conclusion. Radermacher's (p. 218) view is representative: the composer of lines 513–78 was "ein Anhänger des Apoll, der den Ausgleich bis zum letzten führte, aber nicht zugunsten des Hermeskindes."

[151] See Ludwich (1908), pp. 31–36, for a general statement of his "Transpositionstheorie," which is further vitiated by his notions of strophic composition in the hymn. In his text, he has no less than four transpositions in lines 513–80.

[152] I suggest that the transposition occurred when lines 507–12 were first omitted after 575 and then added in the margin. A subsequent scribe, unsure where they belonged but recognizing that the subject of συνήγαγε must be Zeus, mistakenly inserted them after 506.

[153] On the formula, μύθοισιν . . . κερδαλέοισιν (cf. 162 and 260), which is not Ho-

Apollo's preeminence in prophecy. Finally, we may note that the poem as a whole appears to be constructed in three triads: *kluta erga* (lyre, theft, *dais*); followed by three verbal confrontations (Maia, Apollo, Zeus); and culminates in Apollo's three gifts (cattle, wand, bee oracle). With due caution, then, we may attempt to interpret the text before us, always bearing in mind the necessarily tentative character of our conclusions.

An apparently satisfactory exchange of cattle and lyre has been achieved, but, suddenly, Apollo expresses the fear that Hermes may try to rob him of his lyre and bow:[154]

τιμὴν γὰρ πὰρ Ζηνὸς ἔχεις ἐπαμοίβιμα ἔργα
θήσειν ἀνθρώποισι κατὰ χθόνα πουλυβότειραν.

For you have from Zeus the *timē*
to establish deeds of exchange for men on the much-nourishing
earth.
(516–17)

The transition, to be sure, is abrupt but not incomprehensible. After all, the cows were first stolen, and Hermes retained them in his control until he "traded" them for the lyre. The apparent mutuality of the exchange masks a real asymmetry; Apollo was faced with a fait accompli. From such a thievish rascal, Apollo might well expect further attempts to steal his possessions and to extort other privileges. For as Apollo well recognizes, Hermes' domain embraces all "deeds of exchange"—theft as well as trade. The cows themselves have become an emblem of the young god's prerogative; not only were they first stolen and used as the vehicle of the first mutually agreed-upon barter, but in their newly domesticated condition, they also become the very standard by which trade is conducted. In other words, they have become χρήματα (cf. 400);[155] and with their newly acquired ability to reproduce and increase, they become circulating goods and a common basis for all commercial activity. But in

---

meric, see Van Nortwick (1975), pp. 46–47. He claims that in 463 "it might appear that Hermes no longer needs craftiness, since he has won over Apollo completely with his singing." But Van Nortwick also recognizes that "the question of whether κερδαλέοισιν has particular significance in context is important . . . to the controversy over lines 513–580" (which he attributes to "some kind of Apolline revision" [p. 130]). κερδαλέοισιν makes clear that Hermes wants more than he has yet acquired, and that "more" is prophecy.

[154] See Horace, *Odes* 1.10.11. The story of the theft of the bow may go back to Alcaeus.
[155] Cf. Kahn (1978), p. 181.

addition to the movement of material goods, *epamoibima erga* encompass verbal communication, for words, too, are a medium of exchange.[156] The common Greek word for "to reply" or "to answer," ἀμείβομαι, contains the same root as *epamoibima*. All verbal exchanges, conversations, and acts of communication belong to Hermes' domain. Just as theft and trade are but two aspects of the same phenomenon, so the verbal sphere under Hermes' patronage embraces lies, deceptions, and perjuries, as well as oaths, contracts, and instruction, which, as we have seen, is described as a dialogue. What unites the various manifestations of *epamoibima erga* is movement and passage.

At this juncture, appropriately enough, Apollo solicits a binding oath from Hermes not to rob him or even to approach his "compact house." In return, Apollo promises his eternal friendship. An exchange of oaths follows and guarantees the exchange of goods. The mutual pact between the two brothers becomes the model for all future agreements, a perfect *symbolon*, as Apollo calls it, trustworthy and honored.[157] In addition, Apollo will give Hermes "the lovely staff of prosperity and wealth, golden, with three branches," which will bring to fulfillment the good things Apollo learns from Zeus.[158] With the acquisition of the caduceus, Hermes becomes the divine messenger, the go-between par excellence between gods and mortals, as well as the "giver of good things," δώτηρ ἐάων, and patron of all human heralds.

Both Apollo and Hermes will be mediators between Zeus and mankind, but their mediation will take different forms. Prophecy, as the vehicle of communication between gods and men, would indeed seem a suitable attribute for the divine go-between—which is why Hermes has sought to appropriate it. But Apollo offers his younger brother an alternative means of mediation as herald and messenger of the gods. The kind of prophecy that is properly Apollo's domain—the transmission of Zeus's ὀμφή—is exclusively Apollo's possession; it cannot be shared or transmitted to another divinity. Apollo's oracular art, then, stands in sharp contrast to the arts of Hermes, which can be taught and communicated, and

[156] Cf. Kahn (1978), pp. 184–85.

[157] The text here and in the subsequent lines is extremely difficult. In general, I follow the interpretation of Càssola (1975), p. 540.

[158] Where does the *rhabdos* come from? The other gifts Apollo entrusts to Hermes, the cattle and the bee oracle, are both Apollo's to give. Ludwich (1908), p. 133, seems to be on the right track when he reads κραναιαῖνον at line 460 and equates the "accomplishing" lance by which Apollo swears with the accomplishing (ἐπικραίνουσα, [531]) staff he hands over to Hermes.

whose inventions can be put into circulation. Apollo's description of the functioning of his oracle seems to parallel Hermes' music lesson,[159] but successful consultation depends not on skill or art, but on positive omens. But, just as the lyre player who treats his instrument roughly produces only unpleasant noises, so the man who comes to consult the oracle under adverse conditions or seeks to extort a response, "wanting to know more than the gods who live forever," "his journey will be in vain" (548–49).[160] Although Apollo slyly adds that he will receive gifts from the consultant in any case, the Delphic god here most clearly manifests himself as the enforcer of boundaries dividing gods and men. Furthermore, because his oracle conveys Zeus's intentions for mankind, Apollo never says that it lies.

Apollo's oracle, then, is his exclusive privilege, limited to the communication of Zeus's will.[161] The oracle of the Bee Maidens Apollo now offers to Hermes differs from the Delphic oracle in important respects. For one thing, Apollo can give it away, and it is not intimately associated with Zeus. Not limited to the communication of the plans of the supreme god, it presumably deals with lesser matters. Moreover, this modest form of divination seems duly suited to Hermes; Apollo himself practiced it as a youth while tending cattle. Finally, the bee oracle conveys both truth and falsehood: truth, when the bees are inspired by the divine food of honey; falsehood, when they are deprived of it.[162] As we have seen, Apollo seems to avoid attributing falsehood to his oracle. Whereas successful response from Delphi depends in part on the consultant's frame of mind, Hermes' oracle appears to lack this ethical dimension. For Apollo, the prophecy of the bees was a passing youthful exercise before he acceded to his august station as exclusive mouthpiece of Zeus. The

[159] See Eitrem (1906), pp. 280–81, for the parallels in the descriptions of the oracle and the lyre.

[160] Cf. Euripides, *Ion* 374–80, where Ion dissuades Creusa from attempting to consult Apollo concerning her abandoned son: "We would reach the height of stupidity if we should force the gods against their will to tell what they do not want to, either by slaughtering sheep before their altars or by the flight of birds. For if we should press by force when the gods are unwilling, we would have good things, without profit, lady. But whatever they give willingly, that will benefit us."

[161] Cf. *Hymn to Apollo* 132. On the basis of their common definition of Apollo's prophetic power, Dornseiff (1938), p. 83, argues for the influence of *Apollo* on the *Hymn to Hermes*.

[162] See S. Scheinberg, "The Bee Maidens of the Homeric *Hymn to Hermes*," *Harvard Studies in Classical Philology* 83 (1979): 11; also Detienne (1973), p. 74; and P. Pucci, *Hesiod and the Language of Poetry* (Baltimore, 1977), pp. 19–21, on the poetic/oracular *logos*.

mortal who consults the bees will hear not Zeus's voice, but Hermes'—if he is lucky. An oracle that capriciously conveys both truth and lies seems appropriate to the trickster god, whose domain embraces both.[163]

The gifts Apollo entrusts to Hermes—the bee prophecy, the herald's staff, and patronage not only over cattle but all domestic animals (568)—have mediation as their common denominator and become the basis of Hermes' *timai*. At this point, it appears that our text breaks off. When it resumes after a lacuna of indeterminate length, the construction has changed from direct to indirect discourse. The speaker must be Zeus,[164] who approves and extends Hermes' privileges to include not only those granted by Apollo, but presumably also those conceded by other gods. Lines 569–70 offer a comprehensive catalog of animals, both wild and domesticated. Because there is no reason to identify Hermes as a "master of animals,"[165] I think it likely that Zeus is speaking of an aspect of Hermes' mediating role that links him to the realm of Aphrodite:[166] the ability to unite the male and female of all species in sexual intercourse. After reiterating Hermes' tutelage over flocks, Zeus ends his catalog of *timai* by singling out a prerogative that belongs to Hermes alone of all the Olympians: the exclusive right to penetrate into the underworld and

[163] Elsewhere, Hermes is connected with divination by lots or pebbles (cf. Apollodorus 3.10.2) and chance utterances (*kledones*).

[164] Consider the end of the first *Hymn to Dionysus*, where Zeus also sanctions Dionysus's newly acquired *timai*. In the *Hymn to Hermes*, Zeus's words are also cited in indirect discourse at lines 391–94; in the *Hymn to Demeter*, he is only quoted indirectly. Concerning the identity of the speaker of these verses, see Gemoll (1886), p. 256: "da die Verse in dem Munde Apollons nicht passend sind, so wird sie ein ander gesprochen haben. Das kann nur Zeus sein. Und dass Zeus hier etwas zu thun hatte, lehren auch die Worte (575): χάριν δ' ἐπέθηκε Κρονίων." Cf. AHS (1936), p. 348: "the subject can hardly be other than Zeus." Also Càssola (1975), p. 544: "si allude senza dubbio alle decisione di Zeus." Radermacher (1931), p. 175, retains Apollo as the speaker and asserts that the lacuna after line 568 must have contained something to the effect: "endlich gab Apollon Hermes die Macht." The question abides whether Apollo would have such power.

[165] Cf. the catalog of animals in *Aphrodite* 4–5 and 70–71; and the headband of the arch-seductress in *Theogony* 582. I am not persuaded by the claims of J. Chittenden, "The Master of Animals," *Hesperia* 26 (1947): 102, that the hymn here offers "our first definite literary statement" of Hermes' original function as a master of animals. Wilamowitz (1959), 1: 163, attributes lines 567–71 to an "überarbeitender Rhapsode . . . [der] die Macht des Hermes willkürlich gesteigert." Following Chittenden, Càssola (1975), p. 165, on the principle of bipolarity, regards Hermes both as god of domestic animals and their enemies. Cf. also Herter (1976), p. 239.

[166] For the link between Hermes and Aphrodite in the area of deception and seduction, see Detienne (1973), pp. 65ff.; and Kahn (1978), pp. 54–55, for Hermes' connection with marriage.

to carry messages to Hades. Zeus concludes his enumeration in riddling fashion: even from Hades who had no gifts, Hermes will receive a privilege (γέρας [573]) of no small account.[167]

If my reconstruction of Zeus's speech is correct, then the hymn concludes with a list of Hermes' *timai*, each defined as a *geras* contributed by the other gods to the youngest member of the Olympian pantheon. Despite false starts and detours, Hermes' campaign to achieve full Olympian status has finally met with success, and Zeus's plans for his wayward son have been accomplished: Διὸς νόος ἐξετελεῖτο (10).

The role of Zeus at the end of the hymn returns us to his intentions at its outset when he begot Hermes without the knowledge of gods and mortals (9) to be a troublemaker for both (160–61). At the poem's close, Zeus officially confers on Hermes those *timai* that his young offspring has acquired and exercised in the first days of his existence. Zeus also dominates the center of the composition. As Radermacher has argued, the so-called trial scene occupies a pivotal position in the narrative[168] but, as Lenz demonstrates, it was probably not found in earlier versions and is clearly not even necessary in ours.[169] For, although Zeus orders Hermes to restore the cattle to Apollo, their permanent reconciliation is effected by the two gods themselves through the medium of exchange and does not involve the active intervention of Zeus.

As Lenz has pointed out, the presence of Zeus in the long Homeric Hymns constitutes a common element and one of their recurring generic features. It is not, however, as Lenz seems to suggest, merely an artistic device, what he calls a "secondary epicization,"[170] but rather a basic theological component. Zeus's presence, even when apparently superfluous as, for example, in the trial scene, keeps before us the thoroughgoing Olympian orientation of the hymns. The confrontation between Apollo and Hermes is not merely one between an older, established brother and

---

[167] The *geras* Hermes is to receive from Hades may well be, as Càssola (1975), p. 544, suggests, the cap of invisibility that he uses in the Gigantomachy (cf. Apollodorus 1.6.2) and lends to Perseus (cf. Apollodorus 2.4.2–3). See J. Roeger, ΑΙΔΟΣ ΚΥΝΕΗ (Graz, 1924). Radermacher (1931), p. 175, takes ὅς at 573 to refer to Hermes.

[168] Radermacher (1931), p. 215: "als Drehpunkt des Ganzen ist die Szene vor Zeus im Olympos."

[169] Lenz (1975), pp. 69–73.

[170] Lenz (1975), p. 78. On the trial scene, Lenz comments: "den Rhapsoden dürfte, weil die Olympszene ein festes hymnisches Werkstück ist, zur Einführung seiner Olympszene die Typik der Hymnengattung (mit-)motiviert haben" (p. 74). This will not suffice as an explanation.

his younger, upstart sibling, nor even between rival divinities, but between two members of a highly articulated divine community. Zeus literally engenders the source of the conflict; it is brought before him for adjudication, an action that reveals that both parties belong within the Olympian community; and he, in turn, puts his seal of approval on the final settlement, thereby elevating Hermes to full membership in the pantheon.

Many scholars have felt that the end of the hymn (512–80) must have been composed by a propagandist for Apollo. After all, Hermes ends up having to content himself with an oracle unmistakably inferior to the one belonging to the lord of Delphi; and the newcomer never does fully achieve his stated aim to acquire *timē* and *hosiē* equal to Apollo's.[171] But the apparent putdown of Hermes demonstrates not the hymnist's pro-Apollonian bias, but rather his allegiance to what I have termed Olympianism.[172] To set Hermes above Apollo—even in a poem in Hermes' honor—would have meant to ignore and distort the organization of Olympus. Likewise, in the *Hymn to Apollo*, Apollo cannot be exalted above Zeus, but becomes his faithful ally and follower. Moreover, as we shall see, in the compositions celebrating Aphrodite and Demeter, both fail to carry out crucial parts of their projects and actually suffer a diminution of their power. The will of Zeus always outweighs the interests of the individual divinity. If Hermes cannot seriously rival or challenge Apollo, he nevertheless gains his destined place on Olympus and fulfills an essential function within the pantheon as messenger and mediator, god of *mētis* and of exchange, passage and communication.

The last lines of the *Hymn to Hermes* briefly summarize the main facets of Hermes, now newly inducted into Olympus: his inexhaustible inventiveness in his discovery of the syrinx to replace the lyre (511–12); his mediating function between gods and mortals (576); and his ambiguous role as benefactor and eternal trickster (577–78).[173] But the closing

---

[171] Herter (1976), p. 238, speaks of Hermes' "Niederlage" at the end of the hymn but wonders whose side the poet is on. But cf. Càssola (1975), p. 172: "la superiorità di Apollo è un presupposto del racconto dal principio alla fine."

[172] Cf. P. Raingeard, *Hermès psychagogue* (Rennes, 1934), p. 613: "le sujet [of the *Hymn*] répond à un travail d'unification religieuse: l'hymne à Hermès comme l'hymne à Déméter règle un différand et sanctionne un accord; il semble que nous ayons dans ces poèmes les monuments d'une activité réfléchie qui cherchait à créer un Olympe homogène uni sous le sceptre de Zeus."

[173] Cf. *Iliad* xxiv.334–35, where Zeus addresses Hermes: Ἑρμεία, σοὶ γάρ τε μάλιστά γε φίλτατόν ἐστιν / ἀνδρὶ ἑταιρίσσαι, καὶ τ᾽ ἔκλυες ᾧ κ᾽ ἐθέλησθα. The last phrase may suggest capriciousness. Cf. Clay (1984), pp. 34–35.

verses dwell most emphatically on the mutual and reciprocal bonds of
philotēs established between the two sons of Zeus:

οὕτω Μαιάδος υἱὸν ἄναξ ἐφίλησεν Ἀπόλλων
παντοίῃ φιλότητι, χάριν δ᾽ ἐπέθηκε Κρονίων,
ἄμφω δ᾽ ἐς φιλότητα συνήγαγε. καὶ τὰ μὲν Ἑρμῆς
Λητοΐδην ἐφίλησε διαμπερὲς ὡς ἔτι καὶ νῦν....

Thus lord Apollo loved the son of Maia
with every kind of friendship; and the son of Cronus added grace
and brought them both into *philotēs*. And Hermes
loved the son of Leto continually, even as he still does now....

(574-75, 507-8)

The ties between these two divinities parallel those of Hermes and Hestia
(φίλα φρεσὶν ἀλλήλοισιν / εἰδότες [*Hymn to Hestia* 9, 12]).[174] Inner
cannot do without outer, nor rest without motion. Similarly, the full definition of limits and boundaries requires the possibility of passage and
penetration: Apollo and Hermes. Their complementarities and interdependencies define the new and fully realized Olympus: clearly articulated
and hierarchically ordered but, with the inclusion of Hermes, capable of
movement, change, and mediation.

[174] I follow Càssola's (1975) text and transpose line 9 after line 11. For the complementarities of Hermes and Hestia, see Vernant (1965c) 1: 124-70.

CHAPTER 3

HYMN TO APHRODITE

 The *Hymn to Aphrodite*, recounting the love goddess's seduction of the mortal Anchises, has itself exercised a seductive charm on its readers, one perhaps not diminished by the mysteries surrounding its composition and purpose.

> The Homeric Hymn to Aphrodite is the most admirable of the major *Homeric Hymns*, yet one remarkably obscure in terms of date, place of origin and relation to other poetry; external evidence is entirely lacking, and the poem is hardly quoted or referred to throughout antiquity.[1]

The vacuum in which this admirable poem stands has produced a kind of philological *Angst*. One can characterize the main lines of scholarship as attempts to attach this irritatingly elusive composition to some kind of firm religious, historical, or literary background. The poem's very lack of obvious cultic associations has given rise to speculation linking the story of the love goddess's seduction of a mortal with Anatolian Great Mother cults.[2] On the other hand, the absence of an overtly religious

[1] Janko (1982), p. 151.
[2] See, for instance, Baumeister (1860), p. 250; Wilamowitz (1920), p. 83; H. J. Rose, "Anchises and Aphrodite," *CQ* 18 (1924): 11–16; L. Malten, "Aeneias," *ARW* 29 (1931): 35; Humbert (1936), pp. 143–44; S. Ferri, "L'inno omerico a Afrodite e la tribù anatolica degli Otrusi," in *Studi in onore di L. Castiglioni* (Florence, 1960), 1: 293–307; Nilsson, *GGR*

context has engendered the view of the composition as a piece of purely secular court poetry intended to glorify the princely house of the Aeneadae in the Troad.³ Finally, the similarity between certain lines in the hymn to passages *Iliad* has drawn the poem into the maelstrom of the Homeric Question;⁴ the ensuing controversy concerning authorship and priority has, unfortunately, shed little light on the meaning of the poem as a whole. The older approaches thus betray a measure of desperation. Only recently have critics laid aside tangential issues and subjected the hymn to fresh scrutiny.⁵ I have freely drawn on their results. In this

---

(1955), 1: 522–23; and Càssola (1975), pp. 231–43. I find myself more in sympathy with scholars like Gemoll (1886), pp. 260–61; AHS (1936), p. 351; H. Podbielski, *La Structure de l'Hymne Homérique à Aphrodite à la lumière de la tradition littéraire* (Wroclaw, 1971), pp. 40–41; and N. van der Ben, "De Homerische Aphrodite-hymne 2: Een interpretatie van het gedicht," *Lampas* 14 (1981): 69–70, who reject Near Eastern parallels and find the Hymn's Aphrodite to be thoroughly Greek and Homeric. D. D. Boedeker, *Aphrodite's Entry into Greek Epic* (*Mnemosyne* Supplement 31) (Leiden, 1974), attempts to trace Aphrodite's origins to an Indo-European dawn goddess. On the other hand, P. Friedrich, *The Meaning of Aphrodite* (Chicago, 1978), pp. 9–54, views the Greek Aphrodite as a complex synthesis of both Oriental and Indo-European elements.

³ Cf. A. Matthiae, *Animadversiones in hymnos Homericos cum prolegomenis* (Leipzig, 1800), pp. 66–67 (cited in E. Heitsch, *Aphroditehymnos, Aeneas und Homer* [Hypomnemata 15] [Göttingen, 1965], p. 12): "hoc carmen 'laudes stirpis Aeneadarum' inscribi posset, siquidem eorum gloriam maxime attingit hoc, quod stirpis auctor dea matre genitus perhibebatur"; and K. Reinhardt, "Ilias und Aphroditehymnus," in *Die Ilias und ihr Dichter* (Göttingen, 1961), p. 507 (hereafter cited as Reinhardt [1961b]: "der Aphroditehymnus unterscheidet sich von allen anderen Hymnen zumeist dadurch, dass seine Absicht zuerst verdeckt ist, dass sie zuletzt nicht sakral, sondern profan ist. Er huldigt zuletzt nicht einem Gott, sondern einem Herrschergeschlecht." See also Wilamowitz (1920), pp. 83–84; Malten (1931), p. 33; Humbert (1936), p. 144; Heitsch (1965); Càssola (1975), pp. 243–47; and in a limited fashion, Lenz (1975), pp. 29 and 31. Doubts have been expressed by Baumeister (1860), p. 251; Gemoll (1886), p. 260; AHS (1936), p. 351. For an exhaustive survey of earlier opinion, see N. van der Ben, "De Homerische Aphrodite-hymne I," *Lampas* 13 (1980): 40–55. In different ways, both van der Ben (1980) and Smith (1981), pp. 17–58, have marshaled sufficient convincing arguments against the court poetry hypothesis to render it a dead issue.

⁴ For a thorough account of the controversies as well as a careful examination of the relevant passages in the *Iliad*, see van der Ben (1980), pp. 40–77; also Lenz (1975), pp. 1–6.

⁵ I have profited most from the observations of Podbielski (1971); C. Segal, "The Homeric Hymn to Aphrodite: A Structuralist Approach," *CW* 67 (1974): 205–12; P. M. Smith, *Nursling of Mortality: A Study of the Homeric Hymn to Aphrodite* (Studien zur klassischen Philologie 3) (Frankfurt, 1981) (hereafter cited as Smith [1981a]); and van der Ben (1981). The overall interpretation of the hymn that jibes most closely with mine is that of van der Ben; see now his "Hymn to Aphrodite 36–291: Notes on the *pars epica* of the Homeric Hymn to Aphrodite," *Mnemosyne* 39 (1986): 1–41, which is essentially a restatement of his earlier study. I have not found Sowa's (1984) book very helpful because her thematic approach tends both to fragment and homogenize the hymn's individuality.

chapter, as in the previous ones, I offer an interpretation of the poem that attempts both to respect its particular character and to account for its place within the hymnic corpus.

In the simplest terms each of the major Homeric Hymns sets out to praise and to portray fully one of the Olympians by means of a narrative that conveys the particular character of the chosen divinity. In addition, but by no means secondarily, through its choice and arrangement of narrative material, each hymn focuses on an epoch-making moment in the history of the divine and human cosmos. Both the *Hymn to Apollo* and the *Hymn to Hermes* present the birth of a new god and, in different ways, the problem of integrating the new divinity into the Olympian order. Such a subject is by definition epoch making; the advent of new gods and their accommodation into the pantheon substantially alter the universe. Moreover, because each divinity possesses not only his particular sphere of activity, his *timai*, but also his particular mode of interaction with mortals, his arrival on the divine scene necessarily inaugurates a new era in the relations between gods and men. In the *Hymn to Demeter* as well as the second half of the *Hymn to Apollo*, the establishment of such a novel relationship is given a concrete manifestation in the founding of a cult. In all probability, the fragmentary first *Hymn to Dionysus*, like *Apollo*, embraced both a birth narrative and a cult foundation.

The *Hymn to Aphrodite*, however, celebrates neither the birth of the goddess nor the founding of her cult,[6] but instead recounts Aphrodite's

---

For example, she characterizes *Demeter* and *Aphrodite* as follows: "the plot of the two poems is essentially the same. Both tell of a fertility goddess who wants to make a man immortal, is balked in the attempt, and brings him increase instead" (p. 39).

[6] Matthiae (1800), cited by Heitsch (1965), p. 12, doubted whether the *Hymn to Aphrodite* should be considered a hymn at all. Cf. Schmid (1929), p. 240, who calls the hymn "ein Blatt aus der Sittengeschichte der ionischen Aristokratie, nicht aus der Religionsgeschichte." Similarly, for E. J. Bickerman, "Love Story in the Homeric Hymn to Aphrodite," *Athenaeum* 54 (1976): 229–54, the poem is primarily a "pastoral idyll" and an adaption of common fairy-tale motifs as well as "a document of the Greek attitude to love in the archaic age" (p. 237). Lenz (1975), p. 28, recognizes the hymn's peculiarities: "weder ein erstmaliges Auftreten der Göttin vor Göttern ... üblicherweise Stoff der hymnischen Geburtsgeschichten—noch ein erstmaliges Aufreten vor Menschen—üblicherweise Anlass der Kultstiftungsgeschichte—ist hier der zentrale Gegenstand." Lenz, pp. 28–31, however, tries to sidestep the issue he has raised. Although dissatisfied with the theory that the hymn gives the etiology of the Aeneidai, he nevertheless lists etiology—either in a birth myth or a cult foundation—as one of the generic components of the major hymns. He tries to justify the absence of an aetiology in *Aphrodite* by including the shorter *Hymn to Dionysus* (no. 7) and the subjects mentioned but rejected in *Apollo* 205–17 as examples of hymnic subject matter. *Dionysus*, however, does not belong to the major hymns by Lenz's own criteria, and the subjects mentioned in *Apollo* are, after all,

seduction of the mortal Anchises. From this perspective, the poem stands out among the other long hymns and raises an immediate question: How can this *histoire gallante*, for all its charm and piquancy, be regarded as epoch making? Furthermore, whereas the other hymns seem to end with the triumph of the god celebrated, *Aphrodite* moves from triumph to defeat or, at least, to a partial diminution of the power of the goddess.[7] These are but the most striking peculiarities of the poem of which an adequate interpretation must take account.

Prologue

Μοῦσά μοι ἔννεπε ἔργα πολυχρύσου Ἀφροδίτης
Κύπριδος, ἥ τε θεοῖσιν ἐπὶ γλυκὺν ἵμερον ὦρσε
καί τ’ ἐδαμάσσατο φῦλα καταθνητῶν ἀνθρώπων,
οἰωνούς τε διιπετέας καὶ θηρία πάντα,
ἠμὲν ὅσ’ ἤπειρος πολλὰ τρέφει ἠδ’ ὅσα πόντος·
πᾶσιν δ’ ἔργα μέμηλεν ἐϋστεφάνου Κυθερείης.

Tell me Muse of the works of golden Aphrodite
the Cyprian, who roused sweet longing in the gods
and overcame the tribes of mortal men,
and the birds who fly heavenward and all the beasts,
both those whom the mainland nurtures and the sea;
the works of the lovely wreathed goddess of Cythera concerns
      them all.
    (1–6)

The *Hymn to Aphrodite* begins with an invocation to the Muse more reminiscent of the epic than of the hymnic genre.[8] The uncertainty con-

---

rejected. Van der Ben (1980), p. 53, notes that Lenz cannot dispense with the Aeneidai theory completely, precisely because it provides him with some sort of etiology.

The birth of Aphrodite from the sea and her first introduction into Olympus is treated in the short sixth Homeric Hymn in her honor.

[7] For Aphrodite's defeat, see Matthiae (1800), cited in Heitsch (1965), p. 12; Reinhardt (1961b), p. 514; and Lenz (1975), p. 34, who notes that while the goddess triumphs over Anchises, she is defeated by Zeus. Demeter also suffers a significant setback in the *Hymn to Demeter*. Cf. Lenz, p. 20. The restriction of the power of female goddesses is entirely in keeping with the patriarchal Olympian orientation of the Homeric Hymns. See the discussion in my conclusion.

[8] Of the long hymns, only *Hermes* and *Aphrodite* begin with invocations to the Muse; eight of the short ones do.

cerning the kind of composition before us is heightened by the announcement of the poem's subject: not the goddess herself, but her works.[9] The
"works of Cyprian Aphrodite" can refer not only to the actions of the
goddess, but also to the deeds she inspires. Similarly, just as by meton-
ymy, the "works of Ares" mean "war," the ἔργα Ἀφροδίτης may also
simply signify "sex." Thus, Hesiod can call a young girl "one unac-
quainted with the works of Aphrodite."[10] In the first twenty-one lines of
the poem, ἔργα / ἔργον occurs six times, and each time the "secondary
meaning (i.e., physical love) will inevitably be suggested whenever the
word appears in the poem, no matter how it is used."[11]

What the subject of the poem will be or even whether it is to be a
hymn remains unclear at the outset. Perhaps it will be an epic of some
sort that focuses on, or begins from, "the deeds of Aphrodite." Such a
poem did in fact exist in the archaic period; its title, maybe not entirely
accidentally, is exactly equivalent to the "works of Aphrodite": *Cypria*.[12]
We have only a few scattered fragments from this poem, but fortunately
also an outline of its contents drawn from a summary of Proclus. It re-

[9] *Aphrodite* is unique in this respect. Cf. H. N. Porter, "Repetition in the Homeric
Hymn to Aphrodite," *AJP* 70 (1949): 252, n. 18: "it is noteworthy that in every other
hymn in the collection a god or goddess is named as the immediate subject. Only in this
hymn are the 'works' of the deity particularized as the theme." Cf. Podbielski (1971), p.
18; and Lenz (1975), p. 23.

[10] *Work and Days* 521. Cf. *Hymn to Aphrodite* 6, 9, 21. Compare ἔργον Ἄρηος, (10);
ἀγλαὰ ἔργ' (11).

[11] Porter (1949), p. 252. Cf. Podbielski (1971), pp. 19–20; and E. Pellizer, "Tecnica
compositiva e struttura genealogica nell' Inno ad Aphrodite," *QUCC* 27 (1978): 118–19.

[12] The name of the poem, Κύπρια or Τὰ κύπρια ἔπη, is usually connected with the
island of Cyprus, the presumed birthplace of Stasinus, who was believed to be the author
of the epic. But neither Stasinus nor his Cypriote origins are firmly established in the
tradition. Cf. W. Kullmann, *Die Quellen der Ilias (Troischer Sagenkreis)* (*Hermes* Einzelschriften 14) (Wiesbaden, 1960), p. 215, n. 2. For the testimonia, see A. Rzach, *s.v.* "Kyklos
(Kypria)," *RE* 2, pt. 2 (1922): 2394–95. No other poem of the Epic Cycle is named after
its author, far less his birthplace. As F. G. Welcker, *Der epische Cyclus oder die homerischen
Dichter 2: Gedichte nach Inhalt und Composition* (Bonn, 1849), 1, pt. 2: 154, acutely observed: "die Seele des Gedichts ist Aphrodite, allerdings, und in so fern hatten diejenigen
Grammatiker nicht Unrecht welch seinem Namen selbst auf die Göttin bezogen."

I suggest that the title *Cypria* originally belonged to a shorter poem concerned with
the preliminaries to the Trojan War and Aphrodite's role in them. It was probably two
to five books in length, as are the other poems in the Epic Cycle (*Aethiopis*, 5 books; *Little
Iliad*, 4; *Sack of Troy* and *Telegonia*, 2 each; and *Nostoi*, 5). Perhaps the epic describing the
events from the landing of the Greeks at Troy to the beginning of the *Iliad* was entitled
Troika (cf. Scholium to Euripides, *Andromache* 1139). Then, at a later time, the title *Cypria*
was applied to all eleven books containing the events prior to our *Iliad*. The sense of the
original title was lost, and various explanations were concocted to explain it.

counted the events that brought about the Trojan war and chronicled the first nine years of the war itself up to the point where the *Iliad* begins. This dovetailing with our *Iliad* suggests that Proclus's *Cypria* was composed as part of the so-called Epic Cycle to fill in the events prior to, between, and after the two Homeric epics; yet it unquestionably contained older traditional material.[13] According to the summary, the *Cypria* began from Zeus's plan to diminish the excessive population of the earth by bringing about "the great strife of the Trojan War. . . . And the heroes died at Troy, and the will of Zeus was accomplished."[14] The more immediate cause of the war arose from the quarrel of the goddesses Hera, Athena, and Aphrodite at the wedding of Peleus and Thetis. This in turn led to the Judgment of Paris and his rape of Helen with the help of Aphrodite. The poem's title would appear to derive from the crucial role of the Cyprian goddess in precipitating the great conflict.

The *Hymn to Aphrodite* has frequently been called the "most Homeric" of the hymns.[15] That label should perhaps be slightly modified to "most epic." At any rate, the first line of *Aphrodite* could easily introduce a poem like the *Cypria*; instead, it introduces not an epic but a hymn whose narrative is not completely unrelated to the events of the *Cypria*.[16] The story of Aphrodite's encounter with Anchises is close, both spatially and chronologically, to another meeting of the goddess with a Trojan prince on Mount Ida: the fateful Judgment of Paris. The oblique allusion to the *Cypria*—or a poem similar to it—in the opening line anchors *Aphrodite*, more than any of the other hymns, to an epic framework. This link is confirmed by the narrative material. Although finally remaining within the bounds of the hymnic genre, the *Hymn to Aphrodite* establishes an intimate attachment to the world of the epic, specifically, to the period that preceded the Trojan War, the culminating event of the heroic age.

[13] Cf. E. Bethe, *Homer. Dichtung und Sage II: Kyklos—Zeitbestimmung* (Leipzig, 1922), p. 213; G. L. Huxley, *Greek Epic Poetry from Eumelos to Panyassis* (Cambridge, Mass., 1969), p. 124. Kullmann (1960) believes that the Cyclic poems in some form antedated the Homeric epics.

[14] *Cypria* fr. 1. 6–7 (Allen).

[15] G. H. Groddeck, *Commentatio philologica de hymnorum Homericorum reliquiis* (Göttingen, 1786), p. 42 (cited in Podbielski [1971], p. 8), said that the hymn "ὁμηρικώτατον iure appellari debeat." Hermann (1806), p. LXXXIX, calls it a "carmen Homeri nomine dignissimum." Reinhardt (1961b) actually argues that the hymn's author was the composer of the *Iliad*.

[16] I have not been able to see Groddeck (see above, n. 15), who evidently argued for a close relationship between the *Cypria* and the *Hymn to Aphrodite*. See also Lenz (1975), pp. 93–95 and 139.

To a certain extent, the other hymns can at least be assigned a relative position within the general framework of divine and human history. Thus, as we have seen, *Apollo* clearly alludes to a period prior to *Hermes*. But the *Hymn to Aphrodite* is exceptional in allowing us to pinpoint the narrative temporally to a precise moment in the history of mankind. The union of Aphrodite and Anchises takes place just before the advent of the Trojan War; its issue, Aeneas, will play a prominent role in that heroic conflict.[17] While grazing at the borders of the epic genre, *Aphrodite* nevertheless maintains the divine perspective characteristic of all the hymns. We are therefore justified in expecting some kind of Olympian interpretation of the antecedents of the Trojan War, although the hymnic viewpoint may differ substantially from that of the epic.

The lines that follow (2–6) define the scope and nature of Aphrodite's power: universal, it embraces gods, men, and beasts. The tenses (ὦρσε, ἐδαμάσσατο) must be considered "hymnic aorists," like those at the beginning of *Apollo*.[18] For although the ensuing narrative will recount a unique occasion when the goddess exercised her characteristic powers with unique consequences, she always produces the same effect. Here, the gods, mentioned first, are separated from men and beasts, who are grouped together. But the ambiguous status of mankind surfaces in the poem whose main opposition is not between gods on the one hand and men and beasts on the other, but between gods and men. This is already hinted at by the expression, φῦλα καταθνητῶν ἀνθρώπων "tribes of mortal men" in line 3. A more emphatic form of the commoner θνητός, καταθνητός appears twelve times in the *Hymn to Aphrodite* whereas it occurs a total of ten times in the whole of the *Iliad* and the *Odyssey*. Thus, the poem verbally insists from its outset on the distinction between ἀθάνατοι, immortals, and καταθνητοί, mortals.[19] Yet, in a sense, the problem of the hymn arises from the excessive similarity and intimacy of gods and mortals. That closeness, which blurs orderly distinctions, also is the work of Aphrodite.

After first proclaiming Aphrodite's universality, the poet—surprisingly—proceeds to enumerate three virgin goddesses over whom Aphrodite holds no sway: Athena, Artemis, and Hestia. In addition, he re-

[17] Cf. Lenz (1975), p. 44: "das Subjet des Aphroditehymnus ist von dem aller anderen Hymnen dadurch ausgezeichnet, dass es sich (wie fern auch immer) mit der Heldenepik vom troischen Krieg stofflich berührt."

[18] See my earlier discussion of *Apollo* 2–13. For the power of Eros-Aphrodite over gods and men and the disorder it sows, see Sophocles, *Antigone* 781–801.

[19] Cf. Podbielski (1971), pp. 20–21, 29; and Porter (1949), pp. 259, 264–66.

defines Aphrodite's mode of operation from arousing desire and overcoming (2–3) to persuasion and deceit (πεπιθεῖν, ἀπατῆσαι [7]). Aphrodite's weapons are not the masculine arms of strength and force, but the arms of the weaker.[20] As such, they resemble the strategems of *mētis*, which bring about the defeat of the stronger by means of craft and guile.[21] One may call Aphrodite's characteristic conquest of the stronger by the weaker seduction. Even when the seducer is in fact the stronger, he must hide his strength and forgo its use to achieve his ends by the gentler means of deception and persuasion. Pindar's *Ninth Pythian* offers a charming and apt illustration. There, Aphrodite inspires "a common marriage uniting a god and a maid" (13). When he sees Cyrene wrestling a lion with bare hands, Apollo is immediately smitten. The god then asks Chiron whether "he may lay his famous hand on her and clip her grass, the honey-sweet favor of her bed" (36–37). Revealing his counsel (μῆτις) with a smile, the wise centaur commends a subtler approach:

> κρυπταὶ κλαῖδες ἐντὶ σοφᾶς
> Πειθοῦς ἱερᾶν φιλοτάτων,
> Φοῖβε, καὶ ἔν τε θεοῖς τοῦτο κἀνθρώποις ὁμῶς
> αἰδέοντ᾽, ἀμφανδὸν ἀδεί-
> ας τυχεῖν τὸ πρῶτον εὐνᾶς.

Hidden are skilled Persuasion's keys
to the holy rites of love,
Phoebus; and among gods and men alike, there is
a sense of shame openly
to obtain the bed of pleasure from the beginning.

(39–41)

Not force but persuasion and guile constitute the secret tools of successful seduction.

The description of the three goddesses for whom Aphrodite and her works have no appeal continues and deepens the definition of Aphrodite's sphere by means of a complex set of oppositions.[22] The first goddess,

---

[20] Consider, for example, Hector's rebuke of Aphrodite's favorite, Paris, in *Iliad* III.41–57.

[21] For the *mētis* of Aphrodite, see Vernant (1974), pp. 267–68; Detienne, (1973), pp. 64–66; and Friedrich (1978), p. 90.

[22] Cf. Smith (1981a), p. 34: "the common traits of the three exceptions to Aphrodite's rule can help to define by contrast the range and character of her own power." Friedrich (1978), pp. 72–103, adopts a strategy very similar to the hymn-poet's in attempting to

Athena, takes her pleasure in war, the "works of Ares," and the "splendid works" of craftsmanship.[23] Lines 8–11 would suffice to characterize Athena, but the poet is interested in including not only her sphere of activity but also her manner of action. As a teacher of both men and women, Athena's instruction produces both the arts of peace and of war.[24] As a *first* teacher, she plays the role of a civilizer, one who raises humans from the status of brutes. The "arts" of Aphrodite, while in some sense natural and innate, are not deprived of artfulness and artifice. One need think only of her connection with the seductive arts of music and dance, of cosmetics, or of erotic conversation. But Aphrodite does not teach these arts so much as exploit them for her own ends, ends that remain always the same. The ἔργα ʾΑφροδίτης do not produce artifacts useful in war and peace as do those of Athena; rather, they promote sexual union.

Second, Aphrodite cannot overcome (δάμναται [17]; cf. ἐδαμάσσατο [3]) Artemis, whose realm encompasses both the wilds (mountains and shadowy groves) and, surprisingly, the "city of just men." Artemis has special associations with the open public space of the city, the *agora*,[25] which can be opposed to Aphrodite's domain, the bedroom. Taking her pleasure in the hunt, Artemis conquers wild beasts by killing them, whereas Aphrodite, also a huntress of sorts, vanquishes them in a quite different way. Like Artemis, Aphrodite has a place in the city, for she is necessary for its propagation, yet she has little interest in the city as a political community. In fact, to be just, the *polis* must limit and legislate sexual activity through laws concerning marriage, incest, and adultery.

---

define Aphrodite by contrasting and comparing her to the goddesses Hera, Athena, and Artemis. Characteristically, van Groningen (1958), p. 106, finds the digressions on the three goddesses, as well as those on Ganymede, Tithonus, and the nymphs, typical of the archaic style in which the poet is seduced into recounting a story unrelated to his main narrative. Cf. J. van Eck, "The Homeric Hymn to Aphrodite: Introduction, Commentary and Appendices" (diss. Utrecht, 1978), p. 12.

[23] Cf. *Iliad* v.428–429, where Zeus consoles the wounded Aphrodite: "Not to you, my child, have the works of war been granted / but rather you look after the desirable works of marriage." In the theomachy (*Iliad* xxi.423–25), Athena gleefully attacks Aphrodite and lays her low with one blow.

[24] For Athena as teacher, see, for instance, *Odyssey* 6.232–34; *Hymn to Hephaestus* 3; and Solon 13.49–50 (West). On σατίνας in line 13, see Càssola (1975), p. 545, who claims they are the light carriages used by women. If so, they balance the martial chariots of the warrior.

[25] For Artemis as *Agoraia*, in Olympia, see Pausanias 5.15.4. Smith (1981a), p. 35, argues unnecessarily that the poet's Ionian origins led him to stress Artemis's civic role.

Not the community as a whole, but the couple, exclusive and private, constitute Aphrodite's sphere.

The poet devotes considerable space to Hestia, the last of the goddesses impervious to Aphrodite's influence (21–32). Rather than merely offering a catalog of her prerogatives, he produces a short narrative, probably of his own invention.[26] He introduces Hestia as the firstborn but youngest daughter of Cronus "by the will of Zeus who wields the aegis." This description alludes unmistakably to an episode in the Hesiodic Succession Myth: the tale of Cronus's swallowing his children as they were born and regurgitating them after the substitution of a stone for the last-born Zeus (*Theogony* 453–97). Only as first born but last out can Hestia be simultaneously eldest and youngest of Cronus's children. In accordance with her high status, Poseidon and Apollo courted her, but she refused them both. On the head of "father" Zeus, Hestia swore to remain a maiden forever, and "father Zeus granted her a fine privilege instead of marriage" (29). Honored as the personified hearth in all houses by all men and as the sacrificial altar in all the temples of the gods, Hestia rivals Aphrodite in her universality, though hers is, to be sure, different in kind. Aphrodite's place is neither at the chaste focus of the domestic hearth[27] nor in the public world of religious festivals and ceremonies. She belongs rather to the private enclave of the bedroom and the secret trysting places of lovers.[28]

As Solmsen has pointed out,[29] the short episode of Hestia links the hymn to the theogonic traditions of Hesiod, not only in its portrayal of the goddess as youngest and eldest daughter of Cronus, but also in the role it assigns to Zeus. Moreover, the Hesiodic account of Hestia contradicts the Homeric description of Hera as Cronus's oldest daughter.[30] The hymn-poet tries to reconcile the two versions by emphasizing Hera's out-

[26] Cf. Gemoll (1886), p. 263; and Podbielski (1971), p. 24. F. Jouan, "Thétis, Hestia et Athéna," *REG* 69 (1956): 290–302, believes the hymn-poet drew on elements from the Hesiodic account of Thetis's courtship. Cf. F. Dornseiff, "Der homerische Aphrodite-hymnos," *ARW* 29 (1931): 203.

[27] On the chastity and the purity of the hearth, cf. Vernant (1965b), 1: 125–44.

[28] Thus, for example, Hera refuses to make love to Zeus on Ida where all the gods can watch them and insists on returning to the privacy of their bedroom until Zeus promises to cover them with a golden cloud (*Iliad* xiv.330ff.). On the other hand, in *Odyssey* 8.302–27, the discovery of Ares and Aphrodite *in flagrante* provokes "unquenchable laughter" among all the gods.

[29] F. Solmsen, "Zur Theologie im grossen Aphrodite-hymnus," in *Kleine Schriften* (Hildesheim 1968), 1: 55–67.

[30] Solmsen (1968), pp. 65–66. Cf. *Iliad* iv.58–61.

standing beauty and position while giving Hestia primacy of age. If this attempt to harmonize the two traditions renders the poet, in Solmsen's words, a "theologian,"[31] it remains unclear why he created the problem in the first place. His desire to invent a mythology for the shadowy figure of Hestia offers a partial explanation, but his little vignette throws as much light on Zeus as on Hestia herself. Paradoxically, Zeus is twice called "father," though he cannot logically be father to his older sister. Yet in a sense, Zeus constitutes the father of all the gods and of men, according to the common formula, πατὴρ ἀνδρῶν τε θεῶν τε. It is, as we shall see, his paternity of *men* that is problematic. At any rate, the poet is at pains to introduce Zeus as the only one who can distribute *timai* to the other gods[32]—and, presumably, modify them as well. Here, he can even grant exemption from the common lot, in Hestia's case, from marriage. The subsequent narrative presupposes our understanding of the position and power of Zeus vis-à-vis the other gods as adumbrated in the Hestia story.

We have already noted the peculiarly epic quality of the *Hymn to Aphrodite*. We can now recognize the importance of certain Hesiodic elements as well, above all in its depiction of Zeus. The particular character of the poem, I suggest, derives from its double link to both the heroic epic and to the theological traditions of Hesiod.

Restating line 7, which opened the enumeration of goddesses immune to Aphrodite's wiles, line 33 closes off the excursus, while lines 34–35 reemphasize the universality of her domain over all others (cf. 2–6).[33] This time, only gods and men are mentioned, and it is on this opposition that the subsequent narrative will focus.[34] After thus defining and delimiting the nature of Aphrodite's power, the introductory section culminates in a crowning example of its triumphant exercise: Aphrodite's conquest of Zeus himself.

καί τε παρὲκ Ζηνὸς νόον ἤγαγε τερπικεραύνου,
ὅς τε μέγιστός τ' ἐστί, μεγίστης τ' ἔμμορε τιμῆς·

[31] Solmsen (1968), p. 66.

[32] Solmsen (1968), p. 64. Cf. Smith (1981a), p. 37, who recognizes the portrait of Zeus within the framework of the Hestia story "as the unquestioned head of the world's government, the maintainer of order, the giver and protector of rights and honours."

[33] Smith (1981b), p. 32, aptly entitles the proem embracing lines 1–35 "The Boundaries of Aphrodite's Realm."

[34] Lenz (1975), p. 23, notes the narrowing of focus between line 6 and line 34.

καί τε τοῦ εὖτε θέλοι πυκινὰς φρένας ἐξαπαφοῦσα
ῥηϊδίως συνέμιξε καταθνητῇσι γυναιξίν.

And she even led astray the mind of Zeus who takes pleasure in
    thunder,
he who is the greatest and received the greatest honor,
deceiving even his compact wits whenever she wished,[35]
easily she caused him to mingle with mortal woman.

(36–39)

The goddess's deception of Zeus constitutes the supreme paradigm
of all her seductive power. As presented here, Zeus is not only the greatest and most powerful, but clearly also the mastermind of the gods. Yet
easily and at will, the weaker Aphrodite overcomes the mightiest and
most intelligent. Such a situation in which the supreme god who possesses the greatest *timē* is at the mercy of a lesser divinity threatens to
undermine the entire Olympian hierarchical system in which Zeus alone
distributes and confirms divine *timai*. In addition, by causing Zeus to
mate with mortal women, Aphrodite makes him forget his legitimate
wife, who is in every way a suitable consort for him. As the most beautiful and splendid of the immortal goddesses, Hera is perfectly matched
with her husband; as simultaneously wife and sister, she shares his august
parentage from Rheia and Cronus.[36] Yet Aphrodite easily disrupts this
apparent marriage of true minds.

    All this talk of Hera (40–44)[37] might suggest that she would indeed

---

[35] Hermann (1806), p. 88, incorrectly preferred εὖτ᾽ ἐθέλῃ but noted that the optative
is appropriate "si solum de re praeterita, neque etiam de praesente et futura, sermo esset."
As will become clear, we are indeed dealing with a *res praeterita*. Cf. Baumeister (1860),
p. 255; van der Ben (1981), pp. 92–93; and van Eck (1978), p. 27: "the statement that
Aphrodite makes Zeus fall in love with mortal women, is no longer valid in the poet's
day."

    Compare also the description of Aphrodite's girdle in *Iliad* xiv.215–17, whereby
Hera manages to seduce Zeus: "in it were wrought all kinds of charms; / there was love,
there was desire, and there was seductive / converse, which steals the mind even of those
with steady thought."

[36] For endogamy among the Olympians, see J. S. Clay, "Aeolia, or Under the Sign of
the Circle," *CJ* 80 (1985): 290.

[37] The attention given to Hera is not quite justified by the need to compensate for her
loss of primacy to Hestia, as Solmsen (1968), p. 65, claims, nor, as Fränkel (1962), p. 286,
suggests, by the poet's desire to balance his praise of Hera with that of Aphrodite. Cf.
Smith (1981a), p. 110, n. 26. The presentation of Hera raises an expectation in the mind

CHAPTER 3

have good reason to attempt to put an end to her husband's incessant infidelities, which—as we know from countless stories of her jealousies—she endures with very bad grace. On the basis of her seduction of Zeus in the fourteenth book of the *Iliad*, we might even expect some campaign on the part of the aggrieved wife, perhaps even in alliance with Aphrodite, to recapture Zeus's affections. Instead, however, Zeus himself will take steps to curtail Aphrodite's activity.

Abruptly and surprisingly, the dramatic action of the hymn begins not from Aphrodite or even Hera, but from Zeus:

τῇ δὲ καὶ αὐτῇ Ζεὺς γλυκὺν ἵμερον ἔμβαλε θυμῷ
ἀνδρὶ καταθνητῷ μιχθήμεναι, ὄφρα τάχιστα
μηδ᾽ αὐτὴ βροτέης εὐνῆς ἀποεργμένη εἴη
καί ποτ᾽ ἐπευξαμένη εἴπη μετὰ πᾶσι θεοῖσιν
ἡδὺ γελοιήσασα φιλομμειδὴς Ἀφροδίτη
ὥς ῥα θεοὺς συνέμιξε καταθνητῇσι γυναιξὶ
καί τε καταθνητοὺς υἱεῖς τέκον ἀθανάτοισιν,
ὥς τε θεὰς ἀνέμιξε καταθνητοῖς ἀνθρώποις.

Even in her [Aphrodite] Zeus cast sweet longing in her heart
to mingle with a mortal man, so that quickly
not even she would be kept from a mortal bed,
and then boastfully speak among all the gods,
while laughing sweetly, how she, smile loving[38] Aphrodite
caused the gods to mingle with mortal women
—and they bore mortal sons to the immortals—
and how she joined goddesses to mortal men.

(45–52)

Because Aphrodite's power lies precisely in her ability to overcome the stronger, the weapons normally used by the stronger prove worthless against her onslaught. Zeus can only turn the tables on the goddess by utilizing her own weapons against her.[39] It is intriguing to realize that

of the audience that she will play a role in the narrative. The thwarting of that expectation throws Zeus's intervention into relief.

[38] Aphrodite's standing epithet, "smile loving," usually suggests the pleasures of love. Here, the context modifies the sense to the laughter of mockery and superiority. Cf. Podbielski (1971), p. 30; and Boedeker (1974), p. 33.

[39] Cf. Lenz (1975), p. 33: "Zeus kann alles. Der Zusammenhang zeigt, dass (der allgewaltige) Zeus nicht beliebig in andrer Götter Funktion und τιμή eingreift, sondern an dem Punkt, da diese sich gegen das Interesse der Götter insgesamt zu kehren drohen."

164

Zeus can avail himself of Aphrodite's methods when necessary to pursue his own ends. The action of Zeus suggests that the division of prerogatives among the gods that characterizes the Olympian regime may be not a necessary arrangement, but a voluntary one, under the benign authority of Zeus. Moreover, if Zeus can distribute and guarantee *timai*, he can equally increase or diminish them, as well as take them away. This, after all, was the import of the Hestia story.

Zeus's intervention initiates the narrative action of the poem. Elsewhere, Aphrodite's union with mortal Anchises is recounted without the agency of Zeus.[40] This omission results in a completely different story— one unsuited to the hymnic genre, but fully appropriate to the epic— which accounts for origins of the hero Aeneas.[41] In the hymn, Zeus's initiative transforms a heroic genealogy into a divine intrigue of cosmic significance, whose consequences will alter all future relations between gods and mortals. The poem hints at the wide-ranging implications of Zeus's action by describing the Olympian as "knowing imperishable counsels" (ἄφθιτα μήδεα εἰδώς [43]). In the *Theogony*, this epithet occurs in the context of Zeus's confrontation with Prometheus in which Zeus exercises his supreme intelligence to defeat his wily opponent.[42] There, Zeus sets into motion a plan whose ultimate success is assured from the outset and whose consequences for gods and mortals are eternal. Similarly, in the *Hymn to Aphrodite* behind the intervention of Zeus lies a far-ranging plan and a purpose that will not only reinforce his supreme authority among the gods, but will also inaugurate a new age for mankind.

Most critics interpret Zeus's purpose only in narrow or immediate terms. Thus, some claim that Zeus gives Aphrodite a taste of her own medicine merely to make her stop boasting of her power and mocking

---

[40] AHS (1936), p. 349, list the other versions. Lenz (1975), p. 37, rightly notes that the poet has added the plan of Zeus to the episode. So does Rose (1924), p. 12, although he does not understand its significance: "the action of Zeus in starting the whole affair . . . is clearly no part of the real myth, being just such a thoroughly human motive as the Ionians, and after them the Alexandrians, loved to ascribe to the deities in their half-serious handling of them."

[41] Lenz (1975), pp. 34–35, notes that, in the epic, unions of gods and mortals are mentioned *for the sake* of their divine offspring. A significant exception: *Odyssey* 5.121–27. Van Eck (1978), p. 2, claims that "the form as well as the contents of the *pars epica* of the present hymn have been strongly influenced by the genre of the *Eoeae*." For thematic similarities between the *Hymn to Aphrodite* and genealogical poetry, see Pellizer (1978), pp. 137–43. It is, however, the differences that matter. Cf. van der Ben (1986), p. 7.

[42] *Theogony* 545, 550, and 561. Compare *Hymn to Demeter* 321 and the discussion of that passage below.

the helpless gods.[43] Or, alternatively, in teaching Aphrodite a lesson, Zeus intends to diminish the goddess's excessive power and thus to redress the imbalance within the Olympian hierarchy.[44] Finally, it has been maintained that Zeus wants Aphrodite to suffer the same pain and humiliation deriving from intercourse with a mortal that she herself has inflicted on the other gods.[45]

Although these explanations of Zeus's intention are valid as far as they go, they stop short of grasping his ultimate goal. Not only does Aphrodite embarrass and humiliate the gods; not only does she cause them grief and pain and undermine the delicate balance of power that constitutes the Olympian family; but she causes the gods to produce offspring who are half divine and half human. Ultimately, Aphrodite not only disseminates disorder on Olympus, she perpetuates it through the production of a mixed race of demigods or heroes, which blurs the clear distinction between gods and humans. The final upshot of Zeus's intervention is to make Aphrodite cease and desist from bringing about these inappropriate unions between the gods and mortals, which, in turn, will mean the end of the age of heroes.[46]

At this point, it may be useful to review cursorily the mythology surrounding the genesis and demise of the heroic epoch. The Myth of the Ages in Hesiod's *Work and Days* (109–201) offers the broadest tableau of mankind's decline from the Golden Age, when men lived like the gods, to our own Age of Iron. After the disappearance of the first three races of Gold, Silver, and Bronze, Zeus creates "a divine race of hero-men, who

---

[43] Cf. Rose (1924), p. 11: "Zeus, to prevent Aphrodite having the laugh over all other deities, causes her to fall in love with Anchises." Bickerman (1976), p. 240: "Zeus ... led her astray ... so that she could no longer mock the other gods for their incontinence." Similarly, J. C. Kamerbeek, "Remarques sur l'Hymne à Aphrodite," *Mnemosyne* 20 (1967): 394: "Zeus a voulu qu'Aphrodite devienne victime de sa propre puissance à elle en lui inspirant une passion pour un mortel afin de l'humilier et de la faire se taire sur ses victoires remportées sur les autres immortels." For Podbielski (1971), p. 54, the main point is the humorous effect of watching Aphrodite fall into her own trap; but, then, he generally views the whole poem as an ironic parody of the epic gods, intended to divert a sophisticated audience (cf. pp. 30–31). Yet the comic dimension of the hymn in no way precludes its underlying seriousness.

[44] Cf. Lenz (1975), p. 93: "Zeus' Absicht bei diesem Unternehmung ist, bestimmte intern olympische Verhältnisse in Ordnung zu bringen." Also p. 129: "die Sondermacht dieser Göttin stört die innere Ausgewogenheit der olympischen Hierarchie." Lenz is wrong, however, when he claims that Zeus "legitimiert die Liebschaft zwischen Göttern und Menschen wieder als unanstössig für die Götter, indem er Aphrodite Ausnahmestellung aufhebt" (p. 33).

[45] Cf. Smith (1981a), pp. 39–40.

[46] To the best of my knowledge, only van der Ben (1981), pp. 89 and 93, has grasped this essential point. Lenz (1975), p. 35, hints at it, but then backs away.

are called demigods" (159–60). More just and better than the previous generation, these heroes are the offspring of one divine and one human parent. Exceptionally, a few—one thinks of Dionysus and Heracles—become immortal, but the heroes proper are the mortal progeny of such unions. Two factors bring about the end of the heroic age; many die violently in the great conflicts at Thebes and, above all, at Troy (161–65). But the death knell for the heroes is sounded when the gods withdraw from intercourse with mortals, and their race is not replenished.[47] The increased distance between the gods and mortals marks the Age of Iron, which is our own.

Two other works of Hesiod bear on this question. The *Theogony* concludes with a brief account of unions between goddesses and men (965–1020).[48] Its continuation, the *Catalog of Women*, enumerates the far longer list of unions between mortal women and the gods, as well as their progeny; it spans the entire heroic period. Its invocation stresses the intimacy obtaining between gods and men during that era (fr. 1. 6–7 [Merkelbach-West]).[49] A lengthy but unfortunately badly damaged fragment from the last book (fr. 204.41–95 [Merkelbach-West]) enumerates the suitors of Helen and describes the oath they took to come to the aid of the successful aspirant. In time, they will become the leaders of the Greek contingents at Troy. A brief mention of Helen's marriage to Menelaus precedes an abrupt transition: we suddenly discover a quarrel breaking out among the gods and Zeus pondering how to bring about the destruction of the heroes (96ff.).[50] Nagy comments: "besides entailing the death of the heroes in the Trojan War ... the Will of Zeus also entails *the permanent separation of gods and men*" (cf. 102–3).[51] As we have already seen, the plan of Zeus at the beginning of the *Cypria* has a similar point

---

[47] Cf. Clay (1983), p. 173; and Rudhardt (1981), pp. 247–49.

[48] For the problems of the authenticity of this passage, see West's (1966) commentary to the *Theogony*. I myself am tempted to believe that lines 1008–10 concerning Anchises and Aphrodite ("Lovely garlanded Cythereia bore Aeneas, / joining in love with the hero Anchises on the peaks of windy Ida of many folds") brought the poem to its conclusion. The position of the episode in the catalog of unions between goddesses and mortal men may, then, reflect a tradition, elsewhere unknown, that Aeneas was the last-born of the heroes.

[49] "At that time, both the feasts and the sitting places were common / to both the immortal gods and mortal men." On the proem to the *Catalog*, see K. Stiewe, "Die Entstehungszeit der hesiodischen Frauenkataloge," *Philologus* 106 (1962): 291–99.

[50] On this difficult fragment, see K. Stiewe, "Die Entstehungszeit der hesiodischen Frauenkataloge (Fortsetzung)," *Philologus* 107 (1963): 1–29. Less convincing is the interpretation of M. L. West in *The Hesiodic Catalogue of Women* (Oxford, 1985), pp. 115–21, and "Hesiodea," *CQ* 55 (1961): 132–36.

[51] G. Nagy, *The Best of the Achaeans* (Baltimore, 1979), p. 220.

of departure and goal. The parallelism in our sources, then, suggests a well-developed tradition linking the beginning of the end of the age of heroes to the period just before the Trojan War.[52]

Although less explicit, the Homeric epics contain numerous indications that the heroic era is coming to a close.[53] Thus, Nestor can disparage the heroes at Troy in comparison with the mighty warriors of his youth:

κείνοισι δ᾽ ἂν οὔ τις
τῶν οἳ νῦν βροτοί εἰσιν ἐπιχθόνιοι μαχέοιτο.

With those men, no one
of mortals who is now living on earth could do battle.

(*Iliad* 1.271–72)

The distance separating gods and mortals seems to be increasing. They last feasted together at the wedding of Peleus and Thetis (xxiv. 62) Now the gods generally come upon men unseen or in disguise. The time when elect heroes might achieve immortality through a special dispensation also seems to belong to the past. Now only few of the heroes can lay direct claim to a divine parent.[54] The best of them, Achilles, curses his mixed parentage (xviii.86–88); for his divine mother, her son's mortality constitutes a source of boundless grief. Sarpedon's death gains in tragic poignancy when we recognize him to be the last son of Zeus. Other heroes must search back several generations to discover a divine ancestor; most acknowledge their fathers and their forefathers to be better than they. Tlepolemus, son of Heracles and grandson of Zeus, can even taunt Sarpedon:

ψευδόμενοι δέ σέ φασι Διὸς γόνον αἰγιόχοιο
εἶναι, ἐπεὶ πολλὸν κείνων ἐπιδεύεαι ἀνδρῶν
οἳ Διὸς ἐξεγένοντο ἐπὶ προτέρων ἀνθρώπων.

[52] Cf. Nagy (1979), p. 219, n. 14, 2: "there is no need to assume that the text of Hesiod *fr*. 204 M W is based on one or several other *texts*; it is enough to say that the text is based on various *traditions* that occur also in the *Cypria* and in the *Iliad*." Cf. Thalmann (1984), pp. 102–6.

[53] Cf. Clay (1983), pp. 174–76; Rudhardt (1981), pp. 257–58, n. 66. Compare Griffin (1980), p. 170: "the poet offers no explanation for the fact that once there were heroes, and now there are not, but only the inferior men of today."

[54] Cf. van der Ben (1981), p. 89, who offers a list.

They lie when they say you are the offspring of Zeus of the aegis,
since you are far inferior to those men
who sprang from Zeus among men of the past.

(*Iliad* v.635–37)

The *Iliad* itself reveals an awareness of the declining nature and transience of its own epoch. At the beginning of the twelfth book, the poem momentarily looks forward to a time when all traces of the war, including the great Achaean wall, will be effaced (XII.13–33). Only in this passage does Homer use the term demigods (ἡμιθέων γένος ἀνδρῶν [23]).[55] From the perspective of our own age, the heroes who fought at Troy will have become the vanished race of demigods. The *Odyssey*, where the ghosts of the heroes twitter bloodlessly in Hades, already looks back on the heroic age as a thing of the past.[56] At its end, gods and men join not in feasting, but in lamentation, to mourn the great Achilles and the epoch he embodied (24.64).

Both the Hesiodic catalog tradition and the epic pinpoint the destruction of the heroes at Troy as a pivotal moment in human history. This, however, forms only part of the story. The Homeric poems and the *Catalog* implicitly acknowledge a second factor in the passing of the heroic age; as the gods cease mating with mortals, the generation of new heroes likewise ceases.

It is within this framework that the *Hymn to Aphrodite* must be understood and that its epoch-making character stands revealed. Its action takes place at a decisive moment in human and divine history. The plan of Zeus, from which the narrative springs, has as its goal the permanent and absolute separation of gods and mortals. In accomplishing his purpose, Zeus will institute a new order, one that Hesiod calls the Age of Iron and the epic poet describes as the time of "men as they are now." Far from merely being a tale of seduction or even a parable of "the tables turned," the hymn, for all its risqué charm and wit, offers an etio-

[55] On this passage, consider the remarks of K. Reinhardt, *Die Ilias und ihr Dichter* (Göttingen, 1961), p. 267: "Es ist das einzige Mal, dass der Dichter jener Heldenzeit, die er besingt, als einer fernen Zeit von seiner eigenen Gegenwart sich ansichtig wird. . . . Es ist aus dieser Perspektive, dass die Heroen zum einzigen Male in der Ilias 'das Geschlecht der halbgöttlichen Manner' (ἡμίθεοι) heissen. . . . Der Rhapsode, der dies Wort in den Mund nimmt, tritt damit als heutiger Mensch der Heroenwelt betrachtend und bewundernd gegenüber." Cf. Nagy (1979), pp. 159–61; and R. Scodel, "The Achaean Wall and the Myth of Destruction," *HSCP* 86 (1982): 33–50.

[56] Cf. Clay (1983), pp. 183–85.

logical myth that explains why those splendid but problematic *Misch-wesen*, whom the Greeks called heroes and demigods, no longer exist in the world as we know it.[57]

The story of Aphrodite's seduction of Anchises and their union is thus both a typical exemplar of all erotic activity, a graceful meditation on the eternal meaning of Aphrodite,[58] and at the same time a uniquely portentous event of universal consequence: the last time a god mates with a mortal to produce the last hero. The hymn combines a celebration of Aphrodite and her "works," which are everywhere and always the same, with a singular narrative whose outcome radically alters the configuration of the cosmos and all future relations between gods and mortals.

Seduction

The remainder of the hymn can easily be divided into two parts: the seduction (53–167), and its aftermath (168 to the end), most of which is taken up by Aphrodite's great speech (191–290). With the exception of some so-called disgressions in Aphrodite's speech, the hymn exhibits none of the abrupt transitions or leaps of thought that characterize *Apollo* and *Hermes*. *Aphrodite*'s remarkably smooth and linear narrative progress has been widely admired, and even the finicky nineteenth-century critics found few grounds for questioning the unity or integrity of the composition.[59]

Ἀγχίσεω δ᾽ ἄρα οἱ γλυκὺν ἵμερον ἔμβαλε θυμῷ.

For Anchises, then, did he [Zeus] cast sweet desire in her heart.

(53)

Desire is not for the general but for a particular object: Anchises, who grazes his cattle on the peaks of Ida. It is kindled by beauty (he resembles "the immortal gods in his build") and inflamed by sight:

[57] Cf. van der Ben (1981), p. 89.

[58] Cf. Fränkel (1962), p. 285: "am Beispiel des einen Abenteuers offenbart sich Aphrodites Wesen und Wirken wie es immer ist." Also Porter (1949), p. 270: "the perfection of the hymn form is found in the perfect synthesis of the dramatic and the metaphysical, the temporal and the timeless."

[59] G. Freed and R. Bentman, "The Homeric Hymn to Aphrodite," *CJ* 50 (1955): 157, use the excellent condition of the text to argue for a Hellenistic date for the poem, which is "unmarred by either lacunae or corrupt readings."

τὸν δὴ ἔπειτα ἰδοῦσα φιλομμειδὴς Ἀφροδίτη
ἠράσατ᾽, ἐκπάγλως δὲ κατὰ φρένας ἵμερος εἷλεν.

Then, on seeing him, smile-loving Aphrodite
fell in love, and terribly did desire seize her in her heart.

(56–57)

The goddess of love finds herself in the grip of desire, but first she must make herself an object of desire. Going to her temple at Paphos, Aphrodite is washed and anointed with the ambrosial oil of the gods by her attendant Graces; then, the goddess dresses and adorns herself with gold. The seductive odor of perfume and incense dominates the scene.[60] Her preparations resemble those of a warrior arming for battle:[61] seduction, like war, requires preparation. There are also echoes of similar Homeric episodes: when Hera prepares to seduce Zeus in the *Iliad*, and when Athena beautifies the sleeping Penelope so that "she might flutter the hearts of the suitors."[62] But both these epic seductions are means to very different ends: Hera's, to distract Zeus from the Trojan battlefield; Penelope's, to extract gifts from her wooers. Aphrodite, by contrast, has no ulterior motives; for her, it is pure seduction with no purpose but consummation.[63] Zeus's intentions remain unknown to her.

When all is ready, Aphrodite rushes through the clouds, from Cyprus to Troy, until she reaches wooded Ida, "mother of beasts" (66–69). At the goddess's coming, the fiercest animals are rendered tame by her presence and fawn on her.

---

[60] Cf. Porter (1949), pp. 268–69; Podbielski (1971), p. 37; and van der Ben (1981), p. 69. For the erotic associations of scents and perfumes, see M. Detienne, *Les Jardins d'Adonis: La Mythologie des aromates en Grèce* (Paris 1972).

[61] Cf. Smith (1981a), p. 41.

[62] Lines 60 and 63 correspond to *Iliad* xiv.169 and 172, where Hera prepares for the seduction of Zeus. For a comparison of the two passages, see Lenz (1975), pp. 118–23; and Podbielski (1971), pp. 36–39. Lines 58–59 parallel *Odyssey* 8.362–63 and 364–65, where Aphrodite retires to Cyprus *after* being caught *in flagrante* with Ares. The very fact that the lines can be used both as preparation and aftermath of erotic activity suggests that they are formulaic in Homer. There is, then, no need to assume that the hymn-poet imitates here. Cf. Pellizer (1978), pp. 132–33. In the Penelope passage, Athena prepares the queen by anointing her with the "ambrosial beauty" Aphrodite uses when she joins the "lovely dance of the Graces" (*Odyssey* 18.192–94).

[63] As Reinhardt (1961b), p. 515, comments on the difference between Hera's seduction and Aphrodite's: "Was bei Hera Trug ist, ist bei ihr [Aphrodite] Wesen."

ἡ δ' ὁρόωσα μετὰ φρεσὶ τέρπετο θυμὸν
καὶ τοῖς ἐν στήθεσσι βάλ' ἵμερον, οἱ δ' ἅμα πάντες
σύνδυο κοιμήσαντο κατὰ σκιόεντας ἐναύλους.

> Seeing them, she rejoiced in her heart,
> and she cast desire in their hearts; and all of them at once
> lay down in twos in their shadowy lairs.

(72–74)

The proem proclaimed Aphrodite's conquest over the beasts of land, sea, and air: here we see her exerting her power as she passes among them. For the brutes, unlike for humans and gods, persuasion and deception and the other arts of Aphrodite prove unnecessary; they do what comes naturally and mate only with their own kind.

Between the city and the dens of savage beasts, at the boundary between civilization and the wilds, lies the realm of Aphrodite.[64] In this liminal area, the goddess comes upon Anchises, who has been left behind, wandering aimlessly and playing his lyre[65] while his companions are off grazing their cattle (78–80). His solitude and leisure, preconditions for *eros*, are duly emphasized, as is his physical beauty:

τὸν δ' εὗρε σταθμοῖσι λελειμμένον οἶον ἀπ' ἄλλων
Ἀγχίσην ἥρωα θεῶν ἄπο κάλλος ἔχοντα.

> She found him alone, left behind by the others,
> Anchises, the hero, who had his beauty from the gods.

(76–77)

Line 77 might appear to be merely formulaic or conventional, but it is not.[66] "Hero" occurs only here in the Homeric Hymns.[67] In fact, Anchises has his beauty from the gods (cf. 55) because he is a hero and sprung from

---

[64] Cf. Segal (1974), p. 210; and Friedrich (1978), pp. 74 and 143–45.

[65] Cf. *Iliad* III.54, where the lyre is conjoined with the "gifts of Aphrodite." Achilles plays the lyre after he has withdrawn from battle. For Anchises' aimless wandering, compare *Iliad* II.779, where the Myrmidons pass their time in enforced leisure. It seems likely that the *Cypria* depicted Paris playing the lyre when the three goddesses approached him for the fateful judgment. For the evidence from vase painting, see C. Clairmont, *Das Parisurteil in der antiken Kunst* (Zurich, 1951), pp. 19–22 and 104.

[66] The closest parallel to the last half of the line occurs at *Odyssey* 8.457, a description of Nausicaa. Cf. *Odyssey* 6.18; Hesiod fr. 171.4 and fr. 215.1 (Merkelbach-West). The expression is elsewhere applied only to women.

[67] Anchises is called a hero in *Theogony* 1009.

them. The description of Anchises and his situation is framed by the arrival of Aphrodite.[68] The narrative can now proceed.

στῆ δ' αὐτοῦ προπάροιθε Διὸς θυγάτηρ 'Αφροδίτη
παρθένῳ ἀδμήτῃ μέγεθος καὶ εἶδος ὁμοίη,
μή μιν ταρβήσειεν ἐν ὀφθαλμοῖσι νοήσας.

She stood before him, the daughter of Zeus, Aphrodite,
alike in size and form to an unbroken maiden,
so that, in observing her with his own eyes, he would not be
frightened.
(81–83)

Seduction, as we have said, is the erotic conquest of the stronger by the weaker; its tools are deception and persuasion. In this particular case, Aphrodite is a goddess and hence more powerful than the mortal Anchises. Her epiphany in her true form would arouse not love but fear in Anchises, the fear evoked by being in the presence of a superior being who has the potential for doing one harm. The stronger must then disguise herself as the weaker. Not only does the love goddess transform herself into a mortal; she disguises herself as an innocent maiden, "unbroken,"[69] that is, without sexual experience, who appears to Anchises in an isolated spot without protectors in a position of extreme vulnerability. The piquant irony of this reversal of appearance and reality offers a perfect example of Aphrodite's wiles.[70]

On seeing her, Anchises marvels at her beauty, her gleaming clothes, and shining ornaments (84–90). In the dressing sequence, Aphrodite's appearance was treated with relative brevity. We can now see that it has been deferred to be elaborated here, as she appears before Anchises' eyes. Previously, scents predominated; here it is sight, as the many words for brightness and light attest.[71] Anchises' reaction to this wondrous shining vision is laconically stated: *"Eros* seized Anchises"

[68] Cf. Smith (1981a), p. 44. For a comparison with typical epic arrival sequences, see Lenz (1975), pp. 123–24.
[69] In *Odyssey* 6.109 and 228, Nausicaa is called a παρθένος ἀδμής.
[70] Cf. Podbielski (1971), p. 52: "L'autoportrait d'Aphrodite [est] diamétralement opposé à son portrait traditionnel et à celui crée par l'auteur de l'*Hymne* au début de celui-ci."
[71] For Aphrodite's shining quality, see Smith (1981a), p. 45. For the dramatic character of the description, see Podbielski (1971), p. 43.

(91).[72] Nevertheless, he greets the lovely stranger with a pious prayer and addresses her as an unknown goddess. She must be one of the blessed ones—perhaps Artemis or Leto or golden Aphrodite, or Themis or Athena, or perhaps one of the Graces or even a local nymph. The lengthy list of possibilities demonstrates both Anchises' ignorance and his caution. While unaware of which of the immortals has appeared to him, he rehearses all the possible candidates to avoid giving offense. Unbeknownst to him, he has, in fact, hit the mark. Whoever she may be, Anchises continues, he promises her an altar in a conspicuous place and fine sacrifices in all seasons (100–2).[73] Upon this promise, in accordance with the normal sequence of prayer, follows a request. May the unknown goddess be well disposed and grant him to be outstanding among the Trojans, to have thriving offspring, to live well and long, and to grow old prosperously among his people (102–7). Anchises' prayer contains nothing excessive or inappropriate for a young man in his situation.[74] It is the prayer of a moderate and sensible man who recognizes the superiority of the gods and the limitations of the human condition.

At least one critic has raised the question of Anchises' sincerity here. Because this first speech is important for establishing our hero's character, the issue deserves consideration. Does he really believe he has encountered a god or is he employing "prudent flattery" or "adopting the same diplomatic attitude Odysseus used to address Nausikaa"?[75] In the *Odyssey* (6.149–58) the briny and naked stranger asks the virginal princess whether she is a god or a mortal: if a god, he likens her to Artemis; if a mortal, he counts her parents most blessed. The whole matter is then quickly dropped. Odysseus offers no prayer or promise of worship, and

[72] The same expression occurs again after Aphrodite's speech of seduction at line 144, a fact that has troubled critics. Lenz (1975), p. 37, n. 1, claims that it means different things in the two passages and that the poet has committed "eine psychologische Ungenauigkeit" by reusing the same formula. Van der Ben (1981), p. 71, argues similarly that *eros* in line 91 implies only a "general disposition," whereas *eros* plus *himeros* in lines 143–44 signifies an invincible desire that demands immediate gratification. None of this special pleading is necessary, and it destroys the dramatic progress.

[73] Podbielski (1971), pp. 46 and 85, as well as Càssola (1975), p. 549, assume an etiological reference to a cult of Aphrodite on Ida. But both Lenz (1975), p. 27, and van der Ben (1981), p. 72, note that Aphrodite makes no response to Anchises' offer either here or at the end of the poem.

[74] Smith (1981a), p. 47, thinks Anchises' prayer "show[s] him to be most untypically concerned with his old age and with the future of his family." But part of it resembles Hector's prayer for his son (cf. *Iliad* vi.476–78) and the rest can be compared to Odysseus's prayer to the nymphs (*Odyssey* 13.360) and the end of Teiresias's prophecy to him (*Odyssey* 11.134–37).

[75] Smith (1981a), pp. 46–47.

his request is a decidedly lowly and commonplace one: some clothing to cover his nakedness. The parallel to the hymn proves unpersuasive.[76] Moreover, on purely internal grounds, we must postulate Anchises' sincerity. Otherwise, a great deal of the high comedy and playful irony of the sequel is lost. For one thing, despite her attempt to tone down her beauty and desirability, Aphrodite nevertheless overwhelms the mortal with her *superhuman* beauty. One might recall the passage in the third book of the *Iliad* where the goddess likewise appears to Helen in the guise of an old woman. Yet her lovely neck, desirable bosom, and sparkling eyes give her away (III.396–97). The love goddess, it appears, cannot be other than lovely and desirable. Even more important, Anchises' sincerity is essential to the dramatic progress of the narrative. His genuine piety must be established. Although he is in the very grip of *eros*, religious scruples restrain him from any impropriety. Anchises is emphatically not a *hybristēs*, an impious fool like Ixion or Orion whose lust drove them to violate goddesses. Finally, if Anchises is only pretending, Aphrodite's response becomes unnecessary; she has no need to overcome his resistance or to persuade him. Her speech of seduction becomes pointless, an empty charade. Although, as the text tells us (91), Anchises falls victim to desire from the moment he lays eyes on Aphrodite, nothing in his words betrays his aroused state. The pious Anchises can and does control his sexual appetite so long as he believes that the strange woman before him is a goddess. To achieve her ends, she must convince him otherwise; in other words, she must seduce him. Unlike the wild beasts in whom desire leads to immediate consummation, humans are subject to certain scruples and constraints, whether social or religious, that restrict sexual license. Human beings, like animals, copulate, but the art of seduction, used to overcome inhibitions and restrictions, distinguishes them from beasts.

Aphrodite's task is clear: she must remove the remaining obstacle to the fulfillment of her desire by convincing Anchises that she is not a divinity. Anchises is her dupe. But she in turn is the unwitting pawn of Zeus; in accomplishing her end, she fulfills the plan of Zeus. It is rendered somewhat easier by Anchises' desire to believe her. The persona that Aphrodite constructs for herself in the following speech (108–42) is the verbal complement to her physical disguise. While adopting the pretty prattle of a modest maiden, she must also account for her sudden appearance and increase Anchises' already inflamed lust through indirec-

---

[76] Cf. Podbielski (1971), pp. 45–46, who points out the essential differences between the two passages. Also van der Ben (1981), p. 72.

tion and innuendo. She begins, surprisingly, by addressing Anchises by name and a flattering epithet: "most glorious of earth-born men."[77] A god, of course, would know his name, but she will later have to explain how she came by it. After first vehemently denying her divinity (109–10), the goddess launches into an account of her background, filled with circumstantial details that lend an air of verisimilitude to her tale (110–16). Her father is Otreus, ruler of Phrygia, "if perhaps you have heard of him somewhere."[78] With a pretty touch, she adds that she learned to speak Anchises' language from her Trojan nurse.[79] Next, Aphrodite neatly solves the awkward question concerning how she came to this isolated spot in all her finery, while she manages at the same time to stress her desirability. Hermes, it seems, carried her off from the "chorus of Artemis" where she was dancing with other maidens "worth many cattle," while a great crowd looked on.[80] Frequently mentioned in Greek legends, the dance in honor of Artemis by girls approaching the age of marriage performed the function of a debut or showcase for the display of marriageable maidens, who were generally kept in seclusion.[81] So far, Aphrodite has established her credentials as a nubile maiden of royal stock, who has been properly brought up and sheltered in accordance with the standards of aristocratic society; in addition to her evident beauty and desirability, she is a valuable commodity.

Twice Aphrodite mentions that Hermes snatched her away from the dance of Artemis, the traditional locus of rape or abduction. The verb she uses, ἁρπάζω, is in fact the proper term for abduction; moreover, a passage in the *Iliad* describes just such an abduction on the part of Hermes.[82] Of course, in the hymn, Hermes merely transports the would-be maiden, but why does Aphrodite allude to the common abduction

[77] χαμαιγενέων occurs only once again in the Homeric Hymns at *Demeter* 352. Smith (1981a), pp. 50–51, notes that Aphrodite never manufactures a false name for herself.

[78] In *Iliad* iii.184–89, Priam relates that, in his youth, he aided Otreus, lord of the Phrygians, in a campaign against the Amazons. Apollodorus 3.12.3 mentions a Placia, daughter of Otreus, as the wife of Laomedon. Such an alliance would establish close familial ties between the royal houses of the Phrygians and the Trojans, of which Anchises might indeed have heard.

[79] On the language question, see Smith (1981a), p. 50; and Reinhardt (1961b), p. 517.

[80] Smith (1981a), p. 51, calls Aphrodite's account a "story of innocence overpowered" and notes the breathless girlish naiveté of lines 119–23 (p. 52).

[81] For the χορός of Artemis, see Boedeker (1974), pp. 47–49; and C. Calame, *Les Choeurs de jeunes filles en Grèce archaïque* (Rome, 1977), 1: 174–90.

[82] *Iliad* xvi.181–86. ἁρπάζω is the appropriate term for abduction. See the *Hymn to Demeter* 3, 19, etc. Both Podbielski (1971), p. 51, and Reinhardt (1961b), pp. 517–18, remark on the high incidence of divine rape in Anchises' family. Cf. *Aphrodite* 203 and 218.

motif here? I suggest that she wryly insists on it to titillate and inspire Anchises—to give him "ideas." Seduction, we should note, in which the weaker overcomes the stronger, is the polar opposite of forcible rape. Throughout, Aphrodite has made herself appear the weaker; now she hints at rape to Anchises, for the moment, apparently the stronger.

Be that as it may, Hermes then carried her over the inhabited and uninhabited land, both "the works of mortal men" and the "undistributed and unbuilt" land frequented by wild beasts. Inevitably, we are reminded of the realm of Aphrodite, which encompasses both. Now it appears that Hermes, far from being an abductor, turns out to be a matchmaker:

Ἀγχίσεω δέ με φάσκε παραὶ λέχεσιν καλέεσθαι
κουριδίην ἄλοχον, σοὶ δ᾽ ἀγλαὰ τέκνα τεκεῖσθαι.

He told me over and over that in the bed of Anchises I would be
    called[83]
your wedded wife and bear you splendid children.

                                         (126–27)

(So that's how she learned Anchises' name!)[84] Thus, the marriage foretold by Hermes is duly sanctioned by the gods: Anchises need have no fear. Ironically, of course, the union (but no marriage) is not only sanctioned but planned by Zeus himself.

Having explained how she got there and for what divinely ordained purpose, all the while indicating her present helplessness, Aphrodite now appeals to Anchises by Zeus and his own parents, who must surely be excellent people to have such a fine son; let him introduce her, "unbroken" and sexually inexperienced as she is, to his parents and brothers, for she will be a seemly sister-in-law to them.[85] Meanwhile, he should send word to her parents—her mother may be worried. They, in turn, will send gifts appropriate to a girl of her social standing.[86]

[83] For the diction of this line, see Càssola (1975), p. 550; and Kamerbeek (1967), pp. 391–92.
[84] Note the emphatic initial position of the name in line 126.
[85] Van der Ben (1981), p. 75, thinks the reference to brothers is an indirect compliment to Anchises. But could the reference to *his* brothers draw attention to the fact that her natural protectors are not present?
[86] J. J. Keaney, "*Hymn. Ven.* 140 and the Use of ᾽ΑΠΟΙΝΑ," *AJP* 102 (1981): 261–64, convincingly argues that the use of the puzzling ἄποινα, "ransom," in line 140 furthers Aphrodite's pose as Anchises' suppliant and serves to underline her complete help-

ταῦτα δὲ ποιήσας δαίνυ γάμον ἱμερόεντα
τίμιον ἀνθρώποισι καὶ ἀθανάτοισι θεοῖσιν.

Having done these things, arrange the feast for the desirable
marriage,
honored by both men and the immortal gods.

(141–42)

In the course of her speech, Aphrodite manages to allude to her virginity,
which makes her more desirable as a wife,[87] her elevated social status,
and the wealth that marriage to her will bring to Anchises—all in all, a
masterful selling job on someone who hardly needs to be sold. At the
same time, however, her insistence on observing the proprieties and complex formalities prior to the wedding—with the clear understanding of
no premarital sex—sets roadblocks in the path of immediate satisfaction
and serves to tease Anchises all the more. There is an additional irony
here in Aphrodite's elaboration of the social conventions regulating marriage. Aphrodite, we remember, is not the patroness of legitimate marriage, which involves a regulated exchange between two families, but the
patroness of sex.

I have dwelt on the preceding speech in some detail. This little masterpiece of trickery and persuasion, in which every word is chosen for its
calculated effect on Anchises, reveals Aphrodite in her element as perfect
mistress of seduction and desire.[88] At the same time, the speech keeps
before us in an ironic perspective the theological implications of the plan
of Zeus. Literally from her first words to her last, the problematic nature
of the conjunction of god and mortal stands revealed. Union, however
temporary, can only be achieved through deception and self-deception,
of which Aphrodite herself is the emblem.

ὣς εἰποῦσα θεὰ γλυκὺν ἵμερον ἔμβαλε θυμῷ.
᾿Αγχίσην δ᾿ ἔρος εἷλεν.

So speaking, the goddess cast sweet desire in his heart,
and love seized Anchises.

(143–44)

---

lessness. She presents herself as totally within his power—and he immediately takes advantage of the situation.

[87] Cf. van der Ben (1981), pp. 74–75.

[88] Cf. Lenz (1975), p. 126:, "man darf wohl sagen, dass der Dichter mit der Verfüh-
rung, deren Glanzstück die Rede 107 ff ist, quasi-homerisch eine Art Aristie der betör-
ungsmächtigen Aphrodite darbietet."

Despite his state of passionate arousal, Anchises nevertheless responds with caution.[89] If indeed she is, as she claims, a mortal, born of mortal mother, and Otreus is her father, and if she has come by the will of Hermes.... His rehearsal of the goddess's lying tale sounds at once as if he is protecting himself and as if the mere repetition of her falsehoods would make them true. He will indeed marry her, as she had asked; but no man or god will keep him from possessing her here and now.[90]

> ... οὐδ' εἴ κεν ἑκηβόλος αὐτὸς Ἀπόλλων
> τόξου ἀπ' ἀργυρέου προΐῃ βέλεα στονόεντα.
> βουλοίμην κεν ἔπειτα, γύναι εἰκυῖα θεῇσι,
> σῆς εὐνῆς ἐπιβὰς δῦναι δόμον Ἄϊδος εἴσω.

> ... not even if far-darting Apollo himself
> should shoot his grievous arrows from his silver bow.
> I would be willing, thereafter, woman who resembles the
>   goddesses,
> once having mounted your bed, to go into the house of Hades.

(151–54)

Hyperbolically, Anchises declares his willingness to die after he has slept with the girl. The pious hero who refused to violate religious taboos even in the heat of passion turns out to be quite willing to ignore human social conventions. But the hero's passionate declaration contains a deeper irony: whereas the gods may strike down the mortal lovers of goddesses, they do not, as a rule, intervene in purely human unions, nor do they generally consider premarital sex a punishable offense.[91] But Anchises' defiant statement, born of his impulsive passion, points to his true danger.

After these words, Anchises takes the goddess by the hand and leads her to his bed, while she, with her "fine eyes cast down" (156)[92] modestly

[89] Van der Ben (1981), p. 76, speaks of Anchises' almost judicial caution here. Smith (1981a), p. 55, on the other hand, notes that the lack of a vocative suggests a kind of impulsiveness.

[90] Note the postponement of αὐτίκα νῦν in line 151. Compare the similar treatment of the ways of a man with a maid in Archilochus's *Cologne Epode*, fr. S 478, in D. Page, *Supplementum lyricis graecis* (Oxford, 1974), pp. 151–54.

[91] In the first book of the *Iliad*, Apollo's arrows unleash a plague upon the Greeks because of Agamemnon's mistreatment of Chryses. His "gentle arrows" bring death to the inhabitants of Eumaeus's Syria (*Odyssey* 15.410–11); and the nasty goatherd Melanthius prays that the god strike Telemachus (*Odyssey* 17.251). The only divinity who punishes unchaste behavior seems to be Artemis.

[92] Aphrodite's gesture suggests modesty, but it may also be intended to hide her divinity, since the sparkling eyes of the gods often give them away. Cf. the *Hymn to Demeter*

follows. Anchises, as Smith points out, plays the "dominant man here in control of the encounter."[93] But that control remains illusory; the powerful goddess, who for the moment appears the passive partner, has accomplished her purpose. The bed to which they repair is covered with soft blankets and draped with "the hides of bears and roaring lions whom he himself had killed on the lofty mountains" (159–60)—an appropriate symbol of the half-wild, half-civilized character of *eros*.[94] Then, first taking off the jewelry Aphrodite had so carefully donned for just this moment, Anchises undresses the goddess and neatly places her clothing in a chair.

> ... ὁ δ' ἔπειτα θεῶν ἰότητι καὶ αἴσῃ
> ἀθανάτῃ παρέλεκτο θεᾷ βροτός, οὐ σάφα εἰδώς.

> ... and then by the will and destiny of the gods,
> he lay beside the immortal goddess, a mortal, not clearly knowing
> what he did.
> (166–67)

Ominous words climax this union of god and mortal. Anchises' human ignorance[95] of his divine bedfellow is matched by Aphrodite's ignorance of the will of the gods. Unwitting tools of Zeus, both the goddess and her mortal lover are united in their ignorance of his plan.

Aftermath

The remainder of the poem involves at least the partial dissipation of the lovers' ignorance. The simpler and shorter recognition of Anchises follows immediately on the epiphany of the goddess (168–90). Aphrodite's more complex psychological *anagnōrisis* is dramatically conveyed in her long speech (192–291); it involves more than merely recognizing what stands before her eyes, but a realization of the trap into which she has fallen.

Anchises sleeps until evening, the time that herdsmen return from

---

194. Thalmann (1984), p. 95, I think wrongly, interprets the gesture as a "sign of her self-abasement."

93 Smith (1981a), p. 59.

94 Cf. Segal (1974), p. 210; and Smith (1981a), p. 59.

95 Smith (1981a), p. 61, speaks only of Anchises' "incomplete knowledge"; van der Ben (1981), p. 77, emphasizes the ignorance of both parties.

pasture (168–71). With this generic indication of time,[96] the poet reminds us of the hero's absent comrades who have been tending their flocks while the lovers have been dallying. *Eros* demands both leisure and privacy; the lovers' realm, circumscribed by the dimensions of a bed, begins to give way to the work-a-day considerations of the larger world. Meanwhile, the "shining goddess" dresses and assumes her true stature and superhuman splendor:

ἔστη ἄρα κλισίῃ, εὐποιήτοιο μελάθρου
κῦρε κάρη, κάλλος δὲ παρειάων ἀπέλαμπεν
ἄμβροτον, οἷόν τ᾽ ἐστὶν ἐϋστεφάνου Κυθερείης.

She stood up in the hut, and her head grazed
the well-wrought roof beam, and from her cheeks shone beauty
immortal, such as belongs to well-garlanded Cythereia.

(173–75)

Previously, the disguised deity shone on account of her jewels; the revealed goddess radiates a divine glow from within. Such radiance is a hallmark of epiphany.[97] The increased height of the goddess recalls the description of the gods on Achilles' shield.[98] Intercourse between gods and mortals literally requires a diminution of divinity.

Aphrodite awakens her lover in a commanding tone ("Arise, offspring of Dardanus"[99]), and then asks with teasing sarcasm whether she looks the same as before. On seeing her "neck and fine eyes," Anchises is terror stricken, averts his eyes, and hides his face under the bedcovers. Earlier, the goddess correctly anticipated the fear her true appearance would inspire (cf. 83). Now, there is no question as to who is the superior. The submissive maiden has become the imperious goddess, and the formerly bold lover Anchises, a frightened suppliant.[100] In a beseeching tone, Anchises asserts that he knew right away from the beginning that she

---

[96] Cf. Smith (1981a), pp. 61–62.

[97] Cf. *Apollo* 202–3, 440–42, 444–45; *Demeter* 275–80. See also F. Pfister, "Epiphanie," *RE* suppl. 4 (1924): 315–16. For divine epiphany as a regular feature of the hymnic genre, see Lenz (1975), pp. 19–20.

[98] *Iliad* XVIII.519.

[99] Dardanus is not only the founder of the Trojan line, but a son of Zeus. Cf. the genealogy in *Iliad* XX.215–41 and 304.

[100] Cf. Smith (1981a), p. 65. Lenz (1975), p. 40, notes that now (line 181) Anchises averts his eyes, whereas before (line 156), it was the disguised Aphrodite who did.

was a goddess, but she deceived and misled him. Then he begs her by Zeus

μή με ζῶντ' ἀμενηνὸν ἐν ἀνθρώποισιν ἐάσῃς
ναίειν, ἀλλ' ἐλέαιρ'· ἐπεὶ οὐ βιοθάλμιος ἀνὴρ
γίγνεται ὅς τε θεαῖς εὐνάζεται ἀθανάτῃσι.

not to leave me to live without strength among men,
but take pity; since not flourishing is the life of the man
who goes to bed with immortal goddesses.

(188–90)

Having recognized the goddess and her deception, Anchises pleads for mercy, but what does he fear?[101] Some commentators adduce the examples of Tityus, Orion, and Ixion, who slept, or attempted to sleep, with goddesses; all received exemplary punishment for their *hybris*. Other scholars cite *Odyssey* 5.119–29, where Calypso enumerates instances of mortals beloved by goddesses whom the gods, jealous of their happiness, struck down.[102] Yet Anchises' situation does not comfortably fit into either category. It was not he who tried to rape the love goddess, but she who seduced him. As for Calypso's accusations, they belong to a time emphatically after the events recounted in the hymn and, in fact, presuppose them. Anchises, then, fears neither punishment for *hybris* nor divine jealousy—not some hostile action on the part of the gods—but, as Giacomelli has recently argued,[103] the immediate consequences of the act itself: the loss of μένος. As she points out, one need not look to Oriental myths of the Great Mother and her consort to find a close parallel.[104] In the tenth book of the *Odyssey*, Circe preemptorily invites Odysseus to her bed. Fearing that the goddess will make him "weak and unmanned"

[101] Smith (1981a), p. 65, sees Anchises' plea here as a "negative and fearful" formulation of the request he made earlier in lines 102–6. Van der Ben (1981), p. 79, believes that Anchises is asking the goddess for immortality, i.e., "do not leave me *here* to live among men, but take me with you." I am not convinced.

[102] Podbielski (1971), pp. 63–64, considers Calypsos's speech the model for Anchises', but he takes no account of the hymn's temporal framework. AHS (1936), p. 363, recognize the difference between the examples adduced by Calypso and Anchises' situation, and they conclude: "probably the fears of Anchises here are based upon a vague dread of the supernatural."

[103] A. Giacomelli, "Aphrodite and After," *Phoenix* 34 (1980): 1–19.

[104] Giacomelli (1980), p. 17: "the fear is emphatically Greek." I follow her interpretation of the Circe passage, although I find her citation of the Ixion story in this context misleading.

once he is naked (341), the wily hero exacts an oath that she will not "plot some other evil pain" for him (344). Afterward, Circe offers him a restorative bath and meal to relieve his "heart-destroying weariness" (363), caused, no doubt by his extraordinary sexual activity. Similarly, in the hymn, Anchises is afraid that his union with Aphrodite will leave him permanently debilitated in a state resembling postcoital lassitude. He cannot, however, yet be aware of another peril lying in the future. Beguiled by Aphrodite, but innocent of *hybris*, Anchises has unwittingly crossed the boundary separating gods and mortals at the moment when that boundary is about to be enforced.

The response of Aphrodite, which occupies the rest of the poem, has rightly been termed a commentary on the preceding action.[105] At the same time, as Lenz has observed,[106] it replaces an expected epilogue returning us to the plan of Zeus from which the entire action sprang. We are therefore justified in anticipating that the goddess's speech will illuminate not only her immediate encounter with Anchises, but also the long-range consequences outlined by the plan of Zeus. Throughout the speech, it is essential to bear in mind the epochal character of the events represented in the hymn—not just any union of god and mortal, but the last one. Insofar as the poem signals the end of one era and the start of the new, Aphrodite's discourse serves to explicate both the old order of relations between gods and men as well as to allude to those that will obtain in the new. If Aphrodite's actions in the first half of the hymn are the agency of this change, her words allow us to view simultaneously the old and the new and thus throw light upon the poem's pivotal character. Nevertheless, the goddess herself remains only incompletely aware of the final outcome of her actions. Although her words betray a recognition of Zeus's role in inspiring her desire for Anchises, she never becomes fully cognizant of his ultimate plan, which she unwittingly executes. Only we, the audience, are privy to the ἄφθιτα μήδεα of Olympian Zeus. The sublime intellectual pleasure derived from sharing in the eternal counsels of the supreme god consoles us, to some extent, for the loss of intimacy with the divine, which is the purpose of his plan.

The complex texture of Aphrodite's speech thus results from its triple function. Addressed to Anchises, the goddess's words simultaneously comfort and warn her mortal lover. At the same time, she gives voice to

---

[105] Cf. Podbielski (1971), p. 64.

[106] Lenz (1975), pp. 24–25. Compare the structure of the *Hymn to Demeter*, which begins among the gods and returns to them at the end.

reflections concerning the relation between the human and the divine that spring from her forced contact with mortality and her recognition of the complicity of Zeus. Finally, while she refers prophetically to the future, of whose ultimate contours she is only dimly aware, she invites our participation and understanding of its evolution and necessity.

Addressing Anchises once again as "most glorious of men" (192), Aphrodite substitutes καταθνητῶν for her earlier epithet, χαμαιγενέων (108), thus perhaps insisting more strongly on the distance between her revealed divinity and his mortality.[107] He is not to fear punishment from her or the "other blessed ones,[108] since you are dear to the gods" (195). Anchises' actions have been innocent of *hybris* nor do they provoke divine enmity. Far from begrudging the union, the gods, or at least Zeus, have promoted it. Anchises remains, as before, beloved by the gods, and he will receive not punishment, but a reward—not the sterility he feared, but the male heir for whom he had hoped. Aphrodite announces the birth of a son sprung from their union, who will rule over the Trojans, and a continuous succession for Anchises' line.[109] Her promise corresponds at least in part to the hero's own earlier prayer to her for a "flourishing progeny" (104). But she makes no reference to his request "to be outstanding among the Trojans" (102). Perhaps the favorites of Aphrodite cannot hope for heroic stature.[110] At any rate, the son she has conceived

> ... Αἰνείας ὄνομ' ἔσσεται οὕνεκά μ' αἰνὸν
> ἔσχεν ἄχος ἕνεκα βροτοῦ ἀνέρος ἔμπεσον εὐνῇ.
>
> ... will have the name Aeneas, since dread
> grief possessed me because I fell into the bed of a mortal man.
>
> (198–99)

By saying that she "fell" into Anchises' bed,[111] Aphrodite indirectly acknowledges herself to have been pushed. Moreover, through the name

---

[107] Cf. Smith (1981a), p. 126, n. 79.

[108] μακάρων as a designation of the gods occurs only here and at line 92 in Anchises' prayer to the unknown goddess. The term demonstrates an awareness of the gulf between the blissful gods and human beings.

[109] For the difference between the prophecy given to Anchises and the one given to Aeneas in *Iliad* xx.307–8, see van der Ben (1981), pp. 81–82; and Lenz (1975), pp. 114–5.

[110] For the unheroic character of Paris, another favorite of Aphrodite, see H. Monsacré, *Les Larmes d'Achille* (Paris, 1984), pp. 41–51.

[111] The usual verb for entering a bed is ἐπιβαίνω. Cf. lines 154 and 161. In *Iliad* xviii.85, the gods are said to have cast (ἔμβαλον) Thetis into the bed of a mortal man.

she gives her son, the goddess commemorates her painful fall from untroubled, even irresponsible, divinity to intimate contact with a mortality
whose product will, of necessity, be grief.

Now expanding on her assertion of the gods' love for Anchises,
Aphrodite remarks that, because of its beauty, his race has always been
"near the gods"—that is, it stands in a privileged position of closeness to
the divine.[112] As proof, she offers the example of Ganymede, whom Zeus

ἥρπασεν ὃν διὰ κάλλος ἵν' ἀθανάτοισι μετείη
καί τε Διὸς κατὰ δῶμα θεοῖς ἐπιοινοχοεύοι.

abducted[113] on account of his beauty so that he might live among
   the immortals
and be wine pourer to the gods in the house of Zeus.

                                                    (203–4)

There, honored by all the gods, Ganymede pours the nectar that keeps
the Olympians eternally young and fair.[114] However, after the mysterious
disappearance of his son, Tros grieved incessantly until Zeus took pity,
gave him immortal horses as recompense,[115] and revealed Ganymede's
fate to his father:

    ... εἶπεν δὲ ἕκαστα
Ζηνὸς ἐφημοσύνῃσι διάκτορος Ἀργειφόντης,
ὡς ἔοι ἀθάνατος καὶ ἀγήρως ἶσα θεοῖσιν.

                  ... and he told him everything,
on orders from Zeus, Hermes the messenger,
that he [Ganymede] would be immortal and unaging even as the
   gods.
(212–14)

On hearing the news, Tros ceases his lamentation and rejoices at his son's
extraordinary destiny.

[112] ἀγχίθεοι is used of the Phaeacians in the *Odyssey*.
[113] In *Iliad* xx.234, it is the gods who carry off Ganymede. The *Hymn to Aphrodite*
emphasizes the agency of Zeus in the Ganymede affair. Cf. Lenz (1975), p. 108; and van
der Ben (1981), pp. 83–84, who understands the implication: "quod licet Iovi non licet
Veneri."
[114] Cf. Clay (1981–1982), pp. 112–7.
[115] In *Iliad* v.265–68, we learn that Anchises stole the horses of Tros, mated them, and
gave two to his son Aeneas.

Because it affects the overall understanding of the hymn, I must momentarily digress to take issue with Peter Smith's recent interpretation of this passage.[116] Smith argues for a generally negative valuation of Ganymede's fate, first, because Tros's loss of his son is only inadequately compensated by the gift of immortal horses. But more important, for Ganymede himself, his apotheosis contains undesirable qualities: he will never "grow up"; "he has no potential for development"; and "his immortality is a purely negative escapist gain."[117] Furthermore, his intimacy with Zeus can never compensate for the loss of a normal human relationship between father and son. Finally, on the basis of the choices made by Odysseus and Achilles, Smith concludes: "The heroes of both major epics turn down the chance to live longer when accepting it would mean sacrificing the fulfillment in action of their roles as men. It does not seem hard to imagine how either of them would have chosen had he been offered the immortality of Ganymede."[118] In addition to the obvious error of equating "longer life" with the eternal immortality of the gods, Smith's interpretation of the Ganymede figure is imbued with a modern sensibility that runs counter to the pessimistic Greek assessment of the human condition as well as its understanding of heroism.

Apotheosis is granted to a very few mortals—a Heracles, for his heroic labors and sufferings,[119] a Ganymede, for his superhuman beauty. After a certain period, when the gods begin to separate themselves from mortals, it ceases altogether. Yet to become a god does not become any less desirable or enviable on account of its rarity or even impossibility. The best commentary on the Ganymede story in the *Hymn to Aphrodite* is Pindar's *First Olympian*, which rings the changes on the heroic possibilities of human life through the myths of Tantalus and Pelops. Tantalus, supremely blessed by his intimacy with the gods, proves unable to digest his good fortune and, in attempting to steal the nectar and ambro-

[116] Smith (1981a), pp. 71–77.

[117] Smith (1981a), p. 74. Smith, p. 72, also detects secondary negative overtones in the fact that Ganymede is the passive partner in a homosexual relationship. R. Janko, in his review of Smith (*CR* 31 [1981]: 286), suggests Hesiod's Silver Age as a parallel to "Ganymede's eternal adolescence." But Zeus would hardly be disposed to have those huge babies wait on him in Olympus. In fact, he destroyed them.

[118] Smith (1981a), pp. 76–77. Cf. his wrong-headed interpretation of the choices of Odysseus and Achilles, pp. 75–76. Odysseus's rejection of Calypso's offer of immortality is far too often misunderstood and sentimentalized. Cf. Clay (1983), p. 185. Achilles' choice between a short, splendid life and an obscure, long one is similarly not a rejection of immortality but an acknowledgment of its impossibility in his epoch.

[119] Cf. the *Hymn to Heracles, the Lionhearted*.

sia of the gods, becomes an exemplar of *hybris*. Explicitly called a parallel and predecessor of Ganymede (43–45),[120] Tantalus's son, Pelops, was loved by Poseidon who translated him to Olympus. When the gods discover Tantalus's crimes, they send Pelops down from Olympus "back among the short-lived race of men" (66). Returned to his mortality, precisely *because* he must die, Pelops chooses the dangers of heroic endeavor rather than "nameless old age" (83–84). With the help of Poseidon who loved him, Pelops risks and wins the heroic struggle and is honored in death with heroic cult.

In this meditation on heroism, Pindar makes clear that it remains a *pis aller*, a second best after the loss of immortality. In a famous passage from the *Iliad*, often cited as "the Code of the Hero," Sarpedon voices the same sentiment to his friend Glaucus:

> For if, my friend, having escaped this war,
> you and I could always be ageless and immortal,
> neither would I fight among the first ranks,
> nor would I send you to fight into battle which gives men glory;
> but now that the dooms of death continually surround us,
> countless, which no man can avoid or escape,
> let us go, either to give the boast to another, or to let someone give
>   it to us.[121]
> (*Iliad* XII.322–28)

To be sure, in the Homeric epic, apotheosis already belongs to a prior age, but Ganymede's fate, to become immortal and unaging, nevertheless remains the highest and best imaginable. In the *Hymn to Aphrodite*, nothing in the goddess's account of Ganymede suggests otherwise.

To illustrate further her contention concerning the gods' love for the family of Anchises, Aphrodite proceeds to adduce a second example: the story of the dawn goddess's abduction of the beautiful Tithonus. But while ostensibly beginning as a parallel to the tale of Ganymede, the story of Tithonus develops into a contrasting picture in which the wretchedness of Tithonus stands in sharp opposition to the blissful lot of

---

[120] Cf. D. E. Gerber, *Pindar's Olympian One: A Commentary* (Toronto, 1982), pp. 79–80; and J. T. Kakrides, "Die Pelopssage bei Pindar," *Philologus* 85 (1930): 463–5. Both believe Pindar modeled his Pelops story on that of Ganymede.

[121] Cf. Griffin (1980), pp. 92–93, on this passage: "if the hero were really god-like, if he were exempt, as the gods are, from age and death, then he would not be a hero at all." Smith (1981a), p. 129, n. 94, misunderstands the passage completely.

Ganymede. At the same time, Aphrodite exploits the parable of Tithonus to explain and justify her own situation. The Tithonus example, then, has a double function, shedding new light on the Ganymede story and obliging us to reassess certain of its features, as well as preparing a return to Anchises and the goddess's present dilemma.[122]

Aphrodite recounts how, after Eos had carried off Tithonus, "who resembled the immortals" (219), she asked Zeus to make him immortal. Zeus grants the request, but the dawn goddess had forgotten to ask for youth and "a stripping off of old age."[123] As long as Tithonus retained his "lovely youth," he enjoyed the company of Eos, but the goddess abandons his bed as soon as his first gray hairs appear. She nevertheless keeps him "in her halls," solicitously feeding him with "grain and ambrosia." When, however, "hateful old age" weighs him down completely and Tithonus can no longer move, she hides him away in a chamber behind closed doors. Nothing is left of him but his voice, which "flows unceasing"[124]—with what eternal lament we can only guess. With each successive stage of Tithonus's inexorable deterioration, the dawn goddess increasingly separates herself from her erstwhile lover.[125]

According to one interpretation, Dawn's oversight in requesting eternal life but not eternal youth is due to "her frivolity . . . or rather her love-inspired blindness." Thus, the moral of the tale resides in a condemnation of unreasonable passion.[126] But I believe the burden of the story lies elsewhere. On a narrative level, it emerges that Eos must apply to Zeus to render her mortal lover immortal. He alone, it appears, has the power to grant such a request and to dispense such an exemption from the common lot. Indeed, he exercised a similar function in approving Hestia's request to maintain her chastity. The granting of such extraordinary privileges and honors belongs exclusively to Zeus. The importance of this fact will become clear in the sequel.

In her account to Anchises, Aphrodite spares us nothing of the horror and the pathos of Tithonus's condition. Death itself seems infinitely

---

[122] According to Lenz (1975), p. 111, the Tithonus story has "a double face" as both a parallel and a contrast to the tale of Ganymede.

[123] For the meaning of ἀποξύνω, see van der Ben (1981), p. 86.

[124] For the effect of the switch to the present tense here in the Greek, see Smith (1981a), p. 81. Tithonus's voice continues even now. For an attempt to imagine what it might say, see Tennyson's "Tithonus."

[125] On the stages of this separation, see Smith (1981a), pp. 78–81.

[126] Cf. Podbielski (1971), pp. 71–72: "Le résultat de la légèreté de la 'déesse du matin' ou plutôt de son aveuglement amoureux . . . apparaît comme une condamnation de l'amour irraisonable et fou."

preferable to his eternal aging, which Mimnermus called a κακὸν ἄφθι-
τον, "an imperishable evil."[127] Neither Homer nor Hesiod mentions Tithonus's terrible destiny, and many scholars believe it to be the invention
of the hymn-poet,[128] but the truth cannot be known with certainty. Whatever its source, the story arises from a consideration of the common epic
formula for immortality, which has not one but two components: ἀθάνατος καὶ ἀγήρως ἤματα πάντα, "immortal and ageless forever."[129] Such,
of course, is the blessed state of the gods and of Ganymede, but the two
qualities are separable phenomena. Tithonus is immortal but not ageless.
A pattern can be detected here, and by the end of the hymn, all the possible combinations of these two categories will have been presented to
form a complete system. As such, it readily yields to, and even invites, a
structural analysis involving bipolar oppositions. These will be considered later. But, for the present, we must not lose sight of their dynamic
role in the dramatic logic of the unfolding story.

Aphrodite explicitly links the fate of Tithonus to the situation of
Anchises.[130] The example of Tithonus serves to justify her decision not
to make Anchises her consort:

οὐκ ἂν ἐγώ γε σὲ τοῖον ἐν ἀθανάτοισιν ἑλοίμην
ἀθάνατόν τ᾽ εἶναι καὶ ζώειν ἤματα πάντα.
ἀλλ᾽ εἰ μὲν τοιοῦτος ἐὼν εἶδός τε δέμας τε
ζώοις, ἡμέτερός τε πόσις κεκλημένος εἴης,
οὐκ ἂν ἔπειτά μ᾽ ἄχος πυκινὰς φρένας ἀμφικαλύπτοι.
νῦν δέ σε μὲν τάχα γῆρας ὁμοίιον ἀμφικαλύψει
νηλειές, τό τ᾽ ἔπειτα παρίσταται ἀνθρώποισιν,
οὐλόμενον καματηρόν, ὅ τε στυγέουσι θεοί περ.

I, indeed, would not choose you to be such as he among the
    immortals,
to be immortal and to live forever.

[127] Mimnermus fr. 4.1 (West).
[128] Podbielski (1971), p. 70; Smith (1981a), p. 84; van der Ben (1981), p. 86; and
C. Segal, "Tithonus and the Homeric *Hymn to Aphrodite*: A Comment," *Arethusa* 19
(1986): 45. J. T. Kakrides, "ΤΙΘΩΝΟΣ," *Wiener Studien* 48 (1930): 25–38, on the other
hand, believes the story to be older than the hymn. H. King, "Tithonos and the Tettix,"
Arethusa 19 (1986): 15–35, not only supposes that the hymnist knew the myth, but that in
her speech Aphrodite suppresses its ending, Tithonus's metamorphosis into a cicada, because it would not suit her rhetorical purpose.
[129] Cf. Clay (1981–1982), pp. 112–17.
[130] Van der Ben (1981), p. 85, calls the Tithonus story the major premise of Aphrodite's
argument.

But if as you are now in form and build
you could live and be called my husband,
then grief would not encompass my compact heart.
But, as it is, soon leveling old age will encompass you,
pitiless, which hereafter attends human beings,
baneful, toilsome, and which even the gods loathe.

(239–46)

Aphrodite's argument is illogical and specious, but rhetorically effective. Having dwelt on the horrors of Tithonus's existence, the goddess asserts that she would not wish such a fate on Anchises. She implicitly suggests to him that it would be far better for him to remain the mortal he is than to endure such immortality. Her contention, however, is flawed by the simple fact that there is no reason why Aphrodite should repeat the foolish mistake of Eos. If Anchises could, on the other hand, remain as young and fair as he is now—that is, be like a Ganymede—and become her consort, Aphrodite continues, she would have no cause for grief. This alternative is silently rejected as impossible: "but as it is. . . ." If we have paid attention to the tales of Ganymede and Tithonus, we will understand the hidden grounds for its rejection: Zeus had the power to make his beloved Ganymede immortal; Dawn, on the other hand, had to request immortality for hers from Zeus. Aphrodite would have to apply to Zeus on behalf of Anchises, and this is precisely what she cannot do.[131] For Eos, it may have been unproblematic to approach Zeus with her request. Aphrodite, however, tacitly ignores even the possibility of such an undertaking. Her speech thus reveals an awareness of Zeus's role in the entire affair. Aphrodite knows that her request for Anchises' immortality would meet with scornful rejection on the part of Zeus, who intended from the first to teach her a lesson. By compelling her to desire a mortal, Zeus has set his trap. But it snaps shut only when Aphrodite realizes that there is no escape from the inevitable grief and pain such a union produces, because the sole key to an escape is held by the very one who laid the trap.

It may be objected that Aphrodite's recognition of Zeus's role in her discomfiture is not explicitly stated. It must, however, be postulated on the grounds of both dramatic and narrative logic. As we have seen, her

---

[131] Cf. Boedeker (1974), p. 80: "in the *Hymn*, Aphrodite, like Eos, is apparently unable to offer a deathless existence to her lover of her own accord. That ability rests with Zeus." See also van der Ben (1981), p. 87.

implicit recognition at the moment of her epiphany corresponds to Anchises' recognition of her divinity. Moreover, if we do not assume it, we must sacrifice a coherent interpretation not only of this passage, but of the poem as a whole. The mythical exempla of Ganymede and Tithonus become mere "speculative symbols" without genuine relevance to Anchises' case, and Aphrodite's speech involves a "breakdown of everyday logic."[132] Smith is ultimately led to such a view on the basis of his contention that "if this is to be a serious myth and not simply a fantasy of wish-fulfillment," we must accept the fact that "one of the underlying realities which guide the myth ... is the unchangeable fact of men's mortal nature."[133] I cannot quarrel with the assertion of the seriousness of the myth recounted in the hymn. But that seriousness derives precisely from its explaining how it came about that, formerly, human beings could become immortal, whereas now and forever, immortality can never again be the human lot, and man is henceforth consigned to his mortality.

Having sealed Anchises' future fate with a somewhat Olympian *hauteur*, Aphrodite now turns to her own:

αὐτὰρ ἐμοὶ μέγ' ὄνειδος ἐν ἀθανάτοισι θεοῖσιν
ἔσσεται ἤματα πάντα διαμπερὲς εἵνεκα σεῖο,
οἳ πρὶν ἐμοὺς ὀάρους καὶ μήτιας, αἷς ποτε πάντας
ἀθανάτους συνέμιξα καταθνητῇσι γυναιξί,
τάρβεσκον· πάντας γὰρ ἐμὸν δάμνασκε νόημα.

But for me there will be a great reproach among the immortal
    gods
continually for all time, on account of you,
they who formerly were wont to tremble at my love talk and plots,
    whereby
I at one time mated all the immortals to mortal women;
for my design used to overcome them all.

(247–51)

<hr>

[132] Smith (1981a), pp. 88–89. Cf. p. 90: the poet juxtaposes "the cases of Ganymede and Tithonos with that of Anchises *even though the juxtaposition can lead to nothing in the story*" (italics in original). Smith at least does not ignore the problem of logic and consistency here, although he tends to skirt the issues that it raises. Lenz's comment ([1975]), p. 112, n. 1) is completely unsatisfactory: "der Dichter kann ja nicht gegen den Mythos die Göttin bei Zeus um Unsterblichkeit samt ewiger Jugend für Anchises bitten lassen." Càssola (1975), p. 248, notes "una incrinatura nello sviluppo logico del carme," but attributes it to the contingencies of recitation.

[133] Smith (1981a), pp. 87–88.

Anchises and Aphrodite must go their separate ways. Whereas he remains an earthling, consigned to his mortality, she will return to Olympus. But there her brief encounter with a mortal will prove an eternal source of potential reproach from the gods.[134] In outlining her previously invincible power over the gods, Aphrodite mentions only the liaisons she caused between male gods and mortal women. Perhaps she regards her conquests over female deities as lesser victories insofar as they do not necessarily imply the defeat of the stronger at the hands of the weaker.[135] Although both the unions of gods with mortal women and of the rarer ones of goddesses with mortal males produce mortal heroes, the latter seem to cause attachments more painful because they are more enduring. One thinks immediately of Thetis, the *mater dolorosa*, δυσαριστοτό-κεια, who must endure not only Peleus's aging, but also Achilles' premature death. Despite Aphrodite's attempt to dissociate herself from Anchises and the distance she will shortly put between herself and her child, she acknowledges the painful character of her divine maternity in the name she assigns her son. The goddess's omission of her triumphs over female divinities thus points to her embarrassed awareness of her own predicament.

Aphrodite's universal conquests belong to the past: "now it is no longer . . ." (252). Unfortunately, at this crucial juncture, the text is not entirely clear.[136] As it stands, the goddess appears to say that she will no longer be able "to mention this among the immortals." "This" (τοῦτο [253]) must refer to νόημα, Aphrodite's "design" for the promiscuous mingling of gods and mortals, and encompasses the whole preceding description of her formerly triumphant power. Most critics are content to

---

[134] For the use of ὄνειδος here, see van der Ben (1981), pp. 88–89.

[135] Van der Ben (1981), p. 89, suggests only that the male gods were more active in this respect and hence that such unions were more common.

[136] The manuscripts at line 252 read στοναχήσεται, which is not Greek. στόμα χείσεται, "my mouth will no longer contain me to name," is read by Hermann (1806), Baumeister (1860), Humbert (1936), and AHS (1936), but the sense is terribly strained. Gemoll (1886) and Càssola (1975) accept στόμα τλήσεται, "my mouth will no longer dare to name," which gives better sense, but raises metrical problems. Cf. P. M. Smith, "Notes on the Text of the Fifth Homeric Hymn," *HSCP* 83 (1979): 34–35. Kamerbeek (1967), pp. 392–93, prefers στόμ' ἀχήσεται, "my mouth will no longer cry out to name." Van Eck (1978), pp. 86–87, offers στοναχὴ (ἔ)σεται, "but now that will no longer be a reason for sighing among the immortals to mention," which retains the manuscript reading but does not convince. Van der Ben (1981), p. 90, offers the boldest emendation: νῦν δὲ δὴ οὐκέτι μοι γάμον ἔσσεται ἐξονομῆναι / τοῦτον ἐν ἀθανάτοισιν, "now, it will no longer be possible to name this marriage."

believe that Aphrodite only renounces her previous boasting over her conquests.[137] But as we saw earlier, Zeus's plan went far beyond merely putting an end to Aphrodite's mocking the gods who fall victim to her power. So here, the goddess realizes that she will no longer be able to mention her victories, *because there will be none to speak of*; her days of devising mixed marriages are over forever,

> ἐπεὶ μάλα πολλὸν ἀάσθην
> σχέτλιον οὐκ ὀνομαστόν ἀπεπλάγχθην δὲ νόοιο,
> παῖδα δ᾽ ὑπὸ ζώνῃ ἐθέμην βροτῷ εὐνηθεῖσα.

> since I was gripped by reckless blindness
> —a wretched and unspeakable[138] thing—and was driven out of
> my mind;
> and put a child under my girdle after sleeping with a mortal.

> (253–55)

In conceiving a child by a mortal, Aphrodite has fallen prey to the same blind foolishness[139] and madness as her erstwhile victims. Having learned that the conjunction of divine and human can produce only grief, the goddess now turns her attention to the future of the son she will bear, the child whom we can now recognize as the last of the race of demigods.

In the hymn, the gulf between the human and the divine has been defined by a double set of oppositions: mortal/immortal, and subject to age/unaging. Although these opposing pairs have been operative throughout the poem, they come to the fore here as Aphrodite describes the future nurses of her son (257–73). Although some earlier scholars found the lengthy description of the nymphs to be either an unnecessary or merely picturesque excursus,[140] several modern critics have recognized

[137] For example, Bickerman (1976), p. 239: "she, who had made all the immortals mate with mortal women, would no longer dare to speak out about the lapses of the other gods." See also n. 43, above. The exception is van der Ben (1981), p. 92.

[138] ὀνομαστόν, read by Gemoll (1886), Humbert (1936), Kamerbeek (1967), p. 393, Càssola (1975), Smith (1979), pp. 36–37 is clearly to be preferred to the reading of AHS (1936), ὀνοταστόν.

[139] The closest parallel to the expression πολλὸν ἀάσθην occurs at *Iliad* XIX.113, where Agamemnon describes how even Zeus suffered from *atē* when Hera tricked him at the moment Heracles was about to be born. I wonder if the phrase in Aphrodite's mouth in line 253 does not similarly indicate the goddess's recognition of the trick played on her.

[140] For earlier bracketers of the nymph passage, see Baumeister (1860), p. 252, and Gemoll (1886), p. 274. Cf. van Groningen (1958), p. 106, for whom the lines remain an "intercalary" digression.

the function of this digression within the overall economy of the poem.[141] The nymphs of Ida, who will tend the infant Aeneas, we are told, follow neither the pattern of mortals nor of immortals: they live a long time, and eat immortal food. They dance with the gods and even have intercourse with those minor nature divinities, the Silenes, and with Hermes, the god closest to mortals and, of course, himself born of a nymph. In some peculiar way, the lives of these nymphs are bound up with the mighty oaks and pines growing on the mountains, which are called "precincts of the immortals" (267), and no mortal dares to cut them down. When these trees wither and die, the nymphs simultaneously "leave the light of the sun" (272).

It is fully appropriate that the offspring of the goddess and a mortal be nursed by these intermediate beings who inhabit the very wilds where the child was conceived and which constitute the domain of Aphrodite. But the unusual length and detail devoted to the description of the tree nymphs indicate that their presence in the poem goes beyond their simple narrative function. In fact, the digression on the nymphs completes the series of examples beginning with the story of Ganymede, which can be schematized as follows:

GANYMEDE	TITHONUS	NYMPHS	ANCHISES
Immortal	Immortal	Mortal	Mortal
Unaging	Aging	Unaging	Aging

As Segal has noted, this scheme can be further elaborated to include both the diets and the spatial realms appropriate to each member:

Olympus	Boundaries of Ocean	Wilds of Ida	Troy
Ambrosia/ Nectar	Ambrosia/ Grain	Ambrosial Food	Grain

We can clearly perceive a significant pattern of oppositions and correspondences that articulate the various possibilities and combinations underlying the major preoccupations of the hymn.[142] But it is important to note that the complete pattern emerges only at the end of the poem, with

[141] Cf. Podbielski (1971), pp. 75–77; Segal (1974), pp. 209–11; Smith (1981a), pp. 92–95; and van der Ben (1981), p. 94.

[142] Cf. Segal (1974) for other structural components and correspondences in the hymn; see also his restatement (1986), pp. 37–44.

the introduction of the nymphs.[143] At that point, we can look back upon the tales of Ganymede and Tithonus and reevaluate them from this new perspective.

In Lévi-Straussian terms, the two inner columns would appear to present mediating terms between the polarities of mortality and immortality. But the model of Tithonus can only be considered a failure. His eternal aging constitutes a fate worse than death, and Aphrodite exploits his example to reconcile Anchises to his mortality. The nymphs, on the other hand, offer an example of successful mediation between gods and mortals. On the narrative level, they literally mediate the transfer of Aeneas from his divine mother to his mortal father. Likewise, they have intercourse with both gods and men.[144] But on what we might call a symbolic level, the nymphs, or rather the trees to which their lives are bound, suggest a mediation of the contradiction between mortality and immortality.[145] These oaks or firs spring from the "much-nourishing earth" which is the abode of mankind, but they also constitute groves sacred to the gods. They flourish, constantly renewed throughout their long lives, until the time comes for them to die. Then, they dry up, wither, and drop their branches.

The symbolic connection between trees and mankind is a commonplace of Greek literature. Individuals may be called branches or young shoots that will grow and flourish like trees. In the *Iliad*, Priam uses the same term that the hymn-poet applies to the trees—τηλεθάοντες, "flourishing"—to describe his sons (266).[146] Deriving from the notion of vegetative growth, the same verbal root occurs in Anchises' request for a "flourishing progeny" (θαλερὸν γόνον [104]). Finally, Aphrodite herself will call her son a young shoot (θάλος [278]). A famous passage in Homer develops the relationship between men and trees in an elaborate simile:

---

[143] I emphasize the importance of respecting the linear progress of the composition and the order in which certain crucial motifs emerge during its course. Thus, it seems to me bad criticism to begin by analyzing a thematic pattern or motif without attending to the moment and manner in which it emerges.

[144] As becomes clear from lines 284–85. For the nymphs as nurses of the heroes, see Hesiod, fr. 145.1–2, (Merkelbach-West), where Zeus evidently entrusts his son Minos to the nymphs.

[145] Cf. Smith (1981a), pp. 92–95; and Segal (1974), pp. 209–11.

[146] *Iliad* XXII.423. Cf. especially Thetis's description of the young Achilles in *Iliad* XVIII.437–38: "He shot up like a young tree, / and I tended him like a seedling on the high ground of an orchard."

οἵη περ φύλλων γενεή, τοίη δὲ καὶ ἀνδρῶν.
φύλλα τὰ μέν τ᾽ ἄνεμος χαμάδις χέει, ἄλλα δέ θ᾽ ὕλη
τηλεθόωσα φύει, ἔαρος δ᾽ ἐπιγίγνεται ὥρη·
ὣς ἀνδρῶν γενεὴ ἣ μὲν φύει ἣ δ᾽ ἀπολήγει.

As is the generation of leaves, such too is that of men.
Some leaves the wind pours on the ground, but others the
     flourishing forest
brings forth, and the season of spring comes on.
So also is the generation of men: one grows, but another declines.

(*Iliad* vi.146–49)

The leaves may come and go, but the forest itself abides, renewing itself each spring.[147] To be sure, from the divine perspective, the same image illustrates the miserable brevity of human life. Thus, Apollo can use it to dissuade Poseidon from fighting with him over mortals:

ἐννοσίγαι᾽, οὐκ ἄν με σαόφρονα μυθήσαιο
ἔμμεναι, εἰ δὴ σοί γε βροτῶν ἕνεκα πτολεμίξω
δειλῶν, οἳ φύλλοισιν ἐοικότες ἄλλοτε μέν τε
ζαφλεγέες τελέθουσιν, ἀρούρης καρπὸν ἔδοντες,
ἄλλοτε δὲ φθινύθουσιν ἀκήριοι.

Earth shaker, you would not call me sensible,
if I should fight with you for the sake of mortals,
wretched creatures, who like leaves at one moment
flourish in all their brilliance, while eating the fruit of the field,
but at another, they wither and die.

(*Iliad* xxi.462–66)

However, in human terms, the longevity of the family compensates in part for the brevity of human life. As generation succeeds generation, the race outlasts the individual, and it is in this limited duration that mankind must find solace.[148] The child Aphrodite will bear to Anchises will carry on his line and console him for the loss of immortality and the impossibility of a lasting union with the divine.

[147] For the topos, see M. Griffith, "Man and the Leaves: A Study of Mimnermos fr. 2," *California Studies in Classical Antiquity* 8 (1975): 73–88.
[148] This, according to Smith (1981a), is the central message of the hymn.

In the fifth year, Aphrodite continues,[149] she will bring her son to Anchises:

τὸν μὲν ἐπὴν δὴ πρῶτον ἴδῃς θάλος ὀφθαλμοῖσι,
γηθήσεις ὁρόων· μάλα γὰρ θεοείκελος ἔσται.

When you first see your young shoot with your eyes
you will rejoice at the sight, for he will be very godlike.

(278–79)

In a sense, Anchises' very human prayer at the beginning of his encounter with Aphrodite has been answered. With both apotheosis and sexual union with the divine henceforth denied, prayer and sacrifice remain the appropriate vehicles of communication with the divine. θεοείκελος in line 279 is not merely conventional. Aeneas's resemblance to the gods does not simply testify to his physical beauty; this last offspring of a god and a mortal will be godlike because divine blood flows in his veins. Immediately, Anchises is to take his son to Troy where, after being conceived and nursed in the wilds, Aeneas will join the community of men.[150]

Aphrodite's speech concludes with a solemn prohibition and warning to Anchises:[151] if any mortal should ask about the mother of his son, Anchises must remember to respond that Aeneas is the offspring of one of the Idaean nymphs:

εἰ δέ κεν ἐξείπῃς καὶ ἐπεύξεαι ἄφρονι θυμῷ
ἐν φιλότητι μιγῆναι ἐϋστεφάνῳ Κυθερείῃ,
Ζεύς σε χολωσάμενος βαλέει ψολόεντι κεραυνῷ.

---

[149] AHS (1936), p. 371, argue for the retention of the manuscript text at lines 274–77. Hermann (1806) and Gemoll (1886) bracketed 277–78. Baumeister (1860), Humbert (1936), and Càssola (1975) eject 274–75. Cf. Smith (1979), pp. 39–41. Van der Ben (1981), p. 95, moves 275 between 277 and 278. But it is precisely line 275 that causes difficulties, because there the nymphs are called goddesses, despite the fact that the poet has taken pains to describe them as different from both gods and mortals. I must therefore agree with those who consider lines 274–75 an interpolation.

[150] For the meditating function of the city, see Segal (1974), pp. 206–7.

[151] Smith (1981a), p. 98, correctly notes a "sharp change in subject and tone" here in Aphrodite's speech: "her concern at this point for secrecy and for containment of the truth is different from the general tenor of her behaviour toward Anchises since the moment of her epiphany" (p. 99). But Smith offers no explanation for Aphrodite's altered tone.

εἴρηταί τοι πάντα· σὺ δὲ φρεσὶ σῇσι νοήσας
ἴσχεο μηδ᾽ ὀνόμαινε, θεῶν δ᾽ ἐποπίζεο μῆνιν.

But if you should speak out and boast with a senseless mind
that you mingled in love with well-garlanded Cythereia,
Zeus in his anger will strike you with his smoldering thunderbolt.
All has been told to you. But you, understanding it in your mind,
restrain yourself, nor speak of it; respect the wrath of the gods.

(286–90)

At long last, Aphrodite reveals her identity, but at the same time she enjoins secrecy on her lover. The injunction is puzzling. As Smith observes, because Aphrodite's maternity cannot be concealed from the gods, "what then has she to gain from *men's* ignorance of the affair?"[152] Although Aphrodite's fall may diminish her power on Olympus, its revelation to mankind does nothing to lower her position in the eyes of mortals who are universally subject to her sway. After all, the hymn itself, while recounting the affair, simultaneously celebrates the love goddess's power.

To answer this question, we must bear in mind that the hymn presents a critical juncture in the history of the relations between gods and mortals. Zeus's plan, we recall, aimed at putting an end to sexual unions between gods and humans, thereby bringing a close to the age of heroes. His design has met with complete success; because of her painful and ignominious experience, Aphrodite will no longer cause such matings. The gulf separating gods and mortals has grown deeper and wider in the course of the poem: a new era has dawned. Whereas Aphrodite assured Anchises that his union with her would not meet with retribution, she now threatens punishment merely if he reveals it. Although his intercourse with her was pronounced innocent, its revelation constitutes an act of *hybris*. The language employed by the goddess makes this clear: she speaks of senseless boasting, an angry Zeus, and "the wrath of the gods"—not just her own. μῆνις, divine wrath, is provoked by human

---

[152] Smith (1981a), p. 98, who continues: "very little, one would guess, especially since her involvement with sex is itself no embarrassment to Aphrodite; at any rate, when the secret got out, she lost no respect from mortals for being the mother of Aeneias." Lenz (1975), pp. 42–43, however, believes that the revelation of the affair by Anchises would constitute an additional humiliation for the goddess. But he seems to contradict himself when he claims that in the eyes of the gods, Aphrodite's action is a defeat, but in the eyes of mortals, it is a triumph and a sign of her power.

behavior that tends to erase the distinctions between gods and mortals and to overstep the boundaries separating them.[153] But as the hymn stands on the threshold of a new era, the boundaries themselves have been redrawn. What previously may have been permitted can now no longer even be spoken of without *hybris*.

The punishment Aphrodite predicts Anchises will incur if he does not heed her warning will come from her, but from the thunderbolt of Zeus, with which he strikes the hybristic enemies of his order.[154] There is an apparent paradox here: Zeus, who at the beginning contrived to weaken Aphrodite's power among the gods, now appears as her defender.[155] But the contradiction vanishes as soon as we realize that Zeus's bolts are not intended to punish an offense against Aphrodite alone, but rather to exact retribution for overweening conduct that attacks *all* the gods and challenges the Olympian order.

It is clear that Anchises ignored the solemn warning of the goddess and revealed the secret, for we, the audience of the hymn, are privy to it. Thus, a second question arises: Was the punishment carried out? Or is Aphrodite's threat as ineffectual as her prohibition? The poem's original auditors were doubtless familiar with Anchises' ultimate fate, but we are not quite so fortunate. According to one tradition, which may go back to the Epic Cycle,[156] Anchises was merely lamed or blinded by Zeus's lightning and survived the fall of Troy with his son. These later traditions may be attempts to harmonize the disability feared by Anchises in lines 187–90 with Aphrodite's final threat. But the romantic coloring of some versions of this tale—Aphrodite is said to intercede on behalf of her former lover—suggests that this account mitigates an earlier version in which Anchises was indeed killed.[157] The *Iliad* at least hints at such an

---

[153] Cf. Clay (1983), pp. 65–68.

[154] For the thunderbolt of Zeus, see *Iliad* xv.117–18, xxi.198; and *Odyssey* 5.125–28, 12.415–19. Cf. Typho in the *Theogony* 839–56, and Hesiod, fr. 51 (Merkelbach-West).

[155] Cf. Lenz (1975), p. 150, n. 1: "Zeus nimmt 45 ff das Ansehen der Götterschaft gegen die eine Göttin und 286–88 das Ansehen der Göttin gegen den Menschen in Schutz." Yet the predicted intervention of Zeus at the end of the hymn defends not only Aphrodite, but the whole divine community. Zeus's conduct is perfectly consistent throughout. Cf. van Eck (1978), p. 97: "Zeus protected the τιμαί of the other gods by confining that of Aphrodite; now he protects Aphrodite's τιμή by safeguarding it from disregard among human beings."

[156] See the discussion of Lenz (1975), pp. 144–52.

[157] Servius at *Aeneid* 2.649 recounts that Anchises was merely lamed because Aphrodite deflected the thunderbolt. However, at *Aeneid* 1.617, he claims Anchises was blinded. Rose (1924), p. 16, argues rather perversely that Zeus's thunderbolt actually immortalized

outcome, for Aeneas is there said to have been raised in the house of his brother-in-law.[158] In the final analysis, it is likely on purely internal grounds that the threat so solemnly pronounced was fulfilled. Aphrodite speaks not as an outraged deity who has received some personal offense, but as an august divinity who warns against hybristic conduct.

ὣς εἰποῦσ᾽ ἤϊξε πρὸς οὐρανὸν ἠνεμόεντα.

And having spoken thus, she darted off toward the windy heaven.

(291)

The hymn ends abruptly. Anchises is given no opportunity to respond. On the Olympus to which the goddess returns, order has been restored. No longer insubordinate to her father, Aphrodite has become a true daughter of Zeus. It now becomes clear why the hymn-poet, although apparently acquainted with the *Theogony*, did not adapt Hesiod's version of Aphrodite's birth from the semen of the castrated Uranus (188–200), but chose instead to follow the Homeric account of the goddess as daughter of Zeus. In the *Hymn to Aphrodite*, the goddess's behavior remains on the level of insubordination within the Olympian family and not a challenge to it from without by an older divinity whose origins antedate those of Zeus.[159]

At the end of her speech, Aphrodite speaks not merely on her own behalf, but as a representative and guardian of the new order. Her final words seal the restored solidarity among the Olympians. At the same time, Aphrodite's brusk departure to Olympus signals the end of an epoch in which gods and mortals shared a now vanished intimacy. It her-

---

Anchises. Lenz (1975), p. 147, assumes the hymn presupposes the tradition of Anchises' crippling. Cf. Kamerbeek (1967), p. 394, who thinks Anchises was punished by either blindness or paralysis, while Smith (1981a), p. 99, is noncommittal on the precise nature of Anchises' punishment. Van der Ben (1981), pp. 97–99, agrees that Aphrodite threatens Anchises with death, but believes that Anchises never violated the prohibition.

[158] *Iliad* XIII.465–66. Hyginus, *Fabula* 94, where Anchises is killed for revealing the secret, is generally assumed to be a late version, but it is just as likely to be early, especially since Hyginus also preserves (in 254 and 260) the tradition of Anchises' survival, which had been canonized in the *Aeneid*.

[159] Cf. Boedeker (1974), p. 37: "the identification of Aphrodite as a daughter of Zeus implies that she is also subordinate to him, a theme which generally affects the characterization of Aphrodite in the hymn." Despite his interest in the "Hesiodic" theology of the Hymn, Solmsen (1968), p. 67, n. 1, dismisses the question: "man könnte allenfalls fragen, warum der Dichter ... nicht vor allen Dingen sich über Aphrodites Eltern und γοναί ... äusserte; aber Überlegungen solcher Art haben sehr begrenzten Wert. Unser Hymnendichter hat an die γοναί wenig Interesse."

alds a new age in which they will no longer freely mingle on earth and no longer unite to produce the demigods. Yet from their remote abodes on Olympus, the gods will continue to enforce the new order of separation. We, for our part, must give up thoughts of immortality or hopes for divine union. The watchword of the new era might well be Alcman's dictum: "do not strive to marry Aphrodite."[160] By explaining and justifying our loss of intimacy with the divine, the *Hymn to Aphrodite* bids us to come to terms with our mortal lot.

[160] *Partheneion* 17 (fr. 1, Page).

CHAPTER 4

HYMN TO DEMETER

 The *Hymn to Demeter* is the best known of the major Homeric Hymns, and it is the only one that has received a full-length scholarly commentary within the last fifty years.[1] Both the familiarity of the myth and the charm of the narrative have attracted even those who do not consider themselves students of Greek mythology. Perhaps more than any other Greek myth, the tale of Persephone carried off by the Lord of the Dead, Demeter's search and mourning, and the final joyous reunion of mother and daughter attests to the humane genius of the Greek imagination, which links the eternal cosmic phenomena of the return of the seasons with the divine drama of loss and renewal. The hymn itself, with its combination of *charis* and *semnotēs*, offers a series of captivating scenes: the innocent joy of Persephone gathering flowers; the daughters of Celeus, frisking like calves or deer; the august silent figure of the black-veiled Demeter; and the speechless terror of Metaneira at the epiphany of the awesome goddess in her house.[2]

Before proceeding to a reading of the hymn within the general framework put forward in the introductory chapter, we must clear away some scholarly underbrush. The relation of the hymn to Eleusinian cult has, to be sure, been a focal point of scholarly interest, but it has also

---

[1] Richardson (1974).
[2] Cf. the appreciation of Fränkel (1962), pp. 288–89.

indirectly impeded the study of the poem. As Allen, Halliday, and Sikes comment: "Great as is the poetical value of the Hymn, perhaps its chief interest lies in the fact that it is the most ancient document bearing on the Eleusinian mysteries."[3] Historians of ancient religion have inevitably been drawn to the hymn because it appears to offer significant clues to the best kept secret of antiquity: the sacred Mysteries of the Two Goddesses at Eleusis. Most of our explicit information as to what went on comes from early Christian apologists—not reliable or unbiased sources. Even writers as late as Pausanias and Plutarch kept the holy injunction against revelation of the rites; and we may recall that in the "enlightened" atmosphere of late fifth-century Athens, the charge of profaning the Mysteries led to the exile of Alcibiades and even contributed to the defeat and decline of Athens. Finally, inscriptional evidence, while abundant, deals mainly with the practical administration of the sanctuary. It is thus inevitable that the *Hymn to Demeter*, as the fullest and earliest document relating to the founding of the cult, should be scrutinized for hints and allusions to what transpired during the initiation ceremony held yearly in the great *telesterion*. After all, we have so little else to go on; and scholarship, like nature, abhors a vacuum.

Yet the hunt for clues to the secret rites has, to a certain extent, jeopardized the interpretation of the hymn. Whenever a detail does not appear immediately germane to the narrative, its presence is explained by appeal to ritual practice. For instance, it is often claimed that Hecate is introduced into the narrative merely because she played a role in Eleusinian cult.[4] Her presence in the hymn is thus assumed to be purely etiological, while her important narrative function is overlooked. Similarly, Demeter's carrying of torches during her search for Persephone is thought to reflect the torchlight procession during the celebration of the Mysteries,[5] and the goddess's silence at lines 59–61 is "explained as a feature of cult."[6] More tenuous are suggestions that Demeter's nine-day fast

---

[3] AHS (1936), p. 118. For a thoroughgoing myth-and-ritual approach to the poem, see F. Wehrli, "Die Mysterien von Eleusis," *ARW* 31 (1934): 77–104. Clinton (1986), p. 44, notes that "some aspects of the poem . . . suggest that the poet's knowledge of Eleusinian matters was hardly intimate at all." Clinton concludes his important article by suggesting that scholars have sometimes actually impeded their understanding of what happened at the Mysteries by excessive concentration on the hymn (p. 49).

[4] Richardson (1974), p. 156. For convenience, I have cited many of these "ritual" explanations from Richardson's commentary, although he is generally less dogmatic than other scholars.

[5] Ibid., p. 165.

[6] Ibid., p. 171.

during her search corresponds to "a similar period of abstention by the initiates at Eleusis,"[7] or that the all-night vigil held by the women of the house of Celeus to propitiate the angry goddess is related to the *pannychis* at Eleusis.[8] On a thematic level, certain aspects of the hymn's narrative have been linked to the symbolism of the cult. The recurrent motifs of seeing and hearing in the poem may derive from phases in the ritual.[9] Likewise, Demeter's partial epiphany on entering the house of Celeus, followed by her full revelation upon departure, has been taken as an allusion to the gradations of initiation.[10] Finally, and perhaps on a more abstract level, Demophoon has been identified as a symbol of the first initiate.[11]

Some of these suggestions are, to be sure, more persuasive than others, and they will receive their due consideration. But it must also be admitted that many of these alleged parallels between the myth of the hymn and Eleusinian practice raise more problems than they solve. Often enough, they place us in the uncomfortable position of interpreting *obscura per obscuriora*. In addition, the pursuit of supposed correspondences tends to reduce the hymn to a kind of rebus puzzle. But even more detrimental to an understanding of the hymn is the assumption that such presumed allusions, once detected, provide sufficient explanation of the presence of a narrative element.

The relation between myth and cult, once perceived as a rather simple one-to-one correspondence, has long since been recognized to be a far more complex phenomenon.[12] Moreover, we have learned that, to inter-

---

[7] Ibid., p. 165

[8] Ibid., p. 256; for further examples, see pp. 201 and 293.

[9] Cf. P. Scarpi, *Letture sulla religione classica: L'Inno omerico a Demeter* (Florence, 1976), pp. 9–46.

[10] Cf. Richardson (1974), p. 209.

[11] Cf. D. Sabbatucci, *Saggio sul misticismo greco* (Rome, 1965), pp. 163–65.

[12] Richardson (1974), p. 234, cautions: "one should remember that one cannot expect the relations of myth to ritual to follow the rules of strict logic." Cf. J. Fontenrose, *The Ritual Theory of Myth* (Berkeley, 1966), p. 50, who points to the fact that there are "all sorts of relations between myths and rituals among primitive peoples: a ritual drama may clearly enact the events of a myth, or a myth may account for nearly every act in a rite, each ritual act in order; other myths, however, account for rites in a less systematic way; still others tell only how the rites were introduced. Moreover once ritual and myth become associated, one affects the other. The myth suggests additions to the rite . . . and the rite suggests additions to or interpolations in the myth." On the "multiple contamination of myth and cult in the case of Greek maenadic cult and the *Bacchae*," see A. Henrichs, "Greek Maenadism from Olympias to Messalina," *HSCP* 82 (1978): 122: "the *Bacchae* itself, with its ritualistic interpretation of Dionysiac myth, must be considered a potential

pret a mythic narrative, we must first respect its integrity. In the specific case of the *Hymn to Demeter*, we must not forget that the poet has no qualms about being overtly etiological when he wants to be—but he also repeats the solemn prohibition against divulging the Mysteries.[13] The hymn, then, must be regarded as an exoteric work.[14] Regrettable as it may be, we must give up, or at least defer, the hope of discovering the secret of Eleusis from the hymn and first seek to understand the story it tells.

That story is by no means as simple or straightforward as might first appear. The familiarity of the myth may cause us to overlook or play down the peculiarity of the version recounted in the hymn, in what it includes as well as what it omits, and especially in its structuring of events. Most strikingly, the hymn completely leaves out Demeter's gift of agriculture to mankind. In addition, the motivation for Demeter's journey to Eleusis and for her attempted immortalization of Demophoon appears obscure, as is the treatment of Demeter's first "epiphany" upon entering the house of Celeus. Further questions are raised by the delay between Demeter's apparent promise to instruct the Eleusinians in her rites and its fulfillment, and the seeming displacement of the theme of the famine.

The hymn, then, appears to lack certain crucial links of logic and motivation.[15] But what is especially remarkable about these narrative gaps and inconsequences is that other extant versions of the myth organize many of the same components and motifs into a coherent narrative sequence, in which each change of scene or transition follows with admirable logic and clarity from what has preceded. There is good reason to suppose that at least some of these versions do not constitute later rationalized revisions of elements found in the hymn but, rather, that they preserve traditions older than the hymn itself. Moreover, the hymn shows internal signs of an awareness and self-conscious avoidance of al-

---

source of inspiration for later maenadic cult. We shall never disentangle the intricate web of maenadic myth and cult which the Greeks wove." The situation for Eleusis is surely similar. One must then agree with G. S. Kirk, *Myth: Its Meaning and Functions in Ancient and Other Cultures* (Berkeley, 1970), p. 18: "It is preferable, therefore, to assess the narrative elements independently of their ritual associations."

[13] Lines 478–79.

[14] Cf. Sabbatucci (1965), p. 170; and Lenz (1975), p. 60, who calls the myth of Demeter in the hymn "nicht streng 'sakral' . . . einmal weil die Prooimia stets halbprofan sind."

[15] Cf. Càssola (1975), p. 33: "È facile notare che la trama narrativa manca di nesso logico."

ternate versions. A comparison with these variants draws our attention to those critical points of transition and abrupt changes of direction that seem to characterize the *Hymn to Demeter*. Again and again, the poet seems to take perverse pleasure in thwarting our expectations and rendering the narrative progress problematic.

Faced with such apparent lapses and illogicalities, an older generation of scholars had recourse to varied explanations involving multiple authorship, interpolations, lacunae, later additions, and reworkings.[16] For the most part, modern commentators tend to assume unitary composition for the hymn[17] and account for inconsistencies by the conflation of various versions of the myth and either formal (i.e., poetic or generic) or external (especially religious) constraints on the poet. According to Richardson, for example, the hymn "is evidently combining two separate stories" while further inconsistencies arise from "the requirements of the traditional epic narrative."[18] On the other hand, Càssola believes that the opaqueness of the narrative may be due to the poet's incomplete knowledge of the Eleusinian myth combined with his fear of revealing secret doctrine.[19]

In approaching the hymn, we must, as I have argued, distance ourselves somewhat from Eleusis. But we must also avoid simplistic solutions to narrative problems. More often than not, they merely skirt issues and close a question at the moment it begins to become interesting. To discover a "meaningless digression" demands that we reconsider our notion of what constitutes meaning in a hymnic narrative; to spot a narrative inconsequence requires us to reexamine our understanding of narrative and mythic causality; and to apprehend a "lack of motivation" means to

[16] E.g., Hermann (1806), p. xcix, believed that the hymn contains "ad minimum duas recensiones confusas"; R. Wegener, "Der homerische Hymnus auf Demeter," *Philologus* 35 (1876): 227–54, on the basis of his hyperrational criteria, discovers four separate strands in the poem. V. Puntoni, *L'Inno omerico a Demeter* (Leghorn, 1896), pp. 2–3, has perhaps the most complex scheme: an original hymn A to which were added fragments of two other hymns, B and C. The final version, in turn, was reworked by two distinct redactors. To counter such analysts, one can also discover unitarians such as K. Francke, *De hymni in Cererem Homerici compositione dictione aetate* (Kiel, 1881); and Baumeister (1860), who gives a good history of early editions of the hymn (pp. 274–79).

[17] Cf. Wilamowitz (1959), 2: 47, who rather grudgingly admits: "Er [the hymn] ist einheitlich; zur Ausscheidung grösserer Abschnitte sind wir nicht berechtigt, denn die Möglichkeit, Versreihen zu entfernen, ist kein Beweis, weil nennenswerte Widersprüche nicht vorhanden sind, wenn man nur die Lässigkeit der Rhapsoden in Rechnung setzt."

[18] Richardson (1974), pp. 259 and 85.

[19] Càssola (1975), p. 34.

rethink the possible intentions of the poet. Like the rites at Eleusis, the hymn consists of *legomena* and *dromena*, the narrative of the poet and the speeches and actions of his characters. Mysteries, too, abound, and while we may not solve them all, we can at least hope to pose the proper questions. The final revelation requires no mystical experience but, rather, painstaking attention to the text.

What follows is an interpretation of the hymn rather than an analysis of the myth of Demeter and Kore, which would demand an exhaustive examination of its variants and parallels as well as its structural components.[20] The uniqueness of the hymn resides precisely in the sequence of its episodes and in its ordering of motifs—displacing some and breaking the logical connection between others. This is what gives the hymn its distinctive character, and its distinctive character is equivalent to its distinctive message. In adapting the traditional tale of Demeter and Kore, the poet of the hymn made certain choices and structured his material to give new meaning to what was probably already an old story. At the same time, he integrated the myth into a larger framework of fundamental notions concerning the Olympians and the relations between gods and mortals that follow the great contours of the theological speculations of Homer and, above all, Hesiod. By means of such modifications, the resultant poem transcends local traditions and practices to become a document of Panhellenic thought.

The hymn falls into three easily differentiated sections:[21] the abduction of Persephone and its revelation to Demeter; the sojourn of the goddess at Eleusis; and the aftermath, including her subsequent withdrawal and the return of Persephone, which leads to the final reconciliation. The first and last parts of this drama take place in the divine sphere and involve divine actors, whereas the middle section focuses on the interaction of Demeter with human beings. The hymn thus operates on two levels, the divine and the human, and its structure demonstrates their interdependence. What happens in the one sphere has important consequences for the other. In its form and import, then, the *Hymn to Demeter* most closely resembles the *Hymn to Aphrodite* and contrasts with the largely

---

[20] For a study of the hymn from a structuralist perspective, see Scarpi (1976).

[21] L. J. Alderink, "Mythological and Cosmological Structure in the Homeric Hymn to Demeter," *Numen* 29 (1982): 1–16, insists on a four-part structure and divides the Eleusis episode into a sequence of "disguise" and "revelation." This, I think spoils the intended symmetry. For the importance of threes in the hymn, see E. Szepes, "Trinities in the Homeric Demeter-Hymn," *Annales Universitatis Budapestinensis de Rolando Eötvös nominatae, sectio classica* 3 (1975): 23–38.

Olympian perspective of the *Hymn to Apollo* and the *Hymn to Hermes*. The consequences of the narrative will lead not only to a modification of the *timai* of the gods, but will also inaugurate a new era in the relations between gods and men.

Spatially, the *Hymn to Demeter* embraces the three domains of the cosmos: Olympus, the earth, and the underworld. It explores the relations among these three realms as well as the possibilities of movement and communication between them. In the course of the story, lines of communication will be both opened and closed in turn until finally a stable avenue of relationships embracing these three spheres of activity will be permanently established. The consequences of what happens in the poem introduce an irreversible alteration in the organization of cosmic space.

Each of the major Homeric Hymns, I have argued, is set within a temporal mythological framework situated somewhere between the accession to power of Zeus and the age of "men like us." In one way or another, each hymn moves us closer to the way the world is now. The "mythical" time of the *Hymn to Demeter* is not too far distant from our own. The great division of the cosmos among the three sons of Cronus has already taken place, and Zeus reigns supreme. The other gods have presumably acquired their various functions and *timai* within the Olympian pantheon, and, most important, Demeter is already in charge of agriculture, her gift to mankind. Mortals, on the other hand, inhabit cities and work the land; they also possess temples and perform sacrifices to the gods. As the Greeks would say, the narrative takes place in the post-Promethean age, one much like our own.[22] The question naturally arises as to how the world on which the hymn opens differs from ours. And further: if the divine hierarchy and the conditions of human life are substantially the same, what changes are introduced by the action of the hymn that demarcates "that time" from ours?

The complexity of the hymn arises from the complexity of its concerns, which encompass the relations among the gods, their relations with mortals, and the repercussions of both on the spatial and temporal realms. Interpretation of the poem demands an awareness of the impact of the narrative—the contours of the plot as well as what each of the actors says and does—in terms of the overall cosmic scheme outlined by the poem.

[22] Cf. J. Rudhardt, "À propos de l'hymne homérique à Déméter," *MH* 35 (1978): 10: "La crise prométhéenne a donc déjà eu lieu." Rudhardt's excellent essay focuses on the key notion of the (re)distribution of divine *timai* in the hymn and its chronological and spatial framework.

Abduction and Revelation

Δήμητρ' ἠΰκομον σεμνὴν θεὰν ἄρχομ' ἀείδειν,
αὐτὴν ἠδὲ θύγατρα τανύσφυρον ἣν Ἀϊδωνεὺς
ἥρπαξεν, δῶκεν δὲ βαρύκτυπος εὐρύοπα Ζεύς,
νόσφιν Δήμητρος χρυσαόρου ἀγλαοκάρπου. . . .

I begin to sing of fair-tressed Demeter, awesome goddess,
herself and her slender-ankled daughter, whom Aidoneus
carried off, but deep-thundering Zeus, the wide-seeing gave her,
in the absence of Demeter of the golden rod and splendid fruit. . . .

(1–4)

The hymn begins by naming its subject, Demeter, and, in second
place, her daughter. Demeter will be the primary focus and agent of the
narrative that follows, but her actions—or rather, reactions—are motivated by the abduction and disappearance of Persephone. In turn, the
rape, in which Persephone remains a passive victim (cf. ἣν), though per-
petrated by Hades, Lord of the Dead, ultimately springs from an action
of Zeus. Lines 1–4, then, begin and end with Demeter, but they also
introduce the other main characters in the divine drama: Persephone,
Hades, and, behind it all, Zeus. The collocation of ἥρπαξεν and δῶκεν
in the third line is both shocking and paradoxical. If Zeus gives his
daughter in marriage in accordance with his paternal prerogatives, why
must Hades carry her off? The reasons become immediately manifest:
not only Persephone's unwillingness but also Demeter's resistance or lack
of consent to the union *if* she had known about it. The goddess's reaction
is presupposed. This marriage, then, is no ordinary marriage, and it demands extraordinary measures.[23] The striking juxtaposition of giving

[23] Cf. Richardson (1974), p. 138: "His [Zeus's] consent to the marriage as father was
necessary to make it legal. . . . But the Rape is also his plan." The fact that Zeus not only
consents to, but sets the trap for, the abduction is unique. Cf. Ramnoux (1959), pp. 129–
30. Scarpi (1976), p. 127, is therefore wrong to see an allusion to a primitive institution of
marriage by rape. There are, to be sure, other unwilling maidens and mothers in Greek
mythology; and the legalization of marriages ex post facto must have been common
enough in life as well as myth. This seems to be what Anchises has in mind in the *Hymn
to Aphrodite* 145–51. But I can think of no genuine parallels to the peculiar marriage
arrangements in the *Hymn to Demeter*. The closest analogy might perhaps be the marriage
of Peleus and Thetis, where the goddess is "given" to the mortal by the gods, but Peleus
is obliged to trap her. There, too, the marriage is motivated by Olympian political considerations and involves the forced union of a seemingly mismatched couple.

and carrying off already contains the germ of the whole ensuing narrative. The spare Hesiodic allusion in the *Theogony* with its parallel phrasing (Περσεφόνην ... ἣν ᾿Αϊδωνεὺς / ἥρπασεν ἧς παρὰ μητρός, ἔδωκε δὲ μητίετα Ζεύς, 913–14) suggests that Hesiod followed a similar tradition.[24] This, in turn, would forge an important link between the version of the myth recounted in the hymn and the theogonic tradition.

Various critics have interpreted both the rape of Persephone and the resistance of Demeter to her daughter's marriage largely in psychological terms—that is, in terms of the natural affection between mother and daughter, the painful inevitability of separation from the mother, and the brutal necessity of sexual maturity and marriage.[25] Or, on a feminist reading, Zeus's decision is viewed as an unfeeling exercise of paternal authority symptomatic of the male subjugation of the female, whereas Hades' action symbolizes the violent irruption of male sexuality onto the innocent female consciousness.[26] While the hymn-poet is by no means unaware of the psychological and sexual implications of his narrative, his attention remains fixed on the larger political and theological ramifications of his story within the clearly articulated framework of Greek mythological thought. And this is evident from the emphatic role he as-

[24] Cf. Richardson (1974), p. 137: "The lines are probably traditional, as they occur in almost identical form in Hes. *Th.* 913f. ... This suggests that they are traditional genealogical summaries, and there is no reason to suppose that the hymn is echoing Hesiod here." Lenz (1975), p. 61, tries, I think mistakenly, to distinguish the two passages. According to Lenz, Hesiod meant for Zeus's ἔδωκε to take place after the abduction as a "nachträgliche Sanktionierung dieser Ehe." The hymn-poet, thereupon, misunderstood the passage and made Zeus's consent prior.

[25] The Demeter and Kore story seems to have a special attraction for Jungians. Cf., for instance, K. Kerényi, *Eleusis: The Archetypical Image of Mother and Daughter*, trans. R. Mannheim (Princeton, 1967) (hereafter cited as Kerényi [1967a]); Kerényi's "Kore" in C. G. Jung and K. Kerényi, *Essays on a Science of Mythology: The Myth of the Divine Child* (Princeton, 1967), pp. 101–55; and Jung's essay, "The Psychological Aspects of the Kore," pp. 156–77, in the same volume. See also P. Berry, "The Rape of Demeter/Persephone and Neurosis," *Spring* (1975): 186–98.

[26] M. Arthur, "Politics and Pomegranates: An Interpretation of the Homeric Hymn to Demeter," *Arethusa* 10 (1977): 7–47, claims that the hymn "reveal[s] ... a peculiarly feminine sensibility" and that "on one level Demeter's plight is ... that of all women, who must struggle to achieve self-definition in a social and psychic world which values male attributes more highly and depreciates females" (p. 8). Arthur then proceeds to analyze the poem "by employing the psychoanalytic model of female psychosexual development." Consider also the more sociological orientation of B. Lincoln, "The Rape of Persephone: A Greek Scenario of Women's Initiation," *Harvard Theological Review* 72 (1979): 223–35. Lincoln regards the rape of Persephone not as a marriage to Hades, but as a reflection of women's "initiation by rape" through the agency of a "male oppressor."

signs to the plan of Zeus, which is precisely what lifts a touching tale of maternal love and filial devotion into the realm of theological and cosmological speculation.

Nilsson has remarked that Zeus "does not belong to the circle of the Eleusinian gods,"[27] and that "he plays no role in the Mysteries. In literary versions and in art, if he occurs at all, he is a peripheral figure."[28] Older versions of the Demeter and Kore myth may have done without Zeus altogether.[29] Our literary accounts generally limit his role to giving his consent to Hades' request for Persephone and to arranging the final compromise between Demeter and Hades. Several scholars have, to be sure, drawn attention to the presence of Zeus and the general Olympian orientation of the hymn.[30] According to Lenz, Zeus's role has been superimposed onto the old myth, which results in a certain degree of incoherence in his behavior. At first, Zeus takes the side of Hades, but at the end, he assumes his characteristic role as conciliator of conflicts among the gods.[31] Olympus and the intervention of Zeus, in Lenz's view, constitute typical formal features of the hymnic genre, which, on occasion, are not fully integrated into the narrative.[32] Deichgräber, on the other hand, shows a deeper appreciation of the capital importance of Zeus and his plan within the poem: "Zeus—that is the decisive thing—sees not only the momentary, but the eternal, and that means, what will be."[33]

The plan of Zeus forms the starting point for the entire subsequent action of the hymn and unleashes a crisis among the gods that engulfs the whole cosmos.[34] Thus, a proper appreciation of Zeus's intentions and their cosmological and theological ramifications constitutes the foundation of any interpretation of the hymn. Our understanding of Zeus's design depends, in turn, on our grasping the status quo that obtains at the

[27] M. Nilsson, "Die eleusinischen Gottheiten," *ARW* 32 (1935): 126.

[28] Nilsson, *GGR* (1955), 1: 662.

[29] Cf. Lenz (1975), p. 59: "Wenn Zeus im eleusinischen Kult als Vater Kores und Gatte Demeter nicht heimisch war, dann muss auch entsprechend die eleusinische Kultlegende einmal zeus-los erzählt worden sein."

[30] For example, Rudhardt (1978); and U. Bianchi, "Sagezza olimpica e mistica eleusina nell' inno omerico a Demetra," *SMSR* 35 (1964): 161–93.

[31] Lenz (1975), pp. 65–68.

[32] Lenz (1975), pp. 59–60, calls the "Zeus und Olympmotiv des Demeterhymnus" a "typisch hymnisches Werkstück."

[33] K. Deichgräber, "Eleusinische Frömmigkeit und homerische Vorstellungswelt im Homerischen Demeterhymnus," *Akademie der Wissenschaften und der Literatur in Mainz, Geistes- und Sozialwissenschaftlichen Klasse* 6 (1950): 526.

[34] Cf. Rudhardt (1978), p. 10.

beginning of the hymn and the change Zeus contemplates. At the very outset, the poet repeatedly stresses the unity of the two great cosmic realms: heaven and earth. Heaven, earth, and sea rejoice as Persephone gathers her flowers (13–14); and after the rape, the mountaintops and the depth of the sea reecho with her cry (38; cf. 33). The gods move freely between their homes on Olympus and the earth, the abode of mortals. Thus, Persephone picks flowers on the Nysian plain, and later Demeter will search over land and sea (43) for her daughter. But between the upper world and the realm of Hades, no communication exists. While Persephone is being carried off, "she still hoped to see her mother and the race of the eternal gods" (35–36) as long as she looked upon the earth, heaven, sea, and sun (33–35).[35] But once beneath the earth, all hope is gone. Similarly, when Demeter finally learns of her daughter's whereabouts, she does not go down into the underworld after her daughter, as she does in several other versions of the myth, nor is that possibility ever contemplated.[36] The reason is simple: no route to the underworld exists for the gods, and such an undertaking is impossible. Rudhardt has understood the cardinal importance of the spatial disposition of the cosmos presupposed by the poem:

> Above, the gods reign on Olympus, but are not confined to it; they have the ability to come down and move at will over the whole earth. . . . Below lies Erebus, dark and misty, inhabited by the dead. A boundary separates it from the upper world. . . . The hymn clearly informs us that the dead can never leave their domain. While agreeing with the usual teaching on this point, the hymn also reveals something else that is less immediately evident but of capital importance: with only one exception, the gods cannot cross the boundary of the lower world. The myth of Demeter, Hades, and Persephone is incomprehensible if we do not recognize this impenetrability.[37]

[35] Cf. Richardson (1974) at line 13: " 'Heaven, earth, and sea' is a way of saying 'the whole world'. This poet is fond of such expressions." Richardson is more accurate in his comment on line 33: " 'Earth, heaven, sea, and sun' is a form of expression for 'the (upper) world.' " For parallels, see E. G. Schmidt, "Himmel—Meer—Erde im frühgriechischen Epos und im alten Orient," *Philologus* 125 (1981): 1–24.

[36] For the *kathodos* of Demeter, see *Orphei hymni* 41.5 (Quandt) and Hyginus *Fabulae* 251.

[37] Rudhardt (1978), p. 8. Cf. Bianchi (1964), pp. 164–66, on the division of the upper and lower worlds. He points out (p. 166) the paradox in the fact that the nether world both does and does not belong to Zeus's Olympian realm. See also Ramnoux (1959), pp. 127–29.

The meaning of Zeus's plan now becomes evident: by giving his daughter Persephone to Hades, Zeus intends to create a bridge and alliance between the upper and the hitherto inaccessible lower world. Persephone is a peculiarly appropriate vehicle for such an alliance. As the only daughter of the union of Zeus and Demeter,[38] she is in some sense an *epiklēros*,[39] not herself inheriting, but transmitting her paternal heritage by marriage to her closest relative—who is none other than her paternal uncle, Hades.[40] The marriage, then, is politically motivated by the highest considerations of the highest god in order to unite the Olympian and infernal realms.

The circumstances under which this dynastic marriage are conducted—the separation between the upper and lower regions—are also those that the marriage is ultimately intended to remedy. Accordingly, the "wedding" cannot follow normal procedure: Zeus must resort to secrecy and trickery, while the legitimate bridegroom must make use of force.[41]

As the unsuspecting Persephone plays with her companions and gathers flowers on the Nysian plain, Gaia, the Earth, in accordance with the plan of Zeus, puts forth the narcissus with a hundred heads.[42] The complicity of Gaia is by no means arbitrary. Her role in the hymn can only be understood from the perspective of the theogonic tradition. In the *Theogony*, Gaia brings forth not only the Hundred-Handers, but also the monstrous Typhoeus with his hundred heads.[43] Throughout the prehistory of the gods, Gaia orchestrates the succession in heaven.[44] Only after

[38] Persephone is called μουνογένεια in *Orphei hymni* 29.2 (Quandt).

[39] On the institution of the epiclerate, see W. K. Lacey, *The Family in Ancient Greece* (Ithaca, N.Y., 1968), pp. 139–45; D. M. MacDowell, *The Law in Classical Athens* (London, 1978), pp. 95–98; W. Erdmann, *Die Ehe im alten Griechenland* (Munich, 1934), pp. 68–86; and J. Karnezis, "The Epikleros" (Diss., Athens, 1972).

[40] On the avuncular marriage of an *epikleros*, cf. A.R.W. Harrison, *The Law of Athens* (Oxford, 1968), 1: 23: "In fact her [the epikleros's] father's brother had the first claim to the hand of an ἐπίκληρος."

[41] It is perhaps worth noting that the matrimonial arrangements described in the hymn have no parallel in the exhaustive list (drawn from Vedic texts) of possible types of Indo-European marriages cited by G. Dumézil, *Mariages Indo-Européens* (Paris, 1979), pp. 32–33.

[42] For the mythological associations of the narcissus, especially with death and the underworld, see J. Murr, *Die Pflanzenwelt in der griechischen Mythologie* (Innsbruck, 1890), pp. 246–50; and I. Chirassi, *Elementi di cultura precereale nei miti e riti greci* (Rome, 1968), pp. 143–55.

[43] *Theogony* 147–52, 820–28.

[44] Gaia inspires Cronus to castrate his father (*Theogony* 159–66); she hides the infant

the defeat of the Titans and Typhoeus does she ally herself with the victorious Zeus and instruct him how to safeguard his rule.[45] Temporally, then, Gaia's cooperation with the plan of Zeus in the hymn indicates that the last serious opposition to the Olympian regime has vanished. Gaia demonstrates her acceptance of the new order by mediating appropriately between Zeus and Hades and aiding Zeus's plan to consolidate his universal dominion. Like many of the other prodigious creatures Gaia has brought forth in the past, the narcissus is a monstrosity of nature, but here the awesome fertility of the Earth is put in the service of Olympian Zeus.

While presumably ready for marriage, Persephone still plays like a child and reaches out for the marvelous flower as if it were a pretty toy.[46]

χάνε δὲ χθὼν εὐρυάγυια
Νύσιον ἂμ πεδίον τῇ ὄρουσεν ἄναξ πολυδέγμων
ἵπποις ἀθανάτοισι Κρόνου πολυώνυμος υἱός.
ἁρπάξας δ᾽ ἀέκουσαν ἐπὶ χρυσέοισιν ὄχοισιν
ἦγ᾽ ὀλοφυρομένην.

And the wide-wayed earth gaped open
on the Nysian plain, where the lord who receives many rushed
with his immortal horses, the many-named son of Cronus.
And having seized her against her will on his golden chariot,
he carried her off weeping.

(16–20)

Completely innocent of the plot, Persephone calls on her father, "the son of Cronus, highest and best," as she is borne off.[47] But he has absented

Zeus (*Theogony* 479–80); she plots Cronus's downfall (*Theogony* 494); and she advises Zeus to release the Hundred-Handers before doing battle with the Titans (*Theogony* 626–28).

[45] Gaia gives birth to Typhoeus (*Theogony* 821); through her designs, Zeus becomes king (*Theogony* 884): she warns him of Metis (*Theogony* 888–93).

[46] For the καλὸν ἄθυρμα, cf. *Hymn to Hermes* 32, where the expression is used of the tortoise discovered by the infant Hermes. While clearly of marriageable age, Persephone continues to play like a child. Some versions suggest an overprotective or possessive attitude toward her on the part of Demeter, but there is no sign of it in the *Hymn to Demeter*.

[47] Cf. Richardson (1974), p. 153, on line 20 concerning Persephone's cry: "the cry for help is an important element of primitive justice, especially in cases of rape or abduction, where failure to set up a cry renders the plaintiff's subsequent plea invalid." There is a certain irony in Persephone's crying out to her father as "highest and best." For in this particular case, the political interests of the king of the gods are at odds with his paternal obligations.

himself from the scene,[48] subordinating his role as father-protector to reasons of state. While Zeus sits in his temple receiving fine offerings from mortal men (which soon will be interrupted),

τὴν δ᾽ ἀεκαζομένην ἦγεν Διὸς ἐννεσίῃσι
πατροκασίγνητος πολυσημάντωρ πολυδέγμων
ἵπποις ἀθανάτοισι Κρόνου πολυώνυμος υἱός.

He [Hades] led her,[49] all unwilling, by the behests of Zeus,
her uncle, the ruler over many, the receiver of many,
on his immortal horses, the many-named son of Cronus.

(30–32)

In the meantime, we are told, no god or mortal heard Persephone calling to her father except Hecate from her cave and Helios the sun god (22–26). Only these two divinities can and will reveal the rape to Demeter.

ὄφρα μὲν οὖν γαῖάν τε καὶ οὐρανὸν ἀστερόεντα
λεῦσσε θεὰ καὶ πόντον ἀγάρροον ἰχθυόεντα
αὐγάς τ᾽ ἠελίου, ἔτι δ᾽ ἤλπετο μητέρα κεδνὴν
ὄψεσθαι καὶ φῦλα θεῶν αἰειγενετάων.

As long as the goddess gazed upon the earth and starry sky
and the mighty flowing fishy sea
and the beams of the sun, she yet had hope of seeing her revered
    mother
and the race of the eternal gods.

(33–36)

The syntax here is ambiguous; we could also translate: "she yet hoped that her mother and the gods would see *her*."[50] But it amounts to the same thing. To go to the house of Hades means both to become invisible[51] to those above and to look no longer on the light of the sun. Only while

[48] Cf. Gemoll (1886), p. 283: "natürlich *absichtlich*."
[49] Cf. Scarpi (1976), p. 114, on the tension between ἄγω (= *uxorem ducere*) and ἁρπάζω.
[50] Cf. Gemoll (1886), p. 284, who takes μητέρα as subject and translates: "Solange sie den Himmel ... noch sah, und sie noch hoffte, dass die Mutter und die ewigen Götter [den Raub] sehen würden."
[51] Consider the folk etymology, Ἄιδης from ἀ-ίδης*, "invisible," "rendering invisible."

above the ground can Persephone retain the seductive hope of seeing and being seen.

Now the poet breaks off where we expect him to continue to describe Persephone's descent into the nether regions and her despair.[52] Hermann believed that something had dropped out of our text and made so bold as to supply it.[53] But I think the abruptness here is intentional; the narrator dramatically averts his eyes from the invisible things below.[54] Not even his gaze—no more than that of the gods—can penetrate the barrier separating the upper from the lower world.

All that remains above of Persephone is the terrestrial echo of her immortal voice.[55] "And her mother heard it" (39). As Persephone disappears below the earth, the second movement of the hymn's first section begins: the revelation of her daughter's fate to Demeter. Its progress is precisely articulated into three stages. At first, all that Demeter hears is a muffled, inarticulate echo of Persephone's appeal for help. Yet it is recognizably the voice of her daughter. Demeter cannot yet know her fate, only that something dreadful has happened to her beloved child. Grief stricken, the goddess tears off her headdress, mantles herself in a black veil, and flies over land and sea like a madwoman, in search of her daughter (40–44).[56] No god or mortal was willing[57] to tell her the truth, nor did even an indirect report through an omen bring her news (44–46).

ἐννῆμαρ μὲν ἔπειτα κατὰ χθόνα πότνια Δηὼ
στρωφᾶτ᾽ αἰθομένας δαΐδας μετὰ χερσὶν ἔχουσα,

[52] Cf. Richardson (1974), p. 159: "There is no mention in the *Hymn* of Persephone's descent with Hades. This was important in cult . . . and one expects something about it after *Dem.* 33–6."

[53] Hermann (1806), p. ci, fills the presumed lacuna as follows: "quum vero ipsam terram subiisset, nec quidquam nisi tenebras circumfusas videret, tum vero animum despondit. quum vero hiantem terram ingrederetur, seque ad inferos deduci intelligeret, tum prorsus desperans multo, quam ante, clamavit vehementius: et resonuerunt montium cacumina, et maris cavernae: audiitque mater." Richardson (1974), AHS (1936), and Càssola (1975) all suspect a lacuna here, but it becomes unnecessary as soon as we understand that Demeter hears an echo of Persephone's cry and not a second cry.

[54] Throughout, the hymn avoids mentioning the dead and the underworld. θάνατος occurs only once in the poem at line 262. This euphemism is more than simply a matter of style; we learn literally nothing about the dead or the nether regions from the hymn.

[55] This observation and the subsequent discussion of the sequence of revelation depends heavily on a forthcoming paper of D. Mankin.

[56] Richardson (1974), p. 161, draws attention to the parallel to Andromache in *Iliad* XXII.401–70. Consider also *Iliad* XXIV.94 for the black veil of Thetis, "than which there is no darker garment."

[57] Cf. Gemoll (1886), p. 285: οὐκ ἤθελεν is not equivalent to *non poterat*.

οὐδέ ποτ' ἀμβροσίης καὶ νέκταρος ἡδυπότοιο
πάσσατ' ἀκηχεμένη, οὐδὲ χρόα βάλλετο λουτροῖς.

Then for nine days throughout the earth mighty Deo
wandered, holding burning torches in her hands,
nor did she ever taste of ambrosia or nectar, sweet to drink,
in her grief, nor did she bathe her skin.

(47–50)

Despite the absence of corroborating evidence, some scholars have sought to link the goddess's nine-day abstention from food and washing to Eleusinian practice.[58] Now, it must be admitted that nine days is a long time to fast, even for a god; for a mortal initiate, it borders on the impossible.[59] The nine-day period must rather be taken as a period of transition, as frequently in the epic,[60] a dead or empty time that culminates in a significant change on the tenth day. Ritual meaning has also been attributed to the torches Demeter carries during her wanderings.[61] To be sure, a torchlight procession played an important role at Eleusis, and the final revelation was probably accompanied by the flare of torches. In addition, iconography often represents the goddess with torches. There remains, however, a simple narrative function to the torches in the hymn. Demeter searches both day *and* night, and the beginning of illumination occurs appositely at dawn. Hecate approaches and introduces the second phase in the progressive discovery of Persephone's whereabouts.

Hecate's role in this scene has generally been misunderstood. The poet, it is claimed, introduces her solely because of her cultic associations

[58] Cf. Richardson (1974), pp. 165–67.

[59] As P. R. Arbesmann, *Das Fasten bei den Griechen und Römern* (Giessen, 1929), pp. 80–83, points out. He believes that the fasting of the *mystai* was confined to the single day before the initiation rites proper. Demeter's fasting in the hymn is "nur dichterisches Bild" (p. 82).

[60] Arbesmann (1929), p. 80, notes that the number of days Demeter fasted, that is, until the drinking of the Cyceon, is not even explicitly specified in the hymn. The nine-day period corresponds to Demeter's searching, but not necessarily to her fasting. Nine-day periods figure prominently in the epic. Consider the nine-day plague in *Iliad* 1.53 and the nine-day quarrel of the gods at *Iliad* xxiv.107. In the *Odyssey*, a nine-day storm precedes the arrival at the land of the Lotus Eaters as well as the arrival on Ogygia; nine days of sailing bring Odysseus from Aeolia to Ithaca. Cf. G. Germain, *Homère et la mystique des nombres* (Paris, 1954), p. 13: "Le nombre 9 sert essentiellement à exprimer un temps, au terme duquel, le dixième jour ou la dixième année, arrivera un événement décisif."

[61] Cf. Richardson (1974), pp. 165, 167–68.

with Eleusis, but assigns her no function.[62] In this case, the appeal to external evidence actually interferes with our ability to understand the narrative progress. The text itself sufficiently elucidates Hecate's role as a critical intermediary in the gradual process of revelation. On the dawn of the tenth day, the goddess encounters Demeter:

καί ῥά οἱ ἀγγελέουσα ἔπος φάτο φώνησέν τε.

And, in order to convey a message to her, she spoke and said.

(53)

But instead of the expected announcement, Hecate merely poses a question:

τίς θεῶν οὐρανίων ἠὲ θνητῶν ἀνθρώπων
ἥρπασε Περσεφόνην καὶ σὸν φίλον ἤκαχε θυμόν;
φωνῆς γὰρ ἤκουσ᾽, ἀτὰρ οὐκ ἴδον ὀφθαλμοῖσιν
ὅς τις ἔην.

Who of the heavenly gods or of mortal men
carried off Persephone and grieved the heart within you?
For I heard her voice, but did not see with my eyes
who it was.

(55–58)

[62] Cf. Richardson (1974), pp. 155–56: "In the *Hymn*, she is very much a 'Nebenfigur': she does not tell Demeter anything new.... Her appearance is presumably due to her position in the cult." Cf. p. 169, and Càssola (1975), p. 470. Also Puntoni (1896) p. 5: "Hecate è personaggio inutile nello svolgimento del fatto narrato dal poeta. Ella non svela a Demetra, malgrado che si presenti a lei come ἀγγελέουσα nessun particolare che a Demetra importi di sapere." Richardson explains ἀγγελέουσα as possibly derived from a cult title of Hecate/Artemis as Ἄγγελος, but, then, he does not believe that Hecate "in fact tell[s] Demeter anything that she does not already know." There remains a problem with explaining Hecate's presence in the hymn as due to her role in cult; the representations of Hecate cited by Richardson on p. 155 and pp. 168–69 do not connect Hecate with Eleusinian ritual so much as with myth. O. Kern, "Mysterien," in *RE* 16, pt. 2 (1935): 1213, notes that "irgendein eleusinischer Zug in dem Wesen der Hekate findet sich im homerischen 'Hymnos' nicht." Wilamowitz (1959), 2: 50, points out that in Eleusis Hecate is identified with Artemis Propylaea, "aber das ist noch nicht einmal im homerischen Hymnus geschehen." Clinton (1986), p. 45, notes decisively: "nowhere over a span of ca. 1,000 years does the name Hekate appear at Eleusis." Arthur (1977), p. 13, proposes to interpret Hecate as a vestige of Titan opposition to Zeus's patriarchal power. But Gaia is already firmly in Zeus's camp. For Hecate's mediating function in the *Theogony*, see Clay (1984).

From within her cave (cf. 25), appropriately located in the earth and hence between the upper and lower regions,[63] Hecate was unable to observe the event; yet she heard the girl cry out for help and recognized that someone—she cannot know whether god or mortal—carried Persephone off violently. From Hecate's question, Demeter gathers a vital piece of information: that her daughter has been abducted, but she remains ignorant of the author of the deed. Wordlessly,[64] Demeter, now accompanied by Hecate, proceeds to the only source of complete and reliable information: Helios, who as "watcher of gods and men" has been an eyewitness to the event. Incorporating Hecate's testimony, Demeter implores him to reveal who carried off her daughter:

ἀλλὰ σὺ γὰρ δὴ πᾶσαν ἐπὶ χθόνα καὶ κατὰ πόντον
αἰθέρος ἐκ δίης καταδέρκεαι ἀκτίνεσσι,
νημερτέως μοι ἔνισπε φίλον τέκος εἴ που ὄπωπας
ὅς τις νόσφιν ἐμεῖο λαβὼν ἀέκουσαν ἀνάγκῃ
οἴχεται ἠὲ θεῶν ἢ καὶ θνητῶν ἀνθρώπων.

But you, who look down upon the whole earth and sea
from the shining ether with your beams,
tell me truthfully about my dear child, if somewhere you have seen
who of gods or mortal men it was who came and seized her in my
        absence
against her will, under compulsion.

(69–73)

Helios reassures her; out of respect and pity for her grief, he will tell her what she wants to know. But to our surprise, Helios first names not the agent of the rape, but its ultimate instigator:

οὐδέ τις ἄλλος
αἴτιος ἀθανάτων εἰ μὴ νεφεληγερέτα Ζεύς,
ὅς μιν ἔδωκ' Ἀΐδῃ θαλερὴν κεκλῆσθαι ἄκοιτιν.

[63] Cf. the cave where the newborn Zeus is hidden: ἄντρῳ ἐν ἠλιβάτῳ, ζαθέης ὑπὸ κεύθεσι γαίης (*Theogony* 483).

[64] I do not think Demeter's dramatic silence here has anything to do with ritual silence during the Mysteries, as Richardson (1974), p. 171, suggests. At this point, Demeter's lack of response to Hecate's question is more eloquent and powerful than anything she might say. But, of course, most commentators refuse to recognize that the goddess has received some shocking news from Hecate.

CHAPTER 4

> Nor is anyone else
> of the immortals to blame but cloud-gathering Zeus,
> who gave her in marriage to Hades to be called his tender wife.
>
> (77–79)

The whole anomalous arrangement of this extraordinary marriage is now revealed to Demeter. Because Zeus himself has legitimized the marriage, the deed appears irreversible. Anticipating Demeter's grief and "insatiable anger," Helios immediately attempts to console her for the loss of Persephone: Hades is no unseemly son-in-law; his lineage is as august as her own, for Hades is her own brother.

> ἀμφὶ δὲ τιμὴν
> ἔλλαχεν ὡς τὰ πρῶτα διάτριχα δασμὸς ἐτύχθη·
> τοῖς μεταναιετάει τῶν ἔλλαχε κοίρανος εἶναι.
>
> And as for honor,
> he received his share, when first the threefold distribution was
> made;
> and he lives among those whom he received as his share to be lord
> over.[65]
> (85–87)

Helios here refers to the triple division of the cosmos made among the sons of Cronus, after the victory of the Olympians.[66] The allusion once again serves to underline both the mythological time of the hymn—between the first distribution of divine privileges, which followed the accession of Zeus, and our own times—and the spatial disposition of the cosmos it presupposes. But Helios's immediate purpose is to mollify Demeter by dwelling on the exalted lineage and status of her new son-in-law. The sun god then goes about his ordinary daily business, driving his chariot across the heavens. But the news she has heard contains nothing

[65] Note again the hymn's characteristic euphemism.
[66] On the tripartition of the cosmos, see *Iliad* xv.187–92, where Poseidon protests to Zeus's messenger Iris: "We were three brothers from Cronus, whom Rheia bore / Zeus and I, and third was Hades who rules the nether regions. / In three parts everything was divided, and each received a share of *timē*; / and I received the gray sea to inhabit always / when we drew lots, and Hades received the murky darkness; Zeus received the broad heaven in which are clear sky and clouds." Poseidon adds in the next line: "but earth and tall Olympus is still common to all." This last circumstance does not yet obtain in the *Hymn to Demeter*. Cf. *Orphei hymni* 18.6 (Quandt).

ordinary for the ears of the goddess. Now, for the first time, the fate of Persephone and its full import stand clearly illuminated. With this, the first "act" of the *Hymn to Demeter* comes to a close.

We may pause for a moment to consider the structure of the opening section. First of all, in the hymn as opposed to other versions of the myth, discovery follows immediately upon the abduction. This fact is of cardinal importance for understanding the subsequent narrative progress and will receive further consideration. The detailed elaboration of the revelation itself is also striking. The poet takes pains to emphasize the secrecy shrouding the plan of Zeus. While Demeter searches without direction, neither god nor man is willing to volunteer information. Almost by inadvertence, Hecate gives Demeter the necessary clue that permits the goddess to take the initiative in questioning Helios and thus finally to learn the truth. This gradual discovery (39–87) actually occupies more lines than the description of the rape (2–39) and thus gains in narrative weight. By drawing attention to the precise steps in the revelation sequence, the hymn-poet underlines its significance and its completeness. Demeter learns not only of the immediate cause of her daughter's disappearance, but also comprehends the complicity of Zeus.

Demeter's response is swift and violent:

τὴν δ᾽ ἄχος αἰνότερον καὶ κύντερον ἵκετο θυμόν.

A grief more terrible and beastly came to her heart.

(90)

Initially grieved at her daughter's disappearance, the goddess's anguish increases when she understands its cause. It is further compounded by her rage against Zeus. Again, Rudhardt has clearly grasped the reason:

> In all of Greek mythology, no marriage precipitates a drama like that caused by the marriage of Hades and Persephone, none tears asunder a young bride and her mother to such a degree, because the normal marriages of the gods do not separate them permanently. In the upper world, the gods are accessible to one another, no matter where they live, to the extent they desire. If Demeter and Persephone could cross the boundary of the lower world, the marriage of Hades would resemble other divine marriages and would not have produced the crisis recounted in the Eleusinian hymn.[67]

[67] Rudhardt (1978), p. 8.

This unique marriage, then, provokes on the part of Demeter a unique series of reactions that are motivated by the double passions of grief and rage.

Eleusis

χωσαμένη δ᾽ ἤπειτα κελαινεφέϊ Κρονίωνι
νοσφισθεῖσα θεῶν ἀγορὴν καὶ μακρὸν Ὄλυμπον
ᾤχετ᾽ ἐπ᾽ ἀνθρώπων πόλιας καὶ πίονα ἔργα. . . .

Then angered with the dark-clouded son of Cronus [Zeus],
she absented herself from the assembly of the gods and high
    Olympus
and came to the cities of men and their rich works. . . .

(91–93)

As the abduction was carried out in Demeter's absence (4), and Zeus absented himself from the scene of the crime (27), so now Demeter absents herself from Olympus and takes up her abode among mortals. At the beginning of the hymn, the separation of upper and lower realms led to the violent separation of mother and daughter. This separation, in turn, provokes the self-exile of Demeter from the company of the gods. Disunity and separateness characterize relations among the gods as well as the cosmic spheres.[68] Still further separations and displacements must occur before the final reunion and reconciliation.

The goddess comes to Eleusis, which will be the arena for the middle section of the poem. Here too scholarly controversy has centered. Narrative cruces abound at the beginning, middle, and end of the Eleusis episode. The motivation for Demeter's going there in the first place; the significance of her actions there, especially her attempt to render the infant Demophoon immortal; and finally her epiphany and angry withdrawal—all appear tangential and unconnected to the framing theme of the abduction and recovery of Persephone. One critic summarizes:

[68] Cf. νόσφιν (4) of Demeter's absence; θεῶν ἀπάνευθε (28) of Zeus in his temple; νοσφισθεῖσα (92) of Demeter's absenting herself from Olympus; and μακάρων ἀπὸ νόσφιν ἁπάντων (303) of Demeter's shutting herself in her temple. Cf. C. Segal, "Orality, Repetition and Formulaic Artistry in the Homeric 'Hymn to Demeter,'" in Brillante (1981), pp. 131–33.

If one surveys the poem as a whole, then it is immediately apparent that the Rape of Persephone and the Eleusis story are pieced together. As soon as one removes Eleusis, a coherent connection emerges. When Demeter has heard that her daughter is in Hades' power, and therefore inaccessible to her, she abandons her searching and exerts pressure on Zeus through the cessation of vegetation. This myth has nothing to do with Eleusis.[69]

Similarly:

One of the places at which in its present form the Homeric hymn breaks apart is around verse 95. After the goddess has learned the identity of the abductor from Helios, she betakes herself to the cities of men. . . . Why does Demeter go to Eleusis? Not on account of her daughter; Helios has already revealed the abductor to her. For all their piety, the Eleusinians are unable to restore her stolen daughter. Without a word does the goddess even inquire after her daughter in Eleusis; as far as the Eleusinians are concerned, both Persephone and her fate have been completely forgotten.[70]

Finally, Richardson notes: "Demeter's wanderings on earth and visit to Eleusis have no special purpose."[71] For all their inherent interest and even charm, two hundred lines—almost half the poem—seem unrelated to the main story.

In other versions of the myth, Demeter's stay in Eleusis raises no such problems but is fully integrated into the central narrative. There,

---

[69] Wilamowitz (1959), 2: 50.

[70] L. Malten, "Altorphische Demetersage," *ARW* 12 (1909): 433, n. 4. Cf. G. Zuntz, *Persephone* (Oxford, 1971) p. 79: "Demeter has roamed the earth 'for nine days' in search of her daughter (vv. 48ff.); thereafter she learns from the sun-god that Persephone has been abducted, with the consent of Zeus, by the Lord of the Netherworld (v. 77). This knowledge must be the end of her search, and since in the Netherworld her daughter is beyond her reach, this is the point for the angered goddess to force the issue by withholding her gift. The rhapsode, however, makes her resume her wanderings—so as to be able to bring her to Eleusis; after he has narrated her doings there the situation is exactly as before (v. 91–304) and the action now takes the expected course."

[71] Richardson (1974), p. 81. Cf. the weak defense of K. Stiewe, "Der Erzählungsstil des homerischen Demeterhymnos" (Diss., Göttingen, 1954), p. 82: "Wenn die Persephone- und die Eleusishandlung relativ selbständig angelegt sind, wenn sich in v. 91ff. und dann wieder nach v. 302 fast schlagartig der Gesichtskreis ändert, spricht das nicht mehr gegen die Einheit des Hymnos, sondern für die Eigenheit seines Dichters, der eine stärkere kompositorische Zusammenfassung wohl gar nicht erstrebte."

the goddess comes to Eleusis in the course of her search for Persephone and learns of her daughter's whereabouts from the local inhabitants. In gratitude, Demeter rewards them with the gift of agriculture and, in some cases, the establishment of her Mysteries.[72]

This form of the myth with sundry variants is first attested in some so-called Orphic compositions dated to the sixth century B.C. or later and which subsequently gain wide currency.[73] There is, however, good reason to suppose that it is as least as old as the alternative version told in the hymn. Richardson expresses himself cautiously: "it is possible that in some respects the 'Orphic' versions may represent earlier and more genuine traditions than those of the Homeric poet."[74] I would like to go further and suggest that the hymn-poet assumes a knowledge of this common version on the part of his audience and has deliberately modified it. Moreover, he draws attention to his modifications by short-circuiting the expected narrative connections and reshaping the story to his own purposes. Two examples may serve as illustrations. When Demeter leaves Olympus, she comes to the "cities and rich works of men" (93). The epic phrase, πίονα ἔργα, unmistakably means "agricultural works." Its presence at this particular juncture precludes what is the climax of the

---

[72] For the variants, see R. Förster, *Der Raub und Rückkehr der Persephone* (Stuttgart, 1874). The influence of these other versions is so strong that even careful critics occasionally misrepresent the narrative of the hymn. For instance, in the citation from Zuntz in n. 70, the poem will not support the statement that Demeter resumes her wanderings before reaching Eleusis. The misleading summary of the hymn by R. Wünsch, *s.v.* "Hymnos" in *RE* 9, pt. 1 (1914): 155, offers several good examples. He makes no mention of the end of Demeter's search and implies that the famine is coincident with her grief. Cf. Bianchi (1964), p. 168: "durante il lutto di Demetra cessa il ritmo delle stagioni." Cf. p. 173, n. 10; and n. 136 below.

[73] Malten (1909) proposed to date the "Orphic version" to the time of the Peisistratids. F. Graf, *Eleusis und die orphische Dichtung Athens in vorhellenistischer Zeit* (Berlin, 1974), pp. 151–81, however, points to the difficulty of determining which versions are really "Orphic." In his view, an Orphic poem, incorporating the Mission of Triptolemus, should be dated to Athens between the years 468–405 B.C.

[74] Richardson (1974), p. 85. F. R. Walton, "Athens, Eleusis, and the Homeric Hymn to Demeter," *Harvard Theological Review* 45 (1952): 105–14, puts forth the argument that the hymn was composed not before the Athenian takeover of Eleusis, as is generally believed, but after it. In his view, the poem presents a polemical statement against Athenian claims to Eleusis and Athenian propaganda. Nilsson *GGR* (1955), 1: 655, n. 1, calls Walton's thesis "nicht unwahrscheinlich." The very fact that the thesis can be maintained at all reveals how little we know of the circumstances of the hymn's composition. Wünsch (1914), p. 155, considers the "Urform" of the myth closer to the Orphic version preserved in the Berlin Papyrus (= *Orphicorum Fragmenta* 49, Kern). Cf. Wehrli, (1934), p. 84, and now also Clinton (1986), pp. 47–48.

myth in other versions: Demeter's gift of agriculture to mankind. Similarly, by recounting Demeter's discovery of the rape immediately after its occurrence, the poet does away with the usual motivation for the goddess's journey to Eleusis; her searching has already come to an end. The poet thus signals to his audience that his justification for Demeter's sojourn in Eleusis will be different. While I am convinced that a version of the myth resembling in its outlines those found in the Orphic and later traditions was well known to the poet and to his audience, the interpretation of the hymn presented here does not depend on this view, nor do I insist on it. If, however, we posit the existence of such a parallel tradition, the narrative strategies adopted in the hymn gain in significance and coherence.

Be that as it may, the problem of the motivation for Demeter's sojourn in Eleusis remains whether or not we view it as a conscious divergence from a traditional version. Scholars generally assume that Demeter forgets both her grief over Persephone and her anger at Zeus during her stay at Eleusis. But the first of these assumptions can easily be disproved. On entering the house of Celeus, the goddess succumbs to what may fairly be called a mute paroxysm of grief over the loss of her daughter (197–201). Nor is there any reason to believe that the rage that motivates Demeter's departure from Olympus is abruptly set aside upon her arrival in Eleusis. On the contrary, her anger abides until her grief is assuaged. Yet her opposition to Zeus does not take the form of impotent raging, but surfaces in a considered plan of action, whose intention is to avenge herself upon Zeus. The original *boulē* and *dolos* of Zeus demand a counterplan and strategem on the part of Demeter. The game of Olympian politics is not limited to Zeus alone, but can be played by the other gods as well.

An understanding of Demeter's plan emerges from an analysis of her actions in Eleusis, actions that display nothing of the arbitrary or random; from the very outset, they point to a specific end. If Zeus has deprived Demeter of her daughter for his own political purposes, then she will adopt a mortal child for hers. The nursing of Demophoon does not simply constitute an expression of frustrated maternal instincts or an attempt to replace the lost Persephone. In that case, a girl would have been a far more appropriate substitute, yet a daughter would not suit the goddess's political purpose. Ramnoux comes close to understanding Demeter's purpose and grasping the link between Persephone's abduction and her mother's activity in Eleusis:

What can Demeter do to avenge herself? Rob Hades of his natural prey, a child of mortals, a child born mortal. In exchange for her stolen child, a child stolen in return. And, at the same time, Demeter satisfies her resentment against all the gods. By an act no less serious than Prometheus's theft of fire, she steals immortality for the benefit of her mortal infant, conferring upon him the privilege of all the gods.[75]

Yet Demeter's anger is aimed not so much at Hades or all the gods as against Zeus, the instigator of her daughter's disappearance. However, the enormity of Demeter's undertaking is fully analogous to Prometheus's challenge to Zeus. For if Prometheus's actions led to the separation of gods and mortals and the establishment of strict lines of demarcation dividing them, then Demeter's attempt to confer immortality on a human infant violates the post-Promethean order Zeus has decreed. But Demeter's choice of a male child has further and more ominous implications for an audience familiar with the theogonic tradition. Adopting a male child and rendering him immortal would allow the goddess to defy the authority of Zeus. In other words, Demeter's plan, *mutatis mutandis*, parallels the plan of Hera in the *Hymn to Apollo*. Although Demeter's intentions are not made explicit, her actions speak for themselves. Moreover, the hymn's audience would recognize the pattern not only from Hera's opposition to Zeus in *Apollo*, but also in the behavior of Gaia throughout the *Theogony*. In fact, the opposition of a powerful female deity to presumed tyrannical action on the part of the supreme male divinity generally follows this paradigm. Prior to the accession of Zeus, it constitutes the primary impetus for the succession in heaven. But after Zeus's dominion is assured, all such attempts prove doomed to failure. As soon as we grasp the pattern underlying Demeter's plan, much that first appears irrelevant or incoherent in the events at Eleusis begins to make sense. Far from being grafted onto the hymn for no apparent purpose, the Eleusinian episode firmly links the poem to the theogonic and cosmogonic tradition of which it forms a part.

The events at Eleusis take place among mortals, and the hymn's focus now shifts from the divine and cosmic spheres to the interaction between Demeter and the inhabitants of Eleusis. The central contrast that informs this part of the poem is the difference between gods and mortals—more precisely, the ignorance of mortals in relation to the gods.

[75] Ramnoux (1959), pp. 131–32.

As a whole, the action in Eleusis can be divided into three sequences: the first culminates in Demeter's reception at the palace of Celeus; the second focuses on her nursing of Demophoon; and the last depicts the aftermath of the interrupted apotheosis. The main movement of the first section involves the gradual physical penetration of the goddess from the out-skirts of Eleusis to the *megaron* of the palace of the king and her simul-taneous spiritual progress from a homeless stranger to a trusted member of the royal household.

Upon arriving in Eleusis, Demeter sits down by a well at the edge of town. To accomplish her purpose, she "blots out her form" (94) and adopts an unusual disguise:

γρηΐ παλαιγενέϊ ἐναλίγκιος, ἥ τε τόκοιο
εἴργηται δώρων τε φιλοστεφάνου 'Αφροδίτης,
οἷαί τε τροφοί εἰσι θεμιστοπόλων βασιλήων
παίδων καὶ ταμίαι κατὰ δώματα ἠχήεντα.

... resembling an ancient old woman, who is shut off from
    childbirth
and the gifts of wreath-loving Aphrodite,
like those who are nurses of the children of decree-giving kings
and housekeepers in echoing halls.

(101–4)

The persona assumed is manifestly ungodlike, for the gods, eternally in their prime, are exempt from the ravages of old age that beset mortals. In the case of Demeter, the mask chosen is particularly ironic: the great divinity of fertility and fecundity presents herself as a barren old woman. Allen, Halliday, and Sikes allow that "the metamorphosis of Demeter into an old woman need have no special significance."[76] But in the epic, a god's choice of disguise is determined by the circumstances and moti-vation for his or her intervention.[77] Here, Demeter's disguise is carefully chosen to elict pity and respect but, above all, to promote her acceptance as trusted nursemaid to a royal princeling.

The daughters of Celeus come to the well to draw water. Ironically, while Demeter has "blighted her form," the young girls are described as

---

[76] AHS (1936), p. 142. I do not find the psychological interpretation—that Demeter adopts the appearance of an old woman as a sign of her depression—very convincing. Cf. Arthur (1977), pp. 15ff.
[77] One need think only of "Mentor" in the *Odyssey*.

being "like goddesses in the bloom of their youth" (108), but they are unable to recognize the goddess in their midst.

οὐδ' ἔγνων· χαλεποὶ δὲ θεοὶ θνητοῖσιν ὁρᾶσθαι.

Nor did they know her; the gods are difficult for mortals to behold.

(111)

The outcome of what happens in Eleusis will reaffirm the disjunction between human mortality and the deathlessness of the gods. Richardson notes an additional irony in this scene; if one compares it with other encounter sequences found in the epic, "the normal roles are reversed, since the goddess is the suppliant."[78]

The eldest girl now asks the old woman's identity and remarks at the strangeness of finding an old woman outside the city rather than in her proper place within the house, in the company of women of her own age "who would welcome you in word and deed" (117). The goddess responds by giving an account of herself that forms the verbal counterpart of her disguise and serves to flesh out her adopted persona. She has been abducted from Crete, "by force, against my will by compulsion" (124) by pirates, but managed to make her escape, "so that selling me without payment, they would not profit from my price" (132). The fact that Demeter manufactures a Cretan origin for herself reminds us of the Cretan tales Odysseus concocts on his return to Ithaca. It indicates not only that the goddess is lying, but that she is—in the manner of an Odysseus—manipulating the truth to her own ends. We must remember that the Cretan tales of Odysseus are not simply lies but lies that "resemble the truth."[79] The false tale of Demeter's abduction parallels the truth of Persephone's. Persephone is carried off by her future husband for the purpose of marriage; the old woman is carried off by pirates for the sake of gain. In both cases, women are precious commodities. But while the passive Persephone cannot make good her escape on her own, the old woman was able to elude her captors. All of Demeter's activity in Eleusis will be directed toward avenging the loss of her daughter, and her efforts will ultimately meet with partial success.

[78] Richardson (1974), p. 180.
[79] Cf. Arthur (1977), p. 19: "like the similar tales of Odysseus . . . the falsity is only superficial, for the message of the tale is true." There is no reason to find a reference to a Cretan origin of the Demeter cult here.

As is typical in such speeches, the goddess asks for pity and prays for the prosperity of her interlocutors:

ἀλλ' ὑμῖν μὲν πάντες 'Ολύμπια δώματ' ἔχοντες
δοῖεν κουριδίους ἄνδρας καὶ τέκνα τεκέσθαι
ὡς ἐθέλουσι τοκῆες· ἐμὲ δ' αὖτ' οἰκτείρατε κοῦραι

But to you may all those who inhabit Olympian homes
grant wedded husbands and to bear children
as your parents desire; but, maidens, pity me in turn.

(135–37)

The prosperity appropriate to young girls is a husband and a family in accordance with their parents' wishes. We are inevitably reminded of Demeter's lack of consent to her own daughter's marriage; but we should also note that she is not opposed to *all* marriage but only to the uniquely wrenching one between Persephone and the lord of the netherworld. With the appeal for pity, the goddess's speech should now come to an end.[80] Instead, she abruptly moves on to another subject and applies for a position as nurse and housekeeper—which has been her goal all along.[81]

In response, the fairest of the girls, Callidice, consoles the old woman for her misfortunes:

μαῖα θεῶν μὲν δῶρα καὶ ἀχνύμενοί περ ἀνάγκῃ
τέτλαμεν ἄνθρωποι· δὴ γὰρ πολὺ φέρτεροί εἰσιν.

Granny, the gifts of the gods, even to our grief, by necessity
must we human beings endure; for they are much more powerful.

(147–48)

This gnomic utterance encapsulates much that is characteristic of archaic Greek thought concerning the relations between gods and human beings: the ethic of endurance in the face of the "gifts" the gods apportion to mortals; the very ambiguity of those divine gifts that they must accept willy-nilly; and the powerlessness of mankind.[82] However commonplace,

[80] In epic speeches of this sort, the request for pity and the wish for prosperity generally flank the request for help in the middle. Cf. Richardson (1974), p. 190.

[81] Note the description of her disguise at lines 103–4: "such women are nurses of the children of decree-dispensing kings and housekeepers in echoing houses."

[82] Cf. Deichgräber (1950), pp. 529–31. Bianchi (1964), p. 171, notes the correspondence between Callidice's speech and that of Helios: both teach resignation. But while mortals must resign themselves to the order of Olympus, Demeter refuses to do so.

the sentiment nevertheless remains a profound statement of the fragility and helplessness of mankind in relation to powerful gods, whose designs remain incomprehensible to them. In the present context, however, the solace offered by the lovely Callidice has patently ironic overtones. In her ignorance, she addresses the goddess who calls herself the "Giver"[83] and whose greatest gift is mankind's sustenance, the grain that renders human life possible. Moreover, Demeter will soon attempt to bestow an even greater gift, not just life but immortality, on the infant Demophoon. But, once again, human ignorance, which comprehends nothing of the ultimate purposes of the gods, will thwart those plans to its own cost.

Callidice now names the most powerful men among the Eleusinians; none of their wives will dishonor or cast out[84] the stranger, "for you are godlike" (159). The young girl's list of the four "kings" of Eleusis might well arrest our attention. Triptolemus, while mentioned first, is simply one of the four. The hymn offers no hint of his role as the culture hero who disseminates Demeter's gift of agriculture throughout the world.[85] It is generally held that the particular prominence of Triptolemus and the story of his Mission develops only after the Athenian takeover of Eleusis and is later further exploited as a vehicle of Athenian cultural propaganda. Beginning in the late sixth century and culminating in the fifth, the profusion of vase paintings depicting Triptolemus and his chariot attests to the popularity of the subject. Indubitably, the story served as a justification for the Athenian claim to firstfruit offerings from Greek cities during the fifth and fourth centuries. The fact, however, that Triptolemus is exploited by Athenian propaganda does not mean that he is its invention. His firm local ties to Eleusinian legend as the first man to plow the Rarian plain suggest otherwise. The hymn itself seems to display an awareness of that story in its somewhat awkward allusion to the place in lines 450–56.[86] Walton has argued that the hymn is an Eleusinian composition postdating the Athenian incorporation of the sanctuary.[87] In that case, the absence of any special reference to Triptolemus's

[83] The manuscript offers the unmetrical Δώς at line 122. Δωσώ "is the most satisfactory solution" (Richardson [1974] p. 188).

[84] For the thematic importance of the expression ἀπονοσφίσσειεν, see above n. 68.

[85] For Triptolemus, see Richardson (1974), pp. 194–96; and F. Schwenn, "Triptolemus," RE 7A (1939): 213–30.

[86] See my subsequent discussion of this passage. The Marmor Parium, lines 23–29 (F. Jacoby, Das Marmor Parium [Berlin, 1904]), gives both versions.

[87] Walton (1952), pp. 105–14. Cf. Clinton (1986), pp. 46–47, who questions the historical evidence and emphasizes "the Hymn's ignorance even of important Eleusinian matters."

role constitutes a conscious Eleusinian suppression with a view to countering Athenian claims. Correct or not, Walton's argument demonstrates how scanty the historical evidence for the dating of our poem is and encourages caution in basing an interpretation on assumed chronological criteria.

The downplaying of Triptolemus may be due to factors other than historical circumstances. It is, after all, not an isolated phenomenon in the hymn. In the very next line, Eumolpus too appears stripped of his special status as founder of the hereditary *genos* of the Hierophant of the Mysteries.[88] And no one has yet to suggest that the outstanding role of the Eumolpids in the cult is an Athenian invention. The hymn's silences, then, may suggest another avenue of interpretation. The treatment of both Eumolpus and Triptolemus accords well with certain other tendencies in the poem. The first may point to a general deemphasizing of local cult in the interest of a broader Panhellenic perspective. Minimizing Triptolemus's role, on the other hand, forcefully points to the exclusion within the hymn of a version that culminates in Demeter's gift of grain to mankind. The rejection of the agrarian myth in the interest of Olympian theological speculation and the shift from the interests of local cult to a Panhellenic orientation—these, I submit, constitute the fundamental coordinates of the hymn's innovations.

The daughter of Celeus now suggests that the old woman should wait while they go home to their own mother, Metaneira, and tell her the whole story of their encounter. Indeed, Metaneira may invite the old woman to their own house to look after her son, one who is late-born, much-prayed-for, and greatly cherished:

εἰ τόν γ᾽ ἐκθρέψαιο καὶ ἥβης μέτρον ἵκοιτο
ῥεῖά κέ τίς σε ἰδοῦσα γυναικῶν θηλυτεράων
ζηλώσαι· τόσα κέν τοι ἀπὸ θρεπτήρια δοίη.

If you should nurse him up and he should come to the measure of
    his prime,
easily would someone of female women on seeing you
feel envy: so great would be your payment for his nurture.

(166–68)

---

[88] Cf. Clinton (1986), pp. 45–46, on the hymn's neglect of Eumolpus and Keryx, as well as Triptolemus.

This child, the only male among the girls, born to his mother late in life, and sole heir to the family, is an object of special concern. The hopes of the house are fixed upon him. His preciousness, the importance of his nurture, as well as his safe passage through the perils of infancy are emphatically stated. The goddess silently assents to this proposal, and the girls run off to report to their mother. A simile likening them to deer or calves frisking in the spring charmingly describes their youthful enthusiasm as they return to bring the stranger to their house. By contrast, Demeter, following behind with her head veiled, continues to grieve in her heart.

As Demeter crosses the threshold, something remarkable happens:

ἡ δ' ἄρ' ἐπ' οὐδὸν ἔβη ποσὶ καί ῥα μελάθρου
κῦρε κάρη, πλῆσεν δὲ θύρας σέλαος θείοιο.

She stepped on the threshold with her feet, and, lo,
her head touched the roofbeam, and she filled the gates with a
divine flash of light.

(188–89)

This has often been called an epiphany or a "partial epiphany," but the scene is unique. None of the supposed parallels cited by scholars is convincing. In typical epiphanies, a divinity wants to be recognized. Such, in fact, is Demeter's self-revelation in lines 275–80. In other cases, a disguised god partially reveals himself intentionally, or inadvertently raises the suspicion of a divine presence. For instance, in the *Hymn to Aphrodite*, in a scene adduced as the prototype of ours, Aphrodite disguised as a nubile young woman suddenly appears before Anchises (81–110).[89] He suspects that she may be some goddess, and Aphrodite is obliged to deny her divinity vehemently before proceeding with her intended seduction. The poet might well have exploited the ironies of human ignorance inherent in the situation, as he does elsewhere, but nothing of the sort happens in our passage. Although Metaneira is impressed and even frightened by the stranger's appearance, she nowhere appears to suspect the old woman before her might be a god. She does, however, recognize that there is something awe-inspiring and uncanny about the stranger, some kind of mysterious power, perhaps benign, perhaps not.[90] Demeter's im-

[89] Cf. Lenz (1975), p. 56; and Heitsch (1965), pp. 39–40.
[90] Cf. Scarpi (1976), p. 181: "per Metaneira, quindi, Demeter non è ancora la 'dea,' ma una 'straniera' carica di valenze."

pressive entrance must be acknowledged to be part and parcel of her assumed disguise. How Demeter presents herself to the household and how Metaneira sizes up her strange guest will prove crucial to the outcome of the events in the house of Celeus.

As has long been recognized, the next section of the poem (192–211) is overtly etiological, reflecting the preliminary ritual preceding initiation. Each uniquely conditioned gesture of the goddess in the myth—her silence, her fasting, her sitting on a stool covered with a fleece, and her drinking of the *kykeon*—is imitated and infinitely repeated by her followers in cult. Her actions are both rooted in the unique time of myth, "*illo tempore*," and transcend it, as the initiates rehearse her movements in preparation for the revelation of the Mysteries. In this passage where myth and cult momentarily coalesce, the style of the narrative changes perceptibly. The poet gives Demeter's words only in indirect discourse (ἔφασκε [207]) and only hints at the content of Iambe's raillery. One has, in fact, the impression that the entire sequence of action is veiled and speech somehow muffled, perhaps against the eyes and ears of the profane.

As the goddess enters the palace, an awestruck Metaneira yields her chair. At first, Demeter refuses to sit down but remains standing silently with her eyes cast down. Now Iambe offers her a "jointed stool" covered with a fleece,[91] and on this the goddess takes her place in an attitude of silent grief:

ἔνθα καθεζομένη προκατέσχετο χερσὶ καλύπτρην·
δηρὸν δ᾽ ἄφθογγος τετιημένη ἧστ᾽ ἐπὶ δίφρου,
οὐδέ τιν᾽ οὔτ᾽ ἔπεϊ προσπτύσσετο οὔτε τι ἔργῳ,
ἀλλ᾽ ἀγέλαστος ἄπαστος ἐδητύος ἠδὲ ποτῆτος
ἧστο πόθῳ μινύθουσα βαθυζώνοιο θυγατρός.

Sitting there, she held before her a veil with her hands;
and for a long time, she sat on the chair without speaking, in grief,
nor did she address anyone in word or deed;
but, unsmiling and without touching food or drink,
she sat, wasting away with longing for her deep-girdled daughter.

(197–201)

---

[91] For the significance of this stool in the preliminary rituals of initiation, see Richardson (1974), p. 212. I do not believe its cultic use precludes its narrative function, as outlined later.

Finally, Iambe, who "knew excellent things," breaks the spell by mocking and scolding the grieving goddess and, by distracting her from her woes, causes Demeter first to smile, then to laugh, and finally "to have a cheerful heart." We are not told exactly what Iambe said to amuse the goddess, perhaps out of the poet's sense of decorum.[92] Interpreters generally assume some form of ritual obscenity or *aischrologia*, which we know had a place in Eleusinian cult. But the so-called *gephurismoi*—insults hurled against prominent citizens as they crossed the bridge on their way from Athens to Eleusis—formed part of the procession rather than the preparatory rites at Eleusis itself.[93]

Other versions of this curious incident point perhaps toward a different line of interpretation that coheres more closely with the dramatic situation in the hymn.[94] In one variant, it is the maid Baubo[95] who makes Demeter laugh by lifting her skirts. But the gesture goes beyond the mere shocking display of what is usually covered and seems to indicate the display of the female genitals in their reproductive capacity. For as Baubo exhibits herself, a laughing infant peeps forth from her belly.[96] With this parallel in mind, it may be possible to interpret what Iambe may have said to make Demeter laugh. First, we should note that χλεύης and παρασκώπτουσ᾽ (202–3) do not refer to making jokes or telling funny stories, obscene or not, but instead involve personal abuse and invective directed *at* someone.[97] Second, the posture of the silent goddess may re-

[92] Cf. Arthur (1977), p. 21: "The account of Iambe and her joking . . . probably conceals a reference to the grosser and more explicitly sexual aspects of Demeter's fertility powers." It is possible that the concealment goes beyond decorum; many scholars suspect that one of the objects shown forth at the culmination of the Mysteries may have been a vulva.

[93] Apollodorus 1.5.1 considers the Iambe story an etiology for the jesting by women at the Thesmophoria, but he evidently knew of no similar ritual at Eleusis. Wilamowitz (1959), 2: 52, n. 2, assumes that the obscene jesting at Eleusis was at some point transferred to the procession: "das ἰαμβίζειν . . . gehörte wohl zu vielen Frauenkulten, aber in Eleusis war es nicht erhalten, sondern auf die γεφυρισμοί abgeschoben." I am not quite satisfied with this assumed transfer.

[94] *Orphicorum Fragmenta* 52 (Kern). For a discussion of the sources in Clement and Arnobius, see Graf (1974), pp. 194–99.

[95] The word βαυβώ apparently means vulva. Cf. Hesychius, who cites a meaning, κοιλία, from Empedocles; also Herondas, Φιλιαζουσαί 19, where it means dildo.

[96] Compare the terracotta figurine found in Priene of a female figure with a child's face on her abdomen, reproduced in Nilsson, *GGR* (1955), pl. 45, no. 3.

[97] Cf. Aristole, *Rhetoric* 2.2.12, of people prone to anger: ὀργίζονται δὲ τοῖς τε καταγελῶσι καὶ χλευάζουσι καὶ σκώπτουσιν· ὑβρίζουσι γάρ ("Men are angry at those who ridicule, mock, and scoff at them, for this is an insult." *Aristotle: The "Art" of Rhetoric*, trans. J. H. Freese [London, 1926], p. 181).

semble that of mourning, as many critics have noticed. But mourners usually sit on the ground,[98] whereas Demeter sits on a stool. I suggest, then, that Demeter's attitude resembles nothing so much as a woman in labor on a birthing stool, about to give birth.[99] Iambe notes the resemblance—and its absurdity. For Demeter has disguised herself as an old woman well past the age of childbearing. In her good-natured ignorance of the goddess's identity, Iambe jeers and mocks the ridiculous figure cut by the old woman. But Demeter does not react the way the gods usually do when insulted by mortals; not anger, but laughter follows upon Iambe's raillery. As a result, Iambe "even afterward continued to please her in her rites" (205). The explanation proposed here must, to be sure, remain tentative, but it has the advantage of taking into account the dramatic situation of the narrative as well as reinforcing the motif of children and childbearing so prominent in this part of the hymn.

Metaneira proceeds to offer the restored goddess wine, which she refuses because it is not lawful for her to drink it. Instead, she instructs the queen to prepare a mixture of barley and mint, the famous *kykeon* drunk by the *mystai* before initiation. Here again, the poet is explicitly etiological:

[98] Compare Penelope at *Odyssey* 4.716–17: "nor could she bear to sit on a chair, of which there were many in the house, but she sat on the threshold." See also Richardson (1974), pp. 218–19 and 220.

[99] Cf. Soranus's detailed description of such a birthing stool in Περὶ Γυναικείων 2.3 (Ilberg) (= *Corpus Medicorum Graecorum* 4 [1927]). Soranus clearly considered the use of a stool preferable to a bed, at least for a healthy woman. On the basis of Leto's posture in *Hymn to Apollo* 117, it is generally assumed that the normal birthing posture involved kneeling while leaning forward. This ignores line 17 of *Apollo* where Leto is said to lean back and, more important, the anomalous mythological context of giving birth on a desert island. Cf. G. Most, "Callimachus and Herophilus," *Hermes* 109 (1981): 188–96, who argues that Callimachus's reversal of Leto's position in his hymn is based on contemporary medical views (i.e., those of Herophilus). Both F. G. Welcker, "Entbindung" in *Kleine Schriften* (Bonn 1850), 3: 185–208, and E. Samter, *Geburt, Hochzeit und Tod* (Leipzig, 1911), pp. 6–15, insist that the kneeling position was the usual one in antiquity and identify various kneeling figures with birth goddesses. P. Baur, *Eileithyia* (University of Missouri Studies 1.4) (Chicago, 1902), p. 44. expresses doubts, because Eileithyia is not represented thus. The entire theory of a kneeling birth posture has been conclusively disproved by J. Morgoulieff, *Étude critique sur les monuments antiques représentant des scènes d'accouchement* (Paris, 1893). His conclusions (p. 75): "Dans la Grèce antique, à l'époque la plus ancienne, l'accouchement *se fait généralement sur des sièges à dossier* ou sur des chaises se rapprochant des chaises longues" (italics mine). The *Nixi Dii*, mentioned by Festus 174b, 33, as well as some of the kneeling figures discovered in Greece should perhaps be understood as kneeling midwives or attendants at birth. Alan Hall has pointed out to me some figures of a seated goddess giving birth on a similar type of chair from the neolithic period at Catal Hüyük. See J. Mellaart, *Catal Hüyük: A Neolithic Town in Anatolia* (London, 1967), p. 184 and pl. 67, 68, IX.

ἡ δὲ κυκεῶ τεύξασα θεᾷ πόρεν ὡς ἐκέλευε·
δεξαμένη δ᾿ ὁσίης ἕνεκεν πολυπότνια Δηώ.

And she [Metaneira], having prepared the *kykeon*, gave it to the
goddess as she had ordered;
but she took it, Deo, mistress over many, for the sake of the rite.

(210–11)

Much has been written about the Eleusinian *kykeon*;[100] here it must suffice to point out that this peculiar beverage forms a link between Demeter
and mortals. Standing somewhere between the divine nourishment, nectar and ambrosia, which Demeter had rejected on her departure from
Olympus, and the mortal wine forbidden to the gods, the barley drink
belongs both to Demeter as the goddess of agriculture and to mankind
as the recipient of her gift. In the drinking of this potion, mortality and
immortality are momentarily joined.

After this parenthetical scene, in which god and mortal, myth and
ritual are briefly united, and our time and "that time" mysteriously in-
tersect, the poet returns to the full epic mode of narration. At the same
time, the revived goddess returns to the implementation of her plan.

The return to epic narration is signaled by the return of direct discourse, as Metaneira now formally greets the stranger. Her apparent
grace and respectability suggest to the queen that the old woman too may
be of royal stock. In words that echo those of her daughter, Metaneira
offers consolation to her guest for her evident fall from an earlier prosperity (216–17; cf. 147–48). But for the young girl's general statement—
"the gods are stronger"—the queen substitutes an expression of bitter
resignation, born, no doubt, from her greater experience: "for the yoke
of necessity lies on their neck" (217). Now, however, that the stranger has
come, let her share in the fortunes of the house and look after the child
in her arms,

. . . τὸν ὀψίγονον καὶ ἄελπτον
ὤπασαν ἀθάνατοι, πολυάρητος δέ μοί ἐστιν.

[100] See A. Delatte, *Le Cycéon: Breuvage rituel des mystères d'Eleusis* (Paris, 1955), pp.
23–56, who points out that while the ritual of drinking the *kykeon* must have preceded
the myth, the myth, on the contrary, offers an explanation for the rite insofar as the
initiates are deemed to imitate the actions of the goddess. See also A. Battegazzore, "Eraclito e il ciceone eleusino," *Maia* 29/30 (1977–1978): 3–12.

*the Cretan origin must
have something to do [with?]
their willingness
to hire her.*

... whom late born and unexpected
the immortals granted; for he is one much prayed for by me.

(219–20)

Once again, the special status of this child is mentioned, as well as the
ample reward for seeing him safely through childhood (219–23; cf. 164–
68). The epithet ὀψίγονος (165, 219) gains special poignancy if we realize
that Metaneira is now well past the age of childbearing. Born late and
against all expectation, the only son could not be replaced if any disaster
were to befall him.

The goddess in turn greets the queen and wishes her prosperity. She
consents to look after the baby:

> κοὔ μιν ἔολπα κακοφραδίῃσι τιθήνης
> οὔτ' ἄρ' ἐπηλυσίη δηλήσεται οὔθ' ὑποτάμνον·
> οἶδα γὰρ ἀντίτομον μέγα φέρτερον ὑλοτόμοιο,
> οἶδα δ' ἐπηλυσίης πολυπήμονος ἐσθλὸν ἐρυσμόν.

> nor do I expect that by the ill-will of his nurse
> nor even that an attack will destroy him or poison herb;
> for I know an antidote more powerful than the herb cutter,
> and I know an excellent defense against painful spells.

(227–30)

Here Demeter employs the language of an adept, a witch, albeit a benign
one, a witch who knows all the magical countermeasures necessary to
defend the child against spells, poisons, and the mysterious "attacks" to
which infants are especially vulnerable.[101] In presenting herself as a witch,
Demeter remains within the confines of her disguise and moves closer to
her ultimate goal. The magical knowledge she claims as her own makes
her appear even more ideally suitable in the eyes of Metaneira to be the
chosen nursemaid of her beloved son. Demeter's words also reinforce the
aura of uncanniness that accompanied the goddess's entrance into the
palace. But in the sequel, both will serve as well to arouse the queen's
suspicions.

---

[101] On the magical and incantatory quality of these lines, see Scarpi (1976), pp. 165–70
and 179–80. For Demeter's self-presentation as a witch, see pp. 170–71: "Demeter inoltre,
proprio per il suo intento di 'proteggere' il fanciullo, si presenta come 'maga benefica,' del
tipo *medicine-man*, il che pero non esclude da lei gli stessi poteri che connotano chi è grado
di inviare influssi malefici" (p. 170).

237

Joyfully, Metaneira entrusts the child, first named here, into Demeter's "immortal hands." As the goddess receives the babe into her "fragrant bosom," the significance of this moment, which concludes the first phase of her plan and opens the second, is signaled in a summarizing sentence:

ὣς ἡ μὲν Κελεοῖο δαΐφρονος ἀγλαὸν υἱὸν
Δημοφόωνθ᾽, ὃν ἔτικτεν ἐΰζωνος Μετάνειρα,
ἔτρεφεν ἐν μεγάροις.

So she nursed in the palace
the splendid son of wise Celeus,
Demophoon, whom well-girdled Metaneira bore.

(233–35)

Demeter's attempt to render the son of Celeus immortal forms the focal point of her visit to Eleusis:

ὁ δ᾽ ἀέξετο δαίμονι ἶσος
οὔτ᾽ οὖν σῖτον ἔδων, οὐ θησάμενος ⟨γάλα μητρὸς⟩
Δημήτηρ
χρίεσκ᾽ ἀμβροσίη ὡς εἰ θεοῦ ἐκγεγαῶτα,
ἡδὺ καταπνείουσα καὶ ἐν κόλποισιν ἔχουσα·
νύκτας δὲ κρύπτεσκε πυρὸς μένει ἠΰτε δαλὸν
λάθρα φίλων γονέων.

And he grew like a daemon,
not eating grain or nursed ⟨on mother's milk⟩.
⟨By day⟩[102] ..... Demeter ...
anointed him with ambrosia, as if he were the offspring of a god,[103]
breathing down on him sweetly and holding him in her bosom;
but during the nights, she would hide him in the strength of fire
like a firebrand,
in secret from his own parents.

(235–40)

Shunning all mortal nourishment, Demeter gives the child ambrosia—a preservative[104]—and inspires him with her own divine breath. The iter-

---

[102] The words in brackets are supplied to fill the lacuna in line 236–37.
[103] Compare the nursing and rapid growth of Apollo in the *Hymn to Apollo* 123–29.
[104] For the preservative powers of ambrosia, see Clay (1981–1982), pp. 112–17; and Scarpi (1976), pp. 184–85.

atives show that the transformation is not instantaneous, but requires time and effort. But the most curious part of this process remains Demophoon's "baptism of fire." It has frequently been compared with the domestic rite of *Amphidromia*, in which a newborn child is run around the familial hearth and thereby officially adopted into his family.[105] The analogy, however, is a poor one. This hearth belongs to Celeus, whose offspring Demophoon is already acknowledged to be; moreover, the child is placed *in* the fire—surely no ordinary procedure, as Metaneira's horrified reaction proves. The story of Heracles' fiery apotheosis on the pyre offers a better parallel.[106] There, as in similar tales, placing the living body into the fire seems to "burn off" mortality.[107] Still, we must note that Demeter intends not only to immortalize, but also to adopt, the infant as her own; her maternal gesture of holding the babe to her bosom indicates as much.[108]

The miraculous growth and godlike appearance of the child arouse Metaneira's curiosity and perhaps also goad her suspicions. The strange nurse's earlier claims to being an adept as well as her uncanny entrance into the palace may already have provoked a certain anxiety in the mother. In any case, Metaneira spies on the goddess at night,[109] observes her precious child[110] in the flames, and cries out in terror. Ignorant of the

[105] Cf. Richardson (1974), pp. 231–36; and especially J. G. Frazer's appendix, "Putting Children on the Fire," in his edition of Apollodorus (Cambridge, Mass., 1921), 2: 311–17. For the *Amphidromia*, see also E. Samter, *Familienfeste der Griechen und Römer* (Berlin, 1901), pp. 59–64. C.-M. Edsman, *Ignis divinus: Le Feu comme moyen de rajeunissement et d'immortalité* (Lund, 1949), pp. 224–29, gives an overview of the varied interpretations of Demophoon's "baptism of fire." In addition to the connection with the *Amphidromia*, links have been proposed to Eleusinian consecration rituals, initiation rites, and certain beliefs and practices involving cremation. Cf. Scarpi (1976), pp. 202–4. Nilsson, *GGR* (1955), 1: 659–60, denies the etiological character of the scene: "Bei näherer Überlegung erkennt man, dass hier kein Aition, sondern freie Dichtung vorliegt" (p. 660).

[106] Cf. Edsman (1949), pp. 233–49; and F. Stoessel, *Der Tod des Herakles* (Zurich, 1947), esp. pp. 15–18.

[107] Cf. Apollonius Rhodius 4.869–72, and Apollodorus 3.13.6 for Thetis's similar treatment of the infant Achilles. Both passages may well be inspired by the *Hymn to Demeter*. See also Plutarch, *De Iside et Osiride* 16, and Iamblichus, *De mysteriis* 5.12.

[108] Cf. line 187, where Metaneira παῖδ' ὑπὸ κόλπῳ ἔχουσα; and line 286, where one of Demophoon's sisters takes over the maternal function: παῖδ' ἀνὰ χερσὶν ἑλοῦσα ἑῷ ἐγκάτθετο κόλπῳ.

[109] The expression, νύκτ' ἐπιτηρήσασα (244), is unique and suggests that Metaneira lay in wait, watching for the right opportunity. Cf. the phrase, ἐπιτηρητέον τὸν καιρόν. The words clearly indicate that Metaneira's interruption is no accidental affair, but a premeditated action based on her growing suspicions.

[110] Richardson (1974), p. 242, comments on line 252: "The line, with its change of subject, is slightly awkward," which is true enough, although I would not follow Rich-

goddess's intentions, Metaneira inevitably assumes that her son is being murdered in some nefarious magic ritual. Metaneira's outcry breaks the spell. Upon hearing it, Demeter angrily takes the child from the fire and sets him on the ground. Her gesture means that he will forever be an earthling. In her fury, Demeter indicts not just Metaneira, but all of mankind:

νήϊδες ἄνθρωποι καὶ ἀφράδμονες οὔτ' ἀγαθοῖο
αἶσαν ἐπερχομένου προγνώμεναι οὔτε κακοῖο.

Ignorant men and senseless, incapable
of foreknowing the lot of coming good or evil.

(256–57)

Metaneira's reckless interference with the goddess's purpose merely constitutes a signal example of the general rule of human folly. The hymn has previously drawn attention to the disparity between divine knowledge and human ignorance. Yet, in this instance, it is difficult to ignore the parallel between Metaneira's maternal grief for her son and that of Demeter for Persephone.[111] Metaneira mistakes the goddess's intention and believes that Demophoon is doomed to a horrible death. Is it possible that Demeter, on her part, similarly mistakes the plan of Zeus for Persephone and can only conceive of it as signifying a permanent and total separation from her daughter—a kind of death?

However that may be, Demeter swears that she would have made Demophoon "immortal and ageless forever" and granted him "imperishable honor." The blame for her failure lies squarely with Metaneira and her ruinous folly. Now, however, although the child is doomed to mortality, Demeter will nevertheless give him "imperishable honor," because "he sat in her lap and lay in her arms":

---

ardson in considering it "unnecessary" or a "fill-line." Here again, the poet goes out of his way to emphasize the special status of the irreplaceable infant and thereby renders Metaneira's horror and grief comprehensible.

[111] N. Rubin and H. Deal, "Some Functions of the Demophon Episode in the Homeric Hymn to Demeter," *QUCC* 34 (1980): 7–21, draw attention to the parallel: "Grief and anger lead each to obstruct a divine plan (Demeter, the will of Zeus; Metanira, the plan of Demeter)" (p. 9). The authors also note that Metaneira's reaction to the presumed loss of her son results in helplessness, whereas Demeter's leads to a purposive plan. Some of the other supposed parallels between the Demophoon episode and the Demeter/Persephone story appear a bit forced.

ὥρῃσιν δ᾽ ἄρα τῷ γε περιπλομένων ἐνιαυτῶν
παῖδες Ἐλευσινίων πόλεμον καὶ φύλοπιν αἰνὴν
αἰὲν ἐν ἀλλήλοισι συνάξουσ᾽ ἤματα πάντα.

And in due season,[112] as the years come around, for him
the children of the Eleusinians will join in war and dread strife,
always, among themselves, for all time.

(265–67)

In lieu of immortality, Demophoon will receive the honors of hero cult
after his death.[113] It is generally thought that Demeter refers to the *Balletys*, an obscure local festival involving a mock battle among the young
men of Eleusis.[114] The hymn's audience will have understood the prophetic allusion, but Metaneira might well be troubled by the goddess's
ominous words.

At this point, the goddess solemnly reveals her identity:

εἰμὶ δὲ Δημήτηρ τιμάοχος, ἥ τε μέγιστον
ἀθανάτοις θνητοῖσί τ᾽ ὄνεαρ καὶ χάρμα τέτυκται.

I am Demeter, holder of honor, who am the greatest
benefit and joy to immortals and mortals.

(268–69)

Agriculture constitutes the *timē* Demeter claims as her own and the benefit she confers upon gods and mortals.[115] How agriculture benefits not
only mankind but the gods as well will soon become manifest. Once
again, Demeter's declaration situates the hymn firmly in the post-Promethean age, where agriculture and sacrifice form essential elements of
human life.[116]

Somewhat abruptly, the goddess now orders a temple to be built for
herself outside the city by the whole people:

[112] So, correctly, Richardson, (1974), p. 245. AHS (1936), p. 160, take ὥρῃσιν etc. as
"when he has grown to manhood," but see my discussion of line 289 below.
[113] Cf. Nagy (1979), pp. 181ff.
[114] For the *Balletys*, see Richardson, (1974), pp. 245–47, and O. Kern, *s.v.* "Βαλλητύς,"
RE 2 (1896): 2830–31. Cf. Clinton (1986), p. 44, n. 6: "The Demophon story as aetiology
for the game Balletys ... may postdate our poem. The poem merely mentions civil strife
as a punishment."
[115] Gemoll (1886), pp. 299–300, misinterprets τιμάοχος (268), calling it "auffällig, da
Demeter selber ihren Dienst erst ordnet."
[116] Cf. Rudhardt (1978), p. 10.

ὄργια δ' αὐτὴ ἐγὼν ὑποθήσομαι ὥς ἂν ἔπειτα
εὐαγέως ἔρδοντες ἐμὸν νόον ἱλάσκοισθε.

And I myself will prescribe the rites, so that afterward,
in performing them purely, you may propitiate my mind.

(273–74)

In assuming that the *orgia* of line 273 refer to the Mysteries, scholars light
upon an apparent contradiction.[117] For Demeter does not in fact establish
her Mysteries until the very end of the hymn (473–79). Her promise, then,
is strangely postponed or, in Richardson's view, interrupted by the introduction of the motif of the famine.[118] But it is essential not to anticipate
any reference to the Mysteries at this point in the narrative. Demeter only
asks the Eleusinians to "appease my mind" (274).[119] In its immediate context, Demeter's demand for a temple and sacrifices[120] is nothing more

[117] Cf. AHS (1936), p. 118, who note that the "foundation of the Mysteries is ordained
in v. 273 and carried out in vv. 473 sqq."

[118] Richardson (1974), pp. 260 and 330.

[119] ἱλάσκομαι can mean both "to make gracious" and "to appease" (LSJ); "chercher à
se rendre favorable, à se concilier" (P. Chantraine, *Dictionnaire étymologique de la langue
grecque* [Paris, 1968–1980]); "gnädig machen" and "entsündigen" (G. Kittel, ed., *Theologisches Wörterbuch zum Neuen Testament* [Stuttgart, 1938], 3: 314–17). In Kittel's *Wörterbuch*, F. Büchsel speaks of the "Doppelbedeutung" of the word. Its exact nuance depends
on its context. Here and in its other occurrences in the hymn (292 and 368), ἱλάσκομαι
has its strong sense of propitiating or placating an angry divinity. Compare *Iliad* 1.100,
147, 386, 444, and 472 in reference to propitiating Apollo for the plague sent against the
Greeks. Cf. Büchsel, p. 316: "Die Kulthandlung, die mit den Verben bezeichnet wurde,
hatte zum Zweck, dem Schuldigen die Gnade der Götter *wieder zu verschaffen*" (italics
mine).

[120] N.M.H. van der Burg, ΑΠΟΡΡΗΤΑ—ΔΡΩΜΕΝΑ—ΟΡΓΙΑ (Amsterdam,
1939), pp. 91–101, argues that the earliest meaning of ὄργια (related to ἔρδω, ἔργον, etc.)
is simply any religious or cultic activity, especially "sacrifices." Only later does the term
become associated with mystery cults, possibly through a false etymologizing from ὀργάω,
ὀρέγω, or ὀργή. Cf. the intriguing remarks of Clement, *Protrepticus* 2.13.1: καί μοι δοκεῖ
τὰ ὄργια ... δεῖν ἐτυμολογεῖν ... ἀπὸ τῆς ὀργῆς τῆς Δηοῦς τῆς πρὸς Δία γεγε-
νημένης. Despite his argument, Burg, p. 94, equates the use of ὄργια at *Demeter* 273 with
line 476, even though it contradicts his own evidence. But cf. J. Casabona, *Recherches sur
le vocabulaire des sacrifices en Grec* (Aix-en-Provence, 1966), p. 66, who remarks on ὄργια
... εὐαγέως ἔρδοντες in lines 273–74: "la comparaison de ces vers avec 368/9 (θυσίαισι
... εὐαγέως ἔρδοντες) suggère même une équivalence, au moins en certains de leurs
emplois, de ὄργια et de θυσία." Note that here the goddess simply establishes or prescribes the usual sacrificial worship; but when she establishes the Mysteries, she must
"reveal the conduct of the sacred acts and explain the rites to all" (474–76). For a discussion of the topographical question of the relationship of the temple Demeter orders for
herself here and the Eleusinian Telesterion, see Richardson (1974), pp. 328–30; and
G. Mylonas, *The Hymn to Demeter and Her Sanctuary at Eleusis (Washington University
Studies* n.s. 13) (St. Louis, 1942), pp. 28–63. Clinton (1986), p. 44, remarks that "the poet's
knowledge of Eleusinian topography is not as good as it is supposed to be."

than a means of propitiating her anger at mankind for Metaneira's stupidity.[121] The establishment of the Mysteries can occur only after Demeter's reconciliation with both gods and mortals; and much will have to happen before then.

Demeter now puts off her disguise and, before departing, reveals herself in all her divine splendor. Stunned by the epiphany and, no doubt by the goddess's angry words, Metaneira faints and forgets to pick up her cherished son. Rushing from their beds as they hear his pitiful cries, his sisters pick him up, relight the fire that had gone out, and raise up Metaneira. Then their attention returns to the disconsolate child:

ἀγρόμεναι δέ μιν ἀμφὶς ἐλούεον ἀσπαίροντα
ἀμφαγαπαζόμεναι· τοῦ δ᾽ οὐ μειλίσσετο θυμός·
χειρότεραι γὰρ δή μιν ἔχον τροφοὶ ἠδὲ τιθῆναι.

Gathering round about him, they washed him, as he panted out
    his life,
and hugged him. But his heart was not comforted,
for worse nurses were holding him.

(289–91)

This is the last we shall hear of poor Demophoon in the *Hymn to Demeter*. In some other versions, the child is immediately burned up in the fire,[122] but the hymn-poet nevertheless clearly alludes to his approaching death. In Homer, ἀσπαίρω (289) is used exclusively of the heroes' death-agony;[123] here it indicates that the infant is doomed to die very soon.

Given the importance of Demophoon's role in the hymn, attempts have been made to link him closely to Eleusinian ritual or to consider him in some sense a prototype of the initiates.[124] But here again, the connection between myth and ritual is not so simple. After all, Demeter had intended to make the child immortal—which is quite a different matter from initiation—and the attempt failed. Similarly, Demophoon's ulti-

---

[121] Cf. the comment of Hermann (1806), p. cvii on line 300: "[the poet] could not very well mention the Eleusinian mysteries here; for it would be ridiculous for Ceres to institute rituals to which she would soon show herself so unjustly disposed that she would punish the piety of her worshipers with starvation."

[122] *Orphicorum fragmenta* 49.101 (Kern); Apollodorus 1.5.1–2.

[123] Cf. LSJ. Consider also Aeschylus, *Persians* 977, concerning the defeated army of Xerxes: τλάμονες ἀσπαίρουσι χέρσῳ, and H. D. Broadhead's (*The Persae of Aeschylus* [Cambridge, 1960]) comment: "ἀσπαίρουσι calls up a vivid picture of the Persians, who as they are washed up on the shore, gasp for breath like the dying fish in the net." Admittedly, Herodotus 1.111.3 offers a counterexample.

[124] Cf. Richardson (1974), pp. 233–36; and Sabbatucci (1966), p. 163.

mate fate—to be honored in cult—does not parallel the lot of the initiates after death. Moreover, the cult dedicated to him remains a local Eleusinian affair and has, as far as we know, no obvious connection with the Panhellenic Mysteries.[125] It then seems mistaken to attempt to identify Demophoon with the mystical divine child Demeter is supposed to bear at the culmination of the Mysteries.[126] Finally, the fact that Demophoon "never appears in Eleusinian inscriptions or in art"[127] can scarcely be ignored.

And yet a connection, albeit a negative one, exists between Demophoon and the initiates. If Demeter had succeeded in making Demophoon a god, there would be no need for initiation.[128] In the context of the hymn, the case of Demophoon and his failed apotheosis guarantees for all time that no man can become immortal; henceforward, mankind cannot hope to escape its mortality. To this extent, the hymn reaffirms the absolute distinction between gods and human beings that forms the fundamental principle of the Olympian hierarchy. On the other hand, it will, in the end, mitigate the lot of mortals through the institution of the Mysteries. One may say, then, the fate of Demophoon forms a precondition to the possibility and desirability of initiation.[129] Only once the avenue of immortality is permanently closed, can the path of initiation be opened.

After Demeter's startling self-revelation and departure, the women of the house of Celeus, quaking with fear, attempt to propitiate the angry goddess all through the night.[130] At dawn, they convey Demeter's commands to Celeus:

[125] Cf. Nilsson, *GGR* (1955), 1: 660, who says of the *Balletys* dedicated to Demophoon, that it "in keinem erkennbaren Zusammenhang mit den Mysterien steht; er ist ein eleusinischer Ritus ohne Zusammenhang mit den Mysterien."

[126] Cf. Richardson (1974), pp. 233–34, and the testimony from Hippolytus, *Refutatio omnium Haeresium* 5.8.39: ἱερὸν ἔτεκε πότνια κοῦρον βριμὼ βριμόν. For Plutus as a child of Demeter, see my discussion of lines 487–88 below.

[127] Richardson (1974), p. 237.

[128] Cf. Sabbatucci (1965), p. 165: "se ci fosse stata l'immortalazione [sic] non ci sarebbe stata l'iniziazione." Cf. Bianchi (1964), pp. 173–75.

[129] Cf. Scarpi (1976), p. 218; and Bianchi (1964), pp. 175–76: "la divinizzazione di persone singole . . . fanno parte della tipologia olimpica, non de quella misterica, giacché si tratta di eccezioni che confermono la regola della mortalità e della deperibilità degli uomini comme categoria."

[130] Richardson (1974), p. 256, suggests that this passage contains a reflection of the ritual *pannuchis* that followed the arrival of the future *mystai* on the night of Boedromion 20. But Richardson also notes that "the atmosphere of dread (*Dem.* 293) might be consid-

αὐτὰρ ὅ γ᾽ εἰς ἀγορὴν καλέσας πολυπείρονα λαὸν
ἤνωγ᾽ ἠϋκόμῳ Δημήτερι πίονα νηὸν
ποιῆσαι καὶ βωμὸν ἐπὶ προὔχοντι κολωνῷ.

And he, calling the multitudinous host to assembly,
commanded them to build a rich temple for fair-haired Demeter
and an altar on the projecting hill.

(296–97)

The construction of the temple constitutes a public activity carried out by
the whole *laos*, that is, the men of Eleusis. The goddess's earlier activity
involved (with the exception of Demophoon) only women and took place
within the palace, in the women's quarters.[131] The shift from indoors to
outdoors, from female to male, and from private to public is a significant
one. It accompanies Demeter's shedding of her disguise as an old woman
and witch and the revelation of her true godhead. In this light, the goddess's attempt to make Demophoon a god appears as a form of magic: a
private ritual performed for a specific private end, conducted in secret by
an adept, and usually involving the transformation or change of state of
a person or a thing.[132] The failure of Demeter's private magic signals, as
we have seen, the impossibility of individual apotheosis. In its stead, the
goddess now establishes a public shrine and sacrifices to appease her anger. Only at the end of the poem will she reveal the "conduct of her holy
rites," accessible to all the initiates.

---

ered inappropriate to a παννυχίς ... and especially to what we know of the Eleusinian
ceremony."

[131] Several versions have not the mother but the father interrupt the process of immortalization. In Hyginus, *Fabulae* 147, for example, the father (called Eleusinius) discovers Ceres' nocturnal activities with the child (here Triptolemus) and is killed by the
angry goddess. Cf. Frazer (1921), p. 312.

[132] Consider the remarks of M. Mauss, *A General Theory of Magic*, trans. R. Brain
(London, 1972), pp. 23–24: "Magical rites are commonly performed in woods, far away
from dwelling places, at night, or in shadowy corners, in the secret recesses of a house or
at any rate in some out of the way place. Where religious rites are performed openly, in
full public view, magical rites are carried out in secret. ... Isolation and secrecy are two
almost perfect signs of the intimate character of a magical rite ... both the act and the
actor are shrouded in mystery. ... Magical rites are anti-religious ... they do not belong
to those organized systems we call cults. Religious practices, on the contrary, even fortuitous and voluntary ones, are always predictable, prescribed and official. ... A magical rite
is *any rite which does not play a part in organized cults*—it is private, secret, mysterious and
approaches the limit of a prohibited rite." See also B. Malinowski, *Magic, Science and
Religion and Other Essays* (Boston, 1948), pp. 20–21 and 68–70, for an attempt to define
magic and to distinguish it from religion. Cf. Scarpi (1976), pp. 191–96. Bianchi (1964), p.
176, speaks of the "aspetto magico" of the process of immortalizing Demophoon.

CHAPTER 4

Famine, Reunion, and Reconciliation

But the time is not yet ripe. The third act of the *Hymn to Demeter* begins with the resumption of the divine drama after the human drama has drawn to a close. Yet while further action will take place among the gods, these actions will not leave mankind unaffected. Demeter retires into her temple as soon as it is completed:

ἔνθα καθεζομένη μακάρων ἀπὸ νόσφιν ἁπάντων
μίμνε πόθῳ μινύθουσα βαθυζώνοιο θυγατρός.

Sitting there, far from all the blessed ones,
she remained, wasting in longing for her deep-girdled daughter.

(303–4)

Demeter's endeavors in Eleusis have come to naught; her plan of re-venge, frustrated. In the meantime, her anguish over her daughter re-mains undiminished. Line 304 echoes line 92. The intervening activity in Eleusis afforded no relief for the goddess's anger and grief. But if she had previously abandoned Olympus for the earth, she now cuts herself off[133] not only from the gods, but also from the community of men.

There is a cruel irony in Demeter's shutting herself off in her own temple, for a temple is the place where mortals come to sacrifice to the gods and the gods come to receive the offerings due them.[134] In other words, it forms the locus of communication between gods and men. Per-verting the function appropriate to it, Demeter here uses the temple to isolate herself both from mankind and the gods. In addition, she will disrupt all sacrifices, the chief medium of communication between them.

αἰνότατον δ᾽ ἐνιαυτὸν ἐπὶ χθόνα πουλυβότειραν
ποίησ᾽ ἀνθρώποις καὶ κύντατον, οὐδέ τι γαῖα
σπέρμ᾽ ἀνίει· κρύπτεν γὰρ ἐϋστέφανος Δημήτηρ.

She made a most terrible year on the much-nourishing earth
for men, and a most beastly one,[135] nor did the earth
bring forth any seed; for well-garlanded Demeter hid it.

(305–7)

---

[133] Note νόσφιν (303). Cf. lines 4, 92, and 114, and ἀπάνευθε in lines 355 and 27.
[134] Cf. Rudhardt (1958), pp. 56–57.
[135] Cf. line 90: ἄχος αἰνότερον καὶ κύντερον corresponds to the αἰνότατον δ᾽ ἐνι-αυτὸν . . . καὶ κύντατον (305–6).

246

The motif of the famine or drought plays a role in many other versions of the myth. As a grief-stricken Demeter searches in vain for her daughter, the crops cease to grow.[136] The famine thus constitutes an outward manifestation of the overwhelming grief of the goddess of vegetation. As we have seen, the *Hymn to Demeter* suppresses the theme of the Search for Persephone, and the famine is deferred until after the events in the palace of Celeus. This striking shift in events has puzzled scholars, among them, Càssola: "Thereupon the goddess refuses to let crops grow in order to destroy mankind—including the inhabitants of Eleusis—and thereby to take revenge on the gods. . . . Why this action is taken so much time after the rape of Persephone . . . is incomprehensible."[137] The famine must remain incomprehensible unless we grasp the overall economy of the hymn's narrative. The postponement of the famine completely alters its significance. Instead of merely being an accompaniment to the goddess's anguish, the famine becomes an independent motif with its own role in the poem. Demeter's first plan, to immortalize and adopt a human child—and thereby to subvert the order of Zeus—has been thwarted. After its failure, the goddess conceives a second plan (cf. line 345 and n. 150 below): to starve men so that they can no longer bring offerings to the gods. While Demeter may still be irritated at mankind for interfering with her designs, the true object of her wrath remains the gods, Zeus, above all. But she is quite willing to sacrifice mankind to her own purpose. The cessation of vegetation is consciously—and somewhat heartlessly—willed and planned by Demeter to achieve her goal.

If Demeter's first plan failed, her blockade of Olympus will succeed. One can surmise the reasons for its success. First, Demeter makes use of the power that is peculiarly her own: the influence over agriculture that forms the basis of her *timē*. Second, human ignorance thwarted her first plan and made manifest the limitations and fragility of the human condition. Now, Demeter will exploit the weakness of mankind, its dependence on agriculture to sustain life, to bring the gods to their knees. For the gods too are not completely autonomous; they depend on mortals not, to be sure, for their lives, but for their *timai*.[138] One might then say that Demeter finally succeeds because she acts in accordance with the princi-

---

[136] For the famine as the accompaniment to Demeter's grief-stricken search, see, for instance, Carcinus the Younger, fr. 5 (*Tragicorum Graecorum fragmenta* 1, ed. B. Snell [Göttingen, 1971], pp. 213–14); and Ovid, *Metamorphoses* 5.477–86.

[137] Càssola (1975), p. 34.

[138] Aristophanes' *Birds* offers a comic treatment of the same motif.

ples of the cosmic hierarchy, whereas her former plan ran counter to them.

καί νύ κε πάμπαν ὄλεσσε γένος μερόπων ἀνθρώπων
λιμοῦ ὑπ' ἀργαλέης, γεράων τ' ἐρικυδέα τιμὴν
καὶ θυσιῶν ἤμερσεν Ὀλύμπια δώματ' ἔχοντας,
εἰ μὴ Ζεὺς ἐνόησεν ἑῷ τ' ἐφράσσατο θυμῷ.

And now she would have completely destroyed the race of men[139]
through grievous hunger and deprived the gods who inhabit
    Olympian homes
of their splendid honor of gifts and offerings,
if Zeus had not noticed and pondered in his heart.

(310–13)

Zeus sends his messenger Iris to Demeter. Here and elsewhere in the poem (and contrary to the practice of the epic), Zeus's words are given in indirect discourse, emphasizing his remoteness and his superiority even to the unfolding cosmic drama.[140] Throughout, the chief Olympian avoids a direct confrontation with the angry goddess. In the course of delivering his message, Iris calls Zeus ἄφθιτα εἰδώς, "he who knows imperishable things" (321). This phrase occurs nowhere else in the hymn, but it is used significantly three times in the Prometheus story in the *Theogony* (545, 550, 561) where, after mutual deceptions and counter-moves, Zeus emerges as the triumphant victor over his cunning opponent.[141] The occurrence of the expression here underlines the supremacy of Zeus in the present encounter also. It further suggests that the resistance of Demeter will finally be overcome and the will of the supreme god ultimately accomplished.

Zeus's command to Demeter is not, as we might expect, that she should make an end to the famine, but rather that she should come back to Olympus, "among the race of the eternal gods" (322). The goddess's return to Olympus would in and of itself signify her reconciliation with the gods and entail her abandonment of the famine and the restoration

---

[139] I omit translating the obscure epithet μέροψ ("Bedeutung, mithin auch Herkunft unbekannt," H. Frisk, *Griechisches etymologisches Wörterbuch* [Heidelberg, 1970]).

[140] Cf. Richardson (1974), p. 262. In Homer, of course, Zeus freely converses with the other gods on Olympus, although he communicates with mortals only indirectly.

[141] Cf. the variants, Ζεὺς ἄφθιτα μήδεα εἰδώς (*Iliad* xxiv.88), and Ζεὺς δ' ἄφθιτα μήδεα εἰδώς (*Hymn to Aphrodite* 43), where again Zeus's supremacy is emphasized. Cf. Deichgräber (1950), p. 525.

of the natural order. To be sure, Demeter rejects Iris's invitation,[142] and for the moment, the messenger's "speech from Zeus" must remain *ateleston*, unfulfilled (324). Zeus now sends forth all the other gods in turn; they offer Demeter "splendid gifts and whatever *timai* she might choose to have among the immortals"[143] (328). The goddess adamantly refuses.

Demeter's self-imposed isolation, her grief, her anger, and her stubborn rejection of both gifts and supplications closely resemble the situation of Achilles in the ninth book of the *Iliad*.[144] In fact, a version of the Demeter myth once began: Μῆνιν ἄειδε θεά, Δημήτερος ἀγλαοκάρπου ("Sing, goddess, of the wrath of Demeter of the splendid fruit" (*Orphicorum Fragmenta* 48); the words could well serve as the opening to our hymn. Nor is it surprising to discover verbal parallels here to phrases found in the Embassy to Achilles.[145] Like an Achilles, Demeter announces her conditions for returning to Olympus:

οὐ μὲν γάρ ποτ᾽ ἔφασκε θυώδεος Οὐλύμποιο
πρίν γ᾽ ἐπιβήσεσθαι, οὐ πρὶν γῆς καρπὸν ἀνήσειν,
πρὶν ἴδοι ὀφθαλμοῖσιν ἐὴν εὐώπιδα κούρην.

For she said that she would not set foot unto fragrant Olympus
nor let the fruit arise from the earth
before she should see her lovely daughter with her own eyes.

(331–33)

In response to Demeter's intransigent demand, Zeus sends Hermes, the only god with the ability to traverse the barrier between the upper and lower worlds, to the Lord of the Dead. His mission is to cajole Hades with "soft words"[146] and to bring Persephone "from the murky darkness into the light, back among the gods, so that her mother . . . might leave off her anger" (334–39). Just as the poet did not describe Persephone's descent into the underworld during her abduction, so too he withholds a

[142] I can think of no instance in Homer where a god simply rejects a command of Zeus.

[143] Gemoll (1886), p. 302, rejects the lines on the ground that "Zeus hat die Ehren zu vergeben," which is quite true; but he here employs the other gods as his spokesmen.

[144] Compare M. L. Lord, "Withdrawal and Return: An Epic Story Pattern in the Homeric *Hymn to Demeter*," *CJ* 62 (1967): 241–48; Segal (1981), pp. 145–48; and Sowa (1984), pp. 108–16.

[145] στερεῶς δ᾽ ἠναίνετο μύθους (line 330); cf. *Iliad* IX.510, where Phoenix warns Achilles of the consequences of rejecting the Litai: ὃς δέ κ᾽ ἀνήνηται καί τε στερεῶς ἀποείπῃ. Also μεταλήξειε χόλοιο (339); cf. *Iliad* IX.157, 261, 299.

[146] Cf. *Iliad* IX.158, where Hades is called ἀμείλιχος ἠδ᾽ ἀδάμαστος.

description of Hermes' journey from Olympus to Hades' domain. Although the world below forms a focal point of the action of the hymn, its geography remains as obscure as before. Despite the poetic possibilities of such a description,[147] the hymn-poet maintains his eschatological reticence.

Hermes comes upon the Lord of the Dead in his palace "sitting on a bed with his revered wife" (343).[148] The posture of Hades and Persephone, and her designation as his wife, indicate that the marriage has been duly consummated and cannot be annulled.[149] While Persephone sits passively grieving, consumed with longing for her mother, Demeter (ἡ δ') is actively pursuing her *boulē* (344–45). That must be the general sense of these corrupt lines:[150] the contrast between Persephone's helpless passivity and her mother's active plan, which is on the point of succeeding. Hermes delivers Zeus's order that Hades permit Persephone to return to the upper world:

> . . . ὄφρα ἑ μήτηρ
> ὀφθαλμοῖσιν ἰδοῦσα χόλου καὶ μήνιος αἰνῆς
> ἀθανάτοις παύσειεν· ἐπεὶ μέγα μήδεται ἔργον
> φθῖσαι φῦλ' ἀμενηνὰ χαμαιγενέων ἀνθρώπων
> σπέρμ' ὑπὸ γῆς κρύπτουσα, καταφθινύθουσα δὲ τιμὰς
> ἀθανάτων.

> . . . so that her mother,
> on seeing her with her own eyes, might put an end to her anger
> and dread wrath[151]
> against the immortals; since she had devised an enormity—

---

[147] Consider Hesiod's description of Tartarus in *Theogony* 736–819 and, of course, the two Homeric Nekyiae.

[148] Gemoll (1886), p. 303, notes: "sicher das Ehebett gemeint." Càssola, (1975), p. 480, misinterprets by translating "sul trono"; while Richardson (1974), p. 265, appears to take ἐν λεχέεσσι as banquet couches.

[149] Cf. Scarpi (1976), p. 120.

[150] For various solutions, see Richardson (1974), p. 266. I cannot see why a "reference to Demeter (reading ἡ δ') is not wanted here." Cf. Baumeister (1860), pp. 316–17. Càssola (1975) takes it as such and reads: ἡ δ' ἐπ' ἀτλήτοις ἔργοις θεῶν μακάρων ⟨δεινὴν⟩ μητίσετο βουλήν ("e la madre, per l'agire / intollerabile degli dei immortali, meditava il suo tremendo disegno"). μητίσετο may well be imperfect.

[151] This is the only time in the hymn that Demeter's anger is called μῆνις. For the meaning of the word, see Clay (1983), pp. 65–68. Also, for the negative connotations of the expression μέγα ἔργον in line 351, see M. Bissinger, *Das Adjecktiv ΜΕΓΑΣ in der griechischen Dichtung* (Munich, 1966), pp. 201–9.

to destroy the powerless tribes of earth-born men
by hiding the seed under the earth, and making the honors (*timai*)
of the immortals wither away.

(349–54)

As Richardson points out,[152] both ἀμενηνά, "used of the dead" in Homer, and χαμαιγενέων "emphasize the helplessness of men." The goddess can easily destroy mankind through starvation. She can also destroy the *timai* of the gods (though not the gods themselves), for those *timai* depend on mankind and will perish along with it.

The normally unsmiling Hades receives Zeus's request with a smile,[153] "nor did he disobey the orders of King Zeus" (358). Quickly, Hades tells "intelligent Persephone" to go to her mother, but to "keep a gentle heart in her breast and not to be excessively angry" (360–61):

οὔ τοι ἐν ἀθανάτοισιν ἀεικὴς ἔσσομ᾽ ἀκοίτης
αὐτοκασίγνητος πατρὸς Διός· ἔνθα δ᾽ ἰοῦσα
δεσπόσσεις πάντων ὁπόσα ζώει τε καὶ ἔρπει,
τιμὰς δὲ σχήσησθα μετ᾽ ἀθανάτοισι μεγίστας,
τῶν δ᾽ ἀδικησάντων τίσις ἔσσεται ἤματα πάντα
οἵ κεν μὴ θυσίαισι τεὸν μένος ἱλάσκωνται
εὐαγέως ἔρδοντες ἐναίσιμα δῶρα τελοῦντες.

Among the gods I shall not be an unseemly husband for you,
a very brother of father Zeus. Going thither,[154]
you will be mistress over all that live and move,
and you shall have the greatest honors among the immortals;
and for all time there will be punishment of those who have
        committed injustices,
whoever, that is, who does not propitiate your might with
        sacrifices,
doing them purely and bringing gifts as appropriate.

(363–69)

---

[152] Richardson (1974), p. 267.

[153] Hades is called unsmiling in the *Palatine Anthology* 7.439.4.

[154] ἔνθα δ᾽ ἐοῦσα is printed by AHS (1936), Humbert (1936), Richardson (1974), and Càssola (1975). The manuscript reading, ἐνθάδ᾽ ἰοῦσα, "coming here" (i.e., returning), is, as Richardson points out, to "give the game away." ἔνθα δ᾽ ἰοῦσα gives the desired ambiguity. For when Persephone goes to the upper world as consort of Hades, she has already become queen "of all that live and move" (i.e., the dead).

The difficulties in Hades' speech arise from the conscious vagueness and ambiguity of his words.[155] Although he does not explicitly mention Persephone's inevitable return to him, he implies that the great honors she will have among both gods and mortals will depend on her being his wife (365–66). These, in turn, will derive from her power as mistress "over all that live and move." In keeping with the hymn's euphemism in matters concerning the dead,[156] and also, perhaps, out of a sense of delicacy, Hades remains somewhat vague as to the nature of Persephone's power. But we know Persephone as Queen of the Dead, and all who live finally come under her dominion. Moreover, she will forever possess the power to punish those who have performed some injustice but refuse or neglect to propitiate her. τίσις ... ἤματα πάντα (367) does not refer to the eternal punishment of sinners after death,[157] but only to the eternal prerogative of Persephone to avenge herself on those who offend her.

We must be cautious here and not anticipate the end of the hymn or introduce anachronisms. As enumerated by Hades, Persephone's future *timai* have nothing to do with either the Mysteries or initiation or, to be sure, with Orphic notions of punishment after death.[158] Only later does the influence of Orphic eschatology with its beliefs in postmortem rewards and punishments infiltrate Eleusinian cult.[159] The *timai* Hades promises his bride are those of the Homeric ἐπαινὴ Περσεφόνεια, the Queen of the Underworld who, along with her consort and the "Erinyes who walk in mist," has the power, when called upon, to curse wrongdoers.[160]

We have noted earlier that the acquisition of *timē* by a god constitutes a central theme in hymnic poetry[161] and in the longer Homeric Hymns in particular. Unlike Demeter, who is already in possession of the *timē* of agriculture, Persephone, a carefree young girl picking flowers with her playmates, had none at the beginning of the poem. As a result,

[155] Cf. Richardson (1974), pp. 269–70.

[156] θάνατος occurs *only* at line 262 of the hymn.

[157] Cf. AHS (1936), p. 168: "the reference is not to the future life."

[158] But see Richardson (1974), pp. 270–75, who tries to argue for some such connection.

[159] Cf. Graf (1974), pp. 79–150.

[160] Cf. Baumeister (1860), p. 321, who cites *Iliad* IX.454–57, where Phoenix's father curses him by calling on the Erinyes, and both Zeus Katachthonios and ἐπαινὴ Περσεφόνεια fulfill his curse; and *Iliad* IX.566–72, in which Meleager's mother invokes Hades and Persephone, "and the mist-walking Erinys, who has a heart that cannot be softened, heard her from Erebus."

[161] Cf. Keyssner (1932), pp. 55–75.

she had, strictly speaking, no place in the divine pantheon, because a god without *timē* is scarcely a god at all.[162] The *timai* here promised to Persephone are identical with those she possesses in the epic.[163] We must wait for the denouement of the hymn for her acquisition of those honors she will share with her mother as one of the "august goddesses" of Eleusis.

With childish delight, Persephone jumps for joy, surely at the prospect of seeing her mother again, but perhaps also on account of the grand privileges just offered her. Or is it purely accidental that only here, both before and after Hades' speech, Persephone is called "circumspect" and "intelligent"?[164] Hades had already[165] secretly given his bride the fateful pomegranate seed, "so that she would not remain forever" by her mother (373–74). The pomegranate, with its double associations with sex and death,[166] offers a perfect emblem for the union of Persephone with the Lord of the Underworld. The eating of its seed is equivalent to the consummation of the marriage and emphasizes the indissolubility of the union.[167]

As Hermes drives the golden chariot of Hades, Persephone's journey to the upper world is quickly accomplished. As soon as the immortal

---

[162] As Demeter's plan of depriving the gods of their *timai* abundantly demonstrates. On Persephone's acquisition of *timai* in the course of the hymn, see Rudhardt (1978), p. 12.

[163] It is possible that the two sets of *timai* Persephone acquires in the hymn may reflect the historical evolution of this goddess. Cf. O. Kern, "Mysterien," *RE* 16, pt. 2 (1935): 1246: "Wenn, wie heute wohl allgemein angenommen wird, Kore-Persephone zuerst eine selbständige Unterweltsgöttin gewesen ist, so ist es wahrscheinlich, dass die enge Verbindung von Demeter und Kore als Mutter und Tochter in Eleusis, wenn nicht entstanden, so doch sicher dort für alle Zeiten gefestigt worden ist." Consider also the discussion of Zuntz (1971), pp. 75–83, on the relation of a pre-Greek Persephone, Queen of the Dead, and the Greek Kore, daughter of Demeter, and the assimilation, but never complete identification, of these two figures. It is striking that in the *Hymn to Demeter*, the name Persephone occurs seven times after she has become the bride of Hades (337, 348, 360, 370, 387, 405, and 493), but only once before (56). Clinton (1986), p. 44, notes that "on all the inscribed monuments at Eleusis, from roughly 500 B.C. to 300 A.D., Demeter's daughter is never in Greek called Persephone." Clinton believes that it was taboo in Eleusis to name either Persephone or Hades because of their underworld associations.

[164] If the list of C.F.H. Bruchmann, *Epitheta Deorum* (Leipzig, 1893), is complete, no other epithets used of Persephone in extant Greek literature ever refer to her intelligence.

[165] Cf. Gemoll (1886), p. 304: "ἔδωκε (373) ist als Plusqpf. aufzufassen." For various interpretations of the mysterious ἀμφὶ ἓ νωμήσας, see Richardson (1974), pp. 276–77.

[166] Cf. Richardson (1974), p. 276; Murr (1890), pp. 50–55; and Chirassi (1968), pp. 73–90.

[167] Cf. Baumeister (1860), p. 321: "symbolum hoc esse videtur irruptorum matrimonii vinculorum."

horses leave the palace below,[168] they reach the seas, rivers, meadows, and mountains, which form the contours of the earth. Flying effortlessly through the dense air, they arrive at the temple "where Demeter of the lovely garland was waiting" (384):

ἡ δὲ ἰδοῦσα
ἤϊξ' ἠΰτε μαινὰς ὄρος κάτα δάσκιον ὕλης.

And upon seeing her,
she rushed like a maenad down the mountain shadowy with its
    forest.
(385–86)

Persephone, for her part, leaps down from the chariot and runs to meet her mother. Although the manuscript has been torn here, we can easily supply the mutual embraces and perhaps the happy tears of the reunited mother and daughter. Soon, however, Demeter interrupts the joyous reunion by asking Persephone if she has eaten anything in the underworld. If not, then her daughter may remain at home[169] in the upper world. Otherwise, she must spend one-third of the year below, and two-thirds with her mother and the other gods:

ὁππότε δ' ἄνθεσι γαῖ' εὐώδε[σιν] ἠαρινο[ῖσι]
παντοδαποῖς θάλλει, τότ' ἀπὸ ζόφου ἠερόεντος
αὖτις ἄνει μέγα θαῦμα θεοῖς θνητοῖς τ' ἀνθρώποις.

And whenever the earth blossoms with fragrant spring flowers
of all kinds, then from the murky darkness
you will rise again, a marvel for gods and mortal men.
(401–3)

In some accounts, the arrangement of Persephone's time above and below the earth results from a compromise decreed by Zeus.[170] In others, the fact that Persephone has eaten while under the earth is only revealed indirectly.[171] The *Hymn to Demeter* deals with all these matters quite dif-

---

[168] διὲκ μεγάρων (379) is all we hear of the underworld. For the avoidance of description of the netherworld in the hymn, see n. 54 above.

[169] κε νέουσα, the reading of the manuscript, is to be preferred. For Demeter, at least, Persephone's home would surely be Olympus. Cf. B. A. van Groningen, "NEOMAI—NEΩ," *Mnemosyne* 4, no. 2 (1949): 42.

[170] See, for instance, Ovid, *Metamorphoses*, 5.564–65; and *Fasti* 4.613.

[171] Through the agency of Ascalaphus, who informs on Persephone. Cf. Apollodorus 1.5.3; and Ovid, *Metamorphoses* 5.538–50.

ferently. It is evident that Demeter immediately knows the consequences of her daughter's eating in Hades. As soon as she recognizes them, the goddess offers no further resistance.[172] Could it be that Demeter acquiesces to the arrangement because she comprehends and accepts its full significance?

Every child knows the meaning of Persephone's annual return, which coincides with the seasonal rebirth of vegetation in the spring. Her absence in the underworld corresponds to the yearly disappearance of the crops during the winter. All other versions of this widespread myth divide Persephone's sojourn in the upper and lower worlds—and hence the agricultural year—into two equal halves.[173] This division, doubtless the original one, suffices to explain the alternation of the seasons, which is the raison d'être of the myth. The hymn, however, offers a unique distribution of Persephone's time above and below the earth. Although the modification may at first appear slight, even insignificant, it reveals that the hymn is not primarily concerned with the origin of the seasons.

The downplaying of the old seasonal myth is also manifest in the formulation of lines 401–3. While Persephone's return coincides with spring, it does not cause it. Nor does the hymn claim, as other versions have it, that Demeter's joy at her daughter's annual return brings about the rebirth of vegetation. The presence of agriculture, upon which the hymn insists from its outset, presupposes the existence of seasons. From the beginning, Demeter is ὡρηφόρος, "bringer of the seasons."[174] In deemphasizing the link between the old seasonal myths and the Persephone story, the hymn points to a different interpretation in keeping with

[172] Cf. Rubin and Deal (1980) p. 13, n. 18: "She [Demeter] did not accept the consequences of her daughter's plucking of the narcissus, nor did she view Persephone's catabasis and abduction as irreversible; but she clearly does accept the consequences of the swallowing of the pomegranate seed and the irreversibility both of Persephone's bond with Hades and of a cyclic life/death, fertility/infertility pattern which results from that bond."

[173] The exception (which proves the rule) is Apollodorus 1.5.3, who clearly follows the hymn in this detail as well as many others.

[174] Such is the influence of the seasonal version that, despite the clear evidence of the text, some scholars still speak of Demeter's instituting agriculture in the hymn. See Bianchi (1964), p. 180, n. 10; and Alderink (1982), p. 11. Rudhardt (1978), pp. 12–14, proposes a subtler interpretation; although he recognizes the presence of agriculture from the beginning of the hymn, he suggests that its seasonal rhythm is inaugurated at the end of the poem by Demeter: "ce fut probablement le premier printemps" (p. 13). Cf. Bianchi (1964), p. 184, n. 9. Attractive as this interpretation may be, I believe it to be wrong. The Greeks could not conceive of agriculture without the existence of the seasons. Eternal spring belongs to the Golden Age (cf. *Works and Days* 109–20; and Ovid, *Metamorphoses* 1.107) and to Olympus (cf. *Odyssey* 6.42–46).

its dominant theological and cosmological concerns.[175] The clue to the meaning of those concerns resides in the poem's innovative division of the year.

The threefold division of the year corresponds to the tripartite division of the cosmos.[176] As set out at the beginning of this study, the relation of the three cosmic realms forms the critical backdrop of the hymn's narrative. The lack of communication between the two upper realms, Olympus and the earth, and the lower world constitutes *the* cosmological problem of the hymn. It is the goal of the plan of Zeus in giving his daughter to the Lord of the Dead to resolve that impasse. The marriage of Persephone is intended to unite the triple spheres of the cosmos and to breach the barrier separating them. The cyclical comings and goings of Persephone, whose temporal distribution mirrors the spatial distribution of the cosmic domains, open the desired path of communication. The annual journey of Persephone fulfills the plan of Zeus.

With a certain abruptness, Demeter now asks her daughter: "By what trick did the One-Who-Receives-Many deceive you?" (404). Persephone first recounts how she was forced to eat the pomegranate seed that seals her future fate. In her charmingly verbose answer, Persephone, as Richardson suggests, does indeed protest too much.[177] For if Hades se-

---

[175] Cf. Sabbatucci (1965), p. 170: "La nuova sacralità che l'inno cognosce e insegna in forma exoterica, ignora o trascende il campo d'azione agricolo ... questo è la rivoluzione mistica." I would modify the last word to "olimpica/mistica." Cf. Kerényi (1967a), p. 120: "The division of the year into three in the Persephone myth corresponds not to a natural process but to a mythological idea." Also W. Burkert, *Homo Necans* (Berlin, 1972), p. 287.

[176] Cf. Richardson (1974), p. 284: "The division into a third and two-thirds perhaps reflects Hades' share in the world." Cf. p. 176. For threes in the hymn, see Szepes (1975). It is noteworthy that the poem thrice repeats the temporal arrangement of Persephone's sojourn: lines 399–400, 445–47, 463–65.

The hymn's tripartition of the year inspired Nilsson (1935), pp. 106–9 and *GGR* (1955), 1: 472–75, drawing on F. M. Cornford, "The ΑΠΑΡΧΑΙ and the Eleusinian Mysteries," in *Essays and Studies Presented to William Ridgeway*, ed. E. C. Quiggin (Cambridge, 1913), pp. 153–66, to create a new myth. Nilsson noted that "es gibt keine viermonatige Ruhezeit im Winter" [in Greece] (p. 473) and that the usual interpretation— that Persephone's return signals the return of vegetation in spring—contradicts the "ausdrückliche Angabe des Mythos, dass Kore vier Monate in dem unterirdichen Reiche zubringen muss" (1935, p. 107). Accordingly, Nilsson took Persephone's absence to coincide with the four summer months, during which the grain is stored underground. His view has not won many adherents, but see Burkert (1972), pp. 287–89.

[177] Cf. Richardson (1974) on lines 406 and 413. Persephone repeatedly insists on the violence done to her. This corresponds to an important legal distinction between sexual assault and μοιχεία. Cf. S. G. Cole, "Greek Sanctions against Sexual Assault," *CP* 79 (1984): 97–113; and U. E. Paoli, "Il reato di adulterio (μοιχεία) in diritto attico," in *Altri studi di diritto greco e romano* (Milan, 1976), pp. 251–307.

cretly administered the pomegranate to her, how was it that she was "compelled by force against my will" (413) to eat it? As we have noted, the pomegranate is a symbol of sexual experience. Persephone reveals herself to be no longer quite the child she was before. Turning now to a somewhat embellished account[178] of the abduction itself, Persephone again stresses her unwilling participation; but she nowhere expresses anger at her abductor.

As mother and daughter spend the rest of the day in mutual happiness, Hecate comes to join them unsummoned. From this time forward, the poet tells us, Hecate will be Persephone's attendant, presumably when the latter makes her annual ascent and descent from the upper to the lower world. ἐκ τοῦ, or similar expressions, elsewhere in the hymn announce a ritual institution;[179] and it may well be that Hecate's apparently unmotivated presence here reflects her role in Eleusinian cult.[180] But her mediating function in this scene also parallels her role at the beginning of the hymn. Hearing the sound of Persephone's cry from her cave between the upper and lower worlds, Hecate proved to be the crucial mediator of the news of the abduction to Demeter. Henceforward, Hecate's role as a go-between will be regularized in her eternal accompaniment of Persephone on her cyclical journey. At the beginning of the hymn, because of her anomalous position between earth and the underworld, Hecate did not appear to belong to either realm and hence had no place in the cosmic scheme. With the unification of the cosmos through Persephone's yearly journey, Hecate too finds a place in the final dispensation. In the course of the narrative, then, Hecate, like Persephone, acquires a *timē* she had not possessed before.

The recapitulation of the abduction and the reappearance of Hecate return us to the beginning of the poem and reveal its ringlike structure.[181] That structure is not merely a matter of form or convention, but a vehicle of meaning. As we have seen, the divine/cosmic drama of the Abduction frames the episode of Eleusis that dwells on divine/human relations. The

[178] See Baumeister (1860), pp. 275–76, for a defense of Persephone's speech. The mention of Artemis and Athena in the catalog of the Oceanids (424) probably is an interpolation.

[179] Cf. lines 205 and 211; also *Hymn to Hermes* 125–26, and *Theogony* 556.

[180] See the remarks of Richardson (1974), pp. 294–95, on line 440. Compare n. 64 above.

[181] For ring composition as a stylistic feature of archaic poetry, see W.A.A. van Otterlo, "Untersuchungen über Begriff, Anwendung, und Entstehung der griechischen Ringkomposition," *Med. d. Kon. Ned. Akad. van Wetensch. Afd. Letterkunde* n.s. 7, no. 3 (1944): 131–76.

CHAPTER 4

restatement of the Rape and the return of Hecate demand that we begin
to reassess the meaning of the intervening events and actions as the hymn
approaches its denouement.

The hymn now moves quickly toward its conclusion. Zeus sends
Rheia, both his own and Demeter's mother, and hence an excellent reminder of the ties that unite them despite their differences, to bring Demeter back "among the tribe of the gods" (443). He renews his offer to
Demeter to give her "whatever *timai* she might chose among the immortal gods" (443–44);[182] and finally he gives his formal consent to the fore-
ordained distribution of Persephone's annual stay in the upper and lower
world (445–47). Quickly, Rheia makes her way down from Olympus:

εἰς δ᾽ ἄρα Ῥάριον ἷξε, φερέσβιον οὖθαρ ἀρούρης
τὸ πρίν, ἀτὰρ τότε γ᾽ οὔ τι φερέσβιον, ἀλλὰ ἔκηλον
ἑστήκει πανάφυλλον· ἔκευθε δ᾽ ἄρα κρῖ λευκὸν
μήδεσι Δήμητρος καλλισφύρου· αὐτὰρ ἔπειτα
μέλλεν ἄφαρ ταναοῖσι κομήσειν ἀσταχύεσσιν
ἦρος ἀεξομένοιο, πέδῳ δ᾽ ἄρα πίονες ὄγμοι
βρισέμεν ἀσταχύων, τὰ δ᾽ ἐν ἐλλεδανοῖσι δεδέσθαι.
ἔνθ᾽ ἐπέβη πρώτιστον ἀπ᾽ αἰθέρος ἀτρυγέτοιο.

And she came to Rarion, the life-sustaining bosom of fields
formerly, but then indeed it sustained no life, but stood idle,
completely without leaves; truly, it kept the white barley hidden
through the designs of lovely ankled Demeter; but afterward
it would bristle with the slender ears of grain
as spring came on; then on the ground, the rich furrows
would grow heavy with ears of grain; and some also would be
    bound into sheaves.
There it was she [Rheia] first descended from the barren ether.

(450–57)

The lengthy description of the fertile plain of Rarion at first seems gratuitous; but the sonorous announcement that Rheia first came to earth
here leads us to expect that the spot has some special significance.[183] Al-

[182] Cf. Richardson (1974), p. 296: "We are not told what τιμαί Demeter chose." But
see below, p. 261.
[183] Cf. Gemoll (1886), p. 309: "die ausdrückliche Bemerkung, dass Rheia zuerst . . . bei
Rarion die Erde betreten habe, macht doch den Eindruck, als wenn es sich hier um die
erste Einführung eines neuen Dienstes handle." Gemoll is thinking (prematurely, I think)

258

though the poet tells us nothing more, the traditional associations of Rarion are well known in antiquity.[184] Among others, Pausanias (1.38.6) relates: "They say that the plain called Rharium was the first to be sown and first to grow crops, and for this reason it is the custom to use sacrificial barley and to make cakes for the sacrifices from its produce. Here there is shown a threshing floor called that of Triptolemus and an altar."[185] The reference to the Rarian plain here alludes to a version of the myth in which Demeter first bestowed the gift of agriculture on the Eleusinians out of gratitude for Persephone's return. "The poet," according to Richardson, "conceals this."[186] I would maintain, on the contrary, that the poet consciously refers to the alternative version in order to emphasize forcefully his divergence from it. Several times in the course of the hymn, he has taken pains to make clear that mankind already possesses Demeter's art of agriculture. Here at its end, the hymn once more draws attention to its own unique narrative by alluding to a version it excludes.

As soon as Rheia arrives, she and Demeter "beheld each other in welcome wise and rejoiced in their hearts" (458). Demeter's warm reception of her mother, before the latter even delivers her message, foreshadows Demeter's reconciliation with the Olympians. Thus, in conveying Zeus's offer (and repeating for the third time the destined arrangement of Persephone's time [464–65]), Rheia scarcely needs to urge her daughter:

[ἀλλ' ἴθι τέκνον] ἐμὸν καὶ πείθεο, μηδέ τι λίην
ἀ[ζηχὲς μεν]έαινε κελαινεφέϊ Κρονίωνι·
α[ἶψα δὲ κα]ρπὸν ἄεξε φερέσβιον ἀνθρώποισιν.

Come now, child, and heed me, nor excessively
rage ceaselessly at the dark-clouded son of Cronus;
but straightway make the life-sustaining fruit grow for men.

(467–69)

---

of the introduction of the cult of Rheia into Attica and her subsequent conflation with Demeter (see Euripides, *Helen* 1301–68) But the poet's πρώτιστον (457) has, I believe, a rather different function here. Stiewe (1954), p. 105, notes that "dem Gang Rheias nach Eleusis doch mehr Aufmerksamkeit geschenkt ist, als der Bedeutung eines solchen Nebenmomente entspricht."

[184] Cf. Richardson (1974), pp. 297–98.

[185] *Pausanias: Description of Greece*, trans. W.H.S. Jones (Cambridge, Mass., 1918), 1: 205.

[186] Richardson (1974), p. 298.

Demeter no longer offers any resistance. After all, she had given up her wrath the moment she learned of Persephone's eating of the pomegranate seed and acknowledged the irreversible consequences of that action.[187] Now comprehending the full meaning of the original plan of Zeus—which was, after all, a plan of reconciliation, of uniting what was formerly separated—Demeter now not only cooperates with that plan, but indeed she undertakes to further and complete it. Her first step is to restore the crops, thereby reinstating the natural order of communication between gods and mortals through the medium of sacrifice. The restoration of the status quo ante precedes the introduction of something completely new:

> ἡ δὲ κιοῦσα θεμιστοπόλοις βασιλεῦσι
> δ[εῖξε,] Τριπτολέμῳ τε Διοκλεῖ τε πληξίππῳ,
> Εὐμόλπου τε βίῃ Κελεῷ θ' ἡγήτορι λαῶν,
> δρησμοσύνην θ' ἱερῶν καὶ ἐπέφραδεν ὄργια πᾶσι,
> σεμνά, τά τ' οὔ πως ἔστι παρεξ[ίμ]εν [οὔτε πυθέσθαι,]
> οὔτ' ἀχέειν· μέγα γάρ τι θεῶν σέβας ἰσχάνει αὐδήν.

> And going to the kings who dispense decrees
> she showed to Triptolemus and horse-lashing Diocles,
> to mighty Eumolpus and to Celeus, leader of the people,
> the conduct of her holy rites and revealed to them all, her rituals
> the awesome ones, which it is not possible to transgress or to hear
> nor to speak of; for a great reverence for the gods restrains human
>   speech.
> (473–79)[188]

Olympian cult centers on the communication between gods and mortals through the medium of sacrifice. The act itself stresses the vertical and ontological distance separating the divine and the human, a distance based on the fundamental distinction between mortality and immortality and the opposition of the terrestrial nature of the one and the celestial character of the other. The language of the lines just quoted as well as those that follow clearly set the Mysteries apart from normal

[187] Cf. Lenz (1975), p. 66: "Der Kompromiss, der 441 ff. Zeus in den Mund gelegt wird, wird 398 ff. von Demeter ohne jede Herleitung schon vorgewusst!" For Lenz, however, this is a sign of an earlier version of the myth in which Zeus had no role.

[188] I assume with Richardson (1974), p. 304, that 477 is an interpolation.

Olympian ritual. Demeter *shows forth* and *reveals* her rites.[189] Initiation, to be sure, involved both *dromena* and *legomena*: but the supreme grade of initiation at Eleusis centered on a visual revelation: ἐποπτεία. The Mysteries, as Aristotle says, are not so much learned or taught as experienced.[190] This direct experiencing of the divine stands in sharp contrast to Olympian cult, which, "as a rule, involves neither epiphany nor revelation."[191] Likewise, the sacred prohibition against revealing the "awesome rites" to the uninitiated as well as the sharp distinction between initiates and the uninitiated have no counterpart in the religion of Olympus. Even if we remain ignorant of what it was that was revealed in the great *telesterion* of Eleusis, the mode of its communication sufficiently attests to a differing conception of the relationship between mankind and the divine.

The establishment of the Mysteries forms the culmination of the *Hymn to Demeter* and the final goal of the narrative. Yet it does not merely symbolize Demeter's reconciliation with mankind; for that, the restoration of agriculture and, with it, the prevailing relations between gods and men would have sufficed. Nor can we view Demeter's action as a reward or sign of gratitude toward the Eleusinians, as some versions suggest. Although the Mysteries are in some sense the goddess's gift to mankind, on a deeper level, they introduce a change in the relationship between gods and mortals that, in turn, reflects the change within the Olympian cosmos. In establishing her rites, Demeter has finally chosen the *timai* that Zeus repeatedly promised her. In accepting those *timai*, Demeter signals her participation in the new cosmic order. As *the* goddess of Eleusis and the Mysteries, Demeter not only acquiesces to Zeus's design, but that design becomes the basis for her new *timai*. The acquisition of new *timai* on the part of a god inevitably introduces a modification within the Olympian hierarchy without, however, destroying it. Analogously, Eleusis inaugurates an alteration in the relations between mankind and the gods without, however, abolishing the abiding distinctions that define them.[192]

[189] On the language here, see Richardson (1974), pp. 302–3. Cf. Graf (1974), pp. 31–33, for δείχνυμι as the *terminus technicus* for the establishment of mystery rituals.

[190] Aristotle, Περὶ Φιλοσοφίας, fr. 15 (Ross): ... Ἀριστοτέλης ἀξιοῖ τοὺς τελουμένους οὐ μαθεῖν τι δεῖν ἀλλὰ παθεῖν....

[191] Burkert (1977), p. 290.

[192] Cf. Rohde (1898), p. 293, who speaks of Eleusinian belief as "in der unbedingten Scheidung und Unterscheidung des Göttlichen vom Menchlichen, sich völlig in den Kreisen griechischer Volksreligion hielt, an deren Eingang gleich, Alles bestimmend, die

ὄλβιος ὃς τάδ᾽ ὄπωπεν ἐπιχθονίων ἀνθρώπων·
ὃς δ᾽ ἀτελὴς ἱερῶν, ὅς τ᾽ ἄμμορος, οὔ ποθ᾽ ὁμοίων
αἶσαν ἔχει φθίμενός περ ὑπὸ ζόφῳ εὐρώεντι.

Happy is he of men on earth who has seen these things:
but he who is not perfected in the rites and has no share in them,
    never a portion of the same things
does he possess even when he perishes under the moldering
    darkness.
        (480–82)

This statement momentarily breaks the narrative sequence to announce the new order of things for mankind and a new status defined by
the word ὄλβιος. Formerly, human existence embraced only two phases:
life and death. Demeter now institutes a third, a *tertium quid*, which
forms in some sense a middle ground between the polarities of life and
death. To be sure, men continue to be ἐπιχθόνιοι, nor are they exempt
from descending into the underworld when they die. Human life remains finite, and death is not transcended. ὄλβιος is not μάκαρ, a word
reserved for the unchanging status of the gods.[193] It must be admitted
that the promise of a better fate for the initiates is left hauntingly vague.[194]
But for mortals, whose greatest limitation according to the hymn resides
in their ignorance of future good or evil (cf. 356–57), that promise must
suffice.

The events leading up to the establishment of the Mysteries define
their significance in the hymn. Without the plan of Zeus, without Persephone's abduction, without Demeter's failure at Eleusis and her subsequent success with the famine, without the return of Persephone and
the institution of her yearly journey, there would be no awesome rites at
Eleusis. A brief recapitulation of those crucial intervening events as I
have interpreted them may be in order. Zeus's intention to unite the separate domains of his realm by marrying Persephone to Hades first leads

---

Worte stehen: ἐν ἀνδρῶν, ἐν θεῶν γένος." Kevin Clinton has pointed out to me that at
Eleusis, "the amount of Olympian sacrifice was enormous. The gods seemed to be very
satisfied. And they allowed their priests and priestesses to march in the procession to
Eleusis." Thus it would seem that Eleusis and Olympus also coalesced on the level of cult.
    [193] Cf. C. de Heer, ΜΑΚΑΡ—ΕΥΔΑΙΜΩΝ—ΟΛΒΙΟΣ—ΕΥΤΥΧΗΣ: *A Study of the
Semantic Field Denoting Happiness in Ancient Greek to the End of the 5th Century* (Amsterdam, 1969), esp. pp. 14–15.
    [194] Cf. Graf (1974), p. 139, who notes that Eleusinian belief remains based on a "sehr
vage Hoffnung auf ein besseres Los nach dem Tode."

to an aggravation of cosmic disunity as Demeter abandons Olympus. In Eleusis, she attempts to obstruct Zeus's plan by making a mortal divine. Had the project been successful, it would have thrown Zeus's authority to rule open to question and led to a blurring of the boundaries defining gods and mortals. Demeter's design fails, however, because of mankind's ignorance and improvidence. Demeter's failed resistance to Zeus reaffirms for all time the unbridgeable gulf between mortality and immortality. Incorporating a recognition of that essential distinction but also a comprehension of the ties that unite gods and mortals, Demeter's second plan succeeds; at the same time, it reveals the full complexities of their mutual interdependencies. Finally, the return of Persephone and the disposition of her time above and below the earth fulfills the plan of Zeus and inaugurates a new cosmic and temporal order.

The new dispensation for mankind instituted by Demeter with her Mysteries corresponds to, although it does not exactly parallel, the new dispensation among the gods.[195] Eleusis does not abrogate the iron law of Olympus and its teaching concerning human mortality. Nor, on the other hand, does human life imitate the cyclical pattern of death and rebirth reflected in Persephone's eternal displacements. The doctrine of metempsychosis is alien to Eleusis.[196] While Persephone opens a divine avenue for communication between the upper and lower realms, the dead remain inaccessible to the living. The analogy between Persephone and mankind remains imperfect. Nevertheless, her annual movement between hitherto isolated domains suggests the mediating term—ὄλβιος—between the formerly uncompromising extremes of life and death.

After instructing the Eleusinians in the conduct of her rites, Demeter, accompanied by her daughter, returns to Olympus "among the gathering of the other gods" (484).

For the first time, Persephone and Demeter take their place in the order to which they as goddesses have a right by virtue of their rank. Here too we notice the etiological moment in the story, but all of that also has meaning in the Homeric world of the gods. The Eleu-

---

[195] Cf. Rohde (1898), pp. 291–93; and Bianchi (1964), pp. 181–87: "non si dà dunque una ciclicità della vita umana ... ma la prospettiva del mista implica pur sempre, con la sua positiva conclusione, una vicenda a tre fasi, non a due ... come nella commune prospettiva 'olimpica' " (pp. 183–84).

[196] Cf. Graf (1974), p. 184: "in Eleusis ... fehlt eine Seelenlehre, erst recht die Seelenwanderung." Also Burkert (1972), p. 323, and Bianchi (1964), pp. 190–93, on the nonmystic nature of Eleusinian religion.

sinian goddesses are, so to speak, taken up into Olympus, into Olympian religion for the first time. . . . Zeus is the god of order, of the will that comes to fulfillment despite all opposition and all apparent impediments. Διὸς δ᾽ ἐτελείετο βουλή.[197]

Like the restoration of vegetation that preceded the gift of the Mysteries, this return constitutes a resumption of the natural order. However, both the divine and the human cosmos have been transformed by the intervening events.[198] That transformation, once established and incorporated into the order of Zeus, becomes everlasting. The shift to the present tense signals the permanence of the new order:

ἔνθα δὲ ναιετάουσι παραὶ Διὶ τερπικεραύνῳ
σεμναί τ᾽ αἰδοῖαί τε· μέγ᾽ ὄλβιος ὅν τιν᾽ ἐκεῖναι
προφρονέως φίλωνται ἐπιχθονίων ἀνθρώπων.

And there they [Demeter and Persephone] live by Zeus of the
    thunder,
august and revered; greatly happy is he
of earth-born men whom they love readily.

(485–87)

The beneficence of the two goddesses toward mankind is also eternal. In what almost appears an afterthought, we learn that their gifts are in fact twofold, encompassing not only life after death, but this life as well. From their homes on Olympus, they send down to the hearths of those mortals whom they love Plutus "who gives riches to mortal men" (488–89). Plutus, wealth personified, is traditionally identified as Demeter's child and so depicted in art.[199] In view of the thematic importance of children in the hymn, his presence at its end takes on special significance. After all, the loss of a daughter precipitated the original crisis, and Demeter tried to adopt Demophoon to compensate for that loss. Now the poem concludes with the sending down from Olympus of Demeter's son Plutus who dispenses her gift of wealth. Plutus, then, forms a counterpart to Demophoon. He offers a paradigm for the appropriate relations between gods and mortals as opposed to the inappropriate model exempli-

---

[197] Deichgräber (1950), p. 528.
[198] Cf. Rudhardt (1978), pp. 12–17.
[199] Cf. Richardson (1974), pp. 316–20. In *Theogony* 969–74, Plutus is celebrated as the child of Demeter and Iasion.

fied in the story of Demophoon. Demeter had attempted to raise the mortal child up to the level of the gods; now the divine child is sent down to the hearths[200] of men. Whereas the goddess's intended gift to Demophoon was immortality, her gift of wealth, especially agricultural prosperity, constitutes a gift appropriate both to Demeter's powers and to the needs of mankind. Hence, in the case of Plutus, the nature of the divine gift, its direction, and its recipients form a suitable expression of the hierarchical relations between gods and men. Furthermore, the goddesses' gift of Plutus corresponds to mankind's gifts to the gods as embodied in the sacrifice, whose savor rises to Olympus. The perfect reciprocity in this exchange of gifts attests to the proper functioning of the cosmos within the Olympian framework.

The most striking feature of the *Hymn to Demeter* is the dominant role assigned to the plan of Zeus. That plan, despite opposition, is finally successful. That means, in turn, that Zeus's antagonist is at least partially defeated. Like the *Hymn to Aphrodite*, although in a subtler way, the *Hymn to Demeter* ultimately presents a diminution or limitation of the power of Demeter. This must be understood in theological terms. Eleusis always offered a potential antagonism to Olympus, and its doctrine posed a possible threat to the Olympian *theologoumenon*, as is abundantly confirmed by the later adoption of Eleusis by the anti-Olympian Orphics and other sects. As a whole, the *Hymn to Demeter* may be understood as an attempt to integrate, and hence absorb, the cult of Demeter and the message of Eleusis into the Olympian cosmos.

The hymn ends with a prayer to the two goddesses to grant the poet a livelihood in return for his song. He then invokes three of their cult places: "fragrant Eleusis," "sea-girt Paros," and "rocky Antron" (490–91). The three epithets draw attention to the contours of the earth—the fertile plains, the sea with its islands, and the mountains. They invite us to consider how the world—our world—has been transformed by the events of the hymn.

[200] ἐφέστιον (488) is reminiscent of the fire by which Demeter attempts to render Demophoon immortal (239). I have appended a schematic diagram of the hymn outlining the comings and goings between the three cosmic realms.

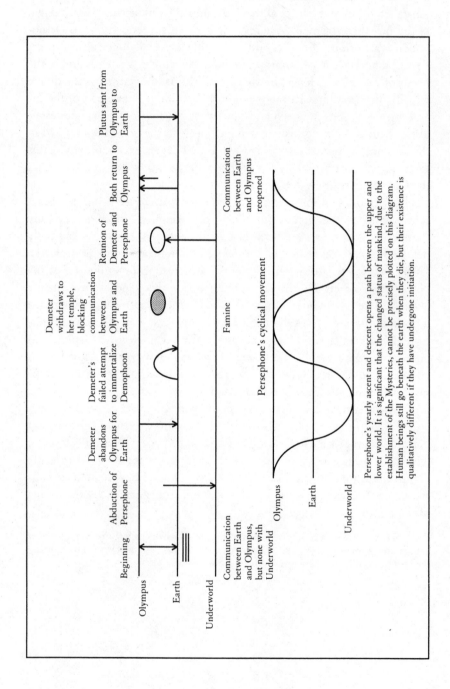

Persephone's yearly ascent and descent opens a path between the upper and lower world. It is significant that the changed status of mankind, due to the establishment of the Mysteries, cannot be precisely plotted on this diagram. Human beings still go beneath the earth when they die, but their existence is qualitatively different if they have undergone initiation.

Conclusion: The Hymnic Moment

My aim throughout the foregoing investigation has been to offer a detailed and coherent interpretation of the four major Homeric Hymns. Some readers may well find certain aspects of this study controversial. And there is no harm in that, especially if it provokes further discussion of these fascinating compositions. At any rate, I believe that the preceding study amply demonstrates that the major Homeric Hymns deserve to take their place alongside epic and theogonic poetry not only as poetic creations of high quality, subtlety, and charm, but also as documents containing some of the most sustained and systematic theological speculation of the archaic period. The hymnic moment presents the intersection of the eternally recurring manifestation of divinity and a series of unique cosmogonic events, a union of timelessness and mythic temporality, of divine being and becoming.[1] Yet the events that define the hymnic narrative are not the birth of Earth and Sky and their offspring, but the genesis and formation of the Olympian order. Not surprisingly, however, the patterns of the primal cosmogony persist into the Olympian era, which forms both the continuation and culmination of the theogonic process.

---

[1] P. Philippson, *Untersuchungen über den griechischen Mythos* (Zurich, 1944), pp. 49–53, speaks of "das Zusammentreffen von äonischen Sein mit chronischen ... Werden."

Although each of the poems offers a wholehearted celebration of its god, that praise is not absolute but is circumscribed and determined by the divinity's place within the Olympian pantheon. The hymns' narrative subjects are further restricted to significant moments in the formation of Olympus, assigning the supreme role in its shaping and ordering to Zeus. In the final analysis, the politics of Olympus are the politics of Zeus. It is he, and he alone, who has the power to distribute *timai* to new gods and to increase or diminish those of existing divinities. Even in those hymns in which his plan does not overtly constitute the springboard of the narrative, his pervasive presence is glimpsed behind the action. In *Apollo*, as we have seen, although Zeus makes only fleeting appearances in the course of the narrative, the new god defines himself in relation to his father, while in *Hermes* Zeus's intervention receives special emphasis, precisely because the story itself does not seem to require it. The apportionment of privileges among the gods and the achievement of a stable balance of power and prerogatives within the pantheon—all this is the accomplishment of Zeus.

The permanence and stability of Zeus's cosmos demands, in turn, a concomitant restriction of the female with her disruptive powers of seduction and her dangerous potential for producing a rival or successor to Zeus. The sexual politics of Olympus has surfaced most clearly in the contrast between Leto and Hera in *Apollo* and the subjection of Aphrodite in her hymn, as well as in the final compromise achieved in the *Hymn to Demeter*. Likewise, the male deities, whether the powerful son who might pose a threat to his father or the disruptive and disorienting runt of the pantheon, must discover their ordained place and *timai* within the framework of the divine hierarchy. Moreover, although the hymns consistently maintain a divine perspective—differing thereby from epic—they also trace the changing orderings in the relations between gods and mortals, both their intimacy and their estrangements and the renewed closeness, which, however, does not obliterate their essential differences.

The Olympian orientation of the major Homeric Hymns goes hand in hand with their pervasive Panhellenism, as is most evident in those cases where we are fortunate enough to possess alternate versions. The radical Panhellenic revisionism arises from the desire to integrate local or other traditions into an Olympian framework.

This brief synthesis of the main features of the narrative hymns returns us to the question of genre from which our inquiry began and the closely related problem of their relation to Hesiod's *Theogony* and the Homeric epic. As we have seen, the Panhellenic hymns complement these two classes of *epos*, seeming, as it were, to fill the mythological gap between them. On the analogy of some of the poems of the Epic Cycle, apparently composed to bridge the events between the *Iliad* and the *Odyssey*, one might argue that the Homeric Hymns were created *in order* to fill the perceived gap between Hesiod and Homer and thus to provide accounts of the major events in the evolution of Olympus. But just as the poems of the Epic Cycle surely draw on far older materials, we may surmise that the hymnic tradition likewise had a lengthy prehistory.

There are, in fact, certain indications that the type of narrative embedded in the hymns is coeval with theogonic and heroic *epos*. As we have observed, the Homeric poems seem to avoid giving anything more than hints at earlier events in the history of Olympus, although certain elements, for instance, Thetis's mysterious hold over Zeus in the *Iliad*, or Calypso's catalog of disastrous marriages between goddesses and mortal men, remain incomprehensible without that background. It may also be significant that our collection of the hymns begins with compositions dedicated to the two gods most ignored by the epic, Dionysus and Demeter, and that there is no narrative Homeric Hymn to Zeus.[2] Similarly, although the *Theogony* mentions Zeus's distribution of *timai* and catalogs his wives and offspring, it quickly moves on to the unions of gods and mortals and does not dilate on the character and organization of the Olympian dispensation.

Such a disposition of mythological materials suggests the existence of distinct genres marked by substantive genre boundaries. Concerning the relation of Homer and Hesiod, Slatkin has recently observed that "genres can be viewed . . . as existing in a relationship of interdependence, in which they have complementary functions in conveying different aspects of a coherent . . . system of beliefs about the world. The crucial point about these distinctions or differentiations is their complementarity: they exist within, and serve to complete, a conception about the way the world

[2] The one Homeric Hymn to Zeus (no. 23) is only four lines long. M. H. Van der Valk, "On the Arrangement of the Homeric Hymns," *L'Antiquité Classique* 45 (1976): 433, suggests, unconvincingly, that religious scruples prevented the poets from composing lengthier hymns to Zeus. We could, of course, say that the *Theogony* is in part a hymn to Zeus.

is ordered."[3] Alongside the Panhellenic genres of heroic epic and theogonic poetry, we can now add the major Homeric Hymns as a distinct and complementary genre, an equal partner, as it were, in the great Panhellenic enterprise that molded a unified and systematic conception of the ordered cosmos for the Greeks.

[3] L. Slatkin, "Genre and Generation in the *Odyssey*," *Mètis* 1 (1986): 260.

Bibliography

Alderink, L. J. 1982. "Mythological and Cosmological Structure in the Homeric Hymn to Demeter." *Numen* 29: 1–16.

Allen, T. W., ed. 1912. *Homeri Opera*, vol. 5. Oxford.

Allen, T. W., W. R. Halliday, and E. E. Sikes, eds. 1936. *The Homeric Hymns*. Oxford.

Allen, T. W., and E. E. Sikes, eds. 1904. *The Homeric Hymns*. London.

Aloni, A. 1980. "*Prooimia, Hymnoi*, Elio Aristide e i cugini bastardi." *Quarderni Urbinati di Cultura Classica* n.s. 4: 23–40.

Altheim, F. 1924. "Die Entstehungsgeschichte des homerischen Apollonhymnus." *Hermes* 59: 430–49.

Amandry, P. 1950. *La Mantique Apollinienne à Delphes: Essai sur le fonctionnement de l'Oracle*. Paris.

Arbesmann, P. R. 1929. *Das Fasten bei den Griechen und Römern*. Giessen.

Arthur, M. 1977. "Politics and Pomegranates: An Interpretation of the Homeric Hymn to Demeter." *Arethusa* 10: 7–47.

Baltes, M. 1982. "Die Kataloge im homerischen Apollonhymnus." *Philologus* 125: 25–43.

Battegazzore, A. 1977–1978. "Eraclito e il ciceone eleusino." *Maia* 29/30: 3–12.

Baumeister, A., ed. 1860. *Hymni homerici*. Leipzig.

Baur, P. 1902. *Eileithyia*. University of Missouri Studies 1.4. Chicago.

Ben, N. van der. 1980. "De Homerische Aphrodite-hymne I." *Lampas* 13: 40–77.

———. 1981. "De Homerische Aphrodite-hymne 2: Een interpretatie van het gedicht." *Lampas* 14: 69–107.

Ben, N. van der. 1986. "Hymn to Aphrodite 36–291: Notes on the *pars epica* of the Homeric Hymn to Aphrodite." *Mnemosyne* 39: 1–41.

Benardete, S. 1967. "Hesiod's *Works and Days*: A First Reading." AΓΩΝ 1: 150–70.

Benveniste, É. 1932. "Le Sens du mot ΚΟΛΟΣΣΟΣ." *Revue de Philologie* 6: 118–35.

———. 1966. *Problèmes de linguistique générale*, vol. 1. Paris.

———. 1969. *Le Vocabulaire des institutions indo-européennes*. 2 vols. Paris.

Bergren, A.L.T. 1982. "Sacred Apostrophe: Re-Presentation and Imitation in the Homeric Hymns." *Arethusa* 15: 83–108.

Berry, P. 1975. "The Rape of Demeter/Persephone and Neurosis." *Spring* 1975: 186–98.

Berthiaume, G. 1982. *Les Rôles du mágeiros: Étude sur la boucherie, la cuisine et le sacrifice dans la Grèce ancienne*. *Mnemosyne* Supplement 70. Leiden.

Bethe, E. 1922. *Homer: Dichtung Und Sage II: Kyklos—Zeitbestimmung*. Leipzig.

———. 1931. *Der homerische Apollonhymnos und das Prooimion*. Berichte der Sächsischen Akademie der Wissenschaften, Leipzig. Phil.-hist. Klasse 83, no. 2. Leipzig.

Bianchi, U. 1964. "Sagezza olimpica e mistica eleusina nell' inno omerico a Demetra." *Studi e Materiali di Storia delle Religione* 35: 161–93.

Bickerman, E. J. 1976. "Love Story in the Homeric Hymn to Aphrodite." *Atheneum* 54: 229–54.

Bielohlawek, K. 1930. "Komische Motive in der homerischen Gestaltung des griechischen Göttermythus." *Archiv für Religionswissenschaft* 28: 185–211.

Bissinger, M. 1966. *Das Adjecktiv ΜΕΓΑΣ in der griechischen Dichtung*. Munich.

Blumenthal, A. von. 1927–1928. "Der Apollontempel des Trophonios und Agamedes in Delphi." *Philologus* 83: 220–24.

———. 1942. "Paian." In *Paulys Realencyclopädie der classischen Altertumswissenschaft* 18, pt. 2: 2345–62.

Bodson, L. 1971. "Hymne homérique à Apollon, 209–213: Un 'locus desperatus'?" *L'Antiquité Classique* 40: 12–20.

Boedeker, D. D. 1974. *Aphrodite's Entry into Greek Epic*. *Mnemosyne* Supplement 31. Leiden.

Böhme, R. 1937. *Das Prooimion: Eine Form sakraler Dichtung der Griechen*. Bühl.

Bona, G. 1978. "Inni omerici e poesia greca arcaica." *Rivista di Filologia e d'Istruzione Classica* 106: 224–48.

Bremer, J. M. 1981. "Greek Hymns." In *Faith, Hope and Worship: Aspects of Religious Mentality in the Ancient World*, edited by H. S. Versnel, pp. 193–215. Leiden.

Brillante, C., M. Cantilena, and C. O. Pavese, eds. 1981. *I poemi epici rapsodici non omerici e la tradizione orale. Atti del Convegno di Venezia, 28–30 settembre 1977*. Padua.

Broadhead, H. D., ed. 1960. *The Persae of Aeschylus*. Cambridge.

Brown, N. O. 1947. *Hermes the Thief*. Madison, Wis.

Bruchmann, C.F.H. 1893. *Epitheta Deorum quae apud poetas graecos leguntur.* Supplement to *Ausführliches Lexikon der griechischen und römischen Mythologie*, by W. H. Roscher. Leipzig.

Bruit, L. 1986. "Pausanias à Phigalie." *Mètis* 1: 71–96.

Bundy, E. 1962. *Studia Pindarica I: The Eleventh Olympian Ode*. Berkeley.

Burg, N.M.H. van der. 1939. ΑΠΟΡΡΗΤΑ—ΔΡΩΜΕΝΑ—ΟΡΓΙΑ. Amsterdam.

Burkert, W. 1972. *Homo Necans*. Berlin.

———. 1977. *Griechische Religion der archaischen und klassischen Epoche*. Stuttgart.

———. 1979a. "Kynaithos, Polycrates, and the Homeric Hymn to Apollo." In *Arktouros: Hellenic Studies Presented to Bernard M. W. Knox*, pp. 53–62. Berlin.

———. 1979b. *Structure and History in Greek Mythology and Ritual*. Berkeley.

———. 1984. "Sacrificio-sacrilegio: Il 'trickster' fondatore." *Studi Storici* 4: 835–45.

Calame, C. 1977. *Les Choeurs de jeunes filles en Grèce archaïque*. 2 vols. Rome.

Cantilena, M. 1980. "Due versi dell' inno omerico ad Apollon." In *Perennitas: Studi in honore di Angelo Brelich*, pp. 109–13. Rome.

Casabona, J. 1966. *Recherches sur le vocabulaire des sacrifices en Grec*. Aix-en-Provence.

Càssola, F., ed. 1975. *Inni omerici*. Milan.

Cessi, C. 1928. "L'inno omerico ad Apollo." *Atti del Reale Instituto Veneto di scienze, lettere ed arti* 87: 864–83.

Chantraine, P. 1968–1980. *Dictionnaire étymologique de la langue grecque*. 2 vols. Paris.

Chirassi, I. 1968. *Elementi di cultura precereale nei miti e riti greci*. Rome.

Chittenden, J. 1947. "The Master of Animals." *Hesperia* 26: 89–114.

Clairmont, C. 1951. *Das Parisurteil in der antiken Kunst*. Zurich.

Clay, J. S. 1981–1982. "Immortal and Ageless Forever." *Classical Journal* 77: 112–17.

———. 1983. *The Wrath of Athena*. Princeton.

———. 1984. "The Hecate of the *Theogony*." *Greek, Roman and Byzantine Studies* 25: 24–38.

———. 1985. "Aeolia, or Under the Sign of the Circle." *Classical Journal* 80: 289–91.

Clinton, K. 1986. "The Author of the Homeric *Hymn to Demeter*." *Opuscula Atheniensia* 16: 43–49.

Cole, S. G. 1984. "Greek Sanctions against Sexual Assault." *Classical Philology* 79: 97–113.

Cornford, F. M. 1913. "The ΆΠΑΡΧΑΙ and the Eleusinian Mysteries." In *Essays and Studies Presented to William Ridgeway*, edited by E. C. Quiggin, pp. 153–66. Cambridge.

Croci, G. 1977–1978. "Mito e poetica nell' Inno a Ermes." *Bollettino dell' Istituto di Filologia greca dell' Università di Padova* 4: 175–84.

Defradas, J. 1954. *Les Thèmes de la propagande delphique*. Paris.

Deichgräber, K. 1950. "Eleusinische Frömmigkeit und homerische Vorstellungs-welt im homerischen Demeterhymnus." *Akademie der Wissenschaften und der Literatur in Mainz, Geistes- und Sozialwissenschaftlichen Klasse* 6: 503–37.

Delatte, A. 1955. *Le Cycéon: Breuvage rituel des mystères d'Eleusis*. Paris.

De Martino, F. 1982. *Omero agonista in Delo*. Brescia.

Detienne, M. 1972. *Les Jardins d'Adonis: La Mythologie des aromates en Grèce*. Paris.

————. 1973. *Les Maîtres de vérité dans la Grèce archaïque*. 2nd ed. Paris.

————. 1976. *Dionysus mis à mort*. Paris.

Detienne, M., and J.-P. Vernant. 1974. *Les Ruses de l'intelligence: La Mètis des Grecs*. Paris.

Deubner, L. 1938. "Der homerische Apollonhymnus." *Sitzungsberichte der Preussischen Akademie der Wissenschaften, Phil.-hist. Klasse* 24: 248–77.

Diano, C. 1968. "La poetica dei Feaci." In *Saggezza e poetiche degli antichi*, pp. 185–214. Vicenza.

Diels, H., and W. Kranz. 1934. *Fragmente der Vorsokratiker*, 5th ed. Berlin.

Dornseiff, F. 1931. "Der homerische Aphroditehymnos." *Archiv für Religionswissenschaft* 29: 203–4.

————. 1933. *Die archaische Mythenerzählung: Folgerungen aus dem homerischen Apollonhymnos*. Berlin.

————. 1935. *Nochmals der homerische Apollonhymnos: Eine Gegenkritik*. Greifswalder Beiträge zur Literatur- und Stilforschung 8.

————. 1938. "Zum homerischen Hermeshymnos." *Rheinisches Museum* 87: 80–84.

Drerup, E. 1937. "Der homerische Apollonhymnos: Eine methodologische Studie." *Mnemosyne* 5: 81–134.

Duchemin, J. 1960. *La Houlette et la lyre*. Paris.

Dumézil, G. 1970. *Archaic Roman Religion*, 2 vols., translated by P. Krapp. Chicago.

————. 1979. *Mariages Indo-Européens*. Paris.

————. 1982. *Apollon sonore et autres essais*. Paris.

Durante, M. 1976. *Sulla preistoria della tradizione poetica greca. Parte seconda: Risultanze della comparazione indoeuropea*. Rome.

Dyer, R. 1975. "The Blind Bard of Chios (*Hymn Hom. Ap.* 171–76)." *Classical Philology* 70: 119–21.

Eck, J. van. 1978. "The Homeric Hymn to Aphrodite: Introduction, Commentary and Appendices." Dissertation, Utrecht.

Edsman, C.-M. 1949. *Ignis divinus: Le Feu comme moyen de rajeunissement et d'immortalité*. Lund.

Eitrem, S. 1906. "Der homerische Hymnus an Hermes." *Philologus*. 65: 248–82.

———. 1909. *Hermes und die Toten*. Christiania.

———. 1938. "Varia, 87: Ad Homericum hymnum in Apollinem." *Symbolae Osloenses* 18: 128–34.

Eliade, M. 1954. *The Myth of the Eternal Return*, translated by W. R. Trask. New York.

———. 1963. *Myth and Reality*, translated by W. R. Trask. New York.

Erdmann, W. 1934. *Die Ehe im alten Griechenland*. Munich.

Fairbanks, A. 1900. *A Study of the Greek Paean*. Cornell Studies in Classical Philology 12. Ithaca.

Farnell, L. R. 1896–1909. *The Cults of the Greek City States*. 5 vols. Oxford.

Ferri, S. 1960. "L'inno omerico a Afrodite e la tribù anatolica degli Otrusi." In *Studi in onore di L. Castiglioni*, 1: 291–307. Florence.

Floratos, Ch. 1952. "Ὁ ὁμηρικὸς ὕμνος εἰς Ἀπόλλωνα." Ἀθήνα 56: 286–309.

Fogelmark, S. 1972. *Studies in Pindar with Particular Reference to Paean VI and Nemean VII*. Lund.

Fontenrose, J. 1959. *Python: A Study of Delphic Myth and Its Origins*. Berkeley.

———. 1966. *The Ritual Theory of Myth*. Berkeley.

———. 1978. *The Delphic Oracle*. Berkeley.

Forderer, M. 1971. *Anfang und Ende der abendländische Lyrik: Untersuchungen zum homerischen Apollonhymnus und zu Anise Koltz*. Amsterdam.

Forrest, G. 1956. "The First Sacred War." *Bulletin de Correspondence Hellénique* 80: 33–52.

Förstel, K. 1979. *Untersuchungen zum homerischen Apollonhymnos*. Bochum.

Förster, R. 1874. *Der Raub und Rückkehr der Persephone*. Stuttgart.

Fowler, A. 1982. *Kinds of Literature: An Introduction to the Theory of Genres and Modes*. Cambridge, Mass.

Francke, K. 1881. *De hymni in Cererem Homerici compositione dictione aetate*. Kiel.

Fränkel, H. 1960. *Wege und Formen frühgriechischen Denkens*. Munich.

———. 1962. *Dichtung und Philosophie des frühen Griechentums*. 2nd edition. Munich.

Frazer, J. G. 1921. "Putting Children on the Fire." In *Apollodorus*, 2: 311–17. Cambridge, Mass.

Freed, G., and R. Bentman. 1955. "The Homeric Hymn to Aphrodite." *Classical Journal* 50: 153–58.

Friedländer, P. 1966. "Das Proömium von Hesiods Theogonie." In *Hesiod*, edited by E. Heitsch. *Wege der Forschung*, 44: 277–94. Darmstadt.

Friedrich, P. 1978. *The Meaning of Aphrodite*. Chicago.

Frisk, H. 1960–1972. *Griechisches etymologisches Wörterbuch*. Heidelberg.

Frolíková, A. 1963. "Some Remarks on the Problem of the Division of the Homeric Hymn to Apollo." In ΓΕΡΑΣ: *Studies presented to George Thomson on the Occasion of his 60th Birthday*, pp. 99–109. Prague.

Gemoll, A., ed. 1886. *Die homerischen Hymnen*. Leipzig.

Gerber, D. E. 1982. *Pindar's Olympian One: A Commentary*. Toronto.

Germain, G. 1954. *Homère et la mystique des nombres*. Paris.

Giacomelli, A. 1980. "Aphrodite and After." *Phoenix* 34: 1–19.

Gill, D. 1974. "*Trapezomata*: A Neglected Aspect of Greek Sacrifice." *Harvard Theological Review* 67: 117–37.

Görgemanns, H. 1976. "Rhetorik und Poetik im homerischen Hermeshymnus." In *Studien zum antiken Epos*, edited by H. Görgemanns and E. A. Schmidt, pp. 113–28. Meisenheim.

Graefe, G. 1973. "Der homerische Hymnus auf Hermes." *Gymnasium* 70: 515–26.

Graf, F. 1974. *Eleusis und die orphische Dichtung Athens in vorhellenistischer Zeit*. Berlin.

Griffin, J. 1980. *Homer on Life and Death*. Oxford.

Griffith, M. 1975. "Man and the Leaves: A Study of Mimneros fr. 2." *California Studies in Classical Antiquity* 8: 73–88.

Groningen, B. A. van. 1948. "Quelques considérations sur l'aoriste gnomique." In *Studia Varia Carolo Vollgraff*, pp. 49–61. Amsterdam.

———. 1949. "NEOMAI—NEΩ." *Mnemosyne* 4, no. 2: 42–43.

———. 1958. *La Composition littéraire archaïque grecque*. Amsterdam.

Guida, F. 1972. "Apollo arciere nell'inno omerico ad Apollo Delio." *Studi Omerici ed Esiodei* (Rome) 1: 7–25.

Hammarström, M. 1921. "Griechisch-etruskische Wortgleichungen." *Glotta* 11: 211–17.

Harrison, A.R.W. 1968. *The Law of Athens*. 2 vols. Oxford.

Heer, C. de. 1969. ΜΑΚΑΡ—ΕΥΔΑΙΜΩΝ—ΟΛΒΙΟΣ—ΕΥΤΥΧΗΣ: *A Study of the Semantic Field Denoting Happiness in Ancient Greek to the End of the 5th Century*. Amsterdam.

Heitsch, E. 1965. *Aphroditehymnos, Aeneas und Homer*. Hypomnemata 15. Göttingen.

Henrichs, A. 1978. "Greek Maenadism from Olympias to Messalina." *Harvard Studies in Classical Philology* 82: 121–60.

Hermann, G. 1806. *Homeri hymni et epigrammata*. Leipzig.

Herter, H. 1976. "Hermes: Ursprung und Wesen eines griechischen Gottes." *Rheinisches Museum* 119: 193–241.

———. 1981. "L'Inno a Hermes alla luce della poesia orale." In *I poemi epici rapsodici non omerici e la tradizione orale*, edited by C. Brillante, M. Cantilena, and C. O. Pavese, pp. 183–201. Padua.

Herwerden, H. van. 1907. "Forma antiquissima hymni homerici in Mercurium." *Mnemosyne* 35: 181–91.

Heubeck, A. 1961. *Praegraeca*. Erlangen.

———. 1972. "Gedanken zum homerischen Apollonhymnus." In *Festschrift K. J. Merentitis*, pp. 131–46. Athens.

Hirsch, E. D. 1967. *Validity in Interpretation*. New Haven.

Hirzel, R. 1902. *Der Eid: Ein Beitrag zu seiner Geschichte*. Leipzig.

———. 1907. *Themis, Dike und Verwandtes*. Leipzig.

Hocart, A. 1936. *Kings and Councillors: An Essay in the Comparative Anatomy of Human Society*. Cairo.

Hoekstra, A. 1969. *The Sub-epic Stage of the Formulaic Tradition: Studies in the Homeric Hymns to Apollo, to Aphrodite and to Demeter*. Verhandelingen der Koninklijke Nederlandse Akademie van Wetenschappen, afd. Letterkunde 75, no. 2. Amsterdam.

Holland, R. 1926. "Battos." *Rheinisches Museum* 75: 156–83.

Hooker, J. 1986. "A Residual Problem in *Iliad* 24." *Classical Quarterly* n.s. 36: 32–37.

Hoz, J. De. 1964. "Poesia oral independiente de Homero en Hesíodo y los Himnos homéricos." *Emerita* 32: 283–98.

Hübner, W. 1986. "Hermes als musischer Gott." *Philologus* 130: 153–74.

Humbert, J. 1936. *Homère: Hymnes*. Paris.

Huxley, G. L. 1969. *Greek Epic Poetry from Eumelos to Panyassis*. Cambridge, Mass.

Immerwahr, W. 1891. *Die Kulte und Mythen Arkadiens. Volume I: Die arkadischen Kulte*. Leipzig.

Jacoby, F. 1933. "Der homerische Apollonhymnos." *Sitzungsberichte der preussischen Akademie der Wissenschaften, Phil.-hist. Klasse* 15: 682–751.

———. 1904. *Das Marmor Parium*. Berlin.

Janko, R. 1981a. Review of *Nursling of Immortality*, by P. M. Smith. *Classical Review* 31: 285–86.

———. 1981b. "The Structure of the Homeric Hymns: A Study in Genre." *Hermes* 109: 9–24.

———. 1982. *Homer, Hesiod and the Hymns: Diachronic Development in Epic Diction*. Cambridge.

Jeanmaire, H. 1939. *Couroi et courètes: Essai sur l'éducation spartiate et sur les rites d'adolescence dans l'antiquité hellénique*. Lille.

———. 1945. "Le Substantif *hosia*." *Revue des Études Grecques* 58: 66–89.

Jouan, F. 1956. "Thétis, Hestia et Athéna." *Revue des Études Grecques* 69: 290–302.

Jung, C. G. 1967. "The Psychological Aspects of the Kore." In *Essays on a Science of Mythology: The Myth of the Divine Child*, by C. G. Jung and K. Kerényi, pp. 156–77. Princeton.

Kadletz, E. 1984. "The Sacrifice of Eumaios the Pig Herder." *Greek, Roman and Byzantine Studies* 25: 99–105.

Kahn, L. 1978. *Hermès passe ou les ambiguïtés de la communication*. Paris.

Kaimio, M. 1974. "Music in the Homeric Hymn to Hermes." *Arctos* 8: 29–42.

Kakrides, J. T. 1930a. "Die Pelopssage bei Pindar." *Philologus* 85: 463–77.

———. 1930b. "ΤΙΘΩΝΟΣ." *Wiener Studien* 48: 25–38.

———. 1937. "Zum homerischen Apollonhymnos." *Philologus* 92: 104–8.

Kalinka, E. 1932. Review of "Der homerische Apollonhymnos und das Prooimion," by E. Bethe. *Philologische Wochenschrift* 52: 385–94.

Kamerbeek, J. C. 1967. "Remarques sur l'Hymne à Aphrodite." *Mnemosyne* 20: 385–95.

Karnezis, J. 1972. "The Epikleros." Dissertation, Athens.

Keaney, J. J. 1981. "Hymn. Ven. 140 and the Use of ᾿ΑΠΟΙΝΑ." *American Journal of Philology* 102: 261–64.

Kerényi, K. 1967a. *Eleusis: The Archetypical Image of Mother and Daughter*, translated by R. Mannheim. Princeton.

———. 1967b. "Kore." In *Essays on a Science of Mythology: The Myth of the Divine Child*, by C. G. Jung and K. Kerényi, pp. 101–55. Princeton.

Kern, O., ed. 1922. *Orphicorum Fragmenta*. Berlin.

———. 1935. "Mysterien." In *Paulys Realencyclopädie der classischen Altertumswissenschaft* 16, pt. 2: 1210–314.

Keyssner, K. 1932. *Gottesvorstellung und Lebensauffassung im griechischen Hymnus*. Würzburger Studien zur Altertumswissenschaft 2. Stuttgart.

King, H. 1986. "Tithonos and the Tettix." *Arethusa* 19: 15–32.

Kirchhoff, A. 1893. "Beiträge zur Geschichte der griechischen Rhapsodik II: Der Festhymnos auf den Delischen Apollon." In *Sitzungsberichte der Preussischen Akademie, Berlin*, pp. 906–18. Berlin.

Kirk, G. S. 1970. *Myth: Its Meaning and Functions in Ancient and Other Cultures*. Berkeley.

———. 1981. "Orality and Structure in the Homeric 'Hymn to Apollo.' " In *I poemi epici rapsodici non omerici e la tradizione orale*, edited by C. Brillante, M. Cantilena, and C. O. Pavese, pp. 163–82. Padua.

Kittel, G., ed. 1932–1972. *Theologisches Wörterbuch zum Neuen Testament*. Stuttgart.

Kolk, D. 1963. *Der pythische Apollonhymnus als aitiologische Dichtung*. Meisenheim.

Koller, H. 1956. "Das kitharodische Prooimion." *Philologus* 100: 159–206.

———. 1968. "Πόλις Μερόπων ᾿Ανθρώπων." *Glotta* 46: 18–26.

Kraus, T. 1960. *Hekate: Studien zu Wesen und Bild der Göttin in Kleinasien und Griechenland*. Heidelberg.

Kroll, J. 1956. "Apollon zum Beginn des homerischen Hymnus." *Studi Italiani di Filologia Classica* 27–28: 181–191.

Kuhn, A. 1886. *Die Herabkunft des Feuers und des Göttertranks*. 2nd edition. Gütersloh.

Kuiper, K. 1910. "De discrepantiis hymni homerici in Mercurium." *Mnemosyne* 38: 1–50.

Kullmann, W. 1956. *Das Wirken der Götter in der Ilias: Untersuchungen zur Frage der Entstehung des homerischen Götterapparats*. Berlin.

———. 1960. *Die Quellen der Ilias (Troischer Sagenkreis)*. *Hermes* Einzelschriften 14. Wiesbaden.

Lacey, W. K. 1968. *The Family in Ancient Greece*. Ithaca, N.Y.

Latacz, J. 1966. *Zum Wortfeld "Freude" in der Sprache Homers*. Heidelberg.

Latte, K. 1939. "Orakel." In *Paulys Realencyclopädie der classischen Altertumswissenschaft* 18, pt. 1: 829–66.

———. 1940. "The Coming of the Pythia." *Harvard Theological Review* 33: 9–18.

Leaf, W., ed. 1900–1902. *The Iliad*. 2 vols. 2nd edition. London.

Lehmann, G. A. 1980. "Der 'Erste Heilige Krieg'—Eine Fiktion?" *Historia* 29: 242–46.

Lenz, L. 1975. *Der homerische Aphroditehymnus und die Aristie des Aineias in der Ilias*. Bonn.

Liderski, J. 1962. "Etruskische Etymologien: zilaθ – und purθ." *Glotta* 40: 150–59.

Lincoln, B. 1979. "The Rape of Persephone: A Greek Scenario of Women's Initiation." *Harvard Theological Review* 72: 223–35.

Lobeck, C. A. 1829. *Aglaophamus*. 2 vols. Königsberg.

Lord, M. L. 1967. "Withdrawal and Return: An Epic Story Pattern in the Homeric *Hymn to Demeter*." *Classical Journal* 62: 241–48.

Ludwich, A. 1908. *Homerischer Hymnenbau*. Leipzig.

MacDowell, D. M. 1978. *The Law in Classical Athens*. London.

Malinowski, B. 1948. *Magic, Science and Religion and Other Essays*. Boston.

Malten, L. 1909. "Altorphische Demetersage." *Archiv für Religionswissenschaft* 12: 417–46.

———. 1931. "Aeneias." *Archiv für Religionswissenschaft* 29: 33–59.

Maltese, E. V. 1982. *Sofocle Ichneutae*. Papyrologica Florentina 10. Florence.

Mauss, M. 1968. "Les fonctions sociales du sacré." In *Oeuvres* 1, edited by V. Karady, pp. 193–307. Paris.

———. 1972. *A General Theory of Magic*, translated by R. Brain. London.

Mellaart, J. 1967. *Catal Hüyük: A Neolithic Town in Anatolia*. London.

Merkelbach, R. 1973. "Ein Fragment des homerischen Dionysos–Hymnus." *Zeitschrift für Papyrologie und Epigraphik* 12: 212–15.

Merkelbach, R., and M. L. West, eds. 1967. *Fragmenta Hesiodea*. Oxford.

Meuli, K. 1946. "Griechische Opferbräuche." In *Phyllobolia für Peter von der Mühll*, pp. 185–288. Basel.

Miller, A. M. 1979. "The 'Address to the Delian Maidens' in the *Homeric Hymn to Apollo*: Epilogue or Transition?" *Transactions and Proceedings of the American Philological Association* 109: 173–86.

———. 1985. *From Delos to Delphi: A Literary Study of the Homeric Hymn to Apollo*. Leiden.

Minton, W. W. 1970. "The Proem-hymn of Hesiod's *Theogony*." *Transactions and Proceedings of the American Philological Association* 101: 357–77.

Mondi, R. 1978. "The Function and Social Position of the *Kêrux* in Early Greece." Ph.D. dissertation, Harvard University.

Monro, D. B., and T. W. Allen, eds. 1912–1920. *Homeri Opera*. 5 vols. Oxford.

Monsacré, H. 1984. *Les Larmes d'Achille*. Paris.

Moran, W. S. 1975. "Μιμνήσχομαι and 'Remembering' Epic Stories in Homer and the Hymns." *Quaderni Urbinati di Cultura Classica* 20: 195–211.

Morgoulieff, J. 1893. *Étude critique sur les monuments antiques représentant des scènes d'accouchement*. Paris.

Most, G. 1981. "Callimachus and Herophilus." *Hermes* 109: 188–96.

Müller, K. O. 1824. *Geschichten hellenischer Stämme und Städte II: Die Dorier*. 2 vols. Breslau.

———. 1833. "Die Hermes-Grotte bei Pylos." In *Hyperboreisch-römische Studien für Archäologie*, edited by E. Gerhard, pp. 310–16. Berlin.

Murr, J. 1890. *Die Pflanzenwelt in der griechischen Mythologie*. Innsbruck.

Mylonas, G. 1942. *The Hymn to Demeter and Her Sanctuary at Eleusis*. Washington University Studies n.s. 13. St. Louis.

Nagy, G. 1979. *The Best of the Achaeans*. Baltimore.

———. 1982. "Hesiod." In *Ancient Writers*, edited by T. J. Luce, pp. 43–73. New York.

Niles, J. D. 1979. "On the Design of the Hymn to Delian Apollo." *Classical Journal* 75: 36–39.

Nilsson, M. P. 1935. "Die eleusinischen Gottheiten." *Archiv für Religionswissenschaft* 32: 79–141.

———. 1955. *Geschichte der griechischen Religion*. 2nd edition. Volume 1. Munich.

Norden, E. 1923. *Agnostos Theos*. Berlin.

Notopoulos, J. A. 1962. "The Homeric Hymns as Oral Poetry: A Study of the Post-homeric Oral Tradition." *American Journal of Philology* 83: 337–68.

Oppé, A. P. 1904. "The Chasm at Delphi." *Journal of Hellenic Studies* 24: 214–40.

Orgogozo, J. 1949. "L'Hermès des Achéens." *Revue de l'histoire des religions* 136: 10–30, 139–79.

Otterlo, W.A.A. van. 1944. "Untersuchungen über Begriff, Anwendung und

Entstehung der griechischen Ringkomposition." *Mededeelingen der Koninklijke Nederlandse Akademie van Wetenschappen, Afd. Letterkunde* n.s. 7, no. 3: 131–76.

Otto, W. F. 1954. *The Homeric Gods*, translated by M. Hadas. New York.

Owen, A. S., ed. 1939. *Euripides Ion*. Oxford.

Page, D., ed. 1962. *Poetae melici graeci*. Oxford.

———. 1974. *Supplementum lyricis graecis*. Oxford.

Pagliaro, A. 1953. "Ἱερός in Omero e la nozione di 'sacro' in Grecia." In *Saggi di critica semantica*, pp. 91–122. Messina.

———. 1971. "Il proemio dell' Iliade." In *Nuovi saggi di critica semantica*. 2nd edition. Florence.

Panagl, O. 1969. "Stationen hellenischer Religiosität am Beispiel des delphischen Sukzessionsmythos." *Kairos* 11: 161–71.

Paoli, U. E. 1976. "Il reato di adulterio (μοιχεία) in diritto attico." In *Altri studi di diritto greco e romano*. Milan.

Parke, H. W. 1940. "A Note on the Delphic Priesthood." *Classical Quarterly* 34: 85–89.

Parke H. W., and D.E.W. Wormell. 1956. *The Delphic Oracle*. 2 vols. Oxford.

Péristérakis, A. E. 1962. "Essai sur l'aoriste intemporel en Grec." Dissertation, University of Paris. Athens.

Pellizer, E. 1978. "Tecnica compositiva e struttura genealogica nell' Inno ad Afrodite." *Quaderni Urbinati di Cultura Classica* 27: 115–44.

Pfister, F. 1924. "Epiphanie." In *Paulys Realencyclopädie der classischen Altertumswissenschaft* supplement 4: 277–323.

Philippson, P. 1944. *Untersuchungen über den griechischen Mythos*. Zurich.

Podbielski, H. 1971. *La Structure de l'Hymne Homérique à Aphrodite à la lumière de la tradition littéraire*. Wroclaw.

Pomtow, H. 1901. "Delphoi." In *Paulys Realencyclopädie der classischen Altertumswissenschaft* 4, pt. 2: 2517–700.

Porter, H. N. 1949. "Repetition in the Homeric Hymn to Aphrodite." *American Journal of Philology* 70: 249–272.

Pötscher, W. 1987. *Hera: Eine Strukturanalyse im Vergleich mit Athena*. Darmstadt.

Powell, J. U., ed. 1925. *Collectanea Alexandrina*. Oxford.

Preisendanz, K., and A. Heinrichs, eds. 1973–1974. *Papyri graeci magicae*. 2nd edition. Stuttgart.

Preller, L., and C. Robert. 1887. *Griechische Mythologie*, 2 vols. 4th edition. Berlin.

Pucci, P. 1977. *Hesiod and the Language of Poetry*. Baltimore.

———. 1987. *Odysseus Polutropos*. Ithaca, N.Y.

Puntoni, V. 1896. *L'Inno omerico a Demeter*. Leghorn.

Quandt, W. 1962. *Orphei hymni*. 2nd edition. Berlin.

Race, W. H. 1982. "Aspects of Rhetoric and Form in Greek Hymns." *Greek, Roman and Byzantine Studies* 23: 5–14.

Radermacher, L. 1931. *Der homerische Hermeshymnus.* Sitzungsberichte Akademie der Wissenschaften in Wien 213, no. 1: 1–263.

Raingeard, P. 1934. *Hermès psychagogue.* Rennes.

Ramnoux, C. 1959. *Mythologie ou la famille olympienne.* Paris.

Regenbogen, O. 1956. "Gedanken zum homerischen Apollon-Hymnus." *Eranos* 5: 49–56.

Reinhardt, K. 1961a. *Die Ilias und ihr Dichter.* Göttingen.

————. 1961b. "Ilias und Aphroditehymnus." In *Die Ilias und Ihr Dichter*, pp. 507–21. Göttingen.

Richardson, N. J. 1974. *The Homeric Hymn to Demeter.* Oxford.

Robert, C. 1906. "Zum homerischen Hermeshymnos." *Hermes* 41: 389–425.

Robertson, N. 1978. "The Myth of the First Sacred War." *Classical Quarterly* 72: 38–73.

Roeger, J. 1924. ΑΙΔΟΣ ΚΥΝΕΗ: *Das Märchen von der Unsichtbarkeit in den homerischen Gedichten.* Graz.

Rohde, E. 1898. *Psyche: Seelencult und Unsterblichkeitsglaube der Griechen.* 2nd edition. Freiburg.

Roscher, W. H., ed. 1884–1937. *Ausführliches Lexikon der griechischen und römischen mythologie.* 6 vols. Leipzig.

Rose, H. J. 1924. "Anchises and Aphrodite." *Classical Quarterly* 18: 11–16.

Roux, G. 1965. "Sur deux passages de l'Hymne homérique à Apollon." *Revue des Études Grecques* 77: 1–22.

————. 1976. *Delphes: Son oracle et ses dieux.* Paris.

Rubin, N., and H. Deal. 1980. "Some Functions of the Demophon Episode in the Homeric Hymn to Demeter." *Quaderni Urbinati di Cultura Classica* 34: 7–21.

Rudhardt, J. 1958. *Notions fondamentales de la pensée religieuse et actes constitutifs du culte dans la Grèce classique.* Geneva.

————. 1962. "La Reconnaissance de la paternité dans la société athénienne." *Museum Helveticum* 19: 39–64.

————. 1978. "À propos de l'hymne homérique à Déméter." *Museum Helveticum* 35: 1–17.

————. 1981. *Du mythe, de la religion grecque et de la compréhension d'autrui.* Revue Européenne des Sciences Sociales 19. Geneva.

Ruijgh, C. 1967. "Sur le nom de Poséidon et les noms en -α-ϝ ον-, ι-ϝ ον -." *Revue des Études Grecques* 80: 6–16.

Russell, D. A., and N. G. Wilson, eds. 1981. *Menander Rhetor.* Oxford.

Sabbatucci, D. 1965. *Saggio sul misticismo greco.* Rome.

Saïd, S. 1979. "Les Crimes des prétendants, la maison d'Ulysse et les festins de l'Odyssée." In *Études de littérature anciennes*, pp. 9–49. Paris.

Samter, E. 1901. *Familienfeste der Griechen und Römer*. Berlin.

———. 1911. *Geburt, Hochzeit und Tod*. Leipzig.

Scarpi, P. 1976. *Letture sulla religione classica: L'Inno omerico a Demeter*. Florence.

Schachter, A. 1976. "*Homeric Hymn to Apollo*, lines 231–238 (The Onchestus Episode): Another Interpretation." *Bulletin of the Institute of Classical Studies* 23: 102–13.

Scheinberg, S. 1979. "The Bee Maidens of the Homeric *Hymn to Hermes*." *Harvard Studies in Classical Philology* 83: 1–28.

Schmid, W., and O. Stählin. 1929. *Geschichte der griechischen Literatur*. Volume 1, part 1, by W. Schmid. Munich.

Schmidt, E. G. 1981. "Himmel—Meer—Erde im frühgriechischen Epos und im alten Orient." *Philologus* 125: 1–24.

Schröder, J. 1975. *Ilias und Apollonyhymnos*. Meisenheim.

Scodel, R. 1982. "The Achaean Wall and the Myth of Destruction." *Harvard Studies in Classical Philology* 86: 33–50.

Seek, O. 1887. *Die Quellen der Odyssee*. Berlin.

Segal, C. 1974. "The Homeric Hymn to Aphrodite: A Structuralist Approach." *Classical World* 67: 205–12.

———. 1981. "Orality, Repetition and Formulaic Artistry in the Homeric 'Hymn to Demeter.'" In *I poemi epici non omerici e la tradizione orale*, edited by C. Brillante, M. Cantilena, and C. O. Pavese, pp. 107–60. Padua.

———. 1982. *Dionysiac Poetics and Euripides' Bacchae*. Princeton.

———. 1986. "Tithonus and the Homeric *Hymn to Aphrodite*: A Comment." *Arethusa* 19: 37–47.

Shelmerdine, S. C. 1981. "The 'Homeric Hymn to Hermes': A Commentary (1–114) with Introduction." Ph.D. dissertation, University of Michigan.

———. 1984. "Hermes and the Tortoise: A Prelude to Cult." *Greek, Roman and Byzantine Studies* 25: 201–7.

———. 1986. "Odyssean Allusions in the Fourth Homeric Hymn." *Transactions and Proceedings of the American Philological Association* 116: 49–63.

Slatkin, L. 1986a. "The Wrath of Thetis." *Transactions and Proceedings of the American Philological Association* 116: 1–24.

———. 1986b. "Genre and Generation in the *Odyssey*." *Mètis* 1: 259–68.

Smith, P. M. 1979. "Notes on the Text of the Fifth Homeric Hymn." *Harvard Studies in Classical Philology* 83: 29–50.

———. 1981a. *Nursling of Mortality: A Study of the Homeric Hymn to Aphrodite*. Studien zur klassischen Philologie 3. Frankfurt.

———. 1981b. "Aineidai as Patrons of *Iliad XX* and the Homeric *Hymn to Aphrodite*." *Harvard Studies in Classical Philology* 85: 17–58.

Snell, B., ed. 1971–. *Tragicorum Graecorum fragmenta*. Göttingen.

———. 1975. *Die Endeckung des Geistes*. 4th edition. Göttingen.

Snell, B., and H. Maehler, eds. 1975–1980. *Pindari Carmina*. 2 vols. Leipzig.

Solmsen, F. 1968. "Zur Theologie im grossen Aphrodite-hymnus." In *Kleine Schriften*, 1: 55–67. Hildesheim.

Sordi, M. 1953. "La prima guerra sacra." *Rivista di Filologia e d'Istruzione Classica* n.s. 31: 320–46.

Sourvinou-Inwood, C. 1987. "Myth as History: The Previous Owners of the Delphic Oracle." In *Interpretations of Greek Mythology*, edited by J. Bremmer, pp. 215–41. London.

Sowa, C. A. 1984. *Traditional Themes and the Homeric Hymns*. Chicago.

Stiewe, K. 1954. "Der Erzählungsstil des homerischen Demeterhymnos." Dissertation, Göttingen.

———. 1962. "Die Entstehungszeit der hesiodischen Frauenkataloge." *Philologus* 106: 291–99.

———. 1963. "Die Entstehungszeit der hesiodischen Frauenkataloge (Fortsetzung)." *Philologus* 107: 1–29.

Stoessel, F. 1947. *Der Tod des Herakles*. Zurich.

Szepes, E. 1975. "Trinities in the Homeric Demeter-Hymn." *Annales Universitatis Budapestinensis de Rolando Eötvös nominatae, sectio classica* 3: 23–38.

Teske, A. 1936. *Die Homer-Mimesis in den Homerischen Hymnen*. Greifswalder Beiträge zur Literatur und Stilforschung 15.

Thalmann, W. G. 1984. *Conventions of Form and Thought in Early Greek Epic Poetry*. Baltimore.

Thompson, D. W. 1895. *A Glossary of Greek Birds*. Oxford.

Toutain, J. 1932. "Hermès, dieu social chez les Grecs." *Revue d'Histoire et de Philosophie Religieuses* 12: 289–329.

Treu, M. 1968. *Von Homer zur Lyrik*. Zetemata 12. 2nd edition. Munich.

Turner, T. 1977. "Narrative Structure and Mythopoesis." *Arethusa* 10: 103–64.

Turyn, A., ed. 1948. *Pindari Carmina*. Cracow.

Unte, W. 1968. "Studien zum homerischen Apollonhymnos." Dissertation, Berlin.

Van der Valk, M. H. 1942. "Zum Worte 'ΟΣΙΟΣ.'" *Mnemosyne* 10: 113–40.

———. 1976. "On the Arrangement of the Homeric Hymns." *L'Antiquité Classique* 45: 420–45.

———. 1977. "A Few Observations on the Homeric *Hymn to Apollo*." *L'Antiquité Classique* 46: 441–52.

Van Nortwick, T. 1975. "The Homeric *Hymn to Hermes*: A Study in Early Greek Hexameter Style." Ph.D. dissertation, Stanford University.

———. 1980. "Apollônos Apatê: Associative Imagery in the Homeric *Hymn to Hermes* 227–292." *Classical World* 74: 1–5.

Van Windekens, A. 1961. "Réflexions sur la nature et l'origine du dieu Hermès." *Rheinisches Museum* 104: 289–301.

————. 1962. "Sur le nom de la divinité grecque Hermès." *Beiträge zur Namenforschung* 13: 290–92.

Verdenius, W. J. 1960. "L'Association des idées comme principe de composition dans Homère, Hésiode, Théognis." *Revue des Études Grecques* 73: 345–61.

Vernant, J.-P. 1965a. "Aspects mythique de la mémoire et du temps." In *Mythe et pensée chez les Grecs*, 1: 80–107. Paris.

————. 1965b. "Hestia–Hermès: Sur l'expression religieuse de l'espace et du movement chez les Grecs." In *Mythe et pensée chez les Grecs*, 1: 124–84. Paris.

————. 1965c. *Mythe et pensée chez les Grecs*. 2 vols. Paris.

————. 1974. *Mythe et société en Grèce ancienne*. Paris.

————. 1979a. "À la table des hommes." In *La Cuisine du sacrifice en pays grec*, edited by M. Detienne and J.-P. Vernant, pp. 37–132. Paris.

————. 1979b. "Manger aux pays du Soleil." In *La Cuisine du sacrifice en pays grec*, edited by M. Detienne and J.-P. Vernant, pp. 239–49. Paris.

Vian, F. 1963. *Les Origines de Thèbes*. Paris.

Vidal-Naquet, P. 1981. "Temps des dieux et temps des hommes." In *Le Chasseur noir: Formes de pensée et formes de société dans le monde grec*, pp. 69–94. Paris.

Wade-Gery, H. T. 1936. "Kynaithos." In *Greek Poetry and Life: Essays Presented to Gilbert Murray on His Seventieth Birthday*, pp. 56–78. Oxford.

Walsh, G. B. 1984. *The Varieties of Enchantment: Early Greek Views of the Nature and Function of Poetry*. Chapel Hill, N.C.

Walton, F. 1952. "Athens, Eleusis and the Homeric Hymn to Demeter." *Harvard Theological Review* 45: 105–14.

Watkins, C. 1970. "Studies in Indo-European Legal Language, Institutions, and Mythology." In *Indo-European and Indo-Europeans*, edited by G. Cardona and H. Hoenigswald, pp. 321–54. Philadelphia.

Webster, T.B.L. 1975. "Homeric Hymns and Society." In *Le Monde grec: Pensée littérature histoire documents: Hommages à Claire Préaux*, pp. 86–93. Brussels.

Wegener, R. 1876. "Der homerische Hymnus auf Demeter." *Philologus* 35: 227–54.

Wehrli, F. 1931. "Leto." In *Paulys Realencyclopädie der classischen Altertumswissenschaft*, supplement 5: 555–76.

————. 1934. "Die Mysterien von Eleusis." *Archiv für Religionswissenschaft* 31: 77–104.

Welcker, F. G. 1849. *Der epische Cyclus oder die homerischen Dichter 2: Gedichte nach Inhalt und Composition*. Bonn.

————. 1850. "Entbindung." In *Kleine Schriften*, 3: 185–208. Bonn.

————. 1857. *Griechische Götterlehre*. 2 vols. Göttingen.

West, M. L. 1961. "Hesiodea." *Classical Quarterly* 55: 130–45.

————. 1975. "Cynaethus' Hymn to Apollo." *Classical Quarterly* 25: 161–70.

West, M. L. 1985. *The Hesiodic Catalogue of Women*. Oxford.

West, M. L., ed. 1966. *Hesiod: Theogony*. Oxford.

————., ed. 1971–1972. *Iambi et Elegi Graeci*. 2 vols. Oxford.

Whitman, C. H. 1970. "Hera's Anvils." *Harvard Studies in Classical Philology* 74: 37–42.

Wilamowitz–Moellendorff, U. von. 1920. *Die Ilias und Homer*. 2nd edition. Berlin.

————. 1922. *Pindaros*. Berlin.

————. 1959. *Der Glaube der Hellenen*. 2 vols. 3rd edition. Darmstadt.

————. 1971. "Hephaistos." In *Kleine Schriften*, 5, pt. 2: 5–35. Berlin.

Wissowa, G., et al., eds. 1894–. *Paulys Realencyclopädie der classischen Altertumswissenschaft*. Stuttgart.

Wolf, F. A. 1985. *Prolegomena to Homer 1795*, translated by A. Grafton, G. Most, and J. Zetzel. Princeton.

Wünsch, R. 1914. "Hymnos." In *Paulys Realencyclopädie der classischen Altertumswissenschaft* 9, pt. 1: 140–83.

Zumbach, O. 1955. *Neuerungen in der Sprache der homerischen Hymnen*. Winterthur.

Zuntz, G. 1971. *Persephone*. Oxford.

Index